FAMINES AND THE MAKING OF HERITAGE

Famines and the Making of Heritage is the first book to bring together groundbreaking research on the role of European famines in the nineteenth and twentieth centuries in relation to heritage making, museology, commemoration, education, and monument creation.

Featuring contributions from famine experts across Europe and North America, the volume adopts a pioneering transnational perspective, and discusses issues such as contestable and repressed heritage, materiality, dark tourism, education on famines, oral history, multidirectional memory, and visceral empathy. Questioning why educational curricula and practices in schools and on heritage sites are region- or nation-oriented or transnational, chapters also consider whether they emphasise conflict or mutual understanding. Contributions also consider how present issues of European concern – such as globalisation, commodification, human rights, poverty, and migration – intersect with the heritage and memory of modern European famines. Lastly, the book considers what role emigrant and diasporic communities within and outside Europe play in the development of famine heritage and educational practices – and whether famine heritage is accessible to them.

Famines and the Making of Heritage provides a crucial resource for museum and heritage scholars, students and professionals working on or with difficult or dark heritages, as well as those interested in the study of famines and legacies of troubled pasts.

Marguérite Corporaal is a Full Professor of Irish Literature in Transnational Contexts at Radboud University Nijmegen.

Ingrid de Zwarte is an Assistant Professor of Economic and Environmental History at Wageningen University and Research.

FAMINES AND THE MAKING OF HERITAGE

Edited by Marguérite Corporaal and Ingrid de Zwarte

Routledge
Taylor & Francis Group
LONDON AND NEW YORK

Designed cover image: Photograph taken by Ingrid de Zwarte of the "Manna" monument by Ram Katzir (2020), located at the Meerwaldtplantsoen in Amsterdam.

First published 2024
by Routledge
4 Park Square, Milton Park, Abingdon, Oxon OX14 4RN

and by Routledge
605 Third Avenue, New York, NY 10158

Routledge is an imprint of the Taylor & Francis Group, an informa business

British Library Cataloguing-in-Publication Data
A catalogue record for this book is available from the British Library

ISBN: 978-1-032-50015-7 (hbk)
ISBN: 978-1-032-48934-6 (pbk)
ISBN: 978-1-003-39152-4 (ebk)

DOI: 10.4324/9781003391524

Typeset in Times New Roman
by MPS Limited, Dehradun

CONTENTS

FIGURES

CONTRIBUTORS

Miguel Ángel Del Arco Blanco is a Full Professor in the Department of Contemporary History at the University of Granada. As a visiting scholar, he has been developing his research agenda at the Università degli Studi Roma Tre, the University of Michigan, and The London School of Economics and Political Science. His work centres on the study of the Spanish Civil War and post-war Francoism. Recently, he has begun to focus on the memory of the civil war and on the study of the Francoist famine. Some of his books include *Mass Killings and Violence in Spain, 1936–52: Grappling with the Past* (co-edited, Routledge, 2014) and *Franco's Famine: Disease, Malnutrition and Starvation in Post-Civil War Spain* (co-edited Bloomsbury, 2021). His latest book is *Cruces de memoria y olvido. Los monumentos a los caídos de la guerra civil española (1936–2021)* (Crítica, 2022).

Anne-Lise Bobeldijk is a postdoctoral researcher at Wageningen University and Research and the NIOD Institute for War, Holocaust, and Genocide Studies. Her research interests include the history and memory of violence within Eastern Europe, and in particular the history and memory of the (former) Soviet Union. In 2022, Anne-Lise defended her PhD thesis at the University of Amsterdam on the history and memory of the Nazi camp and mass grave Maly Trostenets and Blagovshchina forest nearby Minsk, Belarus. Within the NWO-funded 'Heritages of Hunger' project, she investigates the memories of the Holodomor and the Siege of Leningrad.

Charley Boerman is a PhD candidate at Radboud University Nijmegen. Her PhD project, part of the NWO-funded project 'Heritages of Hunger' and titled 'Framing Famines: Memory, Museums and Visual Culture', explores the visual and material memory cultures of nineteenth-century Finnish famines, the Ukrainian Holodomor (1932–33), and the Greek famine (1941–44) that occurred during the occupation by the Axis powers in WWII. Charley holds a Research MA in Cultural Analysis, obtained from the University of Amsterdam, and previously studied Philosophy, Literature, and History at University College Maastricht and at the University of California San Diego. She has written and given talks about the representation and re-enactment of twentieth-century episodes of extreme violence in recent documentary film.

Marguérite Corporaal is a Full Professor of Irish Literature in Transnational Contexts at Radboud University Nijmegen. She is the principal investigator and supervisor of the VICI project 'Redefining the Region' (Dutch Research Council NWO, 2019–24) and PI of the NWO-NWA project 'Heritages of Hunger' (2019–24). Previously, Corporaal was PI of the research programme 'Relocated Remembrance: The Great Famine in Irish (Diaspora) Fiction, 1847–1921', for which she was awarded a Starting Grant for Consolidators by the European Research Council (2010–15). Furthermore, she was project leader and principal investigator of the International Network of Irish Famine Studies, for which she received an Internationalisation Grant from NWO (2014–17). Among her recent publications are *Relocated Memories: The Great Famine in Irish (Diaspora) Fiction, 1847–1870* (Syracuse UP, 2017), *The Great Famine and Social Class* (co-edited, Peter Lang, 2019), *The Great Famine: Visual and Material Cultures* (co-edited, Liverpool UP, 2018), and *Global Legacies of the Great Irish Famine: Interdisciplinary and Transnational Perspectives* (co-edited, Peter Lang, 2014).

Laurence Gouriévidis is a Professor of Modern British History at the University of Clermont Auvergne. As a cultural and social historian, she focuses on the interaction between history and memory, looking at the way societies construct their past, their heritage, and the discourse(s) surrounding these processes. Initially, her research explored the memorialisation of the past of northern Scotland (very specifically the Highland Clearances) in museums, commemorative practices, and monuments, leading her to consider such themes as agricultural changes and their social consequences, such as evictions, famine, migrations, conflict, and land reform. More recently, she has developed a comparative analysis, looking at the representation of migration in museums including Australian and French case studies. She is also working on the ethnographic representations of Highland Scotland, as well as the various modes of exhibiting folk culture since the middle of the nineteenth century. Gouriévidis has been visiting fellow at the University of Canberra in

2005 and received a grant from the Stramartine Trust in 2007. She is a member of the Association of Critical Heritage Studies and the International School for Cultural History. Her publications include *The Dynamics of Heritage: History, Memory and the Highland Clearances* (Ashgate, 2010) and *Museums and Migration: History, Memory and Politics* (Routledge, 2014).

Cormac Ó Gráda is an Emeritus Professor at the School of Economics, University College Dublin. His research focuses on living standards, population, and climate in pre-industrial Europe and on the economic history of famine generally. His many publications include *Black '47 and Beyond: The Great Irish Famine in History, Economy and Memory* (Princeton UP, 1999), *Jewish Ireland in the Age of Joyce: A Socioeconomic History* (Princeton UP, 2006), *Ireland's Great Famine: Interdisciplinary Perspectives* (UCD Press, 2006), *Famine: A Short History* (Princeton UP, 2009), and *Eating People is Wrong, and Other Essays on Famine, Its Past, and Its Future* (Princeton UP, 2015). He is co-editor of *When the Potato Failed: Causes and Effects of the Last European Subsistence Crisis, 1845–1850* (Brepols, 2007) and *Famine in European History* (with Guido Alfani, Cambridge UP, 2017).

Violetta Hionidou is a Professor of Modern European History at the School of History, Classics and Archaeology at Newcastle University. Her research focuses on all aspects of famines: birth control, abortion, and fertility in historical populations; popular and modern Medicine in modern Greece; family history; women's work; identities and experiences of exile of Pontic Greeks from the former USSR; and, more recently, experiences of being a refugee. Her research is interdisciplinary, transcending the fields of Demography, Sociology, Human Geography, and History. In all her work, she has employed oral history, tackling 'difficult' subjects ranging from abortion, birth control, and famine memory in Greece to identity and exile in the Soviet Union. In 2019, she held a Visiting Research Fellowship at Princeton University's Seeger Centre for Hellenic Studies. She is the founder of the Greek Family History website, offering detailed guidance on how to undertake family history with Greek sources. Her research is published in top peer-reviewed journals such as *Medical History, Population Studies, Journal of Refugee Studies, Journal of Contemporary History, Journal of the Social History of Medicine, Europe-Asia Studies*, and *The History of the Family: An International Quarterly.*

Lindsay Janssen is an Assistant Professor at the Department of Modern Languages & Cultures at Radboud University Nijmegen. She wrote a thesis on Irish and Irish diasporic popular fiction from the period 1871 to 1891 concerning the Great Irish Famine and cultural identity formation, and obtained her PhD in 2016. She was awarded a full-time individual Government of Ireland Postdoctoral Fellowship (GOIPD) by the Irish Research Council, and between 2017 and 2019 researched Irish transatlantic periodical culture and uses of Famine memory. For this research, she was affiliated with the School of English and the Humanities Institute at University College Dublin. In 2019, she obtained a grant from the Research Society for Victorian Periodical (RSVP) to do research into textual reuse practices in colonial periodicals at the British Library. From 2020 to 2023, Lindsay was a postdoctoral researcher on the Heritages of Hunger research project, funded by NWO.

Lotte Jensen is a Professor of Dutch Cultural and Literary History at Radboud University Nijmegen and co-applicant of the Heritages of Hunger project. She was Principal Investigator of the project 'Dealing with Disasters: The Shaping of Local and National Identities in the Netherlands (1421–1890)', for which she was awarded a VICI grant by the Dutch Research Council (NWO), and which investigated the impact of natural disasters on Dutch local and national identities from a cultural-historical perspective. Previously, she directed the project 'Proud to be Dutch', for which she was awarded a VIDI grant by NWO, which investigated the roots of nationalism in the Netherlands in a European context. She is a member of the Royal Netherlands Academy of Arts and Sciences (KNAW). Jensen is the author of *Water: A Dutch Cultural History*(Radboud University Press, 2024) and *Celebrating Peace. The Emergence of Dutch Identity, 1648–1815* (Vantilt, 2017). She was co-editor of *Free Access to the Past. Romanticism, Cultural Heritage and the Nation* (Brill, 2010), *The Roots of Nationalism. National Identity Formation in Europe, 1600–1815* (Amsterdam University Press, 2016), and *Dealing with Disasters from Early Modern to Modern Times. Cultural Responses to Catastrophes* (Amsterdam University Press, 2023).

Jason King is an Academic Coordinator of the Irish Heritage Trust and National Famine Museum. Previously, he was a part-time postdoctoral researcher in the Heritages of Hunger project at Radboud University Nijmegen, an assistant professor of Canadian Irish Studies at Concordia University, a lecturer in English at the National University of Ireland, Maynooth and the University of Limerick, a postdoctoral research fellow at the National University of Ireland, Galway, and a visiting professor at the Université de Montréal and University College Cork. His recent publications include *Irish Famine Migration Narratives: Eye-Witness Testimonies, History of the Irish Famine*, volume II (Routledge, 2018, with Christine Kinealy and Gerard Moran) and *Children and the Great Hunger in Ireland* (co-edited, Cork and Quinnipiac University Press, 2018).

Wiktoria Kudela-Świątek holds a PhD in History from the Jagiellonian University in Cracow. In 2015, she was awarded a scholarship from the Lanckoronski Family Fund. She participated in a research residency under the Research and Education Consortium for Holodomor Studies in Toronto (November 2017). She is the author of *Eternal Memory: Monuments and Memorials of the Holodomor* (Canadian Institute of Ukrainian Studies, 2021). From 2014 to 2021, she was engaged in the project 'Social Anthropology of Filling the Void: Poland and Ukraine After the WW2', implemented by the Institute of Philosophy and Sociology, in partnership with the Lviv Center for Urban History.

Deborah Madden is a Lecturer in Hispanic Studies at Lancaster University. She completed her PhD in Hispanic Studies at the University of Sheffield, lectured at Manchester University, and previously was a Leverhulme Postdoctoral Fellow at the Instituto de Investigaciones Feministas, Universidad Complutense de Madrid. Her research interests centre on the intersections of culture, politics, and history in contemporary Iberia, with a particular focus on feminism and biopolitics. She is the author of *Matilde de la Torre: Sex, Socialism and Suffrage* (Legenda 2022). From 2022 to 2023, Deborah was part of the Heritages of Hunger team at Radboud University Nijmegen, working as a postdoctoral researcher on the musealisation of Spanish famine legacies.

Anne van Mourik is a PhD candidate at the University of Amsterdam and the NIOD Institute for War, Holocaust, and Genocide Studies. Her research project within the Heritages of Hunger project is entitled 'Conflicting Legacies of Hunger in Germany' and deals with commemorative practices surrounding the conditions of hunger in Germany during and after the First and Second World Wars. More specifically, she analyses the significance of hunger in educational institutions and the heritage sector over time. Anne is also co-host of the podcast series NIOD Rewind, in which she interviews historians and other experts on the study of mass violence, war, and genocide. Before her PhD, she worked as a research assistant in the project 'Independence, Decolonisation, Violence and War in Indonesia 1945–1950', as a researcher at the Faculty of Governance and Global Affairs at Leiden University, and as a research assistant in a study on the role of the Dutch Red Cross during World War II.

Gloria Román Ruiz is an Assistant Professor at the University of Granada and was previously involved as a postdoctoral researcher in the Heritages of Hunger project. Ruiz completed her PhD at the University of Granada and has been a visiting researcher at the London School of Economics and Political Sciences and at Bristol University. Her line of research has focused on the study of everyday life during Franco's dictatorship (1939–79). In particular, she has analysed the small resistance practices during the Spanish years of hunger and the social politics of the regime to extend its popular support. She published the monograph *Delinquir o morir. El pequeño estraperlo en la Granada de posguerra* (Comares, 2015), and she has been one of the editors of the collective book *Tiempo de dictadura. Experiencias cotidianas durante la guerra, el franquismo y la democracia* (Universidad de Granada, 2019). She is also the author of several articles in peer-reviewed journals such as *Historia Agraria*, *International Journal of Iberian Studies*, *Paedagogica Historica* and *Bulletin of Spanish Studies: Hispanic Studies and Researches on Spain, Portugal and Latin America*.

Ingrid de Zwarte is an Assistant Professor of Economic and Environmental History at Wageningen University and Research. She completed her PhD in History at the University of Amsterdam and the NIOD Institute for War, Holocaust, and Genocide Studies in 2018 with a thesis entitled *The Hunger Winter: Fighting Famine in the Occupied Netherlands, 1944–45*, published by Cambridge University Press in 2020. After her PhD, she was a Niels Stensen Postdoctoral Fellow at Oxford University (2018–19), working on the project 'Hunger as a Weapon: A Comparative Study into the Politics of Famine and Relief'. De Zwarte has published on the Dutch Hunger Winter in journals such as *Population Studies*, *War & Society*, *Food & History*, and *Memory Studies*. She is currently PI of the project 'Food, Famine, and the End of Empire in Indonesia, 1940–1950' and co-director of 'Heritages of Hunger', both funded by the Dutch Research Council NWO. In 2023, she was awarded an Early Career Award by the Royal Netherlands Academy of Arts and Sciences for her work on the politics of famine.

The editors are grateful to the Dutch research council, NWO, for funding the research project from which this volume has ensued: Heritages of Hunger: Societal Reflections on Past European Famines in Education, Commenoration and Musealisation (NWA.1160.18.197).

INTRODUCTION

Famines and the making of heritage

Marguérite Corporaal and Ingrid de Zwarte

The term 'famine' often brings to mind media images of the past as well as ongoing hunger crises, such as those currently faced by millions in the war-stricken regions Gaza, Ethiopia, Yemen, Somalia, and South Sudan. What distinguishes a famine from a food crisis is often subject to debate, but famine is commonly defined as a shortage of food or purchasing power directly leading to excess mortality from starvation, hunger-induced diseases, and fertility decline.[1] The fact that wide-scale famines involving high mortality rates occurred on the European continent, well into the mid-twentieth century, has been widely addressed in seminal scholarship.[2] Yet most people living in Europe—especially the younger generations—will likely not be well acquainted with these episodes of hunger, such as those that occurred in Finland (1866–68), Spain (1939–52), Greece (1941–44), the Netherlands (1944–45), or Germany (1945–49).

At the same time, the memories of European famines have hardly ever been so central to societal debates as over the past five years. The current Russian-Ukrainian war has rekindled international attention for the famine suffered in Ukraine under the Stalinist regime in 1932–33, also known as the 'Holodomor' (meaning 'death through starvation'). Since Russia's invasion in Ukraine in February 2022 and following Ukrainian President Zelensky's repeated calls, countries throughout the world as well as the European Parliament have recently recognised the Ukrainian famine as genocide. What is more, the rich heritage of the Holodomor—in the form of archives, monuments, commemorations, teaching practices, and museums, both in the mother country and in diaspora—is being reframed in relation to the ongoing war and Russia's President Putin's use of hunger as a weapon of warfare, demonstrating how famine pasts are currently used to make sense of the present.

DOI: 10.4324/9781003391524-1

The reinterpretation of the Holodomor in the context of Russia's war in Ukraine illustrates a wider trend that we may witness with regard to European famine heritages. Indeed, past famine legacies are often recalled to give meaning to current problems, for example, with the purpose of emphasising present injustice. During the opening of the photograph exhibition 'The Unknown Famine: Athens 1941–1942' in the European (EU) Parliament in Brussels in March 2017, European MP Stelios Kouloglou drew explicit analogies between the Greek Famine that took place under Axis occupation 75 years earlier and Greece's debt crisis of the present time.[3] As Kouloglou claimed, the restrictions placed by the EU upon Greece to reorganise its financial condition seemed unjust in light of the famine the country suffered during Second World War (WWII). 'Greece is suffering and is accused, wrongfully, for being [...] disorganized under the present government', Kouloglou stated. The exhibition, which brings a forgotten famine under the public's attention, explains why: 'this story reminds us why this happened, because Greece was the last country to start the reconstruction after the Second World War'.[4] In this case, famine heritage was used to express critique of EU's austerity measures and rally support for left-wing Greek politics.[5]

While these famine legacies, on the one hand, still operate in contexts that reinforce tensions between European communities today, on the other hand, they also offer a solid foundation for mutual understanding and expressions of responsibility, solidarity, reconciliation, and reparation. One of these purposes is the evocation of sympathy for those in difficult circumstances, such as refugees. For example, in 2015, Rowan Gillespie's Great Irish Famine Monument (1997) at Dublin's Custom House Quay, which consists of large, bronze sculptures of emaciated figures walking towards an emigrant vessel, became the centre of pro-refugee demonstrations.[6] The drowning of migrants in the Mediterranean sparked an awareness that Ireland too had been a country of refugees, some of whom had lost their lives at sea, turning Gillespie's famine monument into a site of political mobilisation through past remembrance, based on a sense of 'historical duty'.[7]

A similar sense of 'historical duty', in the sense of appreciation for the doctors and nurses who put their lives at risk at the beginning of the COVID-19 pandemic, was evoked during the sober, annual Great Irish Famine commemoration in May 2020, at Edward Delaney's Famine monument in St. Stephen's Green in Dublin. During her speech, Ireland's Minister for Culture, Heritage, and the Gaeltacht, Josepha Madigan, drew parallels between the heroic fortitude shown by 'the doctors and nurses of the fever hospitals, in and outside Ireland, who risked their own lives to care for others' and 'the same qualities of courage and commitment to others in our healthcare staff today'.[8]

European famine memories are thus still omnipresent in societal debates and the public sphere, and, as the above examples reveal, heritage practices play a significant role in the ways in which these legacies are (re-)interpreted. This reinterpretation happens through what James Wertsch calls 'narrative templates': plotlines through which societies organise memory as ways to give meaning to the past.[9] In fact, one could argue that heritages of hunger, while shaped by ideological iconographies and narrative schemata themselves in processes of creation, preservation, and canonisation, may also open up alternative or complementary perspectives in looking at European famine pasts. Heritage is on the one hand an 'expression of the values, historical interpretations and perceived communal pasts of communities';[10] on the other hand, as we have argued elsewhere, the 'shared memory of a culturally active community may form the impetus to the creation of new heritage such as monuments, commemorative rituals and museum collections, or the conservation of material and immaterial artefacts and practices'.[11]

In view of this important function of heritage in the mediation and continuous reconstruction of famine memory, it is remarkable that scholarly research has hitherto predominantly focused on the sociohistorical and economic dimensions of European hunger crises. Major exceptions include pioneering studies by Emily Mark-FitzGerald and Niamh Ann Kelly about monuments and heritage sites related to Ireland's Great Famine, research by Andrew Newby about Finnish Famine monuments, Lisa Kirschenbaum's seminal work on the legacies of the siege of Leningrad, and Lindsay Janssen's and Gloria Román Ruiz' studies into the ways in which recent secondary school textbooks have mediated memories of Ireland's Great Famine and Spain's 'hunger years', respectively.[12] An extensive and comparative study on the role of famines in relation to heritage making has been notably absent. This is striking given the fact that famine is one of the most prominent experiences of the modern era shared by various communities across the European continent that has generated a diverse, yet connected, set of cultural legacies stretching from the mid-nineteenth century to the present day.

This volume is the first to bring together seminal scholarship on famine heritage making, engaging with the legacies of ten different modern European famines that took place between 1845 and 1947. Adopting a pioneering comparative perspective, the contributions address issues such as contestable and repressed heritage, politicisation, materiality, oral history, as well as affect. Questions that are addressed include: are these famine heritages region- or nation-oriented or transnational, and do they emphasise conflict or mutual understanding? How do present issues of European concern intersect with the heritage and memory of these modern European famines? What role do emigrant and diasporic communities within and outside Europe play in the development of heritage practices about these European famines? And how do these heritages develop in societies divided by religion, language, or sectarianism? The included chapters cover various forms of famine heritage making, both from the distant past and the present: ranging from educational textbooks and classroom practices to commemorative ceremonies and from monuments to museum exhibitions. Taking a transnational approach to famine legacies, this volume is the first to uncover the past and present significance of European famines, demonstrating that these troubled pasts are part of a shared European history. Obviously, there are more modern European famines than these contributions could possibly cover, such as the Swedish famine of 1867–69, the 1921–22 Russian famine, and 1946–47 Soviet famines, or the famine conditions created by Nazi Germany in ghettos, concentration camps, and Soviet POW camps during WWII. The many lethal famines that occurred in the global south in the nineteenth and twentieth centuries, not in the least because of European colonial regimes and institutions, also fall beyond the scope of this volume. The chapters in this volume nonetheless discuss the legacies of high-impact European famines in various corners of Europe, selecting case studies that particularly shed light on processes of heritage making in relation to catastrophe, which may very well be applicable to famine legacies in other European and non-European contexts.

Retrieving famine pasts

As the above examples illustrate, cultural legacies of European famines are often utilised and reframed in the context of recent societal issues and developments for different aims. As Cormac Ó Gráda states in the "Afterword" to this volume, this is because famine legacies are intrinsically collective. In this respect, we see a confirmation of Astrid Erll's argument that memory is inherently fluid, as it can travel through time and space, 'across [...] and also beyond cultures', and in that process attain new meanings that serve present agendas and future ambitions.[13] In researching famine heritage making, we should therefore be aware of shifts in the narrative schemata employed to give meaning to these European famine pasts, which can be traced back to watershed developments in historiography, the political and economic conditions of societies which remember these famines, as well as global developments in relation to migration, humanitarian aid, war, and human rights.

Above all, state-sanctioned memory politics strongly impact the development and visibility of famine heritages. There are often tensions between institutionally recognised notions of heritage and 'subaltern and dissenting heritage discourses' that offer alternative but equally valid perspectives on the experiences of legacies.[14] As Aleida Assmann argues, the 'canon' comprises pasts that are recurrently, actively remembered in the public sphere, whereas the 'archive' contains traces and narratives of the past that have either unintentionally fallen 'out of frames of attention' through passive forgetting, or that have been actively forgotten through forms of repression.[15]

With regard to European famine pasts, active forgetting of hunger crises appears to have taken place during the Soviet regime (the Holodomor), and in Francoist Spain and its aftermath (the *años del hambre*). The chapters by Kudela (Part II, Chapter 6) and by Del Arco Blanco and Madden (Part III, Chapter 9) go into the impact of these historical periods of active forgetting, as a result of which famine heritage emerged relatively late in the public sphere (Ukraine) or is still in the early stages of development (Spain). Hionidou's chapter (Part II, Chapter 5) furthermore demonstrates that while famines may not be completely relegated to the realm of oblivion, certain aspects of hunger crises that are inconvenient for national and international politics may be pushed to the margins in favour of a narrative that suits present and future ambitions. As Hionidou argues about Greece's 1940s famine, the national canon narrative, which was reiterated during the 2008 financial crisis over which Greece and Germany clashed, unjustly blames just Germany for the hunger crisis. The complexity of the famine past is not acknowledged in this national canonised narrative, and it is by turning mainly to regional heritage initiatives and archives, from, for instance, Chios and Crete, as well as through creating oral histories that can retrieve alternative perspectives and voices on the famine.

That once-repressed pasts can resurface and lead to the recovery of legacies and new heritage initiatives can be explained by the dynamics between 'available' and 'accessible' memory. As Jefferson Singer and Martin Conway have argued, some pasts are not really forgotten but less accessible in the public sphere: this happens when certain legacies are 'available' but may not be widely 'accessible' at any given time because they remain hidden in archives or because people have kept back testimonies of such a past for personal or political reasons. This implies, however, that such legacies 'can potentially be retrieved and through the retrieval process might enter consciousness and so influence experience and behavior' as well.[16]

While Del Arco Blanco and Madden's Chapter 9 (Part III) mainly focuses on explaining the relative absence of Spanish famine heritage, recent years have also seen budding endeavours to give a due place to these legacies of the hunger years by making them 'accessible' memory. The first chapter, 'Challenges and Opportunities in Teaching European Famines' (Part I), which compares the mediation of various European famine pasts in recent educational textbooks in four European countries, shows that the term '*hambre*' (hunger) is more explicitly identified and actively used with the Franco dictatorship than had hitherto been the case. The acknowledgement of terminology that acknowledges the status of calamities as famines is therefore one important step forward in endorsing its 'available', but often repressed legacies.

One important aspect that educators, policymakers, curators, and museum staff struggle with in constructing famine heritage is the absence of material traces or artefacts. Often, this sense of absence is due to a lack of consciousness. As contributions by Gouriévidis (Part III, Chapter 7), De Zwarte and Jensen

(Part II, Chapter 4), and Boerman (Part III, Chapter 8) point out, societies are often unaware of the rich famine heritage that is available in their proximity, because such monuments or museum exhibits are regional initiatives which have received little to no national endorsement. For example, as De Zwarte and Jensen point out in their chapter, commemorative sites to the Dutch Hunger Winter are first and foremost regional initiatives spread across the country. This dispersion and relative absence of famine memorialisation in the Netherlands, they contend, makes legacies of the Hunger Winter less visible in the public sphere than those related to other events within WWII.

Enhancing the visibility of local famine heritage and encapsulating this in a national narrative is therefore often a matter of collecting dispersed available voices, stories, and even monuments, and the opportunities of using digital tools to create heritage repositories that make these legacies more broadly accessible cannot be underestimated. Providing wider accessibility or even endorsing the visibility of famine-related *lieux de mémoire*, as well as creating new famine heritage through monuments or museums, may furthermore give an impulse to 'dark tourism': travelling visitors interested in 'the memorialisation of the dead [...] concerned with historical atroicity and evil and driven by a desire for education and greater self-awareness'.[17] The 165-km National Famine Way trail that traces the footsteps of the evicted Strokestown tenants from Roscommon to an emigrant ship in Dublin in 1847 is an example of such a venture to turn famine legacies into tourist destinations.[18]

At the same time, as museum studies experts also observe, engaging today's audiences often relies on spectacle or the display of material objects to make the past come alive to visitors. In *Mediating Memory in the Museum* (2013), Silke Arnold-de Simine argues persuasively that 'the museum's representation of the past is intended to generate a sense of belonging that requires emotional investment and identification, sometimes to the extent that it generates the imaginative living through events in order to develop strong forms of affective engagement'.[19] Yet the main challenge seems to be how to evoke this engagement in connection to famine pasts, which have left very few material traces, as these are pasts characterised by dispossession, emigration, and death. Therefore, as Laurence Gouriévidis shows (Part III, Chapter 7) museums rarely mediate a sense of Famine pasts through objects, instead resorting to textual panels.

In recent famine heritage projects, enactment and reconstruction have been used as strategies to evoke what Laurence Gouriévidis has called 'vicarious empathy'.[20] For example, in the Doagh Famine village in County Donegal, tableaux with manikins are being used to represent famine evictions in Ireland to stimulate empathy with Famine victims. However, as Arnold-de Simine also warns, recurrent tension arises in processes of curation between the evocation of generic authenticity and historical specificity. As she remarks, 'There is a fine line between the historian's investment in the authentic object which can provide a wealth of information to the initiated and the fetishist belief that an object has somehow soaked up the events in which it has played a role and allows a spectator to feel that they are in the presence of the past'.[21] Issues of affect versus historical authenticity are thus significant to consider in researching famine heritage, which is a recurrent challenge faced in various European famine contexts.

Three areas of heritage making

The present volume is thematically arranged according to three areas that together encompass the manifold ways in which European famines are mediated in processes of heritage making: through education, memorialisation, and musealisation. Part I focuses on the role of famines in formal education and presents comparative research on European hunger legacies in curricula and textbooks. As Maria Grever and Tina van der Vlies note, curricula and textbooks often serve to endorse national narratives of the past that play an important role in cementing communal identities, and textbooks in particular have a 'canonical function' as repositories of reliable and valid knowledge.[22]

The contributions to Part I are testimony to the fact that formal education, in the form of textbooks, holds a pivotal role in transferring famine heritage to younger generations without living memories of this dark past. As such, textbooks are of vital importance not only in passing on historical awareness but also helping shape present-day and future cultural identities.[23] How famine pasts are represented in textbooks is often strongly influenced by national curricula, historiographical practices, and didactic methodologies, but they are not mere transmitters of 'official memory'.[24] Contributions to Part I show how curricula represent and narrativise famine pasts based on different, and sometimes conflicting, views of the pasts, which are often not in line with the latest scholarly insights. At the same time, chapters in this section demonstrate how education is an important tool in mediating political ambitions for the future.

Significantly, a transnational approach to famine pasts is still largely absent from educational textbooks and practices, even if there are ample opportunities. Chapter 1 in this collection, 'Challenges and Opportunities in Teaching European Famines', compares present-day textbooks for secondary education from Germany, Spain, Ireland, and the Netherlands. The authors show that famine education is usually based on simplified subject positions—often not in line with the latest scholarly insights—leading to problematic misrepresentations of these seminal episodes in history. They conclude that a transnational approach, which not only considers historical hunger periods in a comparative light but also connects hunger pasts to current-day global challenges, is still largely absent. However, as Lindsay Janssen, Anne van

Mourik, Gloria Román Ruiz, and Ingrid de Zwarte show, there is more potential to adopt a transnational approach in teaching European famines. They give evidence for this on the basis of an exploration of victim-perpetrator discourses, common tropes, and representations, as well as surveys among teachers across Europe.

While transnational perspectives on famines can still be notably absent from educational resources and classroom practices, using such a lens in research may generate further insights into the instrumentalisation of these famine pasts in the past and present. Anne-Lise Bobeldijk (Chapter 2) reveals this in her comparative analysis of textbook representations of the Ukrainian Holodomor and the Leningrad blockade of 1941–44 from 1956 until now. The first part of her essay investigates Soviet secondary-level textbooks from 1956 until 1991 in order to establish how these two man-made famines were portrayed during the post-Stalin Soviet era. The second part of her chapter examines how both famines have been taught in Ukrainian and Russian textbooks since the fall of the Soviet Union. As she contends, a comparative, transnational analysis refines our understanding of how education and textbooks are used in the politicisation of history in current political conflicts.

In the case of Ireland's Great Famine, one can speak of a memory culture that transcends national borders and is therefore shared by homeland and Irish diasporic communities descending from Famine emigrants. As a result, the Great Famine is an integral part of American and Canadian memory cultures, and, historically, the Famine and its exodus to North America are recurrent topics in US and Canadian textbooks, as Marguérite Corporaal and Jason King show in Chapter 3. However, as they also illustrate through analyses of textbooks from Ontario and Quebec, and interviews held with teachers, the presence of the Irish Famine and the arrival of Famine immigrants in curricula and educational materials is fading into the background, even more so as the Irish diaspora does not fit comfortably with ethnic, religious, and language politics in both provinces. Visits to heritage sites by educators and school classes may, however, rekindle interests in Ireland's famine past and its connections to Canadian history, Corporaal and King assert.

Part II shifts the focus to the memorialisation of famines: through commemoration practices, through the recording and dissemination of oral histories that often force us to rethink common assumption about the past, and monuments. Commemoration practices serve as a form of redress, providing recognition of the suffering endured by victims, survivors, and successive generations identifying with this past.[25] Furthermore, ceremonies and rituals of commemoration, whether organised top-down or from below, help create a sense of social cohesion, bringing together different groups who identify with these legacies while also socialising populations into a common culture.[26] In this respect, commemorative practices offer informal education to the citizens that participate in them, for example, through workshops, lectures, or educational packages. Moreover, commemorations are often staged in the vicinity of monuments. These memorials are either erected on sites where fateful events of the past occurred, as natural *lieux de mémoire*, or on alternative sites that have become demarcated for crystallising recollections of such pasts, in view of the present politics and economics of societies.[27]

The contributions to Part II investigate the representation of European famines in monuments as well as their function in commemoration practices. As Chapter 4 by Ingrid de Zwarte and Lotte Jensen demonstrates, in the years following the Dutch Hunger Winter (1944–45) only a few, inconspicuous local monuments to this famine were established. Yet even if the Hunger Winter has left few visual objects of commemoration in the Dutch landscape, as De Zwarte and Jensen show, the famine itself did not generate a pervasive, traumatic silence. In the case of the Netherlands, the paradoxical absence of famine monuments stems from a culmination of several factors, which include Dutch war memory politics and the absence of engaged diasporic communities.

Recovering 'accessible' memory that has been subject to neglect or deliberate 'social forgetting',[28] and re-inserting this memory into the public sphere also creates opportunities to revise the narratives that have directed processes of commemoration in a society. Over the past years, personal testimonies and memories—either in written form or as recorded and transcribed oral history—have gained further prominence in both famine research and famine heritage making as resources which can counter existing memory narratives. Violetta Hionidou's Chapter 5 in this collection, '"Remembering" the Greek Famine of the Early 1940s', foregrounds the importance of oral histories undertaken by historians in contesting official, canonised memory that the Greek famine during WWII lasted only during the winter 1941–42, the Germans were solely responsible for this famine, and that Athens suffered the most. These contrasting oral histories nuance the canonised narrative which has undergone a revival in the media since the 2009 economic crisis. A question which Hionidou cannot answer at this stage, but that encourages speculation is the extent to which these oral histories will impact future museum exhibitions and commemorations.

This sense of famine heritage as the key to bring out in the open memories of the past that have remained unarticulated due to state politics also surfaces in Wiktoria Kudela's Chapter 6, 'Holodomor Monuments on the Battlefield'. Kudela shows that remembrance of the Ukrainian famine of 1932–33 in the country itself could only really take shape after Ukraine's independence in 1991. This retrieval of a past soon called Holodomor is reflected in the memorial cultures that came into existence during the post-Soviet era. As Kudela demonstrates, the construction of monuments in the Ukrainian capital of Kyiv progressed or stagnated under the influence of changing governments, and the social significance of these monuments also altered since the Maidan Revolution (2013), Russia's occupation of the Crimean and Donbas regions (2014), and the ongoing war since February 2022. Furthermore, in her analysis of the design for the Holodomor Museum that is still under construction, Kudela illustrates how aesthetics of a heritage site can contribute to the idea of an uncovered past that at last becomes fully accessible to visitors.

Museums are heritage sites where visitors also interact with and learn about past legacies. As Eilean Hooper-Greenhill claims, museums are 'active in shaping knowledge; using their collections, they put together visual cultural narratives which produce views odd the past and thus of the present'.[29] In other words, museums play a significant role in providing templates and interpretive frameworks through which we remember the past, even when, relying on 'spectacle' and 'display', the learning experience is 'more individually directed, more unpredictable'.[30] Part III examines how these past European famines are represented in museums—a much-underexplored subject that sheds further light on how we archive and preserve the legacies of troubled pasts in light of issues of forgetting and silencing.

Scales of heritage making—that is, whether this heritage is created on regional, national or even transnational levels—clearly impact the awareness and interpretation of famine pasts. This is also what Laurence Gouriévidis (Chapter 7) argues in 'Famine Clearances in the Scottish Highlands'. As she explains, the socioeconomic backgrounds of the 1845–46 Scottish potato famine, the effects of which were aggravated by the policy of clearances, primarily feature in regional museums located in the regions that were most affected at the time, the Highlands. The National Museum of Scotland and the National Museum of Rural Life, by contrast, do not specifically feature the famine, merely mentioning it as an event that instigated emigration and technological progress. As she suggests, placing the 1845–46 Scottish Famine in the broader context of similar famines that took place elsewhere in Europe may add to a better understanding of the social inequalities that reinforced the catastrophe.

It is, however, still difficult to integrate this regional famine heritage into a national narrative centred around stamina and progress. This becomes clear from Charley Boerman's contribution to this volume in Part III (Chapter 8), which discusses the memorials found along the so-called 'Skeleton Track', the railway that was built as relief work between Riihimäki and St. Petersburg between 1867 and 1870, and that led to an upsurge in deaths. Boerman examines the local initiatives which led to the erection of memorials to mark these mass graves and, additionally, the extent to which such sites are remembered in very recent exhibitions in national museums across Finland. As she concludes, these monuments to victims of famine and harsh labour sit uneasily with the narratives of the past that have come to shape Finland's post-imperial identity.

As Camilla Orjuela argues, there are various factors that tend to 'make famine memorialisation difficult: narrative challenges, shame and competing traumas'.[31] Nonetheless, the retrieval of famine legacies in contexts which previously allowed little space for memories of these bleak pasts is one of the current trends in famine heritage. This process of recuperating famine memories takes place very slowly in present-day Spain, as Miguel Ángel del Arco Blanco and Deborah Madden argue in Chapter 9. During Franco's long regime (1939–75) both the famine and the wider Years of Hunger were silenced. After Franco's death in 1975, during the so-called Spanish Transition (1975–82), the 'Pact of Oblivion' ensured that the past was left untouched, and no policies of memory recovery were adopted by the new democratic governments. As a result, until the emergence of the movement for the recovery of historical memory (2000) and the first relevant measures of the Government (2007), there were no active policies of memory about the Spanish traumatic hunger years. This might be the main reason to explain the lack of elements that musealise or commemorate both the hunger years and the famine in present-day Spain. As recovery of famine memory can also lay bare societal divisions, as Ó Gráda argues in the 'Afterword', this can be a challenging process.

Transnational perspectives and directions

Together, the chapters shed light on the ways in which famine pasts are mediated in specific forms of heritage making, thereby revealing opportunities and challenges for, amongst others, teachers, policymakers, and museum curators. What is more, the contributions point to potential transnational routes and methodologies for researching famine legacies, as well as discuss existing transnational dimensions of European famine heritage. As such, the chapters to this volume engage with the current transnational turn in European famine heritage, which is arguably rooted in three phenomena: firstly, the exposure of comparable famine conditions across borders and transnational relief operations, as well as transnational cultural repertoires of famine remembrance; secondly, the intersections between the cultural memories of these famines in the homeland on the one hand and those of migrant communities on the other hand; and thirdly, the increasing 'multi-directional' nature of these famine heritages.[32]

There are several recent examples of heritage initiatives which provide comparative perspectives on European famines, and which draw attention to transnational solidarity. These pioneering efforts by heritage makers in the museum sector—to reframe European famines in terms of transnational relief operations—are noticeable in the construction of recent famine monuments, which often commemorate international aid. One example is the Operation Manna monument in Rotterdam (Part II, Chapter 4), designed by Ruud

Reutelingsperger and unveiled on 4 April 2006, which encapsulates the memory of the Allied food drops that took place between 29 April and 8 May 1945 in the western Netherlands. Representing stacked food packages in the steel 'belly' of a plane, the memorial eulogises the British and American military forces who operated more than 5300 flights to distribute food to the starving Dutch. Various chapters in this volume further analyse such heritage initiatives which contextualise famines transnationally: most notably, the chapters by De Zwarte and Jensen (Part II, Chapter 4) and Boerman (Part III, Chapter 8).

Furthermore, this volume includes pioneering examples of comparative research concerning European famine heritage: the chapters by Janssen, Van Mourik, Román Ruiz, and De Zwarte (Part I, Chapter 1) and Bobeldijk (Part I, Chapter 2) show the added value of comparing textbook narratives about various European hunger crises. As their contributions make clear, these comparative approaches help illuminate in what ways certain socio-political contexts—and in particular post-regime and post-war trauma, as well as processes of (postcolonial) identity formation—affect the visibility, recognition, and interpretation of famine pasts in education practices. Furthermore, while focusing on regional and national heritage making, the chapters by De Zwarte and Jensen in Part II and by Gouriévidis (Chapter 7), Boerman (Chapter 8), and Del Arco Blanco and Madden (Chapter 9) in Part III also draw analogies with the monumentalisation and musealisation of other famines, especially Ireland's Great Famine and the Ukrainian Holodomor.

That European famine heritages are often transnational in the sense that they are integral to memory cultures both in the country of origin and in diasporic communities also becomes evident from various examples in this collection. In the case of Ireland's Great Famine, there are also connections between *lieux de mémoire* in the country of origin, where the famine took place, and in diaspora. One example is the bronze statues made by Rowan Gillespie, which connect the Custom house Quay in Dublin as the Famine immigrants' point of departure with monuments at Toronto's Ireland Park on Éireann Quay. 'Famine' (1997) in Dublin represents starving peasants who have walked all the way to the emigrant vessel. 'Migrants' (2006) conveys the hope of the migrants—whose bronze images bear exact likeness to the famishing throng in Dublin—as symbolised by the swollen belly of the expecting female passenger who has disembarked and the way in which one of the male figures stretches out his hands to the waterfront and the heart of the city. The Great Famine is an integral part of American and Canadian memory cultures, and, historically, the Famine and its exodus to North America are recurrent topics in US and Canadian textbooks, as Corporaal's and King's contribution (Part I, Chapter 3) reveals.

Kudela's chapter (Part II, Chapter 6) also testifies to what Thomas Faist calls the 'transnational affiliations [...] shared by both immigrants and natives'.[33]

In 'Holodomor Monuments on the Battlefield', she observes that the Ukrainian global diaspora not only set examples of what Holodomor monuments could look like, such as the first ever memorial in Edmonton, Canada, which was unveiled in 1983; private sponsors of Holodomor monuments in Ukraine were mainly individuals belonging to the Ukrainian diaspora. Indeed, Holodomor heritage is essentially transatlantic in various other respects than those mentioned by Kudela. Ceremonies to commemorate the Holodomor take place in both Ukraine (since 1996) and Canada (since 2008), each fourth Saturday of November. These forms of transnational funding and collaboration are extended to digital heritage: the Ukrainian Canadian Research and Documentation Centre developed a database containing 457 photographs, which maps out all Holodomor monuments in Ukraine.[34]

In today's globalised world, it is by no means surprising that heritage projects function as assemblages of what Michael Rothberg calls 'multidirectional memory'[35]: intersections and interactions between memories related to different pasts that transcend boundaries of time and culture. So far, heritage projects aiming to represent the intersecting famine memories of different cultural communities as pasts of analogous suffering are rare, and those which have been realised continue to spark controversies. Several contributions to this volume show that today's famine heritage, in its multidirectionality, can address present-day issues as well as be more inclusive of new European citizens. Kudela's contribution (Part II, Chapter 6) shows how two Holodomor monuments in Kyiv have attained additional layers of signification through their geographical placement close to memorials to the present Russian-Ukrainian war. As she contends, the Famine monuments are thus sites which also invoke other cultural memories and elicit the creation of other heritage sites related to different pasts.

Moreover, famine legacies can be reinterpreted through analogies with present-day hunger and dislocation. The authors of Chapter 1 show that recent textbooks, such as the German *Kursbuch Geschichte*, ask students to compare the situation of refugees and displaced persons at the end of WWII with the situation of migrants today, thereby suggesting multidirectional approaches to the past. De Zwarte and Jensen (Part II, Chapter 4) furthermore discuss the first Hunger Winter monument that functions 'multidirectionally',[36] by placing the Dutch famine in dialogue with other events, such as the pasts of migrant and refugee communities. The examples of multidirectional and transnational heritage that these chapters discuss provide ground for rethinking future directions for both famine heritage studies as well as heritage practices in multicultural societies. Together, the findings and conclusions of the chapters feed our understanding of famine legacies as forms of cultural memory that are mediated transgenerationally, transnationally, as well as transculturally.

Notes

1 Cormac Ó Gráda, *Famine: A Short History* (Princeton, NJ: Princeton University Press, 2009), 4; Paul Howe and Devereux, 'Famine Intensity and Magnitude Scales: A Proposal for an Instrumental Definition of Famine,' *Disasters* 28, no. 4 (2004): 353–72.

2 See, amongst others, Cormac Ó Gráda and Guido Alfani, eds., *Famine in European History* (Cambridge: Cambridge University Press, 2017); Miguel Ángel del Arco Blanco and Peter Anderson, *Franco's Famine* (London: Bloomsbury, 2021); Andrea Graziosi, et al., eds., *After the Holodomor: The Enduring Impact of the Great Famine on Ukraine* (Cambridge, MA: Harvard University Press, 2013); Violetta Hionidou, *Famine and Death in Occupied Greece, 1941–1944* (Cambridge: Cambridge University Press, 2006); Andrew Newby, *Finland's Great Famine, 1856–68* (London: Palgrave, 2023); Ingrid de Zwarte, *The Hunger Winter. Fighting Famine in the Occupied Netherlands, 1944–1945* (Cambridge: Cambridge University Press, 2020).

3 See Charley Boerman, *Framing Famines: Memory, Museums, and Visual Culture*, (Unpublished PhD Diss., Radboud University Nijmegen, 2024).

4 "The Unknown Famine of Athens 1941–1942—Photo Exhibition—EU Parliament". https://www.youtube.com/watch?v=iJdvhvLbObc, last accessed 11 September 2022.

5 For example, on how legacies of the Dutch Hunger Winter have been recalled in connection to recent famines, see Ingrid de Zwarte and Lindsay Janssen, 'Recalling the Hunger Winter: Evoking Famine Memory Beyond the National', *Memory Studies* 17, no. 2 (2024): 213–27.

6 See David Kearns, 'Thousands Turn Out in Dublin and across Europe for Refugee Support Rally', *The Irish Times*, 12 September 2015. https://www.independent.ie/irish-news/thousands-turn-out-in-dublin-and-across-europe-for-refugee-support-rally-31522118.html, last accessed 29 July 2020.

7 For this concept in relation to refugees in Ireland, see Charlotte McIvor, 'Historical Duty, Palimpsestic Time and Migration in the Decade of Centenaries', *Irish Studies Review* 24, no. 1 (2016): 51. See, for example, Kevin Kenny*, The American Irish: A History* (London: Longman, 2000); and Cian T. McMahon, *The Coffin Ship: Life and Death at Sea During the Great Famine* (New York: NYU Press, 2021).

8 https://www.chg.gov.ie/speech/speech-by-minister-for-culture-heritage-and-the-gaeltacht-josepha-madigan-t-d-at-the-national-famine-commemoration-2020/, last accessed 20 May 2020.

9 James V. Wertsch, *Voices of Collective Remembering* (New York: Cambridge University Press, 2002), 57.

10 Marguérite Corporaal and Ingrid de Zwarte, 'Heritages of Hunger: European Famine legacies in current Academic Debates', *International Journal of Heritage Studies* 28, no. 1 (2022): 31. See also, Veysel Apaydin, 'The Interlinkage of Cultural Memory, Heritage, and Discourses of Construction, Transformation, and Destruction', in *Critical Perspectives on Cultural Memory and Heritage: Construction, Transformation and Destruction* (London: UCL Press, 2020), 16.

11 Corporaal and De Zwarte, 'Heritages of Hunger', 31.

12 See Niamh Ann Kelly, *Imaging the Great Irish Famine: Representing Dispossession in Visual Culture* (London: I.B. Tauris, 2018); Lisa Kirschenbaum, *The Legacy of the Siege of Leningrad, 1941–1995: Myth, Memories, and Monuments* (Cambridge: Cambridge University Press, 2006); Emily Mark-FitzGerald, *Commemorating the Irish Famine: Memory and the Monument* (Liverpool: Liverpool University Press, 2013); Andrew Newby, 'Finland's "Great Hunger Years" Memorials: A Sesquicentennial Report', in Andrew Newby, ed., *The Enormous Failure of Nature'*:

Famine and Society in the Nineteenth Century. CollEgium 22 (2016): 173–214; Lindsay Janssen, 'The Great Irish Famine in Irish and UK History Textbooks, 2010–2020,' *History Education Research Journal* 20, no. 1. (2023): online pre-publication. doi: 10.14324/HERJ.20.1.02; Gloria Román Ruiz, 'Representations of the Spanish Hunger Years (1939–1952) in Recent Secondary School History Textbooks,' *Pedagogica Historica* (2022): 59, no. 6 (2023): 1345–66.

13 Astrid Erll, 'From "District Six" to District 9 and Back: The Plurimedial Production of Travelling Schemata', in Chiara de Cesari and Ann Rigney, eds., *Transnational Memory: Circulation, Articulation, Scales* (Berlin/New York: De Gruyter, 2014), 29.

14 Laurajane Smith, *Uses of Heritage* (London: Routledge, 2006), 29. See also her discussion on pp. 30–41.

15 Aleida Assmann, 'Canon and Archive', in Astrid Erll and Ansgar Nünning, eds., *A Companion to Cultural Memory Studies* (Berlin: Walter de Gruyter, 2008), 97–8.

16 Jefferson A. Singer and Martin A. Conway, 'Should We Forget Forgetting', *Memory Studies* 1, no. 3 (2018): 280.

17 Glenn Hooper, "Introduction," in Glenn Hooper and John J. Lennon, eds., Dark Tourism: Practice and interpretation (London: Routledge, 2016), 2.

18 See www.nationalfamineway.ie.

19 Silke Arnold-de Simine, *Mediating Memory in the Museum: Trauma, Empathy, Nostalgia* (New York: Palgrave, 2013), 12.

20 Laurence Gourievidis, *The Dynamics of Heritage: History, Memory, and the Highland Clearances* (Farnham: Ashgate, 2010), 98.

21 Arnold-de Simine, *Mediating Memory in the Museum*, 84.

22 Maria Grever and Tina van der Vlies, 'Why National Narratives are Perpetuated: A Literature Review on New Insights from History Textbook Research,' *London Review of Education* 15, no. 2 (2017): 288.

23 J. Atkinson, *Education, Values and Ethics in International Heritage* (Farnham: Ashgate, 2014), 101.

24 Román Ruiz, 'Representations of the Spanish Hunger Years'; Janssen, 'The Great Irish Famine in Irish and UK History Textbooks'.

25 See, for example, T.G. Ashplant, Graham Dawson and Michael Roper, 'The Politics of War Memory and Commemoration: Contexts, Structures and Dynamics', in Ashplant, Dawson and Roper, eds., *The Politics of War Memory* (London: Routledge, 2000), 3–84.

26 See Magnus Rodell, 'Monuments as The Places of Memory', in Conny Mithander et al., eds., *Memory Work: The Theory and Practice of Memory* (Frankfurt am Main: Peter Lang, 2005), 125–6.

27 Pierre Nora, 'Between Memory and History: Les Lieux de Mémoire', *Representations* 26 (1989): 7–25. See also, Rudy Koshar, *From Monuments to Traces: Artifacts of German Memory, 1870–1990* (Berkeley: University of California Press, 2000).

28 For the term, see Guy Beiner, 'Disremembering 1798? An Archaeology of Social Forgetting and Remembrance in Ulster', *History and Memory* 25, no. 2 (2013): 9–50.

29 Eilean Hooper-Greenhill, *Museums and Education: Purpose, Pedagogy, Performance* (London: Routledge, 2007), 2.

30 Ibid., 5.

31 Camilla Orjuela, 'Remembering/Forgetting Hunger: Towards an Understanding of Famine Memorialisation', *Third World Quarterly* 44 (2023): 1–18, 45, no. 2 (2024): 259–76.

32 For the term, see Michael Rothberg, *Multidirectional Memory* (Stanford: Stanford University Press, 2009), 19.

33 Thomas Faist, *The Volume and Dynamics of International Migration and Transnational Social Spaces* (Oxford: Oxford University Press, 2000), 240
34 See www.holodomor-monuments.org/, last accessed 9 July 2023.
35 Rothberg, *Multidirectional Memory*, 19.
36 Ibid., 7.

References

Apaydin, Veysel, "The Interlinkage of Cultural Memory, Heritage, and Discourses of Construction, Transformation, and Destruction." In *Critical Perspectives on Cultural Memory and Heritage: Construction, Transformation and Destruction*, Veysel Apaydin, ed., 13–30. London: UCL Press, 2020.

Arnold-de Simine, Silke, *Mediating Memory in the Museum. Trauma, Empathy, Nostalgia*. New York: Palgrave, 2013.

Ashplant, T. G., Graham Dawson, and Michael Roper, "The Politics of War Memory and Commemoration. Contexts, Structures and Dynamics." In *The Politics of War Memory*, T.G. Ashplant, Graham Dawson, and Michael Roper, eds., 3–84. London: Routledge, 2000.

Assmann, Aleida, "Canon and Archive." In *A Companion to Cultural Memory Studies*, Astrid Erll, and Ansgar Nünning, eds., 97–108. Berlin: Walter de Gruyter, 2008.

Atkinson, J., *Education, Values and Ethics in International Heritage*. Farnham: Ashgate, 2014.

Beiner, Guy, "Disremembering 1798? An Archaeology of Social Forgetting and Remembrance in Ulster." *History and Memory* 25, no. 2 (2013): 9–50.

Boerman, Charley, Framing Famines: Memory, Museums, and Visual Culture, Unpublished PhD Diss. Radboud University Nijmegen, 2024.

Corporaal, Marguérite, and Ingrid de Zwarte, "Heritages of Hunger: European Famine legacies in Current Academic Debates." *International Journal of Heritage Studies* 28, no. 1 (2022): 30–43.

Del Arco Blanco, Miguel Ángel, and Peter Anderson, eds., *Franco's Famine*. London: Bloomsbury, 2021.

Erll, Astrid, "From 'District Six' to District 9 and Back. The Plurimedial Production of Travelling Schemata." In *Transnational Memory: Circulation, Articulation, Scales*, Chiara de Cesari and Ann Rigney, eds., 29–50. Berlin/New York: De Gruyter, 2014.

EU Parliament, "The Unknown Famine of Athens 1941–1942." *Photo Exhibition, EU Parliament*. https://www.youtube.com/watch?v=iJdvhvLbObc, last accessed 11 September 2022.

Faist, Thomas, *The Volume and Dynamics of International Migration and Transnational Social Spaces*. Oxford: Oxford University Press, 2000.

Foucault, Michel, "Of Other Spaces: Utopias and Heterotopias." Translated by Jay Miskowiec. *Diacritics* 6, no. 2 (1986): 22–7.

Graziosi, Andrea, Lubomyr Hajda, and Halyna Hryn, eds., *After the Holodomor. The Enduring Impact of the Great Famine on Ukraine*. Cambridge, MA: Harvard University Press, 2013.

Grever, Maria and Tina van der Vlies, "Why National Narratives Are Perpetuated. A Literature Review on New Insights from History Textbook Research." *London Review of Education* 15, no. 2 (2017): 288.

Hionidou, Violetta, *Famine and Death in Occupied Greece, 1941–1944*. Cambridge: Cambridge University Press, 2006.

Hooper-Greenhill, Eilean, *Museums and Education. Purpose, Pedagogy, Performance*. London: Routledge, 2007.

Hooper, Glen, "Introduction." In *Dark Tourism: Practice and interpretation*, Glenn Hooper and John J. Lennon, eds., 1–11. London: Routledge, 2016.
Howe Paul, and Stephen Devereux, "Famine Intensity and Magnitude Scales: A Proposal for an Instrumental Definition of Famine." *Disasters* 28, no. 4 (2004): 353–72.
Janssen, Lindsay, "The Great Irish Famine in Irish and UK History Textbooks, 2010-2020." *History Education Research Journal* 20, no. 1 (2023). Online pre-publication. doi: 10.14324/HERJ.20.1.02
Kearns, David, "Thousands Turn Out in Dublin and Across Europe for Refugee Support Rally." *The Irish Times*, 12 September 2015. https://www.independent.ie/irish-news/thousands-turn-out-in-dublin-and-across-europe-for-refugee-support-rally-31522118.html, last accessed 29 July 2020.
Kelleher, Margaret, *The Feminization of Famine*. Durham, NC: Duke UP, 1997.
Kelly, Niamh Ann, *Imaging the Great Irish Famine. Representing Dispossession in Visual Culture*. London: I.B. Tauris, 2018.
Kenny, Kevin, *The American Irish: A History*. London: Longman, 2000.
Kirschenbaum, Lisa, *The Legacy of the Siege of Leningrad, 1941–1995. Myth, Memories, and Monuments*. Cambridge: Cambridge University Press, 2006.
Koshar, Rudy, *From Monuments to Traces. Artifacts of German Memory, 1870–1990*. Berkeley: University of California Press, 2000.
Mark-FitzGerald, Emily, *Commemorating the Irish Famine. Memory and the Monument*. Liverpool: Liverpool University Press, 2013.
McIvor, Charlotte, "Historical Duty, Palimpsestic Time and Migration in the Decade of Centenaries." *Irish Studies Review* 24, no. 1 (2016): 49–66.
McMahon, Cian T., *The Coffin Ship. Life and Death at Sea During the Great Famine*. New York: NYU Press, 2021.
"National Famine Way". 2019. www.nationalfamineway.ie.
Newby, Andrew, *Finland's Great Famine, 1856–68*. London: Palgrave, 2023.
Newby, Andrew, "Finland's 'Great Hunger Years' Memorials: A Sesquicentennial Report." In Andrew Newby, ed., *The Enormous Failure of Nature: Famine and Society in the Nineteenth Century. CollEgium* 22 (2016): 173–214.
Nora, Pierre, "Between Memory and History: Les Lieux de Mémoire." *Representations* 26 (1989): 7–25.
Ó Gráda, Cormac, *Famine: A Short History*. Princeton, NJ: Princeton University Press, 2009.
Ó Gráda, Cormac, and Guido Alfani, eds., *Famine in European History*. Cambridge: Cambridge University Press, 2017.
Orjuela, Camilla, 'Remembering/Forgetting Hunger: Towards an Understanding of Famine Memorialisation'. *Third World Quarterly* 45, no. 2 (2024): 259–76.
Rigney, Ann, "Portable Monuments. Literature, Cultural Memory, and the Case of Jeanie Deans." *Poetics Today* 25, no. 2 (2004): 361–96.
Rodell, Magnus, "Monuments as The Places of Memory." In *Memory Work: The Theory and Practice of Memory*, Andreas Kitzman, Conny Mithander, and John Sundholm, eds., 105–29. Frankfurt am Main: Peter Lang, 2005.
Román Ruiz, Gloria, "Representations of the Spanish Hunger Years (1939–1952) in Recent Secondary School History Textbooks." *Pedagogica Historica* (2022). 59, no. 6 (2023): 1345–66.
Rothberg, Michael, *Multidirectional Memory*. Stanford: Stanford University Press, 2009.
Singer, Jefferson A., and Martin A. Conway, "Should We Forget Forgetting." *Memory Studies* 1, no. 3 (2018): 279–85.
Smith, Laurajane, *Uses of Heritage*. London: Routledge, 2006.

Wertsch, James V., *Voices of Collective Remembering*. New York: Cambridge University Press, 2002.
Zwarte, Ingrid de, *The Hunger Winter. Fighting Famine in the Occupied Netherlands, 1944–1945*. Cambridge: Cambridge University Press, 2020.
Zwarte, Ingrid de, and Lindsay Janssen, "Recalling the Hunger Winter: Evoking Famine Memory beyond the National." *Memory Studies*. 17, no. 2 (2024): 213–27.

PART I

Education

1

CHALLENGES AND OPPORTUNITIES IN TEACHING EUROPEAN FAMINES

A transnational comparison

Lindsay Janssen, Anne van Mourik, Gloria Román Ruiz, and Ingrid de Zwarte

History textbooks and educational practices are crucial didactic forms to communicate national historical events and developments to learners.[1] They play a vital role in nation-building processes as well as in the formation and dissemination of communal identities among students.[2] This holds especially true for education about difficult pasts, such as natural disasters, wars, and the long-term effects of dictatorships, colonialism, and slavery. Famines take up a particularly interesting position in the education of troubled pasts, as historical events with a tremendous societal impact that are 'remembered' or 'forgotten' depending on their function and role in the social and political present.[3]

Previous studies on European famine education have typically focused on national educational practices, showing how and why national and regional curricula represent and narrativise famine pasts based on different—and sometimes conflicting—views on these pasts, as well as ambitions for the future. They show that famine education is usually based on simplified subject positions—often not in line with the latest scholarly insights—leading to problematic misrepresentations of these seminal episodes in history.[4] At the same time, and given that these studies mostly engage with specific national educational contexts, little remains known about differences and similarities in European famine education. As a result, broader transnational trends, challenges, and opportunities in teaching these difficult pasts are still unexplored.[5]

This chapter analyses famine education in multiple European countries, thereby offering an unprecedented transnational comparison. We comparatively investigate how national periods of hunger are currently (2010–2021) integrated into secondary education in four European contexts: Ireland, Spain, the Netherlands, and Germany. These case studies encompass four major European hunger periods of the nineteenth and twentieth centuries: the

DOI: 10.4324/9781003391524-3

Great Irish Famine of 1845–52, the Spanish Hunger Years of 1939–52, the Dutch Hunger Winter of 1944–45, and post-war German hunger in the years 1945–49.[6] The central position of these episodes of hunger within their respective cultures makes our case studies particularly relevant for a comparative analysis, as all of these historical episodes of hunger continue to inflect contemporary cultural and political discourses.

For this study, we have examined over 50 secondary-level history textbooks in digital and hardcopy format, equally divided over our four case studies. Not all national curricula provide education on their respective hunger pasts at the primary level; to offer a balanced comparison, we focus on secondary education. Through an exploration of victim-perpetrator discourses and possible pathways towards transnational comparisons, our main focus is on the narrativisation of past periods of hunger. In addition to our textual corpus, we have used teacher surveys in order to compare and contrast our textbook analyses with teachers' experiences.

Our transnational comparison allows us to examine the similarities and differences in how recollections of periods of hunger feature in education, thereby revealing present-day challenges and opportunities in teaching European hunger pasts. Our focus on the transnational has two dimensions: in terms of our research corpus, we explore the transnational opportunities offered by history textbooks; in terms of research methods, we adopt a comparative methodology when analysing our findings from the four national contexts. Consequently, our chapter engages with two interrelated questions: firstly, how are histories of hunger and the subjects implicated in these periods narrativised in our European textbook corpus? Secondly, what trends in textbook education transcend national frameworks and can be considered part of a transnational way of narrativising hunger for educational purposes? We argue that a transnational approach, which not only considers historical hunger periods in a comparative light but also connects hunger pasts to current global challenges, is still largely absent.

The chapter's outline is as follows: we will first provide a description of our corpus, theoretical framework, and methodology. The second section focuses on victim-perpetrator discourses in European textbooks, showing the wide variety of approaches to matters of culpability and victimhood. Finally, we engage with the transnational dimension of European famine education, which we argue can provide significant inroads to establishing transnational connections and stimulating mutual understanding among various cultural groups across time and space.

Famine education and textbook analysis

School textbooks are critical to passing on historical awareness to learners.[7] At the same time, textbooks, especially when published in contexts where there is no prior state supervision to their publication, are not mere transmitters of an 'official memory' of the historical past and may, instead, 'reflect a multiplicity of meanings and uses'.[8] Nevertheless, the ways in which textbooks engage with historical awareness are often aligned with the visions and objectives of national curricula; as such, they 'are often regarded as mirroring dominant contents and dominant practices'.[9] Moreover, regardless of whether textbooks offer skewed or incomplete interpretations of history, studies have shown that they possess the ability to shape cultural identities, as students tend to perceive them as 'truthful' and 'neutral' representations.[10]

In our investigation of famine education in school textbooks, we build on the concept of narrativisation; a methodological focus on how (disparate) elements of the past are combined into meaningful narratives for the present and future. In this regard, Astrid Erll speaks of a 'narratology of cultural memory', thereby referring to the close interconnections between narrative, individual and/or cultural memory and identity, and socio-cultural context.[11] Erll furthermore argues that 'different modes of remembering are closely linked to different modes of narrative representation. Changes in representation may effect changes in the kind of memory we retain of the past'.[12] Narrativisation, including the emplotment of famine pasts, typically happens through the use of 'narrative templates' or 'generalized structures [which are] used to generate multiple specific narratives with the same basic plot'.[13] In this chapter, we consider the use of simplified subject positions as a form of narrativisation through the use of a repertoire of pre-existing, familiar plot structures and tropes. This, as we will show, constitutes a recurring feature across our national corpora.

As we will argue, processes of narrative simplification do no justice to the actual historical subject positions and issues of culpability connected to periods of hunger. To be able to sufficiently acknowledge these complexities, we borrow the term 'implicated subject', as formulated by memory scholar Michael Rothberg. The term refers to individuals who are 'neither victims nor perpetrators' but who 'occupy positions aligned with power and privilege without being themselves direct agents of harm' and who 'contribute to, inhabit, inherit, or benefit from regimes of domination but do not originate or control such regimes'. As such, they 'help propagate the legacies of historical violence and prop up the structures of inequality'.[14]

Our focus on the transnational potential of famine memory in education is in line with approaches advocated by memory studies scholars and by the Council of Europe.[15] Both suggest approaching the past, especially the contested or traumatic past, from a transnational perspective. Scholars such as Stef Craps and Rothberg have convincingly argued that national paradigms—which are still the dominant parameters for the narratives of past famines—are undesired when intending 'to help people understand past injuries, to generate social solidarity'. Indeed, such discourses 'insisting on the distinctiveness and difference of one's *own* history' can thus result in an unawareness of or 'a refusal to recognize the larger historical processes of which that history is a part'.[16] By extension, discourses confined by a national framework or which emphasise the uniqueness of the national past can tend 'to deny the capacity for, or the effectiveness of, transcultural empathy'.[17] Similarly, the Council of Europe stresses the importance of 'multiperspectival approaches' in history education, as these can contribute to the promotion of 'historical empathy' and historical understanding.[18] These are significant observations on which we build our analyses in the following two sections.

Our analysis draws on 12 Irish, 13 German, 12 Dutch, and 15 Spanish history textbooks for the secondary level published after 2010 and aimed at students aged 12–18. These include books from the largest publishing houses in each of the national contexts, meaning that our corpus is largely representative of educational publishing in these countries. Our methodology largely consists of a qualitative textual analysis. We believe that a transnational perspective is especially useful for addressing the main challenges and opportunities in teaching European famines. It allows us to attend to the differences and similarities in representations of the periods of hunger, thereby demonstrating that processes of narrativisation transcend national contexts. In so doing, our comparative study serves to demonstrate whether and how educational textbooks offer or support the potential construction of 'transnational'[19] and 'multidirectional'[20] memories of famines.

To enrich our analyses of the textual sources, we also include responses to online surveys provided by secondary-school history teachers working in Ireland (N=16), the Netherlands (N=23), Germany (N=7), and Spain (N=21).[21] These surveys cover the teaching materials and practices that teachers adopt. As, due to these numbers, the survey results can only be considered of limited representability, we discreetly use them as anecdotal evidence. Nevertheless, they offer intriguing insights into the similarities and discrepancies between textbook famine education and educational practices in the classroom, making them a valuable complementary source of enquiry.

Victims, perpetrators, and implicated subjects

Recent studies on the causes and consequences of modern European famines emphasise the complexities surrounding issues of culpability and victimhood. They demonstrate that monocausal explanatory frameworks do no justice to the multifaceted nature of famines, and that not all members of a society are similarly affected by hunger conditions.[22] The latest scholarly insights are, however, not always directly translated into textbooks, as previous studies have also indicated.[23] This section comparatively investigates victim-perpetrator discourses surrounding famine and hunger pasts in selected Irish, German, Spanish, and Dutch textbooks. It shows that these materials offer a wide variety of perspectives on matters of culpability and victimhood, ranging from highly simplified accounts to more complex subject positions. Consequently, our analysis lays bare a problematic gap between scholarship and education, as well as between what textbooks offer and what teachers aspire to in their classes.

Studying contemporary textbooks reveals that simplified, binaristic victim-perpetrator discourses are still pervasive in all four contexts. Many Irish textbooks use simplified, uncritical subject positions in their representations of the Great Irish Famine, for example, by not including landlords as suffering from famine-induced hardships or as trying to alleviate tenant suffering.[24] Moreover, they tend to gloss over differences by presenting 'the Irish' as an allegedly homogeneous victim population.[25] This is problematic as it fails to acknowledge regional and class differences in Irish famine experiences.[26] Some Spanish textbooks echo Franco's propagandistic exculpatory discourses, referring to the famine as the legacy of the previous Republican regime or as the result of the Civil War and the persistent drought, rather than as caused by the autarkic economic policy adopted by the dictatorship for nationalist purposes.[27] In so doing, they convey the idea that Franco's economic interventionism was a necessity, not a political choice.[28]

Several Dutch textbooks similarly perpetuate outdated views on the origins of the Dutch famine, stating, for instance, that 'in 1944 they [the Germans] stopped [food] transports to the western Netherlands, thereby causing the Hunger Winter'.[29] Others incorrectly suggest that the Germans had forcibly exported Dutch agricultural products throughout the conflict, and that the occupying regime did nothing to relieve the famine conditions during the final months of the war.[30] In reality, the famine was caused by a culmination of multiple transportation and distribution problems following the Allied liberation of the south of the Netherlands in the autumn of 1944, preventing adequate food supplies to reach the cities in the urbanised western part of the country.[31] The abovementioned misinterpretations of the role and intent of the German occupier in causing the Dutch famine are, interestingly, also present in some German textbooks,[32] demonstrating the transferability of (erroneous) narrative templates beyond national borders.[33]

Suggestions of a homogeneous victim population, similar to those found in Irish textbooks, are also present in their Dutch and Spanish counterparts. Social categories such as class, gender, or geographical origin, which significantly influence the extent of food deprivation at individual levels, are often neglected in favour of an unnuanced narrative concerning the starving masses. A possible consequence of such uncritical (and indeed ahistorical) depictions is that they can give students the misconception that there was 'a single class of hunger sufferers.'[34] In the Spanish context, regional differences are not always established between the impact of the famine on the poorest and most affected people in the south of the peninsula—especially in Andalusia and Extremadura—and the rest of the population.[35] Furthermore, when referring to post-war scarcity and misery, many textbooks emphasise urban contexts, while scholarship has shown that there was as much or even more hunger in rural areas.[36]

In the Dutch context, the results of our teachers' surveys confirm our argument regarding simplification through homogenisation, as they demonstrate that educators prioritise themes connected to national victimhood over topics that complicate or problematise the victim-perpetrator dichotomy. For example, most Dutch teachers highlight topics such as the 'hunger journeys' that people embarked on in search of food (82.6%), food rationing (73.9%), and the eating of tulip bulbs and sugar beets (69.6%), while relief efforts such as food aid (17.4%) or child evacuations (21.7%), which were allowed and supported by the German authorities, receive relatively little attention.[37]

Contrary to the dominant simplified narratives, some Irish, Spanish, and Dutch textbooks do offer more complex accounts, which is more in line with contemporary historiography. For example, while a minority of Spanish textbooks continue to reiterate the exculpatory rhetoric of Franco's regime by focusing on external causal factors, other textbooks (correctly) recognise that the period of hunger was a consequence of the regime's politics and of the political corruption linked to Francoist economic interventionism.[38] This trend is also confirmed by our teacher survey, with 85.7% of the Spanish respondents stating that in their classes, they address autarkic government measures in connection to the Spanish Hunger Years.

In two Irish textbooks, landlords are acknowledged as victims. The authors include information about landlords who went bankrupt and 'had to sell their estates'[39] and detail how some landlords were murdered.[40] Moreover, these texts are relatively nuanced in their descriptions of landlords, indicating that some tried to help their suffering tenants by reducing or waiving rents during the Irish famine.[41] In the Netherlands, some textbooks include perspectives on the causes of the famine that align with recent scholarly insights, indicating that the famine was caused by a culmination of factors, such as the phased liberation of the country, the national railway strike, heavy winter frost, and fuel scarcity.[42] In the Dutch context, these complexities are addressed in higher level secondary textbooks, while their lower level counterparts tend to forgo the causes of the famine altogether;[43] in the Irish context, complex narratives feature on the junior level, which can be explained by the famine's inclusion in the junior national curriculum.[44]

The German case is particularly intriguing in relation to victim-perpetrator discourses in textbooks due to Germany's role as a 'perpetrator country' in several famines during the Second World War (WWII) (e.g., Greece 1941–44, Leningrad 1941–44, the Netherlands 1944–45), while many Germans suffered from hunger themselves in the immediate post-war years. Generally, German textbooks place these German hunger experiences in a broader normative narrative recognising 'historical responsibility for the atrocities of the Nazi regime', which aligns with what Aleida Assmann refers to as 'hierarchizing memories'.[45] Most textbooks dedicate at least two chapters to the suffering of victims of Nazi Germany, while hunger experiences in German cities (1945–49) are only briefly mentioned, typically on one or two pages.

This memory hierarchy is reinforced by the fact that German textbooks often do not explicitly address the causes of the post-war hunger conditions. While textbooks published before 1990 often simplified the causes of German hunger by blaming Hitler or the Allies, textbooks published after 1990 started to mention the hunger experiences in the context of German defeat and a disrupted infrastructure. As such, many recent textbooks offer a more nuanced view on the hunger conditions, suggesting that multiple factors had an effect on Germany's food provision system. For example, one German textbook explains the hunger conditions by generally referring to 'the completely inadequate supply [of food] to the population in the cities',[46] while another mentions that food consumption had already been sacrificed in favour of Germany's war economy from 1934 onward.[47] Significantly, some textbooks directly link the German perpetrator and victim positions by stating that, after WWII, many Germans used their 'personal suffering through the destruction of their own home, flight or expulsion, hunger and hardship' to avoid historical responsibility for the suffering of others during the war.[48] As such, the hierarchisation of hunger memories in German textbooks serves to acknowledge victimhood without mitigating culpability.

The hunger experiences of one group in particular are typically represented in a simplified manner in German textbooks: those of the so-called expellees (*Heimatvertriebene*)—some 12 million ethnic Germans and German citizens who fled or were expelled from Central and Eastern Europe after 1944.[49] Their experiences are usually characterised by universal victimhood, and neither complicated nor contextualised by issues of German culpability during WWII. Personal memories of former expellees included in many German textbooks often blame the distress on 'the Soviets' or 'Polish militia', who allegedly denied people food even though 'people cried out in hunger'.[50] By contrast, *Zeiten un Menschen* does acknowledge that malnourishment had already started during National Socialism, leaving expellees after the war 'so emaciated that the body was no longer able to resist' extremely low temperatures.[51] By ignoring collective guilt, the book suggests that expellees were doubly victimised by hunger: first during National Socialism and then during the expulsions. The simplified subject positions attributed to the expellees find legitimacy through what Daniel Levy and Nathan Sznaider refer to as the prism of 'universal victimhood', which builds on the premise that 'it does not matter if you start, win, or lose the war because war is a human tragedy affecting all'.[52] In the case of the expellees, simplified victim discourses in textbooks obfuscate an accurate representation of their ambivalent past.

Although universal victimhood is present in all four case studies, famines never affect all groups in society equally. Moreover, famines are typically characterised by, in Rothberg's words, 'complex, multifaced, and sometimes contradictory … modes of implication'.[53] For example, persons suffering from deprivation at the household level might also engage in black marketeering, thereby exacerbating unequal access to food at the communal level.[54] These implicated subjects, who occupy 'positions aligned with power and privilege without being themselves direct agents of harm', do not feature prominently but can indeed be found in some European textbooks.[55] Most German and Spanish textbooks include information on black market activity: in the Spanish context, for example, big *estraperlistas* are included.[56] These estraperlistas owned large trucks and warehouses, which allowed them to illegally trade in large quantities of cereals; they were also in contact with powerful figures in Franco's regime, and their compliance was important to guarantee the political stability of the dictatorship. As such, they helped perpetuate the autarkic economic policy that caused shortages.[57]

Complex subject positions are rarer in Irish and Dutch textbooks, but they do feature. One Irish textbook, *Discovering History*, for instance, discusses the rise in criminal activities such as violence, theft, and food riots during the famine, thereby adding some nuance to how one perceives the actions of Irish victims.[58] The Dutch textbook *Feniks* asks students in an assignment to reflect on the intended and unintended consequences of the Dutch railway strike. As such, the assignment implicates railway workers and the Dutch government-in-exile in London (which instigated the strike) in causing the famine.[59]

Stimulating engagement with implicated subjects among students could potentially contribute to overcoming the simplified victim-perpetrator discourses that currently dominate famine history education. More attention for the implicated subject in times of famine and hunger aligns with the call to move away from 'mono-cultural, ethnocratic, and universalistic' narratives in textbooks towards including 'multiperspectivity'; offering students insight into the perspectives of different historical actors in order to stimulate historical understanding and emotional engagement.[60] At present, this is rarely the case in textbooks that deal with European famine pasts. The few textbooks that do offer engagement with multiple historical experiences or interpretations usually do so in the assignments, and not in the main text. For example, *Discovering History* challenges students to 'write about what it was like to be a cottier in the west of Ireland during the Famine', thereby suggesting regional and class differences in the experiences of famine.[61] In the Spanish case, we find an example in a Castellnou textbook, which invites students to answer the question: 'Do you think the increase in the prices of basic products only happened in Spain during the Civil War or is it common in wartime?'[62] The Dutch textbook *Memo* asks students to reflect on the decision by the Allies not to intervene during the Hunger Winter, thus engendering reflection on complex decision-making processes at the international level.[63]

To stimulate historical empathy and emotional engagement, textbooks sometimes also employ personal accounts from historical actors, such as the memoirs of German expellees; personal testimonies of those who lived through the Spanish Hunger Years;[64] or quotations from, among others, philanthropists, relief inspectors and a famous newspaper illustrator who witnessed the famine in Ireland.[65] Crucially, our teacher surveys suggest that the limited presence of multiperspectivity in textbooks is compensated by supplementary sources that teachers select themselves, including diaries, correspondence materials, documentaries, and films. These sources are vital in helping teachers to engage students with the many diverse voices of historical actors implicated in causing, enduring, or relieving famine.

Transnational perspectives: Opportunities beyond the textbook

Histories of hunger offer opportunities for fostering transcultural understanding between cultural groups. This potential has been recognised in the US, where around the turn of the twenty-first century, the Great Irish Famine study guide became part of the New Jersey Holocaust-Genocide Curriculum,[66] and the Great Irish Famine curriculum became part of the New York State Human Rights Curriculum, with the latter also including American slavery and the Holocaust. Through transnational and diachronic connections, the New York Curriculum speaks to broader societal issues such as government responses to the people's needs, basic rights to food and shelter, and responsibility. In the words of the authors, by 'providing models of compassion and responsible behavior to students', it is concerned with 'how to address contemporary questions of material deprivation in a world of colossal wealth'.[67] These examples demonstrate how famine education can play an important role in forging transhistorical ties and stimulating mutual understanding among various groups.

In recent textbooks, however, German, Dutch, Spanish, or Irish hunger periods are typically placed in their respective national historical narratives—respectively, the German post-WWII experiences, the Dutch experience of WWII, post-war Spain under the Francoist dictatorship, a longer history of famine under British Imperial rule or the struggles for national independence and land rights in Ireland. In Ireland, the national curriculum for the junior cycle also suggests the placement of the Great Irish Famine in a national context, by situating the topic within a national, rather than global history strand.[68] Similarly, the Spanish Hunger Years are dealt with in a national or regional set curriculum; it features subjects specifically dedicated to Spanish history and which include practically no references to other European hunger contexts.

In our case studies, transnational dimensions are not usually highlighted in the textual narratives offered. The Dutch textbooks we examined do not draw any explicit transnational comparisons at all. For the Spanish, Irish, and German cases, there are a few exceptions to this general trend. Spanish textbooks sometimes link Franco's autarkic nationalism to the economic policy adopted by other contemporary dictatorships such as Fascist Italy, Nazi Germany, or Salazar's Portugal.[69] Similarly, the Irish textbooks *Artefact* and *Footsteps in Time* briefly mention that the potato blight also hit other regions in Europe, although the comparison does not go beyond the (valid) remark that nowhere was the result as bad as it was in Ireland.[70] The former includes: 'The potato blight did not affect Ireland alone. Other European countries also lost their potato crops, but they were not as reliant on farming and had other available food. In Ireland, the farming poor would suffer the effects of the famine for years'.[71]

Relatively speaking, German textbooks offer students the most opportunities to engage with histories of hunger in a transnational context, as they dedicate considerable textual space to hunger instigated by Nazi practices or policies. *Buchners Kolleg Geschichte* compares post-WWII shortages in the United Kingdom with contemporaneous hunger conditions in Germany. Explaining why Great Britain aimed for a quick economic stabilisation of Germany after WWII, the book includes the fact that the British population suffered almost 'as much hunger as the population of ruined Berlin'.[72] By contrast, for the three other contexts, it is the case that when textbooks focus on mutual understanding or empathy, the purpose rather seems to be the stimulation of transhistorical empathy for their own national histories than for shared histories across cultures.

It should be noted that the absence of explicit transcultural connections in the narrative texts does not mean that they do not include other periods of hunger at all. Several textbooks mention previous episodes of hunger or famine elsewhere in the world in other chapters. The German textbook *Horizonte 9: Geschichte* and the Irish textbook *Artefact*, for example, quite elaborately discuss the Ukrainian Holodomor of 1932–33, with the former asking learners to reflect on the controversial question whether it was a case of 'catastrophic hunger or genocide' (*Hungerkatastrophe oder Völkermord*).[73] The Berlin Blockade, food shortages, and the Berlin Airlift after WWII are included in the Irish *Timeline*,[74] while another Irish book, *Uncovering History*, includes the impact of the potato blight in Scotland and parts of France in the 1840s.[75]

In Dutch textbooks, many other episodes of hunger besides the Hunger Winter are covered, including the Great Irish Famine, famines in the Soviet Union in the 1920s and 1930s, the Siege of Leningrad, China's Great Leap Forward famine, the Ethiopian famine of the 1980s, and the deprivation experienced in Japanese concentration camps in Indonesia during WWII.[76]

These episodes of hunger are also often connected to major societal developments and events, such as the Great Crash of 1929 or the fight against new episodes of hunger ('never again hunger') as one of the foundations of the European Union.[77] Therefore, although transcultural comparisons largely remain implicit, the inclusion of other histories of hunger in the same textbooks does offer educators and learners the opportunity to draw transcultural connections themselves.

Some textbooks suggest that learners take it upon themselves to draw such links. In assignments, these textbooks prompt higher-level learning skills by asking students to conduct comparative research and formulate their own opinions about these shared histories. Consequently, the transnational dimension lies largely beyond the textbooks. Such incentives are found more often in the Irish sample than in the other contexts. One book slightly predating our corpus deserves mention here: in Aaron Wilkes' *Industry, Reform and Empire. Britain 1750–1900* (2004) students are asked to reflect on parallels between the treatment of the Irish during the famine and the treatment of the Jewish people during WWII: '[do you] think the British Government's actions during the famine were as bad as Hitler's attempts to kill all the Jews?' Students are also asked to hold a class debate on culpability.[78] The book's questions are perhaps understandable in the context of schoolteachers across the Atlantic being instructed by their respective US states 'to teach pupils that the actions of the British Government in Ireland in the 1840s were similar to the actions of the Nazi's against the Jews during the 1930s and 1940s'.[79] This state-level instruction seems to point to the controversy sparked by the inclusion of the Great Irish Famine into the New Jersey Holocaust-Genocide Curriculum.[80]

In more 'hardline' Irish nationalist circles, the Irish-Jewish comparison has even led some to speak of the 'Irish Holocaust' when describing the famine. Feeding into the thesis that the Great Irish Famine was an act of genocide, this Jewish-Irish comparison is highly contentious, as it also runs the risk of an erroneous comparison in terms of premeditation and core objective, projecting Nazi Germany's orchestrated, predetermined policy of ethnic cleansing onto the British case.[81] This is a complicated, polemical question that requires a thorough awareness of both contexts as well as of the concepts of culpability and genocide. As this may be too complex for the secondary level, it is not surprising that the specific Jewish-Irish comparison does not feature in our more recent corpus. *Discovering History* and *History in Focus 1* do ask students to reflect on whether the Irish famine was a genocide, but do not draw transcultural comparisons.[82] This suggests that textbook authors are aware of the ongoing controversies regarding comparative usage of the Holocaust.

In our sample, sometimes different transnational parallels are found in the assignments. In the German textbook *Kursbuch Geschichte*, students are asked to 'analyse and compare the situation of refugees and displaced persons at the end of WWII with the situation of migrants today',[83] thus showing how textbook authors suggest multidirectional approaches, possibly hoping to stimulate a dialogue between past and present periods of hunger.[84] On the whole, Irish history textbooks contain more comparative exercises than their German, Spanish, or Dutch counterparts. For example, under the header 'Historical continuity', *Discovering History* includes a quote by former Irish President Mary Robinson that draws a direct parallel between hunger in Ireland in the 1840s and hunger in Somalia in the 1990s. The accompanying assignment prompts students to analyse the quote and reflect on whether 'Ireland has a greater or lesser responsibility to help countries suffering from famine'.[85] In so doing, the textbook emphasises the moral lessons to be learned from historical famine while simultaneously attempting to stimulate empathetic responses for those suffering hunger in the world today. The inclusion of comparative exercises in the Irish context may likely have been informed by the fact that, nowadays, a transnational awareness with regard to the Great Irish Famine is an established part of political, educational, and commemorative rhetoric in Ireland and its diaspora. This becomes visible in, among other things, the aforementioned educational initiatives in the US, the existence of transnational rhetoric in some memorial plaques, and the inclusion of transnational links in annual state commemorations of the famine.[86]

Despite the relative absence of explicit transnational and transhistorical connections in textbooks, responses to our surveys indicate that, in their teaching practices, teachers working with all four case studies provide this comparative dimension. As one Irish respondent remarked, there are '[s]till famine [sic] in the world today, many of them created by human mismanagement'. Indeed, many teachers state that they relate the Irish famine to present-day contexts and teach the famine in larger transnational contexts. Of the Spanish history teachers that responded to our survey, 48% indicated that they draw connections between the Spanish Hunger Years and hunger in other contexts, such as Germany during and after WWI and WWII, the Ukrainian Holodomor, as well as hunger crises in the Balkans, Syria, Central Africa, or Myanmar. One teacher attempts to connect the Spanish Hunger Years with 'as many [periods of hunger] as possible'. Some teachers pointed out that it was the 'chronological proximity' between the different periods of hunger or their 'relationship to war' or to the crisis that affected the European continent in the 1930s and subsequent decades that led them to make these comparisons. Others argued that they found the comparison useful to underline that famine can occur as a result of the 'economic policies' and 'state violence' of both communist and fascist (or para-fascist) regimes. Various Dutch respondents indicate that they relate the Hunger Winter to other episodes of hunger and/or war, including scarcity during WWI, the Ukrainian Holodomor, hunger in Japanese concentration camps during WWII, in Biafra in the late 1960s, and in North Korea in the 1990s.

When answering a follow-up question on which themes related to the respective period of hunger may be important for the education of future generations, our respondents mention transnational connections and the stimulation of historical and transnational understanding and empathy. In relation to this, they include what famine education can mean in terms of understanding the effects of war, occupation, racism, emigration, and the global environmental crisis. For instance, 90% of the Spanish history teachers surveyed claimed to relate the Spanish Hunger Years to other experiences of current shortages, such as the global economic crisis of 2008, which particularly affected Mediterranean countries. These findings not only suggest that the Dutch and Irish famine pasts inhabit important positions in national configurations of the past, but also that all four famine pasts serve significant present- and future-oriented purposes, as teachers use them to engage their students with the suffering of others in the past, the present, and potentially the future. The fact that textbooks currently lack these explicit transcultural and transhistorical connections in their narrative texts and, for a large part also, in their assignments can therefore be seen as a missed opportunity.

Future directions

There is a considerable discrepancy between recent scholarly insights into Europe's famine pasts and the narratives contained in textbooks. While the former acknowledge complexity, the latter often offer simplistic views. Comparative analysis of recent history textbooks from Ireland, Spain, the Netherlands, and Germany reveals that this simplification is dominant in all four contexts and thus impacts textbooks beyond the national framework.

Relatively speaking, German textbooks offer students the most opportunities to engage with histories of hunger in a transnational context, as they dedicate considerable space to hunger caused by Nazi policies elsewhere in Europe. Irish textbooks also provide learners with opportunities to engage with histories of hunger in a transnational context, although such efforts are limited and should largely be seen as efforts to be undertaken by teachers and learners. In the Netherlands and Spain, a transnational dimension is predominantly absent, possibly because comparative historical analyses of the respective famines are absent in both contexts as well.

Current textbook narratives can limit students' understanding of the full complexities of hunger periods and thus run the risk of impeding perspective taking and historical empathy formation for different subject positions. We therefore suggest two possible future directions in textbook accounts on hunger periods. Firstly, victim-perpetrator discourses in textbooks would benefit from a more nuanced engagement with subject positions. Most textbooks, especially in the Irish and Dutch contexts, still offer simplified accounts of victimhood and culpability by offering inaccurate, one-dimensional content that tends to homogenise victim groups or provides monocausal or incomplete explanations of the hunger periods.[87] Relatively speaking, German textbooks provide the most complex accounts regarding human subject roles, which is likely the result of longer term public and political engagements with the country's perpetrator past. Our study shows that simplification is a form of narrativisation that transcends national contexts and can thus be considered part of an international repertoire of textbook representation. This makes it particularly challenging to counter these simplified narratives. Nevertheless, we argue for a more sustained engagement with historical complexities, as this would benefit the understanding of the human dynamics part of histories of hunger among new generations of learners.

Secondly, the further development of transnational approaches in teaching would help learners to consider historical hunger periods in a comparative light, which in turn could help them realise that their national past is inextricably connected to international events, processes, and developments. Crucially, this would also allow learners to connect past hunger to current-day global challenges. School history textbooks could benefit from a move beyond the national paradigm, as this would offer opportunities for a parallel move from historical empathy to transnational empathy for past, present, and future subjects and cultural groups.

Notes

1 All translations provided in this chapter are by its authors.
2 See, for example, Julian Dierkes, 'The Nation in German History Education', in Hanna Schissler and Yasemin Nuhoglu Soysal, eds., *The Nation, Europe and the World: Textbooks and Curricula in Transition* (New York: Berghahn Books, 2005), 82–104.
3 Guido Alfani and Cormac Ó Gráda, 'Famines in Europe: An Overview', in Guido Alfani and Cormac Ó Gráda, eds., *Famine in European History* (Cambridge: Cambridge University Press, 2017), 23; Marguérite Corporaal and Ingrid de Zwarte, 'Heritages of Hunger: European Famine Legacies in Current Academic Debates', *International Journal of Heritage Studies* 27, no. 1 (2021): 30–43.
4 Gloria Román Ruiz, 'Representations of the Spanish Hunger Years (1939–1952) in Recent Secondary School History Textbooks', *Paedagogica Historica* (2022): 1–22. Lindsay Janssen, 'The Great Irish Famine in Irish and UK History Textbooks, 2010–2020', *History Education Research Journal* 20, no. 2 (2023): 1–16.
5 Jan Germen Janmaat, 'History and National Identity Construction: The Great Famine in Irish and Ukrainian History Textbooks', in Christian Noack, Lindsay Janssen and Vincent Comerford, eds., *Holodomor and Gorta Mór: Histories, Memories and Representations of Famine in Ukraine and Ireland* (London: Anthem Press, 2013), 77–102.
6 For Ireland, we follow the periodisation provided by Alfani and Ó Gráda in 'Famines in Europe', 10. In the case of Spain, there is historiographical consensus that the period 1939–52 constituted the 'hunger years'; recently, Miguel Á. Del Arco Blanco has argued that the worst years of hunger, i.e., 1939–42 and 1946, constituted a real famine. See 'Famine in Spain During Franco's Dictatorship, 1939–1952', *Journal of Contemporary History* 56, no. 1 (2021): 3–27. The timespan

provided for Germany is based on the Allied occupation of the country (1945–49). The authors have chosen to exclude representations of the Berlin Airlift as textbooks often include this topic in a Cold War context, while hunger experienced in German cities is placed in the context of the collapse of the National Socialist regime. For reasons of feasibility, we have chosen to only focus on the latter.

7 Marc van Berkel, 'Plotlines of Victimhood: The Holocaust in German and Dutch History Textbooks', Ph.D. Diss. (Rotterdam: Erasmus University, 2017), 23.

8 John Issit, 'Reflections on the Study of Textbooks', *History of Education* 33, no. 6 (2004): 683–85.

9 Maria Repoussi and Nicole Tutiaux-Guillon, 'New Trends in History Textbook Research: Issues and Methodologies toward a School Historiography', *Journal of Educational Media, Memory & Society* 2, no. 1 (2010): 156.

10 David R. Olson, 'On the Language and Authority of Textbooks', *Journal of Communication* 30, no. 1 (1980): 186–96.

11 Astrid Erll, 'Narratology and Cultural Memory Studies', in Sandra Heinen and Roy Sommer, eds., *Narratology in the Age of Cross-Disciplinary Narrative Research* (Berlin: Walter de Gruyter, 2009), 215.

12 Ibid., 220.

13 The term 'narrative templates' is taken from James V. Wertsch's work. See *Voices of Collective Remembering* (Cambridge: Cambridge University Press, 2002) and 'Collective Memory and Narrative Templates', *Social Research* 75, no. 1 (2008): 140. See also Eviatar Zerubavel, *Time Maps: Collective Memory and the Social Shape of the Past* (Chicago: University of Chicago Press, 2003).

14 Michael Rothberg, *The Implicated Subject: Beyond Victims and Perpetrators* (Stanford, CA: Stanford University Press, 2019), 1–2.

15 Lucy Bond and Jessica Rapson, eds., *The Transcultural Turn: Interrogating Memory Between and Beyond Borders* (Berlin: de Gruyter, 2014).

16 Stef Craps and Michael Rothberg, 'Introduction: Transcultural Negotiations of Holocaust Memory', *Criticism* 53, no. 4 (2011): 518.

17 Ibid.

18 Council of Europe, *Developing a Culture of Co-Operation when Teaching and Learning History* (Strasbourg: Council of Europe Publishing, 2016), 68–74; Tatiana Mininka-Milko, 'Introduction', in Council of Europe, ed., *Shared Histories for a Europe without Dividing Lines 2010–2014* (Strasbourg: Council of Europe Publishing, 2014), 6–8.

19 Chiara de Cesari and Ann Rigney, 'Introduction', in Chiara de Cesari and Ann Rigney, eds., *Transnational Memory: Circulation, Articulation, Scales* (Berlin: de Gruyter, 2004), 3.

20 Michael Rothberg, *Multidirectional Memory: Remembering the Holocaust in the Age of Decolonization* (Stanford, CA: Stanford University Press, 2009), 6, 11.

21 Rather than cap the numbers at the same amounts for every country, we included all survey responses, which explains the disparity in numbers per national context.

22 Alison Ribeiro de Menezes, *Embodying Memory in Contemporary Spain* (Basingstoke: Palgrave Macmillan, 2014), 19; Emily Mark-FitzGerald, 'The "Irish Holocaust": Historical Trauma and the Commemoration of the Famine', in Griselkda Pollock, ed., *The Visual Politics of Psychoanalysis: Art and the Image in Post-Traumatic Cultures* (London: I. B. Tauris, 2013), 86; Ingrid de Zwarte, *The Hunger Winter: Fighting Famine in the Occupied Netherlands, 1944–1945* (Cambridge: Cambridge University Press, 2020), 7; Atina Grossmann, 'Grams, Calories, and Food: Languages of Victimization, Entitlement, and Human Rights in Occupied Germany, 1945–1949', *Central European History* 44, no. 1 (2011): 125.

23 Román Ruiz, 'Representations of the Spanish Hunger Years'.

24 Mark McGowan, '*The Famine Plot* Revisited: A Reassessment of the Great Irish Famine as Genocide', *Genocide Studies International* 11, no. 1 (2017): 93–4.
25 Janssen, 'Great Irish Famine', 12.
26 For scholarship on geographic differences, see Mary Kelly, A. Stewart Frotheringham and Martin Charlton, 'Mapping Population Change in Ireland 1841–1851: Quantitative Analysis Using Historical GIS', in Christian Noack, Lindsay Janssen, and Vincent Comerford, eds., *Holodomor and Gorta Mór: Histories Memory and Representations of Famine in Ukraine and Ireland* (London: Anthem Press, 2012).
27 Carlos Barciela, 'Introducción', in R. Garrabou, C. Barciela and I. Jiménez, eds., *Historia Agraria de la España Contemporánea. 3. El Fin de la Agricultura Tradicional (1900–1960)* (Barcelona: Crítica, 1986), 383.
28 See Jaime Prieto, *Historia de España, 2° Bachillerato* (A Coruña: Bruño, 2016); Eduardo Lama et al., *Historia de España, 2° Bachillerato* (Madrid: SomosLink - Edelvives, 2020).
29 See, for example, Iris van der Brand et al., *Geschiedeniswerkplaats, Geschiedenis Tweede Fase vwo* (Groningen/Utrecht: Wolters Noordhoff, 2021), 151.
30 Eelco Breukers et al., *Memo, 3 havo* ('s Hertogenbosch: Malmberg, 2021), 134; Christa Dekkers et al., *Feniks, Leerboek 1 vmbo-kgt* (Amersfoort: ThiemeMeulenhoff, 2020), 83.
31 De Zwarte, *The Hunger Winter*, 43–59.
32 Maximilian Lanzinner, *Buchners Geschichte Oberstufe [Unterrichtswerk Für Die Gymnasiale Oberstufe] Qualifikationsphase*, North Rhine-Westphalia (Bamberg: Bamberg Buchner, 2015), 259; Ulrich Baumgärter, *Horizonte – Geschichte, Sekundarstufe II Nordrhein-Westfalen Qualifikationsphase: 11./12. Jahrgangsstufe Gymnasium* (Braunschweig: Westermann, 2015), 315.
33 On travelling memory, see Astrid Erll, 'Travelling Memory', *Parallax* 17, no. 4 (2011): 4–18.
34 Emily Mark-FitzGerald, *Commemorating the Irish Famine: Memory and the Monument* (Liverpool: Liverpool University Press, 2013), 90.
35 Vicente Camacho et al., *Geografía e Historia, 4° ESO, Serie Descubre, Proyecto Saber Hacer* (Madrid: Santillana, 2016); Margarita García, Cristina Gatell and Sergio Riesco, *Geografía e Historia, Historia, Andalucía (Digital) (Aula 3D), 4° ESO* (Madrid: Vicens Vives, 2017).
36 Vicente Camacho et al., *Geografía e Historia, 4° ESO*; Fernando García de Cortázar et al., *Historia de España, 2° Bachillerato* (Madrid: Anaya, 2016); Roberto Blanco and Mariano González, *Historia de España, 2° Bachillerato* (Madrid: Editex, 2016). Óscar Rodríguez, 'Cambalaches: Hambre, Moralidad Popular y Mercados de Guerra y Postguerra', *Historia Social*, no. 77 (2013): 149–74; Gloria Román Ruiz, 'El Pan Negro de cada Día. Memoria de los Años del Hambre en el Mundo Rural', in Miguel Á. Del Arco Blanco, ed., *Los Años del Hambre. Historia y Memoria de la Posguerra Franquista* (Madrid: Marcial Pons, 2020), 114–36.
37 For more on these relief efforts, see Ingrid de Zwarte, 'Coordinating Hunger: The Evacuation of Children during the Dutch Food Crisis, 1945', *War & Society* 35, no. 2 (2016); Ingrid de Zwarte, 'Fighting Vulnerability: Child Feeding Initiatives during the Dutch Hunger Winter', in T. Tönsmeyer, P. Haslinger and A. Laba, eds., *Societies under Occupation in World War II: Supply, Shortage, Hunger* (London: Palgrave Macmillan, 2018), 293–310.
38 Ángel Bahamonde and Luis E. Otero, *Historia de España, 2° Bachillerato* (Madrid: SM, 2016); Fernando García de Cortázar et al., *Historia de España, 2° Bachillerato* (Madrid: Anaya, 2016). Carlos Barciela, 'Franquismo y Corrupción Económica', *Historia Social*, no. 30 (1998): 87.

39 Máire de Buitléir et al., *Timeline. A Complete History Text for Junior Certificate History* (Dublin: Edco, 2014), 273.
40 Patsy McCaughey, *Discovering History. New Junior Cycle History* (Dublin: Mentor Books, 2018), 320.
41 Ibid., 314.
42 Breukers et al., *Memo, 3 vwo*; Boonstra et al., *Feniks, Leerboek 4/5 havo,* 106; Conny Bastiaans and Harald Buskop, *Sprekend Verleden – havo Bovenbouw* (Zutphen: Walburg Pers Educatief, 2018), 127.
43 Bert Breeman et al., *Geschiedeniswerkplaats, Geschiedenis vmbo-bk2* (Groningen/Utrecht: Wolters Noordhoff, 2021).
44 See Janssen, 'Great Irish Famine' on this. The junior level is geared to ages 12–16.
45 Aleida Assmann, *Shadows of Trauma: Memory and the Politics of Postwar Identity*, trans. Sarah Clift (New York: Fordham University Press, 2015), 172–73.
46 Maximilian Lanzinner, *Buchners Kolleg: Geschichte 2*, Berlin (Bamberg: Buchners Verlag Bamberg, 2013), 221.
47 Baumgärter, *Horizonte – Geschichte, Sekundarstufe II Nordrhein-Westfalen*, 306–9; Lanzinner, *Buchners Kolleg: Geschichte 2*, 117–221; Lanzinner, *Buchners Geschichte Oberstufe,* North Rhine-Westphalia, 240.
48 Peter Droste Johannes, *Geschichte und Geschehen Qualifikationsphase*, Nordrhein-Westfalen (Berlin: Ernst Klett, 2015), 214.
49 Robert G. Moeller, *War Stories. The Search for a Usable Past in the Federal Republic of Germany* (Berkeley, CA: University of California Press, 2001), 3.
50 Dieter Brückner and Harald Focke, *Das Waren Zeiten: Unterrichtswerk Für Geschichte and Gymnasien, Sekundarstufe I*, North Rhine-Westphalia, 3 (Bamberg: Buchners Verlag Bamberg, 2010), 149.
51 Hans-Jürgen Lendzian, *Zeiten Und Menschen – Geschichte Qualifikationsphase*, Nordrhein-Westfalen (Paderborn: Schöningh, 2015), 408.
52 Daniel Levy and Nathan Sznaider, 'Memories of Universal Victimhood: The Case of Ethnic German Expellees', *German Politics and Society* 23, no. 2 (2005): 4.
53 Rothberg, *Implicated Subject*, 2.
54 Gloria Román Ruiz, 'Pícaros de Posguerra. Turning to Crime to Survive Famine and Malnutrition in Early Francoism (1939-1952)', in Miguel Ángel Del Arco Blanco and Peter Anderson, eds., *Franco's Famine. Malnutrition, Disease and Starvation in Post-Civil War Spain* (London: Bloomsbury Academic, 2022), 114–36.
55 Rothberg, *Implicated Subject*, 1.
56 For Spanish examples of black marketeers, see Leandro Álvarez et al., *Historia de España (Aula 3D), 2° Bachillerato* (Madrid: Vicens Vives, 2016) or José M. Fernández et al. *Historia de España, 2° Bachillerato, Proyecto Saber Hacer, Serie Descubre* (A Coruña: Santillana, 2016).
57 Miguel Á. Del Arco Blanco, 'La Corrupción en el Franquismo. El Fenómeno del Gran Estraperlo', *Hispania Nova*, no. 16 (2018): 620–45.
58 McCaughey, *Discovering History*, 320.
59 Boonstra et al., *Feniks, Geschiedenis voor de onderbouw, 3 havo* (Amersfoort: ThiemeMeulenhoff, 2020).
60 Robert Stradling, *Multiperspectivity in History Teaching: A Guide for Teachers* (Brussels: Council of Europe, 2003), 14; Geerte M. Savenije and Pieter de Bruijn, 'Historical Empathy in a Museum: Uniting Contextualisation and Emotional Engagement', *International Journal of Heritage Studies* 23, no. 9 (2017): 832.
61 McCaughey, *Discovering History*, 312.
62 Ricardo Gorgues et al., *Historia, 4° ESO* (Barcelona: Castellnou, 2008).
63 Breukers et al., *Memo vwo 3*, 150.
64 Margarita García et al., *Geografía e Historia, Historia, Com. Valenciana, (Aula 3D), 4° ESO* (Madrid: Vicens Vives, 2016).

65 Lendzian, *Zeiten Und Menschen*, 408. For Irish textbooks, see for example the quotes included from philanthropist W. E. Forster and Famine Relief Inspector Major Parker in Seán Delap and Paul McCormack, *Time Bound* (Dublin: Folens, 2018), 57–8. Also see the quote by illustrator for the *Illustrated London News* James Mahony, included in Gráinne Henry et al., *History Alive* (Dublin: Edco, 2018), 213. The textbook and activity book to *History Alive* contain many more quotes, including one from influential nationalist politician Daniel O'Connell (*Activity Book*, 127).
66 James V. Mullin, 'The New Jersey Famine Curriculum: A Report', *Éire-Ireland* 37, nos. 1 and 2 (2002): 122.
67 Maureen Murphy and Alan Singer, 'New York State's 'Great Irish Famine Curriculum': A Report', *Éire-Ireland* 37, nos. 1 and 2 (2002): 109, 111, 113.
68 The Irish junior cycle curriculum has three interconnected strands: 'Strand 1: The nature of history; Strand 2: The history of Ireland; Strand 3: The history of Europe and the wider world'. Government of Ireland, NCCA and the Department of Education and Skills, 'Junior Cycle History Specification' (2017), 10.
69 See, for example, Ángel Bahamonde et al., *Historia de España, 2° Bachillerato* (SM, 2016).
70 Gregg O'Neill and Eimear Jenkinson, *Artefact* (Dublin: Educate.ie, 2018), 219; Patricia McCarthy, *Footsteps in Time* 1 (Dublin: CJ Fallon, 2010), 377.
71 O'Neill and Jenkinson, *Artefact*, 219.
72 Lanzinner, *Buchners Kolleg: Geschichte 2*, 224.
73 Christoph Meyer, *Horizonte 9: Geschichte – Materialien für Lehrerinnen und Lehrer*, Berlin (Braunschweig: Westermann, 2019), 147. O'Neill and Jenkinson, *Artefact*, Chapter 24, 340.
74 De Buitléir et al., *Timeline*, 367–68.
75 Seán Delap and Paul McCormack, *Uncovering History. Junior Certificate*, 2nd edn. (Dublin: Folens, 2011), 254.
76 Breukers et al., *Memo, 3 vwo* Part A, 81–2, 90, 135; Part B, 23, 76, 98; Boonstra et al., *Feniks, Leerboek 4/5 havo*, 102, 111; *Feniks vmbo 2bk*, 136.
77 Breukers et al., *Memo, 3 vwo*, Part A, 109; Idem, *Memo vwo 3*, Part B, 44; Boonstra et al., *Feniks, Leerboek 4/5 havo*, 177–8; *Feniks, Geschiedenis voor de bovenbouw vwo*, 199; *Feniks vmbo 2bk*, 132.
78 Aaron Wilkes, *Industry, Reform and Empire. Britain 1750-1900* (Dublin: Folens, 2004), 73.
79 Ibid., 73.
80 Mullin, 'New Jersey Famine Curriculum', 119; Thomas J. Archdeacon, 'The Irish Famine in American School Curricula', *Éire-Ireland* 37, nos. 1 and 2 (2002): 130–52.
81 Christopher Morash, 'Famine/Holocaust: Fragmented Bodies', *Éire-Ireland* 32, no. 1 (1997): 136–50.
82 McCaughey, *Discovering History*, 325; Dan Sheedy, *History in Focus 1. A History of Ireland for the Junior Cycle* (Dublin: CJ Fallon, 2018), 88.
83 Karin Laschewski-Müller and Robert Hübner, *Kursbuch Geschichte Qualifikationsphase* (Berlin: Cornelsen, 2015), 391.
84 Rothberg, *Multidirectional Memory*, 9.
85 McCaughey, *Discovering History*, 324.
86 See, for example, the memorial at Cherryfield Cemetery, Callan, Co. Kilkenny (Action from Ireland, 1994). In his speech for the 2021 Famine Commemoration, Irish President Michael D. Higgins drew attention to the contemporary threat of famine for some 34 million people across the globe and specifically discussed the current situation in war-torn Yemen. See 'Speech at the National Famine

Commemoration 2021', 16 May 2021, https://president.ie/en/media-library/speeches/speech-at-the-national-famine-commemoration-2021, last accessed 20 August 2023.

87 In 'Great Irish Famine', 11–13, Janssen also argues this for Irish and UK History textbooks.

References

Alfani, Guido and Cormac Ó Gráda, 'Famines in Europe: An Overview'. In Guido Alfani and Cormac Ó Gráda, eds., 1–24. *Famine in European History*. Cambridge: Cambridge University Press, 2017.

Álvarez, Leandro, Julio Aróstegui, Margarita García, Cristina Gatell, Jorge Palafox and Manel Risques, *Historia de España (Aula 3D), 2° Bachillerato*. Madrid: Vicens Vives, 2016.

Archdeacon, Thomas J., 'The Irish Famine in American School Curricula'. *Éire-Ireland* 37, nos. 1 and 2 (2002): 130–52.

Assmann, Aleida, *Shadows of Trauma: Memory and the Politics of Postwar Identity*. Trans. Sarah Clift. New York: Fordham University Press, 2015.

Bahamonde, Ángel and Luis E. Otero, *Historia de España, 2° Bachillerato*. Madrid: SM, 2016.

Barciela, Carlos, 'Franquismo y Corrupción Económica'. *Historia Social*, no. 30 (1998): 83–96.

Barciela, Carlos, 'Introducción'. In R. Garrabou, C. Barciela and I. Jiménez, eds., 383–454. *Historia Agraria de la España Contemporánea. 3. El Fin de la Agricultura Tradicional (1900–1960)*. Barcelona: Crítica, 1986.

Bastiaans, Conny and Harald Buskop, *Sprekend Verleden – havo Bovenbouw*. Zutphen: Walburg Pers Educatief, 2018.

Baumgärter, Ulrich, *Horizonte – Geschichte, Sekundarstufe II Nordrhein-Westfalen Qualifikationsphase: 11./12. Jahrgangsstufe Gymnasium*. Braunschweig: Westermann, 2015.

Berkel, Marc van, 'Plotlines of Victimhood: The Holocaust in German and Dutch History Textbooks'. Ph.D. diss. Rotterdam: Erasmus University, 2017.

Blanco, Roberto and Mariano González, *Historia de España, 2° Bachillerato*. Madrid: Editex, 2016.

Boonstra, Robert, Cor van der Heijden, Raymond de Kreek and Idzard van Manen, *Feniks, Geschiedenis voor de onderbouw, 3 havo*. Amersfoort: ThiemeMeulenhoff, 2020.

Boonstra, Robert, Cor van der Heijden, Raymond de Kreek and Idzard van Manen, *Feniks, Geschiedenis voor de bovenbouw vwo*. Amersfoort: ThiemeMeulenhoff, 2021.

Boonstra, Robert, Cor van der Heijden, Raymond de Kreek and Idzard van Manen, *Feniks, Leerboek 4/5 havo*. Amersfoort: ThiemeMeulenhoff, 2021.

Bond, Lucy and Jessica Rapson, eds., *The Transcultural Turn: Interrogating Memory Between and Beyond Borders*. Berlin: de Gruyter, 2014.

Brand, Iris van den, Tom van der Geugten, Bernadette Hijstek, René Raap, Peter Schröer, Rein Tromp and Dik Verkuil, *Geschiedeniswerkplaats, Geschiedenis Tweede Fase vwo*. Groningen/Utrecht: Wolters Noordhoff, 2021.

Breman, Bert, Erica Druif, Tom van der Geugten, Marjette van Koperen, Feike Laffeber, José Ritsma, Pieter Schouten, Michiel Smit and Dik Verkuil, *Geschiedeniswerkplaats, Geschiedenis 2 vmbo-bk*. Groningen/Utrecht: Wolters Noordhoff, 2021.

Breukers, Eelco, Jochem Bootsma, Sanne van den Dries, Eleonoor Geenen, Katja Krediet, Judith Tadema and Mark Verschoor, *Memo, 3 havo.'s*. Hertogenbosch: Malmberg, 2021.

Breukers, Eelco, Jochem Bootsma, Sanne van den Dries, Eleonoor Geenen, Katja Krediet, Judith Tadema and Mark Verschoor, *Memo, 3 vwo.* 's Hertogenbosch: Malmberg, 2021.
Brückner, Dieter and Harald Focke, *Das Waren Zeiten: Unterrichtswerk Für Geschichte and Gymnasien, Sekundarstufe I*, North Rhine-Westphalia, 3. Bamberg: Buchners Verlag Bamberg, 2010.
Buitléir, Máire de, Gráinne Henry, Tim Nyhan, and Stephen Tonge, *Timeline. A Complete History Text for Junior Certificate History*. Dublin: Edco, 2014.
Camacho, Vicente, María Á. Fernández, José M. Fernández, Iñaki Mendoza and Ana Mª. Palacios, *Geografía e Historia, 4° ESO, Serie Descubre, Proyecto Saber Hacer*. Madrid: Santillana, 2016.
Cesari, Chiara de and Ann Rigney, 'Introduction'. In Chiara de Cesari and Ann Rigney, eds., 1–25. *Transnational Memory: Circulation, Articulation, Scales*. Berlin: de Gruyter, 2004.
Corporaal, Marguérite and Ingrid de Zwarte, 'Heritages of Hunger: European Famine Legacies in Current Academic Debates'. *International Journal of Heritage Studies* 27, no. 1 (2021): 30–43.
Council of Europe, *Developing a Culture of Co-Operation when Teaching and Learning History*. Strasbourg: Council of Europe Publishing, 2016.
Craps, Stef and Michael Rothberg, 'Introduction: Transcultural Negotiations of Holocaust Memory'. *Criticism* 53, no. 4 (2011): 517–21.
Dekkers, Christa, Ronald den Haan, Ronald Stroo, Jan-Wolter Smit and Juul Lelieveld, *Feniks, Leerboek 1 vmbo-kgt*. Amersfoort: ThiemeMeulenhoff, 2020.
Dekkers, Christa, Ronald den Haan, Ronald Stroo, Jan-Wolter Smit and Juul Lelieveld, *Feniks, vmbo 2bk*. Amersfoort: ThiemeMeulenhoff, 2020.
Delap, Seán and Paul McCormack, *Time Bound*. Dublin: Folens, 2018.
Delap, Seán and Paul McCormack, *Uncovering History. Junior Certificate*, 2nd edn. Dublin: Folens, 2011.
Del Arco Blanco, Miguel Á., 'La Corrupción en el Franquismo. El Fenómeno del Gran Estraperlo'. *Hispania Nova*, no. 16 (2018): 620–45.
Del Arco Blanco, Miguel Á., 'Famine in Spain During Franco's Dictatorship, 1939–1952'. *Journal of Contemporary History* 56, no. 1 (2021): 3–27.
Dierkes, Julian, 'The Nation in German History Education'. In Hanna Schissler and Yasemin Nuhoglu Soysal, eds., 82–104, *The Nation, Europe and the World: Textbooks and Curricula in Transition*. New York: Berghahn Books, 2005.
Droste Johannes, Peter, *Geschichte und Geschehen Qualifikationsphase*, Nordrhein-Westfalen. Berlin: Ernst Klett, 2015.
Erll, Astrid, 'Narratology and Cultural Memory Studies'. In Sandra Heinen and Roy Sommer, eds., 212–27, *Narratology in the Age of Cross-Disciplinary Narrative Research*. Berlin: Walter de Gruyter, 2009.
Erll, Astrid, 'Travelling Memory'. *Parallax* 17, no. 4 (2011): 4–18.
Fernández, José M., Jesús González, Vicente León and Germán Ramírez, *Historia de España, 2° Bachillerato, Proyecto Saber Hacer, Serie Descubre*. A Coruña: Santillana, 2016.
García, Margarita, Cristina Gatell and Sergio Riesco. *Geografía e Historia, Historia, Andalucía (Digital) (Aula 3D), 4° ESO*. Madrid: Vicens Vives, 2017.
García, Margarita, Cristina Gatell and Sergio Riesco, *Geografía e Historia, Historia, Com. Valenciana, (Aula 3D), 4° ESO*. Madrid: Vicens Vives, 2016.
García de Cortázar, Fernando, Javier Mª Donézar, Julio Valdeón, Mª Isabel del Val, Manuel Fernández and Ángel Gamazo, *Historia de España, 2° Bachillerato*. Madrid: Anaya, 2016.

Gorgues, Ricardo, José Cano, Carmen Calonge and Juan Di Pietro, *Historia, 4° ESO*. Barcelona: Castellnou, 2008.

Government of Ireland, NCCA (National Council for Curriculum and Assessment) and the Department of Education and Skills, 'Junior Cycle History Specification', 2017.

Grossmann, Atina, 'Grams, Calories, and Food: Languages of Victimization, Entitlement, and Human Rights in Occupied Germany, 1945–1949'. *Central European History* 44, no. 1 (2011): 118–48.

Henry, Gráinne, Bairbre Kennedy, Tim Nyhan, and Stephen Tonge, *History Alive (Textbook and Activity Book)*. Dublin: Edco, 2018.

Higgins, Michael D., 'Speech at the National Famine Commemoration 2021', 16 May 2021, https://president.ie/en/media-library/speeches/speech-at-the-national-famine-commemoration-2021.

Issit, John, 'Reflections on the Study of Textbooks'. *History of Education* 33, no. 6 (2004): 683–5.

Janmaat, Jan Germen. 'History and National Identity Construction: The Great Famine in Irish and Ukrainian History Textbooks'. In Christian Noack, Lindsay Janssen and Vincent Comerford, eds., 77–102, *Holodomor and Gorta Mór: Histories, Memories and Representations of Famine in Ukraine and Ireland*. London: Anthem Press, 2013.

Janssen, Lindsay, 'The Great Irish Famine in Irish and UK History Textbooks, 2010–2020'. *History Education Research Journal* 20, no. 2 (2023): 1–16.

Kelly, Mary, A. Stewart Frotheringham and Martin Charlton, 'Mapping Population Change in Ireland 1841–1851: Quantitative Analysis Using Historical GIS'. In Christian Noack, Lindsay Janssen, and Vincent Comerford, eds., 245–68, *Holodomor and Gorta Mór: Histories Memory and Representations of Famine in Ukraine and Ireland*. London: Anthem Press, 2012.

Lama, Eduardo, Manuel Á. García, Francisco Olmedo and Rosa Mª. Pros, *Historia de España, 2° Bachillerato*. Madrid: SomosLink – Edelvives, 2020.

Lanzinner, Maximilian, *Buchners Geschichte Oberstufe [Unterrichtswerk Für Die Gymnasiale Oberstufe] Qualifikationsphase*, North Rhine-Westphalia. Bamberg: Bamberg Buchner, 2015.

Lanzinner, Maximilian, *Buchners Kolleg: Geschichte 2*, Berlin. Bamberg: Buchners Verlag Bamberg, 2013.

Laschewski-Müller, Karin and Robert Hübner, *Kursbuch Geschichte Qualifikationsphase*. Berlin: Cornelsen, 2015.

Lendzian, Hans-Jürgen, *Zeiten Und Menschen – Geschichte Qualifikationsphase*, Nordrhein-Westfalen Paderborn: Schöningh, 2015.

Levy, Daniel and Nathan Sznaider, 'Memories of Universal Victimhood: The Case of Ethnic German Expellees'. *German Politics and Society* 23, no. 2 (2005): 1–27.

McCarthy, Patricia, *Footsteps in Time 1*. Dublin: CJ Fallon, 2010.

McCaughey, Patsy, *Discovering History. New Junior Cycle History*. Dublin: Mentor Books, 2018.

McGowan, Mark, '*The Famine Plot* Revisited: A Reassessment of the Great Irish Famine as Genocide'. *Genocide Studies International* 11, no. 1 (2017): 87–104.

Mark-FitzGerald, Emily, *Commemorating the Irish Famine: Memory and the Monument*. Liverpool: Liverpool University Press, 2013.

Mark-FitzGerald, Emily, 'The "Irish Holocaust": Historical Trauma and the Commemoration of the Famine'. In Griselda Pollock, ed., 60–76, *The Visual Politics of Psychoanalysis: Art and the Image in Post-Traumatic Cultures*. London: I. B. Tauris, 2013.

Meyer, Christoph, *Horizonte 9: Geschichte – Materialien für Lehrerinnen und Lehrer*, Berlin. Braunschweig: Westermann, 2019.

Mininka-Milko, Tatiana, 'Introduction'. In Council of Europe, ed., 8–11, *Shared Histories for a Europe without Dividing Lines 2010–2014*. Strasbourg: Council of Europe Publishing, 2014. http://shared-histories.coe.int.
Moeller, Robert G., *War Stories: The Search for a Usable Past in the Federal Republic of Germany*. Berkeley, CA: University of California Press, 2001.
Morash, Christopher, 'Famine/Holocaust: Fragmented Bodies'. *Éire-Ireland* 32, no. 1 (1997): 136–50.
Mullin, James V., 'The New Jersey Famine Curriculum: A Report'. *Éire-Ireland* 37, no. 1&2 (2002): 119–29.
Murphy, Maureen and Alan Singer, 'New York State's "Great Irish Famine Curriculum": A Report'. *Éire-Ireland* 37, nos. 1 and 2 (2002): 109–18.
Olson, David R., 'On the Language and Authority of Textbooks'. *Journal of Communication* 30, no. 1 (1980): 186–96.
O'Neill, Gregg and Eimear Jenkinson, *Artefact*. Dublin: Educate.ie, 2018.
Prieto, Jaime, *Historia de España, 2° Bachillerato*. A Coruña: Bruño, 2016.
Ribeiro de Menezes, Alison, *Embodying Memory in Contemporary Spain*. Basingstoke: Palgrave, 2014.
Repoussi, Maria and Nicole Tutiaux-Guillon, 'New Trends in History Textbook Research: Issues and Methodologies toward a School Historiography'. *Journal of Educational Media, Memory & Society* 2, no. 1 (2010): 154–70.
Rodríguez, Óscar, 'Cambalaches: Hambre, Moralidad Popular y Mercados de Guerra y Postguerra', *Historia Social*, no. 77 (2013): 149–74.
Román Ruiz, Gloria, 'El Pan Negro de cada Día. Memoria de los Años del Hambre en el Mundo Rural'. In Miguel Á. Del Arco Blanco, ed., 345–66, *Los Años del Hambre. Historia y Memoria de la Posguerra Franquista*. Madrid: Marcial Pons, 2020.
Román Ruiz, Gloria, 'Pícaros de Posguerra. Turning to Crime to Survive Famine and Malnutrition in Early Francoism (1939–1952)'. In Miguel Á. Del Arco Blanco and Peter Anderson, eds., 114–36. *Franco's Famine: Malnutrition, Disease and Starvation in Post-Civil War Spain*. London: Bloomsbury Academic, 2022.
Román Ruiz, Gloria, 'Representations of the Spanish Hunger Years (1939–1952) in Recent Secondary School History Textbooks'. *Paedagogica Historica* (2022): 1–22.
Rothberg, Michael, *The Implicated Subject: Beyond Victims and Perpetrators*. Stanford, CA: Stanford University Press, 2019.
Rothberg, Michael, *Multidirectional Memory: Remembering the Holocaust in the Age of Decolonization*. Stanford, CA: Stanford University Press, 2009.
Savenije, Geerte M. and Pieter de Bruijn, 'Historical Empathy in a Museum: Uniting Contextualisation and Emotional Engagement'. *International Journal of Heritage Studies* 23, no. 9 (2017): 832–45.
Sheedy, Dan, *History in Focus 1. A History of Ireland for the Junior Cycle*. Dublin: CJ Fallon, 2018.
Stradling, Robert, *Multiperspectivity in History Teaching: A Guide for Teachers*. Brussels: Council of Europe, 2003.
Wertsch, James V., 'Collective Memory and Narrative Templates'. *Social Research* 75, no. 1 (2008): 133–56.
Wertsch, James V., *Voices of Collective Remembering*. Cambridge, MA: Cambridge University Press, 2002.
Wilkes, Aaron, *Industry, Reform and Empire. Britain 1750–1900*. Dublin: Folens, 2004.
Zerubavel, Eviatar, *Time Maps: Collective Memory and the Social Shape of the Past*. Chicago, IL: University of Chicago Press, 2003.

Zwarte, Ingrid de, 'Coordinating Hunger: The Evacuation of Children during the Dutch Food Crisis, 1945'. *War & Society* 35, no. 2 (2016): 132–49.
Zwarte, Ingrid de, 'Fighting Vulnerability: Child Feeding Initiatives during the Dutch Hunger Winter'. In T. Tönsmeyer, P. Haslinger and A. Laba, eds., 293–310, *Societies under Occupation in World War II: Supply, Shortage, Hunger*. London: Palgrave, 2018.
Zwarte, Ingrid de, *The Hunger Winter: Fighting Famine in the Occupied Netherlands, 1944–1945*. Cambridge: Cambridge University Press, 2020.

2

CONVEYING SOVIET FAMINES

Representations of hunger as mass atrocity during the Holodomor and the Leningrad Blockade in post-war USSR Textbooks[1]

Anne-Lise Bobeldijk

In 1954, Arthur Koestler, the Hungarian-British journalist and writer, best known for his anti-totalitarian novel *Darkness at Noon*, published his autobiography *The Invisible Writing*. He described his emigration to and travelling through the Soviet Union in the years 1932–33, at the height of the famine in Ukraine, Kuban, Kazakhstan, Belarus, and other regions of the Soviet Union. Despite his membership in the German Communist Party, Koestler was regarded as an outsider by Soviet authorities and was therefore under the strict supervision of both the Joint State Political Directorate (OGPU) and the Department for Agitation and Propaganda (AGITPROP), which tried to prevent him from interacting with locals. Notwithstanding the restrictions, he witnessed starving people in various regions of the Soviet Union in 1932 and, on looking back, stated that 'I have never seen so many and such hurried funerals as during that winter in Kharkov[sic]'.[2]

The Ukrainian famine known as the Holodomor, which Koestler witnessed in Kharkiv, was never part of the official historical state narrative of the Soviet Union: after all, it would expose the repressions of the Soviet population by the Stalinist regime. The Leningrad Blockade, the besieging of the city of Leningrad by the German army from September 1941 until January 1944, which caused the death of approximately 750,000 to a million citizens, held a different position within the grand narrative of the Soviet Union. Although this famine history particularly shows the human losses and vulnerability of the Soviet Union during the Second World War, it also gave Soviet authorities the opportunity to illustrate the strength and perseverance of its people. Contrary to the Holodomor, the perpetrators of this famine did not come from within: it was the German army that inflicted this catastrophe upon the Soviet people. Although it is quite controversial to draw analogies

DOI: 10.4324/9781003391524-4

between the crimes committed by Hitler and Stalin within one article,[3] comparing the Holodomor with the Leningrad Blockade offers the opportunity to see how histories of famines as mass atrocities and attempts to weaponise food have been both instrumentalised and silenced in the construction of grand state narratives. As this chapter will show, history textbooks, as 'collective memory agents' of a nation, are excellent objects to analyse the instrumentalisation of famine pasts: they reveal how these historical narratives surrounding famines developed over time.[4]

Recent studies have shown how hunger memories and hunger representations can contribute to the creation or reinforcement of national identity.[5] Since the fall of the Soviet Union, the Holodomor has particularly informed the identity formation of the Ukrainian nation by addressing the country's suffering under Soviet aggression. This trend intensified after the unprovoked, full-scale invasion of Ukraine by Russia in February 2022, as since then memories of the Holodomor have been invoked as an analogy with the present situation. For example, in November 2022, President of the European Commission, Ursula von der Leyen, tweeted: '90 years after the Holodomor, the Kremlin is again using food as a weapon'.[6] Likewise, the memory of the Leningrad Blockade has been invoked as a historical analogy to current events. Contrary to the memory of the Holodomor, however, this memory of the Leningrad Blockade is not used to alienate Ukrainians from Russians but to unite them in opposing the war in Ukraine. In March 2022, Ukrainian President Volodymyr Zelensky addressed Russian citizens directly by signalling their shared Soviet past of the Nazi occupation, stating: 'Citizens of Russia, how is your blockade of Mariupol different from the blockade of Leningrad during World War Two? [...] We will not forget anyone whose lives were taken by the occupiers'.[7] Zelensky, by recalling the shared Soviet past, aimed to provoke empathy among Russian citizens through a process that memory scholar Ann Rigney calls 'reparative memory', which mobilises a shared past in order to generate a new shared future.[8]

The present attention to and instrumentalisation of these mass atrocities show the importance of their memory for identity formation and interrelationships among former Soviet states. However, the existent excellent body of work on the Leningrad Blockade and the Holodomor rarely engages with the representation of hunger as mass atrocity, nor are both famines discussed as case studies within the same study. Analysing how the representation of these famines developed during the Soviet era as a foundational period for the construction of national identity of both Ukraine and Russia will shed further light on how the memory of these two famines is used in Ukraine and Russia today. The main aim of this chapter is therefore to show to what extent this memory was instrumentalised in Soviet history textbooks for political purposes and identity formation throughout the Soviet period between 1951 and 1991.

This chapter is outlined as follows. The first part offers a description of the methodology, the position of textbooks within the Soviet Union, and the corpus of sources. Subsequently, the historical context of the two Soviet famines as mass atrocities is outlined to understand their extraordinary positions within Soviet history and how this influences their representation within Soviet memory. The third and fourth sections of this chapter focus on the representation of the Holodomor and the Leningrad Blockade in Soviet history textbooks throughout four chronological timeframes that correspond with the reign and influence of the four most important post-war Soviet leaders. The turning points of these periods do not correspond one-on-one with their period of rule, but with watershed moments during or after their rule. This leads to the following periodisation: 1. Joseph Stalin, 1951–56; 2. Khrushchev, 1956–65; 3. Brezhnev, 1965–85; and 4. Gorbachev, 1985–91.

History textbooks as historical sources and their position in the Soviet dictatorship

History textbooks can serve more purposes than simply informing students. Maria Grever asserts that in nation-states, narratives within textbooks are produced 'with different and often competing national plots, vaunting the superiority and longevity of their own country'.[9] Grever regards textbooks as tools to position the indigenous nation against 'the other'. Within Soviet textbooks, this sense of superiority is reflected in the emphasis on the inevitable struggle of communism with capitalism and the superiority of the Soviet state. Aleida Assmann underlines a similar aspect of textbooks, as she observes that 'in the realm of school curricula and textbooks, history automatically becomes applied history. It serves as the backbone for the nation-state and supports its values by constructing heroic and mobilizing patriotic narratives.'[10] Thus, the glorification of the Soviet Union in textbooks serves not only to place oneself against another but also to instil a feeling of patriotism and belonging.

In most authoritarian states, the use of textbooks is more extreme than in democratic ones. Hannah Arendt also observed this in her monograph *The Origins of Totalitarianism* (1951): she underlines the need of propaganda in totalitarian societies like the Soviet Union because 'only the mob and the elite can be attracted by the momentum of totalitarianism itself; the masses have to be won by propaganda'.[11] Likewise John Isitts emphasises that in extreme contexts, 'the textbook is the vehicle for the transmission of authorized dogma' and the 'key mechanism for the production and reproduction of ideas'.[12] Within the Soviet state, history and history education had exactly this function, as historian Janet Vaillant asserts: 'It was expected not only to teach patriotism, but also to present an ideologically determined, monolithic view of the past'.[13] The most important aspect of this view is the focus on success and victory: without a democratic basis, history serves as the legitimisation of the leadership and glorification of the leadership's competence. Thus, viewing textbooks as Soviet propaganda, the analysis of the standardised and centralised textbooks can clarify the position of famines as mass atrocities within Soviet history.

In February 1933, officially approved and centralised history textbooks were introduced as basic learning tools, thus becoming an important medium for the Soviet authorities to reach the (young) masses.[14] The reach of this particular tool broadened as education became more widely accessible, when enrolment of students in school doubled up to 35.5 million students between the late 1920s and 1940s.[15] The Second World War disrupted this pattern of increase of student numbers.[16] In the post-war period, textbooks became focused on Stalin and his achievements due to his cult of personality. As will be discussed, large parts of the history textbooks were based on Stalin's *Kratkii Kurs* (Short Course).

After Stalin's death, his successor, Nikita Krushchev, loosened restrictions on society. This led to the publication of works such as Alexandr Solzhenitsyn's *One Day in the Life of Ivan Denisovich* (1962), while in academic circles, attempts were made to write more nuanced historical studies.[17] Topics within the humanities were 'destalinised', and history courses were reorganised in order to give the 'post-revolutionary' history of the Soviet Union enough attention.[18] From this moment onwards, the cult of Stalin was replaced by the myth of the Great Patriotic War, which developed rapidly into the hegemonic memory representing the strength and perseverance of both the Soviet state as well as the Soviet people. Under Brezhnev, as a response to relative 'Thaw' under Khrushchev, political education became the most important pillar of the educational system.[19] Although there were no major curricular reforms with the coming of *glasnost* under Mikhail Gorbachev, the content of history textbooks changed, as did the public discussion about history in general, because archives concerning Soviet crimes against its own population opened and because it became possible to discuss these topics publicly at last.[20]

The textbook analyses in this chapter are based on a corpus of 32 Soviet textbooks stemming from the above-described periods. Ten of the examined history textbooks were written for students in the fourth or fifth grade, for pupils of approximately 10 years. Twenty-two books were written for the ninth or tenth grade, for children aged approximately 17 years. The textbooks for these specific classes are analysed because they teach the periods during which the Holodomor and the Leningrad Blockade took place. The corpus of sources used for this chapter consists of 2 textbooks stemming from the Stalinist period, 10 from the Khrushchev period, 16 from the Brezhnev period, and 5 from the Gorbachev period. The renewal of books only occurred every few years, and only parts of existing textbooks were rewritten.

Soviet famines, mass atrocity, and collective memory

To understand the representation of these famine pasts, it is important to understand their historical context and what position they hold in relation to each other and to other famines and similar mass atrocities on Soviet soil. After all, the Holodomor and the famine during the Leningrad Blockade were not the only Soviet famines. In 1921–22 and 1946–47, famine struck the Soviet Union as well, with respectively 2.5–5 million and 1–2 million Soviet citizens who died.[21] Contrary to these two famines, the Leningrad Blockade and the Holodomor were different in one key element: whereas in the two other cases, causes of famine were attributed to war, economics, and bad harvests, both the Leningrad Blockade and the Holodomor are considered to be man-made famines.[22] According to Alex de Waal, in both cases, the events can even be considered ‘mass atrocities’, which he defines as ‘widespread and systemic violence against civilians, largely characterized by killing’.[23] The violence in these two cases was the use of food, or rather the deprivation of food, as a weapon to place pressure on the population.

The Holodomor, literally *death by hunger* or *death by starvation*, was the man-made famine in Ukraine that took place between 1931 and 1934, with its culmination in 1932–33. Throughout the Soviet Union, approximately six million people died, of which some three to four million in Ukraine.[24] The famine stemmed from the rapid forced collectivisation of the rural areas of the Soviet Union, in addition to a failed harvest. Terror imposed by authorities struck peasants and specific nationalities because of the policy of *korenitsiia* (indigenisation). Because of Stalin’s fear for Ukrainian nationalism, Ukraine was particularly affected by these politics.[25] The onset of the famine can already be dated back to 1928, with the start of the First Five-Year Plan that restricted the freedom of peasants within the Soviet Union.[26] The forceful integration into collective farms was combined with terror against anyone who was supposedly a *kulak*, a wealthier peasant—even though they were often not much richer than the average peasant—which led to the persecution of 10 million so-called kulaks between 1929 and 1932.[27] Additionally, a grain requisitioning campaign in the years 1932 and 1933 eventually deprived many peasants of their harvest.

Among scholars, there is a recurring debate about whether the Holodomor should be considered a genocide because, in particular, *Ukrainian* peasants fell victim to the famine.[28] However, because of the difficulty of applying a legal concept to a historical event—in which the intent to destroy the Ukrainian nation should be proved—many scholars agree that the famine has at least genocidal characteristics and should be regarded as a mass atrocity.[29] The measures that were taken against the peasantry, such as the restrictions on leaving towns, cities, and regions, the forced requisitioning of grain from already starving peasants in combination with the overall denial of the existence of the famine and the blocking of international relief, constituted a cocktail of genocidal policies with devastating results.[30] The severity of the famine was reflected in widespread cannibalism and necrophagy.[31]

The besieging of Leningrad was also a deliberate act, to put pressure on the Soviet authorities, and was part of a larger exploitative and arguably genocidal policy of the Nazis against the Soviet Union.[32] Prior to the invasion of the Soviet Union, State Secretary of the *Reichsministerium für Ernährung und Landwirtschaft*, Herbert Backe, drafted a policy that would ensure food security for the Nazi troops in the Soviet Union through completely 'living off the land' from 1943 onwards despite the fact that this would cost millions of Soviet civilians their lives.[33] Although this *Hungerplan* or Backe plan was never exactly executed as planned, the reality of the Nazi food policies was detrimental to the Soviet population. Estimates suggest approximately 1.5 million Soviet civilians died of regional famines during the Nazi occupation.[34] Cities were particularly struck by this hunger policy: from halfway through 1941 onwards, the general policy was that major cities should not be occupied but rather had to be besieged for economic and logistic reasons.[35] This shows that the case of Leningrad did not exist in a vacuum but was actually one of the many situations in which the population of Soviet cities was starved. However, Leningrad stands out in that this siege and famine are particularly remembered, as will be discussed.

From September 1941, Leningrad became surrounded by Wehrmacht and Finnish troops and was cut off from the 'mainland'.[36] This led to the almost 900-day blockade of the city, of which the first year of 1941 was the most severe.[37] In the early winter of 1942, an ice road was formed over the frozen Lake Ladoga, enabling transportation of food into the city and of sick and starving citizens to the mainland. Soviet authorities who were still in the city made food available through rationings. However, particularly during the winter of 1941 and 1942, the extremely dreadful situation in the city resulted in cannibalism and necrophagy, similar to what had happened during the Ukrainian famine of 1932–33.[38] Approximately 750,000 citizens of Leningrad died during the three-year blockade.[39]

Both famines have strong characteristics of mass atrocities, and some people who lived through the famine caused by Stalin had to endure similar dreadful situations under Nazi rule. As historian Karel Berkhoff asserts, 'whereas in 1933 peasants had attempted to save themselves by coming to Kyiv, now [during the Nazi occupation] desperate Kyivans tried to barter with well-fed peasants in the countryside', and some of them even viewed the famines under Nazi rule in the early 1940s as revenge of the peasants for '1933'.[40] Similar attitudes towards work and nutrition—in which food is used as a weapon—were central to both Stalin's and Hitler's policies. In February 1933, Stalin asserted that 'those who did not work deserved to starve',[41] while only nine years later, similar areas were struck by the same terror again, as the chief of staff of the 17th Army of the Wehrmacht commented that 'those who do not work will starve to death'.[42] Historian Dieter Pohl also draws the connection between the artificial famines by Stalin and Hitler, contending: 'Like the Stalinist starvations, the starvations from 1941 onwards cannot be attributed to natural disasters or the transport difficulties of the Wehrmacht, but ultimately to inhuman policies'.[43] The similarities between the two famines enable us to elaborate further on whether the representations of these famines are also alike.

The history of these two mass atrocities holds different positions within the Soviet past. For the Leningrad Blockade, the perpetrator-victim paradigm is quite straightforward: the so-called 'German fascist invader' is a rather 'convenient' perpetrator because this figure was an external enemy that was eventually defeated by the Soviets. This view is also prominently present within the hegemonic narrative of the Great Patriotic War (1941–44/45), in which the Soviet people, partisans, and Red Army defeated the German perpetrator of mass atrocities on Soviet soil and Europe as a whole. This narrative is still omnipresent in Russia and Belarus. For example, Russia's President Putin legitimised his invasion of Ukraine by claiming that he would purge Ukraine of so-called Nazis. Thus, he not only reinforced the narrative of Nazi perpetration, but also drew on the victory of the Great Patriotic War as a legitimation for the war in Ukraine. On 22 February 2022, in his speech to the Russian nation to elaborate on the invasion of Ukraine, he said: 'Your fathers, grandfathers and great-grandfathers did not fight the Nazi occupiers and did not defend our common Motherland [the Soviet Union] to allow today's neo-Nazis to seize power in Ukraine'.[44]

The position of the Holodomor is more difficult to grasp within the Soviet context because here the perpetrator came from within society. In a society that did not (yet) go through any process of transitional justice in which the position of the perpetrators was properly addressed,[45] there was no room for the Holodomor within the narrative of the Soviet state. Novels that addressed the Holodomor or related crimes were censored, and although in private the famine was discussed, it was not possible to address the topic in public.[46] Even under Khrushchev, who did address Stalin's crimes, such as the Great Terror of 1937–38, in the denunciation of his predecessor to the 20th Congress of the Communist Party, the Holodomor was not discussed. On a national-state level, Ukrainian communists even publically wondered why the famine was not addressed in the speech, because this was after all a crime of Stalin as well.[47] This is arguably because many Soviet officials, who had only been responsible for parts of the measures that led to the famine and therefore could hardly be pinpointed as perpetrators, could technically only be addressed as, in the words of Michael Rothberg, 'implicated subjects'.[48] This complexity of the Holodomor as a mass atrocity in comparison to the Leningrad Blockade will become clear from the textbook analyses as well.

The Holodomor in Soviet textbooks

Although the history of the famine in Ukraine did not explicitly occur in textbooks until the period of *glasnost* under Gorbachev, the context of the famine—the fast and forced collectivisation—was omnipresent in Soviet educational books. Collectivisation was for the Soviet authorities one of the major successes because it represented the transformation of the Soviet Union as a rural society into an industrial one: the next stage in history that would bring the Soviet Union closer to a utopian society according to Marxist-Leninist theory. In addition, in particular, the diminishing of the group of bourgeoise peasants, here specifically the *kulak*, was regarded as a success, as this was ultimately one of the major goals of the Soviet Union as a socialist utopian state. This process of diminishing was euphemistically referred to as the 'elimination of the kulak as a class', although this in theory meant that 'kulaks' were deported, forcefully integrated into collective farms, incarcerated, or even executed. As the historical context of the Holodomor showed, the famine in Ukraine was the reverse of the medal of the Soviet Union's much-praised collectivisation. Therefore, the analysis of the representation of the Holodomor in textbooks focuses on the collectivisation and its consequences, because the Holodomor or the famine is not mentioned.

During the Stalinist period, the collectivisation of the rural Soviet Union was represented as one of the successes of Stalin's influence. In line with what one would expect, Stalin is a prominent figure in textbooks from this period because after all, history had to serve the legitimisation of the Soviet leadership. Stalin as 'father of the nation' is therefore omnipresent. For example, the tenth-grade textbook *Istoriia SSSR* (1951) is largely based on Stalin's own work and even includes direct quotes from Stalin's infamous *Kratkii Kurs* (Short Course). This short text, published in 1938 and written by ghost-writers, was Stalin's approved history of the Soviet Union's Communist Party and had to serve as *the* guideline of how to view Soviet history.[49] In addition, Stalin's influence on Soviet history itself is also extensively underlined, as according to the textbook for the tenth grade from 1951, it was Stalin who came up with the terminology 'eliminating the kulaks as a class'.[50]

The collectivisation is discussed elaborately in the 1951 tenth-grade textbook, to such an extent that it can be viewed as rather revealing. For example, the book explicitly refers to the 'second group of grain regions—Ukraine, the Central Black Earth Region, Siberia, the Urals, Kazakhstan—[that] was to complete the collectivisation in the spring of 1932'.[51] It was in those regions that famine struck hardest. Considering the famine was a combination of harvest failure and the brutal measures taken by the authorities, the direct follow-up in this textbook about these measures is remarkably open. The 'struggle' against kulaks is underlined by the notion that 'local Soviets were given the right to take all necessary measures to combat the kulaks in areas of complete collectivisation, up to the confiscation of equipment, livestock and the expulsion of kulaks from the area. The kulaks were expropriated, just as the capitalists in industry had previously been expropriated'.[52] The only concealed aspect of the famine here is the fact that this was the consequence of these measures. Considering that the famine was censored and actively silenced, the textbook writers took a risk by disclosing a lot of information about this historical event.

While famine or food shortages during the 1930s are left unaddressed in the textbooks from this period, in the fourth-grade textbook from this period, specific mention is made of famine in Tsarist Russia. Within the section about the creation of the Soviet Union, there is a reference to the economic situation prior to this moment, as the textbook states that in 1914, 'there was famine in the country'.[53] This shows that there was not yet a Cold War paradigm in place in which the communist Soviet Union could be positioned as superior to the capitalist West. In 1951, bourgeois Tsarist Russia had to be portrayed as the 'other', in contrast with the more superior economic situation in the communist Soviet Union. The 1946–47 Soviet famine is left unmentioned because it would not serve the purposes of the Communist Party.

After Stalin's death, textbooks show very explicitly Khrushchev's policy of destaliniation, although this does not seem to affect the way in which collectivisation is addressed. The space devoted to this topic, including the 'elimination of the kulaks', did shrank from 10 pages in the 1951 textbook to only a short 2.5 pages in the 1957 textbook. However, the above-quoted narrative about the collectivisation in Ukraine and other regions in 1932, as well as the measures taken against so-called kulaks, remained exactly the same as in the 1951 version of the book.[54] From the 1957 fourth-grade textbooks onwards, the story of the 'struggle against the kulak' is more extensively addressed (Image 2.1). The most important reason for this is that the influence of Stalin and his mark on Soviet history disappeared completely from the textbooks. This can be observed in the absence of references to Stalin's *Kratkii Kurs* and the overall absence of Stalin in relation to the process of collectivisation and other parts of history.

From the Krushchev period onwards until the collapse of the Soviet Union, a Cold War paradigm started to emerge in the textbooks, especially those written for the tenth grade. The topic of the collectivisation is placed within a larger context of international developments, such as the economic crisis of the late 1920s and the rise of fascism in Germany.[55] As had happened in the context of the Tsarist Russian famine in the 1951 textbook, the success of the collectivisation is placed in juxtaposition to troubles elsewhere in the capitalist world to underline the supposed superiority of the Soviet state. Another aspect of textbooks from the Krushchev era is an increasing tendency to instil patriotic feelings into pupils through underlining Soviet successes. In the 1957 fourth-grade textbook, collectivisation is represented in this fashion, as it states: 'The collective farm

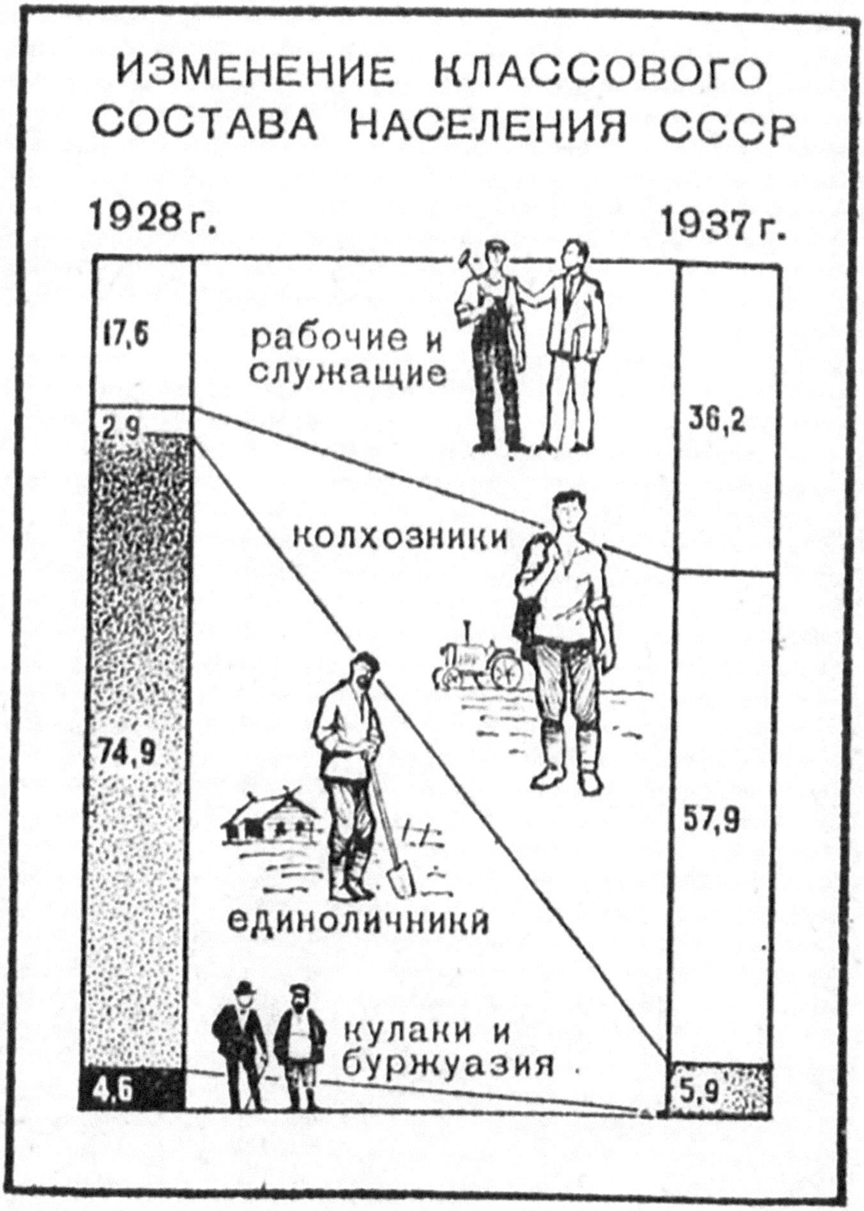

IMAGE 2.1 Figure from the 1976 ninth-grade textbook titled 'Change in the Class Composition of the Population of the USSR', showing the 'elimination of the kulak'. M.P. Kima, ed., *Istoriia SSSR: Uchebnik dlia desiatogo klassa srednei shkoly* (Moscow, 1976), 372.

system won. The whole life of the peasants has changed. Yields began to rise and the incomes of collective farmers began to grow. Schools, hospitals, clubs were built in the villages'.[56] The text is accompanied by an illustration of the difference between sowing and harvesting until the revolution and from the collectivisation onwards. The pre-revolution period is portrayed as rural and somewhat backwards, while collectivisation is shown as a heavily efficient and modern way of farming. The fact that a famine was part of this process of collectivisation is completely disregarded here, like in the other textbooks (Image 2.2).

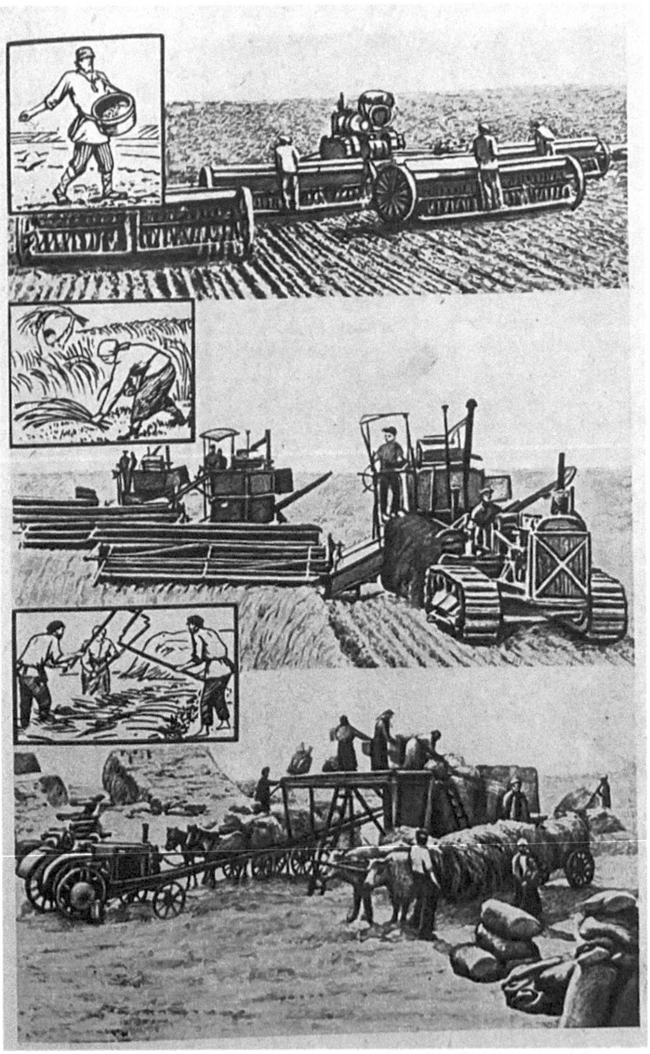

IMAGE 2.2 'Peasant work until the revolution and in the kolkhoz (sowing, harvesting, milling)'. From S.P Alekseev and V.G. Karcov, *Istoriia SSSR: Uchebnaia kniga dlia 4-go klassa* (1957), 121.

Although the textbooks were aimed at conveying a glorified past of the Soviet Union, from the Khrushchev period onwards, the actual belief in this official past apparently started to fade. Historian William Husband observed, 'over time [from the 1950s onwards until the end of the Soviet Union], the manifold contradictions between the overarching message of the official story and existing social memory became evident even to schoolchildren'.[57] James Wertsch makes a similar claim in his research on very early post-Soviet-Latvia: while students who were schooled during the Soviet era did learn the official state narrative, they did not necessarily believe it as they were actively aware of the existence of alternative versions of history.[58] So although within textbooks there was not necessarily more space to discuss the topic of the famine, society itself was more open, and more critical literature was published and even used within the Soviet curricula. For example, Mikhail Sholokhov's novel *Virgin Soil Upturned* (1935) about the collectivisation in Ukraine became even part of literature courses in secondary education.[59] Although the novel is not necessarily critical of the collectivisation, it holds a wide variety of perspectives, including anti-collectivisation.[60] Considering that Soviet students had 2,500 hours of literature courses a year against 500 hours of history lessons, the possibility of being exposed to alternative versions of the past existed outside of history lessons.[61]

The discussion of collectivisation, as taught under Khrushchev, was continued under Brezhnev's rule, with one minor change. Although there were still pictures of the difference between the USA and the USSR in which the USSR was presented more favourably, there were indications of more realistic representations of the Soviet Union's agricultural past. For example, the grain failure of 1946—which contributed to the 1946–47 Soviet famine—is mentioned explicitly in the chapter on the post-war years in the 1983 textbook: 'a heavy blow was the severe drought of 1946, which engulfed the most grain-producing regions of the country: Ukraine, the Lower Volga region, and the Central Black Earth region'.[62] This is accompanied by an illustrated graph showing a decline in production of agricultural products between 1940 and 1946 and again an increase between 1946 and 1950.[63] Although the famine itself is not explicitly addressed, the differences in harvest production serve as an implicit clue to the consequences of the 1946 'severe drought' (Image 2.3).

With the start of Mikhail Gorbachev's rule in 1985, a major change occurred in textbook narratives on the Holodomor because the famine was now explicitly referred to. Whereas earlier on, only implicit indications of a possible famine were present in textbooks, now the famine was addressed in very clear wording: 'In 1932–1933, famine broke out in a number of large rural areas. This cost several million lives'.[64] What was missing in the earlier textbooks, the fact that the measures taken against the peasantry had caused famine, was now openly addressed. However, the 1989 textbook still does

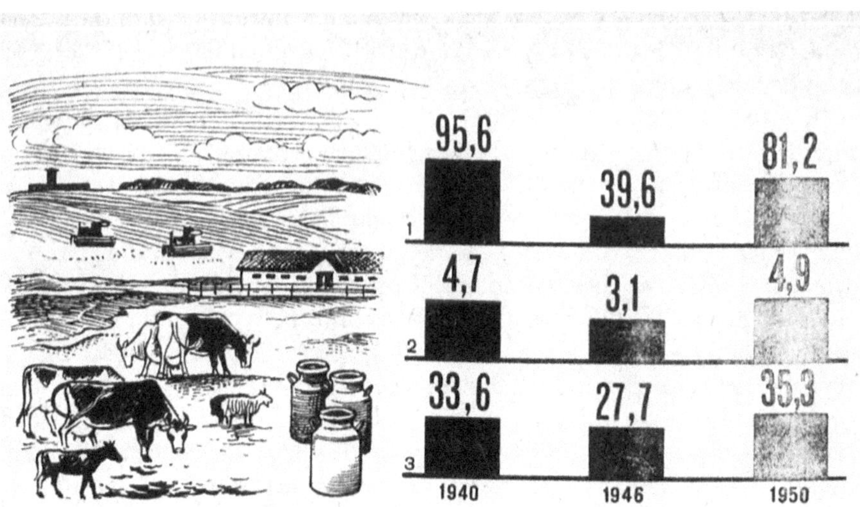

IMAGE 2.3 Diagram in the 1983 tenth-grade textbook, captioned 'Production of agricultural products: 1. grain (in Mt); 2. meat in slaughter weight (in Mt); 3. milk (in Mt)'. M.P. Kima, ed., *Istoriia SSSR: Uchebnik dlia desiatogo klassa srednei shkoly* (1983), 131.

not point to any agents or perpetrators responsible for the hunger crisis. Another significant change is that the measures taken against the peasants are now critically reviewed. The ways in which the measures are described are not radically different: the 1951 textbook employs the term 'expulsion' (выселение), while the 1989 edition speaks of forced relocation (принудительное переселение) as one of the adopted policies. However, in the textbooks from the Gorbachev era, the passport measures against peasants, the confiscation of property, as well as the eviction of entire groups of people who were assumed to have been kulaks are actively condemned. As the 1989 textbook mentions: 'The total number of victims of this policy has not yet been accurately calculated. But there is reason to believe that about 10 million people were subject to repression (репрессиям подверглось). They were mostly peasants'.[65] Whereas the measures were previously represented as justified measures against enemies of the state, the kulaks, now those who suffered from these measures, are actually represented as victims. In addition, the textbook shows that these people were repressed, which indicates that there was no clear justification for these measures at all.

The change in textbook narratives is in line with what happened during the Gorbachev era. Because of the policy of openness, *glasnost*, it became possible to address the crimes that were taken against 'enemies of the people', such as kulaks, but also others who were repressed during the 1930s and thereafter. Whereas during the period of destalinisation only the crimes that could be attributed to Stalin were condemned, in 1989, the crimes that were committed in general were decried.

However, this change did not mean that everything could be criticised or scrutinised. For example, the famine is still described in broad terms without any mention of its severity in Ukraine. Rather, only peasants are mentioned as being the main victims. In addition, the famine is represented as a disaster that simply occurred, without any attribution of guilt to particular perpetrators. Whereas in the case of the Second World War, there was an external enemy that meted out these crimes or repression upon the Soviet population, the fact that Soviet authorities or possibly specific people within the government inflicted these measures and therefore were partially responsible for famine among Soviet civilians was yet to be addressed in the late Gorbachev era. Here, the fact that many people within the Soviet state structure were 'implicated subjects' prevented the next step within the process of transitional justice. This step would only be taken in the post-Soviet era and would then only occur in Ukraine itself and until the early 2000s in Russia.

The Leningrad Blockade in Soviet textbooks

The Leningrad Blockade held a different position within the memory culture of the Soviet Union than the Holodomor and therefore has a different representation in textbooks. Contrary to the Holodomor, it was not a silenced topic, but despite the different positions, it is clear that the overall trends within textbooks follow the same societal changes in both cases. As seen before, Stalin dominated the textbooks in the 1940s and early 1950s. For example, a large part of the tenth-grade textbook from 1951 is based on Stalin's work 'About the Great Patriotic War of the Soviet Union' (1945), Stalin's approved version of the history of the Second World War. The Leningrad Blockade is mentioned explicitly within the context of military events and successes, the hegemonic form of narrating the war in this period. The 1951 textbook mentions that, 'The Stalingrad victory created a radical turning point in the entire course of the Great Patriotic War. The heroic defence of Sevastopol and Odessa, the defeat of the Germans near Moscow, the persistent battles near Leningrad, the greatest battle in history at the walls of Stalingrad, laid a solid foundation for victory over the Nazi armies'.[66] To describe a not so successful military endeavour in this positive way, despite the fact that the city held on for 900 days, arguably posed a problem, as will be discussed. Nonetheless, the successes within this history are underlined, *and* Stalin's influence is emphasised. The textbook mentions that it was Stalin's direct order to establish the 'Road of life', the ice road across Lake Ladoga.[67]

However, outside the realm of military accomplishments, the Leningrad Blockade is discussed more elaborately, in a way in which the heroic attitude of the Soviet population and particularly that of the Leningrad citizens is marketed and emphasised. This is in stark contrast to the conclusions reached by Lisa Kirschenbaum who states that during the direct post-war Stalinist period, the Soviet state 'practically excluded the Leningrad blockade from Soviet histories of the war', while books on Leningrad ceased to appear.[68] In fact, the tenth-grade 1951 textbook elaborately discusses the liberation of Leningrad:

> With the conditions of a complete blockade, Leningrad experienced hunger and cold. [...] Under the conditions of a severe blockade, under continuous bomb and shell attacks, the Leningrad workers did not leave their machine tools and machines, and the factories continued to work for defense. In the besieged city, despite terrible deprivation and constant bombing, ordinary Soviet life continued. Even children and teenagers who did not have time to evacuate continued to study in cold classrooms, and sometimes in bomb shelters. The patriotism, courage and steadfastness of the people of Leningrad helped the besieged hero city survive, while the Soviet Army gathered strength to liberate it.[69]

The heroism of the Soviet population and Leningrad citizens is clearly emphasised. The description of the famine's circumstances is particularly remarkable in comparison to Kirschenbaum's findings: she underlines that the Soviet authorities closed the Museum of the Defense of Leningrad in the late 1940s because it was seen as 'the most dangerous repository of the memory of the siege', which provoked 'empathy and insight through emotional identification', which went against the Soviet *and* Stalinist narrative of the war.[70] However, the narrative in the 1951 textbook actually uses exactly these forms of 'emotional identification' by giving examples of schoolchildren during the siege who studied in bomb shelters and cold classrooms. Additionally, the narrative provokes empathy by using adjectives such as 'terrible' (страшный).[71]

In addition, although the circumstances of the siege are explicitly mentioned, textbook authors arguably seem to have had difficulty in finding space for the Leningrad famine within a narrative that focused on military accomplishments. This is shown by the fact that the siege was framed by the Soviet authorities as a failure of the Nazis: the 1951 tenth-grade textbook mentions that the 'Nazis failed to take Leningrad' in the autumn of 1941.[72] This makes it appear as if the Nazis could not take the city, while the historical context of this chapter has shown that historians agree that it was a deliberate strategy of the Nazis to siege the city. Within this context, the emphasis on the 'steadfastness of the population of Leningrad', which appears later on the same page of this textbook, seems to have had the function of marginalising the Red Army's failures.

From the start of the Krushchev era until the collapse of the Soviet Union, the myth of the Great Patriotic War came to replace the narrative surrounding Stalin. Whereas the fourth-grade textbook from 1951 still speaks of Stalin's strength and inspiration in leading the country to its victory, the 1957 textbook for the fourth grade completely omitted Stalin from the chapter of the Great Patriotic War.[73] Arguably, this replacement resulted from the ongoing process of destalinisation, as a result of which particular parts of history were not to be celebrated, while it was in the best interest of the Soviet state to write a narrative of the glorious and prosperous past. Meanwhile, the narrative of the war started to encompass Soviet civilians, partisans, and others beyond solely glorifying the Red Army. In this period, two parallel developments occurred in perceptions of the past, which were reflected in textbooks: while the narratives grew increasingly personal, the grand narrative, in which sites such as Leningrad had a particular role to play became more orchestrated by the state.

This orchestration of the myth of the Great Patriotic War occurred during all three following periods. From this moment, Leningrad started to have an exceptional position within the grand narrative of the war. Although the history of the siege had already appeared in the earlier textbooks, now specific cities and Soviet Republics were assigned specific roles within this overarching narrative of the Great Patriotic War. For example, in the late 1960s and 1970s, there was a boom in the creation of monuments and memorials, and some Soviet cities were granted the title Hero City of the Soviet Union; Kiev in 1961, Moscow and Brest in 1965, and Minsk in 1974. In textbooks, this trend is also shown: from this moment onwards the story of the 'Unconquered Leningrad' is told within the framework of a subchapter called 'Hero Cities' and is accompanied by narratives of steadfastness displayed in other cities, such as 'Brave Sebastopol'.[74] As discussed, Leningrad was far from the only city under siege, and its population was far from the only people that were starved by the Nazis. Rigney asserts in her article on differential memory that the melodramatic effects of the 'paradoxical combination of victimhood and agency, of powerlessness and empowerment' cause that 'some events are upstaged at the cost of others'.[75] Leningrad holds exactly those characteristics and proves that this differential memory allows the narrative of Leningrad to be used as transnational, multi-interpretable and possibly even 'multidirectional' memory, as becomes clear from the fact that Zelensky recalled it in 2022.

The second development of personalisation of war narratives is also apparent in the textbooks from both the Krushchev and Brezhnev period. According to Kirschenbaum, in this period, personal accounts of the war were no longer banned, as happened under Stalin.[76] This change in how events were represented is overtly demonstrated by the textbooks, in particular the fourth-grade textbook from 1965, which is almost completely told through personal narratives of children. It is unclear whether the stories are real oral narratives or fictive stories, but the representation of Leningrad actually shows a rather realistic image of the besieged city (Image 2.4).

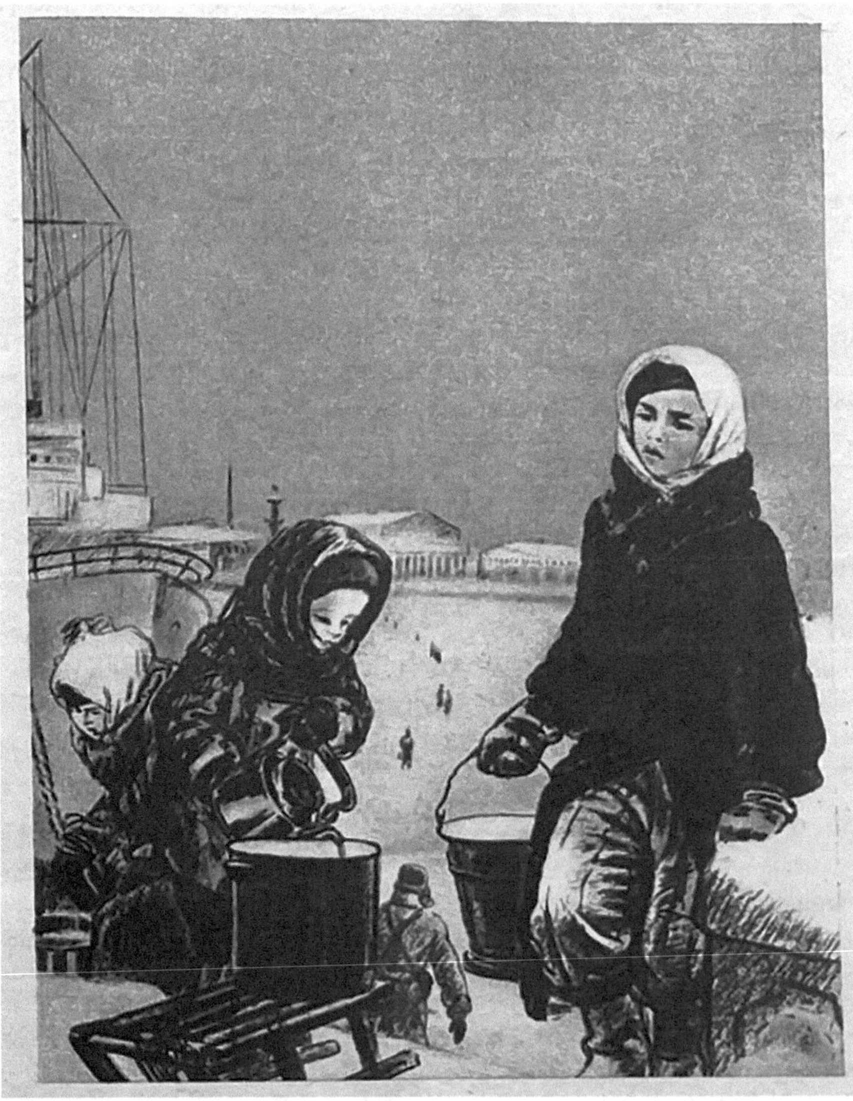

IMAGE 2.4 An illustration of children near the 'Road of Life' across Lake Ladoga from the fourth-grade textbook from 1957. S.P Alekseev and V.G. Karcov, *Istoriia SSSR: Uchebnaia kniga dlia 4-go klassa* (1957), 133.

For Leningrad, a 17-year-old girl, Vera, is introduced, who shares her only 'meager portion of bread (80 grams) with hungry children'. The entire story of the girl is told in detail as an example of life in besieged Leningrad:

> One night Vera came to the post house. She was sick, could hardly move, but she was told that no one had answered the house for a long time, and there was a child in the apartment. In complete darkness, Vera barely could climb to the fourth floor. She opened the door and tripped over something; she lit a match and screamed—a corpse lay under her feet. She quickly ran away from it, from this creepy icy apartment! And suddenly Vera heard a faint childish squeak. Overcoming fear, she stepped over the corpse, found the child in the dark, grabbed it and, gritting her teeth, left the apartment. Vera Shchekina saved 39 children.[77]

The rather horrifying story—in particular for ten-year-olds—shows the exact combination of victimhood and agency that Rigney mentions, and that made the Leningrad Blockade an exemplary case study to endorse dominant state narratives. So although the form—either through personal stories or rather grand storylines—of how to convey this narrative became different, the function of the narrative remained the same.

Vera's story also reveals that the Cold War was now in full swing: specific political aspects within the narrative are emphasised, such as the fact that Vera was a Komsomol member, the political youth organisation of the Communist Party. Indeed, the main message in the 1965 textbook is that Vera's empowerment and agency result from her Komsomol membership. This is emphasised by the description of other heroic figures in the textbook, who are all Komsomol members. For example, despite their own hunger, other Komsomol girls brought disabled people water from the Neva and wood and food from communal kitchens.[78] So the history of the Leningrad Blockade seems to be used with a strong pedagogical goal: to instil Soviet patriotism. The personal accounts that were prominent in the textbooks of the 1960s and 1970s began to disappear in the textbooks of the 1980s. However, the political narratives, such as the references to the Komsomol, remained practically the same until the end of the Soviet Union. Arguably because the narratives of the Holodomor and the Great Terror changed dramatically in this period, the storyline of the Great Patriotic War had to remain the same to bring some stability in the overall historical narrative of the Soviet Union.

Although, from the 1960s onwards, the Leningrad Blockade was fairly realistically represented in textbooks, the victim number of the siege was not. For example, the fourth-grade 1965 textbook speaks of '78 thousand people who died of hunger and famine'[79] and the fourth-grade 1982 textbook argues that 'thousands of people died from starvation'.[80] Because the Soviet Union was known to inflate wartime victim numbers greatly, this aspect stands out. The wartime victim numbers were usually established by the Extraordinary State Commission for the Establishment and Investigation of the Atrocities of the German Fascist Invaders (ChGK). From June 1943 onwards, they had the task to investigate the crimes committed by the Nazis. Although they provided extremely valuable evidence for, among other things, the Nuremberg Trials, the committee was also a propagandistic tool for the Soviet government in establishing the myth of the Great Patriotic War.[81]

The fact that the narrative of Leningrad, despite its role in the storyline of the Great Patriotic War, was not complemented with high victim numbers to showcase the dreadfulness of the situation, suggests that it was not regarded as a mass atrocity, unlike other crimes against the Soviet population. Other cases, such as the Ozarichi camps in Belarus, which were created by the Wehrmacht to imprison and starve the 'useless eaters', that is, the elderly, invalids, and children, of the Bobruisk region in March 1944, were more prominently used within the narrative in order to show Nazi atrocities against the Soviet population and prove the genocidal character of Germany's war against the Soviet Union. The Leningrad Blockade continued to have a different role to play, possibly because it would threaten to expose the incapabilities of the Red Army, as well as the duration of the atrocity, over 900 days. It shows that in the Soviet context, hunger as a form of 'slow violence', does not lend itself as easily to depictions of suffering than more spectacular forms of violence.[82] The prominent presence of Leningrad in the textbooks throughout the entire Soviet period was foremost invoked to show the perseverance and strength of the Soviet people, instead of showing any form of suffering.

Conclusion

The analysis of Soviet history textbooks reveals that both the representation of the Leningrad Blockade and the Holodomor were used for political purposes and identity formation throughout the entire post-war Soviet period. Although the Soviet Union, as an authoritarian state, used history for political purposes, the way in which these histories were used and represented might be considered as more surprising than expected.

Firstly, even though the Holodomor was *never* explicitly mentioned in any of the textbooks studied for this research, it was not deliberately forgotten or silenced in textbooks, as would be expected for such a controversial topic. From the Stalinist period until the Gorbachev era, all the measures that eventually led to the excruciating famine are mentioned in detail. The only, but most important, step in the line of argumentation that is missing in these textbook narratives is that these measures eventually caused this famine. However, considering that from the Krushchev period onwards, students' beliefs in what was told in these educational sources diminished, it can be questioned whether students themselves did not take this last step in their thoughts about the Holodomor past. After all, if Arthur Koestler was able to witness 'so many hurried funerals' in the winter of 1932, students could have known about this as well.

Secondly, textbook analysis shows that there is more continuation in the narrative of the Leningrad Blockade than has been assumed. In scholarly literature, it is portrayed as an undiscussed topic that was even omitted from the Stalinist war narrative, while the textbooks show that this was quite the contrary. The circumstances of the famine and the role of the Leningrad population are mentioned elaborately in a way that clearly sought to provoke empathy for the situation that occurred. Indeed, shortly after the events, the narrative of the Leningrad Blockade was most raw and less frequently used for political purposes.

Thirdly, the process of destalinisation changed textbooks because it erased Stalin's role within Soviet history. In particular, in the case of the Holodomor, this is quite remarkable because, presently, in the discussion of whether the Holodomor was a genocide or not, Stalin is often portrayed as the main genocidaire. Other crimes of Stalin, such as the Great Terror or the post-war terror, were addressed during this period, and their representation in textbooks changed (albeit little). Arguably, the reason why the famine was not addressed in this period is that the Soviet Union needed to interpret the period of collectivisation as a narrative of economic innovation and prosperity in order to battle the Cold War internally. Fourthly, during the Khrushchev and Brezhnev eras, the Cold War paradigm and the use of textbooks to instil patriotic feelings in students becomes more apparent in the representation of both famines. In the case of the collectivisation, it is portrayed as a grand success of Soviet economics, in a similar manner in which the Leningrad Blockade was used to promote the good and strong Soviet citizen.

Fifthly and finally, the fact that both famines are mass atrocities is not apparent in any of the textbooks. When the 1930s famine is represented from the Gorbachev era onwards, then it is portrayed as something that just happened: 'famine broke out', as if it was a natural disaster. No mention of agency can be found in the textbooks except for the policy of dekulakisation that caused the repression of millions of people. Interestingly, the representation of famine as mass atrocity is still rather meagre, as it is represented as an unintentional consequence of collectivisation. The fact that the additional measures against peasants did not have an economic purpose remains unmentioned. A perpetrator is also nowhere to be found in the narrative, not even Stalin. One would assume that in the case of the Leningrad Blockade, a stronger image of the perpetrator, conveniently an outsider, would occur. However, this is actually not obvious from the examined textbooks. This famine is also not considered as a mass atrocity but is portrayed as a challenge that people did not suffer from but overcame, contrary to other events during the Second World War that were actively used as representation of mass atrocity. While recent historiography suggests that both the Holodomor as well as the Leningrad Blockade are to be considered mass atrocities, the Soviet use of history deviated from this idea. Both famines, although often implicitly represented, had to showcase success and glory in order to invoke identity formation and to instil patriotism. It shows that in the Soviet case and arguably in other authoritarian regimes, explicit hunger *and* suffering do not lend themselves as a unifying trope to processes of nation-building.

Notes

1 I would like to thank Anne van Mourik, Charley Boerman, Marguérite Corporaal, and Ingrid de Zwarte for their feedback on earlier drafts of this chapter. The transliterations are according to the modified Library of Congress transliteration system. The translations are my own, except where indicated otherwise.
2 Arthur Koestler, *The Invisible Writing: Being the Second Volume of Arrow in the Blue: An Autobiography* (London: Collins, 1954).
3 The comparison between the regime and the crimes of Hitler and Stalin is subject of an entire field of historical and philosophical research. Building on the theory of totalitarianism of Hannah Arendt and developed through theories military historians, historians of the Soviet Union and of the Third Reich and the Holocaust, the discussion of the field of 'comnaz'—the portmanteau of Communism and Nazism—became even more political since the collapse of the Soviet Union because it would open discussion to equalising the Holocaust to communist crimes. See Michael Geyer and Sheila Fitzpatrick, eds., *Beyond Totalitarianism: Stalinism and Nazism Compared* (Cambridge: Cambridge University Press, 2009); Klas-Göran Karlsson, Johan Stenfeldt, and Ulf Zander, eds., *Perspectives on the Entangled History of Communism and Nazism* (Lanham: Lexington Books, 2015).
4 Tina van der Vlies, *Echoing Events: The Perpetuation of National Narratives in English and Dutch History Textbooks, 1920–2010* (Leiden: Brill, 2022), 29.
5 Marguérite Corporaal and Ingrid de Zwarte, 'Heritages of Hunger: European Famine Legacies in Current Academic Debates', *International Journal of Heritage Studies* 28, no. 1 (2022): 4.
6 Ursula von der Leyen, '90 Years After the Holodomor, the Kremlin Is Again Using Food as a Weapon', *Twitter*, 29 November 2022, https://twitter.com/vonderleyen/status/1596520142673825793.
7 Lorenzo Tondo and Isobel Koshiw, 'Zelenskiy Compares Mariupol to Leningrad Siege', *The Guardian*, 17 March 2022, https://www.theguardian.com/world/2022/mar/17/ukraines-zelenskiy-compares-mariupol-to-leningrad-siege-as-russia-launches-fresh-strikes-on-kyiv.
8 Ann Rigney, 'Ongoing: Changing Memory and the European Project', in Chiara De Cesari and Ann Rigney, eds., *Transnational Memory; Circulation, Articulation, Scales* (Amsterdam: De Gruyter, 2014), 344.
9 Maria Grever, 'Plurality, Narrative and the Historical Canon', in Maria Grever and Siep Stuurman, eds., *Beyond the Canon; History for the Twenty-First Century* (Basingstoke: Palgrave Macmillan, 2007), 34.
10 Aleida Assmann, 'Transformations between History and Memory', *Social Research* 75, no. 1 (2008): 65.

11 Arendt, *The Origins of Totalitarianism*, 341.
12 John Issitt, 'Reflections on the Study of Textbooks', *History of Education* 33, no. 6 (2004): 688.
13 Janet Vaillant, 'Reform in History and Social Studies Education in Russian Secondary Schools', in Anthony Jones, ed., *Education and Society in the New Russia* (New York: Routledge, 1994), 308.
14 Mervyn Matthews, *Education in the Soviet Union: Policies and Institutions since Stalin* (London: Routledge, 1982), 5–6.
15 Ibid.
16 Alexis Peri, 'Lessons of the Leningrad Blockade: Schoolchildren's Diaries as Sites of Learning, 1941–1943', *Peterburgskii Istoricheskii Zhurnal* 3 (2019): 193.
17 Roger D. Markwick, *Rewriting History in Soviet Russia: The Politics of Revisionist Historiography, 1956–1974* (Basingstoke: Palgrave, 2001), 114, 146.
18 Matthews, *Education in the Soviet Union*, 18, 27.
19 Joseph I. Zajda and Edmund King, *Education in the USSR* (Oxford: Pergamon Press, 1980), 35.
20 William B. Husband, 'History and History Education in Soviet and Post-Soviet Russia', in Anthony Jones, ed., *Education and Society in the New Russia* (New York: Routledge, 1994), 269.
21 Steven Wheatcroft, 'Famine and Epidemic Crises in Russia, 1918–1922: The Case of Saratov', *Annales de Démographie Historique* (1983): 329; Michael Ellman, 'The 1947 Soviet Famine and the Entitlement Approach to Famines', *Cambridge Journal of Economics* 24 (2000): 610–16.
22 Some scholars argue that the famine of 1946–7 would fit this category as well, because of certain analogies with the Holodomor: Oleksandra Veselova, 'Famine in Ukraine after the Second World War', in Andrea Graziosi, Lubomyr Hajda, and Halyna Hryn, eds., *After the Holodomor: The Enduring Impact of the Great Famine in Ukraine* (Cambridge: Harvard University Press, 2013), 190–4.
23 Alex De Waal, *Mass Starvation: The History and Future of Famine* (Cambridge: Polity Press, 2018), 21.
24 Andrea Graziosi, 'The Uses of Hunger: Stalin's Solution of the Peasant and National Questions in Soviet Ukraine, 1932 to 1933', in Declan Curran, Lubomyr Luciuk, and Andrew Newby, eds., *Famines in European Economic History: The Last Great European Famines Reconsidered* (Oxon: Routledge, 2015), 223.
25 De Waal, *Mass Starvation*, 100–101; Terry Martin, *Affirmative Action Empire: Nations and Nationalism in the Soviet Union, 1923-1939* (Ithaca: Cornell University Press, 2001), 304–5.
26 Norman Naimark, *Stalin's Genocides* (Princeton: Princeton University Press, 2010), 54.
27 Ibid., 57–9.
28 Robert Conquest, *The Harvest of Sorrow: Soviet Collectivisation and the Terror-Famine* (London: Hutchinson & Co., 1986).
29 Cormac Ó Gráda, *Famine: A Short History* (Princeton: Princeton University Press, 2009), 236–9.
30 Robert Davies and Steven Wheatcroft, *The Years of Hunger: Soviet Agriculture, 1931–1933. The Industrialisation of Soviet Russia. Vol. 5* (Palgrave Macmillan, 2004), 441; Anne Applebaum, *Red Famine: Stalin's War on Ukraine* (New York: Anchor Books, 2017), 216, 240.
31 Oksana Kis, 'Women's Experience of the Holodomor: Challenges and Ambiguities of Motherhood', *Journal of Genocide Research* 23, no. 4 (2021): 542.
32 Alex J. Kay, *Exploitation, Resettlement, Mass Murder; Political and Economic Planning for German Occupation Policy in the Soviet Union, 1940–1941* (New York: Berghahn Books, 2006), 187.

33 C. Gerlach, *Kalkulierte Morde; Die deutsche Wirtschafts- und Vernichtungspolitik in Weißrußland, 1941 bis 1945* (Hamburg: Hamburger Edition, 1999), 46.
34 Nicholas Ganson, *The Soviet Famine of 1946–47 in Global and Historical Perspective* (New York: Palgrave Macmillan, 2009), 105.
35 Karel Berkhoff, *Harvest of Despair: Life and Death in Ukraine under Nazi Rule* (Cambridge: Harvard University Press, 2004), 165.
36 Jörg Ganzenmüller, 'Hungerpolitik als Problemlösungsstrategie', in Jörg Morré and Babette Quinkert, eds., *Deutsche Besatzung in der Sowjetunion 1941–1944* (Paderborn: Ferdinand Schöningh, 2014), 38–9.
37 Dieter Pohl, *Die Herrschaft der Wehrmacht* (Frankfurt aM: Fischer Verlag GmbH, 2011), 186.
38 Boris Belozerov, 'Crime during the Siege', in John Barber and Andrei Dzeniskevich, eds., *Life and Death in Besieged Leningrad, 1941-1944* (Basingstoke: Palgrave Macmillan, 2005), 222–4.
39 Ó Gráda, *Famine*, 241.
40 Karel Berkhoff, 'The Great Famine in Light of the German Invasion and Occupation', in Graziosi, ed., *After the Holodomor*, 175–6.
41 Naimark, *Stalin's Genocides*, 73.
42 As cited in Christoph Dieckmann, 'Das Scheitern des Hungerplans und die Praxis der selektiven Hungerpolitik im deutschen Krieg gegen die Sowjetunion', in Christoph Dieckmann and Babette Quinckert, eds., *Kriegsführung und Hunger 1939-1945* (Göttingen: Wallstein Verlag, 2015), 114.
43 Pohl, *Die Herrschaft der Wehrmacht*, 199–200.
44 Vladimir Putin, 'Address by the President of the Russian Federation', *Kremlin*, 24 February 2022, http://en.kremlin.ru/events/president/news/67843.
45 The process of transitional justice is the 'confrontation of crimes of their predecessor state by postconflict, postauthoritarian, postrepressive successor states' through international crimes tribunals, national or local legal proceedings, truth commissions, restitution, the accurate revision of history, public apologies, the establishment of monuments and museums, and official commemorations. Nanci Adler, 'Introduction; On History, Historians and Transitional Justice', in Nanci Adler, ed., *Understanding the Age of Transitional Justice; Crimes, Courts, Commissions, and Chronicling* (New Brunswick: Rutgers University Press, 2018), 1.
46 Alexandra Popoff, *Vasily Grossman and the Soviet Century* (New Haven: Yale University Press, 2019), 71.
47 As quoted in Valeriy Vasylyev, 'The Holodomor through the Eyes of the Soviet Ukrainian Leadership, 1950–1580', in Graziosi, ed., *After the Holodomor*, 254.
48 Michael Rothberg, *The Implicated Subject: Beyond Victims and Perpetrators* (Stanford: Stanford University Press, 2019).
49 Felix Wemheuer, 'Regime Changes of Memory: Creating the Official History of the Ukrainian and Chinese Famines under State Socialism after the Cold War', *Kritika* 10, no. 1 (2009): 34.
50 A.M. Pankratovoi, ed, *Istoriia SSSR: Uchebnik dlia 10 klassa srednei shkoly* (Moscow: Gosudar. Učebno-Pedag. Izdat. Minister. Prosv. RSFSR, 1951), 328, 383.
51 Ibid., 328.
52 Ibid.
53 A.V. Shestakova, ed., *Istoriia SSSR: Uchebnik dlia 4 klassa* (Moscow: Prosveščenie, 1951).
54 A.M. Pankratovoi, ed., *Istoriia SSSR: Uchebnik dlia 10 klassa srednei shkoly* (Moscow: Gosudar. Učebno-Pedag. Izdat. Minister. Prosv. RSFSR, 1957), 203.
55 Ibid., 200–1.
56 S.P Alekseev and V.G. Karcov, *Istoriia SSSR: Uchebnaia kniga dlia 4 klassa* (Moscow: Gosudar. Učebno-Pedag. Izdat. Minister. Prosv. RSFSR, 1957), 122.

57 Husband, 'History and History Education in Soviet and Post-Soviet Russia', 265.
58 James V. Wertsch, 'Is It Possible to Teach Beliefs, as Well as Knowledge about History?', in Peter N. Stearns, Peter Seixas, and Sam Wineburg, eds., *Knowing, Teaching & Learning History* (New York: New York University Press, 2000), 39.
59 R.W. Davies, *Soviet History in the Gorbachev Revolution* (Basingstoke: Macmillan, 1989), 47.
60 Mikhail Sholokhov, *Virgin Soil Upturned* (Harmondsworth: Penguin Books, 1935).
61 Matthews, *Education in the Soviet Union*, 19.
62 M.P. Kima, ed., *Istoriia SSSR: Uchebnik dlia 10 klassa srednei shkoly* (Moscow: Prosveščenie, 1983), 131.
63 Ibid., 131.
64 A. Fedosov and J.R. Borisov, *Istoriia SSSR: Uchebnik dlia 10 klassa srednei shkoly* (Moscow: Prosveščenie, 1989), 326.
65 Ibid.
66 Pankratovoi, *Istoriia SSSR (10th grade, 1951)*, 380.
67 Ibid., 328, 383.
68 Lisa Kirschenbaum, *The Legacy of the Siege of Leningrad, 1941–1995: Myth, Memories, and Monuments* (Cambridge: Cambridge University Press, 2006), 116.
69 Pankratovoi, *Istoriia SSSR (10th grade, 1951)*, 383.
70 Kirschenbaum, *The Legacy of the Siege of Leningrad*, 152.
71 Pankratovoi, *Istoriia SSSR (10th grade, 1951)*, 383.
72 Shestakova, *Istoriia SSSR (4th grade, 1951)*, 383.
73 Ibid., 272–3.
74 T.S. Golubeva and L.S. Gellershtein, *Rasskazy po istorii SSSR dlia 4 klassa* (Moscow: Prosveščenie, 1965), 145–6.
75 Ann Rigney, 'Differential Memorability and Transnational Activism: Bloody Sunday, 1887-2016', *Australian Humanities Review*, no. 59 (2016): 92.
76 Kirschenbaum, *The Legacy of the Siege of Leningrad*, 152.
77 Golubeva and Gellershtein, *Istoriia SSSR (4th grade, 1965)*, 147–8.
78 Ibid., 147.
79 Ibid.
80 T.S. Golubeva and L.S. Gellershtein, *Rasskazy po istorii SSSR dlia 4 klassa: Uchebnaja Kniga* (Moscow: Prosveščenie, 1982), 203.
81 M.A. Sorokina, 'People and Procedures: Toward a History of the Investigation of Nazi Crimes in the USSR', *Kritika* 6, no. 4 (2005): 801.
82 Rob Nixon, *Slow Violence and the Environmentalism of the Poor* (Cambridge: Harvard University Press, 2011).

References

Adler, Nanci, 'Introduction; On History, Historians and Transitional Justice'. In Nanci Adler ed., 1–17. *Understanding the Age of Transitional Justice; Crimes, Courts, Commissions, and Chronicling*. New Brunswick: Rutgers University Press, 2018.

Alekseev, S.P, and V.G. Karcov, *Istoriia SSSR: Uchebnaia kniga dlia 4-go klassa*. Moscow: Gosudar; Minister. Prosv. RSFSR, 1957.

Applebaum, Anne, *Red Famine: Stalin's War on Ukraine*. New York: Anchor Books, 2017.

Arendt, Hannah, *The Origins of Totalitarianism*. New York: Harvest, 1979.

Assmann, Aleida, 'Transformations between History and Memory'. *Social Research* 75, no. 1 (2008): 49–72.

Belozerov, Boris, 'Crime during the Siege'. In John Barber and Andrei Dzeniskevich, eds., 213–8. *Life and Death in Besieged Leningrad, 1941–1944*. Basingstoke: Palgrave Macmillan, 2005.

Berkhoff, Karel, *Harvest of Despair: Life and Death in Ukraine under Nazi Rule*. Cambridge: Harvard University Press, 2004.

Berkhoff, Karel, 'The Great Famine in Light of the German Invasion and Occupation'. In Andrea Graziosi, Lubomyr Hajda, and Halyna Hryn, eds., 165–81. *After the Holodomor: The Enduring Impact of the Great Famine on Ukraine*. Cambridge, MA: Harvard University Press, 2013.

Conquest, Robert, *The Harvest of Sorrow: Soviet Collectivisation and the Terror-Famine*. London: Hutchinson & Co, 1986.

Corporaal, Marguérite, and Ingrid de Zwarte, 'Heritages of Hunger: European Famine Legacies in Current Academic Debates'. *International Journal of Heritage Studies* 28, no. 1 (2022): 30–43.

Davies, Robert, and Steven Wheatcroft, *The Years of Hunger: Soviet Agriculture, 1931–1933. The Industrialisation of Soviet Russia*. Vol. 5. Palgrave Macmillan, 2004.

Davies, R.W., *Soviet History in the Gorbachev Revolution*. Basingstoke: Macmillan, 1989.

De Waal, Alex, *Mass Starvation: The History and Future of Famine*. Cambridge: Polity Press, 2018.

Dieckmann, Christoph, 'Das Scheitern des Hungerplans und die Praxis der selektiven Hungerpolitik im deutschen Krieg gegen die Sowjetunion'. In Christoph Dieckmann and Babette Quinckert, eds., 88–122. *Kriegsführung und Hunger 1939-1945: Zum Verhältnis von militärischen, wirtschaftlichen und politischen Interessen*. Göttingen: Wallstein Verlag, 2015.

Ellman, Michael. 'The 1947 Soviet Famine and the Entitlement Approach to Famines'. *Cambridge Journal of Economics*, 24 (2000): 603–30.

Fedosov, A., and J.R. Borisov, *Istoriia SSSR: Uchebnik dlia 10 klassa srednei shkoly*. Moscow: Prosveščenie, 1989.

Ganson, Nicholas, *The Soviet Famine of 1946-47 in Global and Historical Perspective*. New York: Palgrave Macmillan, 2009.

Ganzenmüller, Jörg, 'Hungerpolitik als Problemlösungsstrategie. Der Entscheidungsprozess zur Blockade Leningrads und zur Vernichtung seiner Zivilbevölkerung'. In Jörg Morré and Babette Quinkert, eds., 34–53. *Deutsche Besatzung in der Sowjetunion 1941–1944: Vernichtungskrieg, Reaktionen, Erinnerungen*. Paderborn: Ferdinand Schöningh, 2014.

Gerlach, C., *Kalkulierte Morde; Die Deutsche Wirtschafts- und Vernichtungspolitik in Weißrußland, 1941 bis 1945*. Hamburg: Hamburger Edition, 1999.

Geyer, Michael, and Sheila Fitzpatrick, eds., *Beyond Totalitarianism: Stalinism and Nazism Compared*. Cambridge: Cambridge University Press, 2009.

Golubeva, T.S., and L.S. Gellershtein, *Rasskazy po istorii SSSR dlja 4 klassa: Uchebnaja Kniga*. Moscow: Prosveščenie, 1965.

Golubeva, T.S., and L.S. Gellershtein. *Rasskazy po istorii SSSR dlja 4 klassa: Uchebnaja Kniga*. Moscow: Prosveščenie, 1982.

Graziosi, Andrea, 'The Uses of Hunger: Stalin's Solution of the Peasant and National Questions in Soviet Ukraine, 1932 to 1933'. In Declan Curran, Lubomyr Y. Luciuk, and Andrew G. Newby, eds., 223–60. *Famines in European Economic History: The Last Great European Famines Reconsidered*. London: Routledge, 2015.

Grever, Maria, 'Plurality, Narrative and the Historical Canon'. In Maria Grever and Siep Stuurman, eds., 31–47. *Beyond the Canon; History for the Twenty-First Century*. Basingstoke: Palgrave Macmillan, 2007.

Husband, William B., 'History and History Education in Soviet and Post-Soviet Russia'. In Anthony Jones, ed., 263–306. *Education and Society in the New Russia.* New York: Routledge, 1994.
Issitt, John, 'Reflections on the Study of Textbooks'. *History of Education* 33, no. 6 (2004): 683–96.
Karlsson, Klas-Göran, Johan Stenfeldt, and Ulf Zander, eds. *Perspectives on the Entangled History of Communism and Nazism; A Comnaz Analysis*. Lanham: Lexington Books, 2015.
Kay, Alex J. *Exploitation, Resettlement, Mass Murder; Political and Economic Planning for German Occupation Policy in the Soviet Union, 1940–1941*. New York: Berghahn Books, 2006.
Kima, M.P., ed. *Istoriia SSSR: Uchebnik dlia desiatogo klassa srednei shkoly*. Moscow: Prosveščenie, 1983.
Kirschenbaum, Lisa. *The Legacy of the Siege of Leningrad, 1941–1995: Myth, Memories, and Monuments*. Cambridge: Cambridge University Press, 2006.
Kis, Oksana, 'Women's Experience of the Holodomor: Challenges and Ambiguities of Motherhood'. *Journal of Genocide Research* 23, no. 4 (2021): 527–46.
Koestler, Arthur, *The Invisible Writing: Being the Second Volume of Arrow in the Blue: An Autobiography*. London: Collins, 1954.
Leyen, Ursula von der Leyen, '90 Years after the Holodomor, the Kremlin Is Again Using Food as a Weapon'. *Twitter*, 29 Nov. 2022, https://twitter.com/vonderleyen/status/1596520142673825793.
Markwick, Roger D., *Rewriting History in Soviet Russia: The Politics of Revisionist Historiography, 1956-1974*. Basingstoke: Palgrave, 2001.
Martin, Terry, *Affirmative Action Empire: Nations and Nationalism in the Soviet Union, 1923-1939*. Ithaca: Cornell University Press, 2001.
Matthews, Mervyn, *Education in the Soviet Union: Policies and Institutions since Stalin*. London: Routledge, 1982.
Naimark, Norman, *Stalin's Genocides*. Princeton: Princeton University Press, 2010.
Nixon, Rob, *Slow Violence and the Environmentalism of the Poor*. Cambridge: Harvard University Press, 2011.
Ó Gráda, Cormac, *Famine: A Short History*. Princeton: Princeton University Press, 2009.
Pankratovoi, A.M., ed., *Istoriia SSSR: Uchebnik dlia 10 klassa srednei shkoly*. Moscow: Gosudar. Učebno-Pedag. Izdat. Minister. Prosv. RSFSR, 1951.
Pankratovoi, A.M., ed., *Istoriia SSSR: Uchebnik dlia 10 klassa srednei shkoly*. Moscow: Gosudar. Učebno-Pedag. Izdat. Minister. Prosv. RSFSR, 1957.
Peri, Alexis, 'Lessons of the Leningrad Blockade: Schoolchildren's Diaries as Sites of Learning, 1941–1943'. *Peterburgskii Istoricheskii Zhurnal* 3 (2019): 192–210.
Pohl, Dieter, *Die Herrschaft der Wehrmacht; Deutsche Militärbesatzung und einheimische Bevölkerung in der Sowjetunion 1941–1944*. Frankfurt am Main: S. Fischer Verlag GmbH, 2011.
Popoff, Alexandra, *Vasily Grossman and the Soviet Century*. New Haven: Yale University Press, 2019.
Putin, Vladimir, 'Address by the President of the Russian Federation'. *Kremlin*. 24 February 2022, http://en.kremlin.ru/events/president/news/67843.
Rigney, Ann, 'Differential Memorability and Transnational Activism: Bloody Sunday, 1887–2016', *Australian Humanities Review*, no. 59 (2016): 77–95.
Rigney, Ann, 'Ongoing: Changing Memory and the European Project'. In Chiara De Cesari and Ann Rigney, eds., 339–61. *Transnational Memory; Circulation, Articulation, Scales,*. Amsterdam: De Gruyter, 2014.
Rothberg, Michael. *The Implicated Subject: Beyond Victims and Perpetrators*. Stanford: Stanford University Press, 2019.

Shestakova, A.V., ed. *Istoriia SSSR: Uchebnik dlia 4 klassa*. Moscow: Prosveščenie, 1951.

Sholokhov, Mikhail, *Virgin Soil Upturned*. Harmondsworth: Penguin Books, 1935.

Sorokina, M.A., 'People and Procedures: Toward a History of the Investigation of Nazi Crimes in the USSR'. *Kritika: Explorations in Russian and Eurasian History* 6, no. 4 (2005): 797–831.

Tondo, Lorenzo, and Isobel Koshiw, 'Zelenskiy Compares Mariupol to Leningrad Siege as Russia Launches Fresh Strikes on Kyiv'. *The Guardian*, 17 March 2022, https://www.theguardian.com/world/2022/mar/17/ukraines-zelenskiy-compares-mariupol-to-leningrad-siege-as-russia-launches-fresh-strikes-on-kyiv.

Vaillant, Janet G., 'Reform in History and Social Studies Education in Russian Secondary Schools'. In Anthony Jones, ed., 307–65. *Education and Society in the New Russia*. New York: Routledge, 1994.

Vasylyev, Valeriy, 'The Holodomor through the Eyes of the Soviet Ukrainian Leadership, 1950–1980'. In Andrea Graziosi, Lubomyr Hajda, and Halyna Hryn, eds., 251–63. *After the Holodomor: The Enduring Impact of the Great Famine on Ukraine*. Cambridge, MA: Harvard University Press, 2013.

Veselova, Oleksandra, 'Famine in Ukraine after the Second World War'. In Andrea Graziosi, Lubomyr Hajda, and Halyna Hryn, eds., 183–98. *After the Holodomor: The Enduring Impact of the Great Famine on Ukraine*. Cambridge, MA: Harvard University Press, 2013.

Vlies, Tina van der, *Echoing Events: The Perpetuation of National Narratives in English and Dutch History Textbooks, 1920–2010*. Leiden: Brill, 2022.

Wemheuer, Felix, 'Regime Changes of Memory: Creating the Official History of the Ukrainian and Chinese Famines under State Socialism after the Cold War'. *Kritika: Explorations in Russian and Eurasian History* 10, no. 1 (2009): 31–59.

Wertsch, James V., 'Is It Possible to Teach Beliefs, as Well as Knowledge about History?' In Peter N. Stearns, Peter Seixas, and Sam Wineburg, eds., *Knowing, Teaching & Learning History; National and International Perspectives*, 38–50. New York: New York University Press, 2000.

Wheatcroft, Steven, 'Famine and Epidemic Crises in Russia, 1918–1922: The Case of Saratov'. *Annales de Démographie Historique* (1983): 329–52.

Zajda, Joseph I., and Edmund King, *Education in the USSR*. Oxford: Pergamon Press, 1980.

3

NEW FUTURES FOR FAMINE PASTS?

Teaching Ireland's Great Famine in Ontario and Quebec

Marguérite Corporaal and Jason King

Among the Irish Famine emigrants who settled in the Canadas during the Great Famine (1845–49), there were many who found careers in teaching and advocated for French as well as English-language Catholic education. For example, Teresa Dease, who had left famine-stricken Ireland behind and arrived in Canada in September 1847, established the clerical order of the Loretto sisters and, in that capacity, founded various Catholic schools across Canada West (now the province of Ontario): primarily in Toronto but, as Mark McGowan has shown, also in Brantford and London, Ontario, in 1853.[1] Educators of Irish descent from the Famine generation onwards left their mark on teaching practices in Quebec and Ontario. Nonetheless, the Great Irish Famine itself has left relatively little imprint in either province's curricula or formal educational settings, and this presence of the Famine past in curricula and textbooks has further diminished over the past few decades.

Teaching practices are 'influenced by the values, beliefs and understandings that exist within societies', as Carmel Roofe and Christopher Bezzina argue,[2] and these include prominent narratives in a community's cultural memory. This waning presence of Ireland's Famine past and its diaspora in curricula and textbooks in English and French Canada—where many Famine emigrants disembarked—may seem remarkable in view of the omnipresence of Famine memory in public places.[3] The dire events which unfolded with the arrival of Irish immigrants in the summer of 1847, such as the spread of disease, the confinement of sick passengers in quarantine stations, and the subsequent disintegration of immigrant families have been widely commemorated such as at Grosse Île and the Irish Memorial National Historic Site of Canada.

What is more, the Famine has become even more prominent in public memory spaces with the unveiling of Ireland Park in Toronto in 2007, which

DOI: 10.4324/9781003391524-5

commemorates the arrival of Irish Famine immigrants at the city's waterfront. Five bronze statues made by sculptor Rowan Gillespie signify new beginnings for those who survived the journey on the coffin ships, as well as a five-metre-high limestone sculptural installation that records the names of passengers.[4] Moreover, on 14 July 2021, a monument paying tribute to doctors, nurses, and others who lost their lives while caring for the gravely ill Irish Famine immigrants in the fever sheds was unveiled at Grasett Park, Toronto.[5] The Black Rock Famine memorial on the site of Montreal's fever sheds and mass grave containing six thousand Irish emigrants has recently become the focus of community efforts to create a memorial park around it.[6]

Why is it then that the Famine, and especially its Canadian legacies, have never been so prominent in educational practices? This chapter aims to explain the relatively minor role of Ireland's Great Famine in past and present secondary education in Ontario and Quebec on the basis of an examination of a corpus of early and very recent history textbooks as well as interviews with teachers and student teachers. We have selected textbooks that went through several reprints and therefore had a longer term impact on school-going generations. In making these selections, we have carefully considered a fair diachronic spread, from 1891 until the present day. Furthermore, we have made sure to include textbooks used in both Ontario and Quebec and in French and English language schools: after all, in Quebec, children from English-speaking parents are entitled to education in that language. Chau Vu proposes a methodology for studying history textbooks by focusing on 'story line and content analysis, narrative tone and perspective, and treatment of history from a disciplinary perspective'.[7] In broad lines, we have followed this approach while focusing specifically on the 'narrative templates'—the recurring plots and motifs—used to give meaning to the Famine past and its Irish-Canadian diaspora.[8]

As we will illustrate in the first part of this chapter, in Ontario textbooks, the story of the Famine generation was often downplayed in a larger narrative of the British Empire, which foregrounds the formation of a British Canadian identity. In Quebec, some attention is paid to the outbreak of famine fever in the colonies, and the fever sheds after the arrival of sick immigrants in 1847, but the main emphasis is on the construction of a French Quebec identity. Since 2019, more emphasis has been placed in compulsory Quebec French and English language history textbooks on '1845–1847 Massive Irish immigration' that 'prompted hundreds of thousands of Irish people to settle in the British North American colonies', but there is little mention of their contributions to Quebec society.[9] The Irish were 'Other' in terms of either religion or language, and textbooks reflect this.

In the second part of this chapter, we will focus more closely on representations of Famine Irish immigrants in Quebec's current history curriculum. They provide a historical example of Canada and Quebec's first sizeable immigrant group whose experiences of conflict and accommodation remain relevant for contemporary teaching practices. More specifically, we will argue that the Famine Irish story has become a potential vehicle for a number of English-speaking students and teachers in Quebec who often feel excluded from the curriculum and draw upon it to reposition themselves as protagonists of their own history.[10] Building on the research of Quebec educational theorists—Marie McAndrew, Stéphane Lévesque, and Jean-Philippe Croteau, and especially Paul Zanazanian—we will examine some testimonials of English-speaking students and teachers who invoke the Famine Irish historical experience to both question and attempt to write themselves into the Quebec history curriculum.

Religion, language, and the development of school systems

Before turning to our objects of study, it is important to briefly sketch the historical influence of religion and language on teaching practices in both provinces. The establishment of the United Province of Canada in 1840 (providing one government for Canada East and West, formerly Lower and Upper Canada) was followed by the Education Act of 1841 that 'introduced the principle of "separate" or denominational schooling'.[11] This was an important watershed in that it made it possible for Catholics and those of other religious convictions to set up 'denominational schools'.[12] In 1855, 'by the weight of French Canadian Catholic votes', the so-called Taché Act was passed, which extended the rights to Canada West's Catholic minority and Canada East's Catholic majority 'to create and manage their own schools'.[13]

The British North America Act of 1867 delegated the responsibility for education to the provinces. In Quebec, this led to the establishment of Protestant and Catholic school commissions that received taxes paid by parents based on their religious denomination. By the turn of the century, French language instruction in Catholic separate schools was subject to increasingly restrictive legislation in Manitoba (in the 1890s) and Ontario. The implementation of the highly controversial Regulation 17 in Ontario in 1912 restricted French-language education in Catholic separate schools to grades 1 and 2.[14] 'The goal was to gradually assimilate French Canadians into the mainstream. But French Canadians had no intention of remaining quiet', note Stéphane Lévesque and Jean-Philippe Croteau.[15]

Significant Irish clergy support in Ontario for Regulation 17 (1912) 'incensed French-Canadians and aggravated ethno-linguistic and religious tensions'.[16] However, there were also prominent Irish-Canadians who spoke in defense of the rights of linguistic minority students. The most remarkable one was, in fact, a Famine orphan in Quebec who became a priest, the Reverend Thomas Quinn (1841–1923).[17] Father Quinn made it his life's mission to defend and safeguard the rights of his French-speaking parishioners as well as those of French language students in Ontario. As he mentioned in his speech at the First Congress of the French Language in Canada, held in Quebec City, shortly before Regulation 17 was issued in Ontario, his French-Canadian clerical predecessors not only brought him to his father's deathbed and rescued him from the quarantine station on Grosse Île, but also gave him a vocation. In this address entitled 'Une Voix d'Irlande', Father Quinn stated that:

> It was in 1847. A famine [...] threatened the Irish people with total extinction. The most astonishing part of the awful spectacle was, not to see the people die, but to see them live through such great distress [...] Like walking skeletons they went, in tears, seeking hospitality from more favoured lands.[18]

In his speech, Father Quinn also explicitly recollected his formative experience of linguistic and religious suppression in relearning his mother tongue when his adoptive French-Canadian parents 'enrolled me in an English school, run by two old women, who were imbued with a sense of narrow bigotry'.[19] In recounting his childhood humiliation, Quinn was also encouraging commiseration with Franco-Ontarian students whose linguistic and religious liberties were under similar threat. Yet despite his prominence as a defender of French language education, Quinn's legacy was soon forgotten and has only recently been rediscovered. His passionate oratory was never reproduced in textbooks in Ontario or Quebec. Decades later, the Quiet Revolution in 1960s Quebec, and especially the passing of the Charter of the French Language in 1977, defined French as the official language of education in the province, except for the children of Canadian-born English-speakers, who came to see themselves increasingly like Franco-Ontarians as a minority community.[20]

In these educational contexts, Irish-Canadians were often on the side of the minority. In Canada West, later Ontario, the Irish of the Famine generation and their descendants initially faced restrictions in organising and enrolling in Catholic education while speaking the language of the majority. In Canada East, later Quebec, the Irish shared their religious creed with French Canadians, but not their language. At the same time, the Irish played a crucial role in the development of the school system in Ontario and Quebec. The free, compulsory education in public schooling in both provinces was largely modelled on the Irish National School system under the auspices of Egerton Ryerson who had travelled to Ireland in 1845 and was instrumental in the passage of the Common Schools Act in 1846.[21]

The children of Famine Irish emigrants provided much of the student population and helped shape teaching practices in English-speaking Catholic school boards in both provinces. In the case of Ontario, one can trace a thin line of continuity between Toronto Bishop Michael Power's role in establishing Catholic schools before he perished while caring for the city's Famine emigrants on 1 October 1847 and vestigial references to 'Irish refugees in Canada' in recent textbooks.[22] An example of the latter is offered in the 2015 primary school textbook *Many Gifts: Social Studies for Catholic Schools* which explores how the Famine Irish often 'faced discrimination because they were poor and because of their religion'.[23]

From Corn Laws to crowded vessels: Textbook representations of the Famine and its diaspora

Textbook representations of the Famine Irish migration in Canada in both the distant and more recent past tend to concentrate on the British imperial economic context and harrowing experiences of Irish emigrants in 1847 rather than their lasting contributions to Canadian society. When one looks at older textbooks launched on the market in Ontario from the 1890s until before WWII, one notices that the Famine is almost without exception incorporated in a narrative about Robert Peel's repeal of the Corn Laws, a measure taken to protect the domestic food market through an abolition of tariffs on food trade, and his subsequent downfall as Prime Minister. The suffering in Ireland, the tensions between landlords and tenants, and relief operations are left out of consideration, thereby making the Famine part of a broader imperial narrative about food importation and exportation. For example, W.J. Robertson's *Public School History of England & Canada*, authorised by the Education Department of Ontario and published in 1892, states that due to 'the distress among the poor and the failure of the harvest in 1845 [...] in England and Scotland' and 'the potato blight' which had 'destroyed the chief article of food of the Irish', Peel 'saw that he had to choose between leaving thousands of people to die of starvation, and taking off the duty on food'. Robertson's textbook also suggests that this decision indirectly led to the end of his career as PM, as his decisions made enemies who did not support him on the Coercion Law in 1846: 'The Corn Laws were repealed, but Peel's political career was ended'.[24]

High School History of *England & Canada* (1891), also authorised by the Education Department of Ontario, and co-authored by Arabella Buckley and W. J. Robertson likewise contextualises the Famine in a broader narrative about Peel's decision to repeal the Corn Laws and imperial relations between 'England and her colonies': 'In 1845 the harvest failed in England, and the potato disease broke out and destroyed the chief food of Ireland. Famine was close at hand [...] Peel, who had gradually become convinced that Cobden was right, now proposed to bring in a Bill to repeal the duties on corn'.[25] The textbook *Great Britain: Its History to 1901* (1960), published by the Toronto branch of Oxford University Press for the Ontario market, also frames Ireland's Great Famine in the context of the Corn Laws, but the accompanying illustration of suffering Irish peasants, designed for the textbook, serves to elicit empathy for their dreadful plight: as the caption reads, 'Their misery is hard to imagine'.[26] As such, the paratext—a term which includes cover, illustrations and prefaces—provides an alternative narrative that stresses the Irish population's distress. Christopher Culpin's *Making Modern Britain* (1987, reprinted in 1997) includes an engraving depicting a workhouse in Ireland to accentuate Famine suffering in connection with its narrative about Britain's free trade policies, though one that is not from the Famine era itself.

All in all, we see that in Ontario textbooks, Ireland's Famine does not receive much attention of its own and is integrated in a template concerning food distribution as a broader British problem. Empathy for the afflicted in Ireland can therefore be found in the most recent textbooks, albeit in the paratexts rather than the texts themselves. A noteworthy exception is the grade six textbook *Many Gifts* (2015), which focuses on Canada's historical role in global issues such as migration, human rights, and disaster relief. Chapter 6 considers the historical presence of Irish refugees in Canada, and the evictions that many of them had endured in famine-stricken Ireland.[27]

When it comes to the subject of the Irish Famine diaspora, one may notice that early textbooks for the market in Ontario tend to gloss over the presence of the Irish among nineteenth-century migrant waves to Canada. They do not delve into the trauma of the 1847 fever sheds. For instance, George W. Brown's *Building the Canadian Nation* (1942) includes a chapter entitled 'A Wave of Immigration from Overseas' which discusses assisted emigration with 'help from the British government or from charitable organizations',[28] and which outlines the overall poor conditions and many deaths on board of the emigrant vessels: 'Disease often broke out on crowded vessels, and conditions became so bad that descriptions of immigrant ships written at the time now seem almost unbelievable'.[29] While reminiscent of the coffin ships arriving in Canada in 1847, the Irish exodus is not mentioned; the included engraving of 'departure of Emigrants from Waterloo Docks, Liverpool', taken from *Illustrated London News*, seems to hint at the history of Ireland's diaspora, but this is never explicated. Some textbooks address the Irish diaspora primarily in terms of the Fenian raid into Canada, an Irish-American nationalist attack aimed at pressuring Britain to grant home rule to Ireland. The often-reprinted *Flashback Canada* (1978–2007) mentions the battle at Ridgeway. The text suggests that the Fenians aimed 'to free Ireland, their homeland, from British control', but also that Canada would have become 'New Ireland' if their invasion had been successful. The assignment that accompanies the text requires that students try to imagine how they would have felt if they had lived in Canada at the time, with the reassurance that 'Fortunately British soldiers arrive from other parts of the colony'.[30]

Textbooks used in Ontario generally do not explore the 1847 Famine diaspora and quarantine stations in further detail. The exception is the aforementioned *Many Gifts*, which discusses the fateful journey of the Irish on the coffin ships and the quarantine stations where many of them died. What is more, this textbook encourages students to analyse the reasons for the mass emigration from Ireland to Canada, such as the fact that 'many landlords evicted their starving tenants', while some 'paid ships to transport their tenants to Canada'.[31] In this way, the broader context of the Famine diaspora is addressed, probably with the aim of making students aware of the difficult conditions faced by migrants in general.

The textbooks targeting schools in Quebec generally do not examine the Great Famine itself but mention in passing the arrival of sick immigrants from Ireland in 1847, a seminal event in Quebec's history in particular. By comparison, more coverage is devoted to the 1832 outbreak of cholera in Quebec after the arrival of emigrant ships. For example, *Notre Histoire* (1952), published by Copp Clark in Toronto, places more emphasis on the cholera epidemic that led to the establishment of the quarantine station at Grosse Île than the Irish Famine migration of 1847.[32] The textbook features the fictional 1832 diary entries of a fifteen-year-old girl who migrated from England, travelling third-class ('*en troisième classe*'), and who witnesses the many deaths on board as a result of an outbreak of cholera: 'It is impossible to convey our misery. The cholera is spreading rapidly, and within a week eleven people have died'.[33]

In similar fashion, volume 6 of Jacques Lacoursière's *Notre Histoire: Quebec-Canada* (1971) compares the calamitous years 1832 and 1847, only to conclude that the 1847 epidemic was less serious than the one of 1832:

> The summer of 1847 was sobered by the death of several thousands, the majority of whom were Irish immigrants. The typhus did not only wreak havoc among immigrants, but also among the Canadian population. This epidemic was less serious than the one of 1832.[34]

A textbook in English for schools in Quebec, John Alexander Dickinson's *Diverse Pasts: A History of Quebec and Canada* (1995), likewise emphasises the outbreak of cholera in Quebec in 1832, when 'in a few weeks the epidemic spread from the seaports through the colonies'.[35] The textbook also discusses the outbreak of ship fever on the emigrant vessels in 1847 and its impact on the host society: 'Ship fever, as it was called, broke out and spread in a few weeks even to remote settlements, causing thousands of deaths'.[36] However, the main focus remains the year 1832, which shows that the 1847 diaspora is often marginalised in historical representations of Canada's immigration.

As the example of *Diverse Pasts* indicates, references to the epidemic during the summer of 1847 in Quebec textbooks often stress the disastrous effects of the outbreak of diseases on Canada's population. The dire fates suffered by the Irish immigrants who lost loved ones upon entering the host country fade into the background.[37] Quebec's resolute Catholicism is stressed in some schoolbooks as the primary means of integration into French-Canadian society. Thus, *Notre Histoire* (1984) features a short fictional narrative about the impoverished Irish immigrants Olivia and Sullivan who left their homeland but ended in a 'pavillon de quarantaine' after the outbreak of cholera on board of their steamer: 'une épidémie de choléra se déclare sur le bateau'. Both suffer from malnutrition but do not contract the contagious disease. After leaving the quarantine station, Olivia and Sullivan build a successful family life, and their children are brought up as loyal French-Canadian citizens who remain true to their Catholic creed: 'They themselves were Canadian citizens, for born in this country. They attended the French village school. As faithful Catholics, they refused to go to the Protestant English school'.[38] Their religious fidelity and explicit rejection of an English-language Protestant education are key to their integration into French-Canadian society.

The most recent two-volume history textbook introduced into Quebec classrooms in 2019—Francis Campeau et al.'s *Reflections.qc.ca, Origins to 1840* (2016) and Sylvain Fortin et al.'s *Reflections.qc.ca, 1840 to Our Times* (2016)—does make reference to Famine Irish emigrants but not to their role in community building or contributions to Quebec society. The first volume of the textbook, *Reflections.qc.ca, Origins to 1840*, notes that even prior to 1847, 'while some were well-to-do, others were fleeing intolerable living conditions due to famines or epidemics. Victims of the epidemic that swept Europe around 1815 and 1825 and of agricultural crises, many English, Scottish, and Irish people set out for North America in search of a better life'.[39] Below the text is a pie chart with a breakdown of immigrant places of origin in Lower Canada between 1829 and 1840, which shows that 60.8% are from Ireland, more than twice the second largest group of English immigrants (26.6%). Despite their preponderance, the Irish remain for the most part undifferentiated from 'British emigrants' in the textbook's discussion.[40]

The one exception is an image caption entitled 'The hold of a ship from Ireland', accompanying the *Illustrated London News* engraving 'Emigration Vessel—Between Decks' (10 May 1851) that remains unattributed but is a depiction of Famine Irish emigrants. The image is accompanied by a paratextual description: 'Crossings by ship were often in unsanitary and crowded holds' followed by the leading question: 'The majority of Irish immigrants came from which group?' A second *Illustrated London News* image of Famine Irish emigrants—'The Embarkation, Waterloo Docks, Liverpool' (6 July 1850)—also appears, though it is mistakenly captioned 'Boarding ship in Waterloo, England, for the Port of Quebec'. The accompanying text seems anachronistically to refer to Irish migrants in the mid-1840s rather than the preceding decades: 'Dozens upon dozens were crowded into poorly ventilated holds. Lack of hygiene and the food served on these ships led to the outbreak of severe epidemics, such as cholera and typhus'.[41] The iconography and paratexts of the Irish Famine migration thus set the tone for this ostensible discussion of the earlier immigrant arrivals.

The harrowing conditions Irish emigrants experienced during the transatlantic crossing are also emphasised in the second volume of *Reflections.qc.ca, Origins to 1840* (2016). It notes that 'Immigration from the United Kingdom intensified in the 1840s. The Great Famine that ravaged Ireland in 1845 prompted hundreds of thousands of Irish people to leave their country and settle in the British North American colonies'.[42] This is followed by a subsection entitled 'TAKE NOTE!' that features an image of the Celtic Cross memorial on Grosse Île accompanied by the following text:

> 1847, a deadly year. In 1847, hundreds of ships left Ireland for the Province of Canada. On board were tens of thousands of emigrants fleeing famine. A typhus epidemic broke out on the overcrowded and unsanitary ships, whose passengers were already weakened by famine. Many of them died during the crossing or upon their arrival at the quarantine station on Grosse Île. In 1847 alone, some 5000 immigrants died at this station. A Celtic cross was erected there in 1909 to honour the memory of the thousands of Irish people who perished on Grosse Île or during the crossing.

The calamitous arrival of Famine Irish emigrants and their memorial on Grosse Île are vividly described, but not their experiences of community building and integration in the years that followed.[43]

Their negative impact in exacerbating 'epidemics that swept through the colony following a large influx of immigrants, most of whom were from Ireland' is also noted in the textbook's supplemental *Teaching Resources Guide*.[44] In a later review section on immigration to Quebec, the authors observe that Loyalist settlers from the United States 'were joined by a wave of immigrants from the United Kingdom and by many Irish people who were fleeing their harsh living conditions. It may be relevant to remind students', they suggest, 'that migrants generally left their countries of origin to escape a difficult situation, to find better living conditions'.[45] Despite this reminder, there is little consideration of Irish migrant historical experiences after the moment of arrival. The textbook remains fixated on those who perished in 1847 rather than those who survived, thereby showing continuities with narrative scripts used in earlier textbooks.

Cultural heritage and the opportunities for curriculum renewal

While the story of the Famine Irish in Canada features in past and more recent textbooks used in both provinces, Zoom interviews that we conducted with educators from Ontario and Quebec in 2021–23 suggest that there is very little curricular space for engaging with the Great Famine and the Irish diaspora in the classroom. Joseph Stafford, a retired history teacher who taught in the History Education Program at Queen's University in Kingston, Ontario (interviewed on 4 May 2021), feels that the rather subdued presence of the Irish Famine and its diaspora in present-day Ontario secondary education may be explained by a historical tradition of anti-Catholicism in that province that has since disappeared and subsequently a lack of interest in the Irish Catholic minority and its history as descendants from the Famine diaspora. However, Stafford suggests that the provincial curriculum offers space to teach migration into Canada and migrant integration in grade 10, although the focus tends to be on history after 1914. As a result, the societal groups that are usually discussed in history classes are racialised minorities and Indigenous people.

One of the leading experts on the Irish in Quebec, Simon Jolivet, who is also a staff member of Centre de services scolaires Marguerite-Bourgeoys-CSSMB in Montreal, and Gabrielle Palmieri, teacher of history at École secundaire Honoré-Mercier (also in Montreal), concur that there is relatively little coverage of the Irish Famine diaspora in Quebec history curricula.[46] In a Zoom interview that we conducted with them on 10 April 2021, both observed that in secondary schools in Quebec, migration and integration are central topics. The focus, however, is often on contemporary migration, from Latin America to North America and from North Africa to Western Europe, and especially from recent war-afflicted areas such as Kosovo, Rwanda, and Darfur.[47] Interconnecting past and present migration histories and memories hardly ever occurs in schools nowadays.

There are additional obstacles to integrating the Great Irish Famine and its diaspora in history classes in secondary education. As Palmieri explains, when exploring topics like migration, teachers tend to look at the immediate surroundings of their students. In her own case, this implies that she focuses on Arab-African migration due to the presence of these communities in the school's neighbourhood. Excursions to sites connected to the Irish Famine diaspora, such as Grosse Île, are not feasible in terms of distance, and Palmieri states that her school usually visits a mosque in the proximity of the school when teaching on religion and ethics. According to Jolivet, the fact that the Irish are regarded as a historically English rather than French-speaking minority militates against their more prominent inclusion within the Quebec history curriculum. Furthermore, he maintains that the history of the Famine Irish generation foregrounds uncomfortable issues of religion and especially language that have historically divided Quebec's population, especially when it comes to the integration of migrant communities. Persistent linguistic tension marginalises the Irish Famine diaspora within the Quebec history curriculum.

The challenge of reconciling these divisive issues of collective memory, historical identity, and the integration of migrant and minority students in the contemporary classroom is explored by Marie McAndrew. McAndrew contends that 'Francophones teaching in French and Anglophones teaching in English have radically different ideas about the purpose of teaching history', with the former encouraging their students from all backgrounds 'to share the historical memory of Francophones, something they believe is necessary to ensure authentic integration'. She also suggests that the Quebec history curriculum offers little opportunity for the 'discussion of the different nature of group identities'.[48] Hence, she helped initiate a number of twinning projects between Francophone and Anglophone teacher training programmes, including a visit to Grosse Île to enable future teachers 'to broaden the definition of their own identity and to develop empathy for the other group's perspectives and preoccupations'. More specifically, she notes that:

> [...] a site such as Grosse Île calls into question the traditional definition of Francophones as Catholic and Anglophones as Protestant. It also helps future history teachers to grasp concretely the concepts of divergent memories and historical consciousness. [...] The visit resulted in a bilingual video [*Exploring Collective Memory: rencontre à Grosse-Île*] that is used regularly in various courses at universities to sensitize students to the role of the school in the promotion of relations between Francophones and Anglophones and to make them aware of the long history of the immigrant presence within this dynamic.[49]

In this film, *Exploring Collective Memory*, McAndrew explains that the Famine Irish provide a historical model of integration that has lessons for future generations.

Yet if the Irish were exemplary immigrants, their lesson of integration begs the question of which community they sought to join. McAndrew makes the point that their arrival in Quebec represented 'the first time that Francophones were faced with a group who was not the Anglophone conqueror and who, from a religious perspective, resembled themselves'. They were 'supposedly forced to choose which side they would take and subsequently split in two', she adds. 'They maintained a stronger identity when they integrated with the Anglophones than when they integrated with the Francophones'.[50]

This heightened historical consciousness of Irish ancestry is reflected in English-speaking but not French-speaking student and teacher testimonials. Stéphane Lévesque and Jean-Philippe Croteau combine memory and narrative theory with an empirical study of 600 students in Quebec and Ontario who were asked to 'please tell us the history of French Canadians in this country as you know it'.[51] They note that for Franco-Ontarians:

> […] the pivotal moment in students' narratives was the Regulation 17 crisis. This episode plays a fundamental role in the identity construction of Franco-Ontarians, as does the [British] Conquest for young Québécois. […] It allowed French Canadians from Ontario to overcome a minority situation and to acquire the right to exist as an official community.[52]

By contrast, English-mother-tongue students comprised only 1% of their Quebec sample, although their responses are revealing. Lévesque and Croteau quote an English-speaking student from Gatineau who attaches great importance to Irish immigration:

> What I consider most important in history is the Irish potato crisis. This forced the inhabitants to come to settle in Quebec. Irish culture is very present in Quebec culture, so Ireland and its culture are linked to Francophone history. Also, many Quebeckers have Irish origins in Quebec today […] When the teacher taught on this topic, I found it sad that thousands of people died of malnutrition had to come by boat [… and] were piled up.[53]

What is significant about this student's response is its redefinition of the question to include Irish immigration as an integral feature of 'French Canadian history' and the Quebec curriculum. Where Franco-Ontarian students repeatedly insisted on the role that Regulation 17 played in marking 'the birth of their own community', this Anglophone student attributes a similar role to 'the Irish potato crisis' in a communal origin story.

This point is made more cogently and eloquently by Paul Zanazanian who employs similar methods to study English-speaking student, teacher, and community leader testimonials, which often reflect a sense of exclusion from Quebec's history curriculum and society at large. In an article with Nathalie Popa, he develops a 'Narrative Template tool [that] addresses the English-speaking minority's absence from Quebec's official state history' and 'the silencing of the core historical experiences of various historic groups, such as the Irish and Blacks'.[54] Zanazanian elaborates on how to break this silence, quoting at length from an English-speaking Montreal teacher who describes an extracurricular approach in discussing the city's Irish Famine memorial with students:

> I've always taken one full day away from the official program to talk about the Black Rock. The Black Rock is the memorial to 6000 Irish immigrants who died of fever on the shores of Montreal in the late 1840s. The Black Rock acts as a catalyst to get my students to recognize the immensity of what is forgotten, or omitted in the official Quebec government history program. […] The fact that Montreal's greatest single tragedy is forgotten

> allows other doors to be opened for my students. [...] Illuminating these events allows for [them ...] to recognize that a lot of their collective pasts get left out. The question that I ask at the end of this lesson is why? Why is it that their stories, their past, is not as important?[55]

This Montreal teacher, like the Gatineau student, seeks to redefine 'the official Quebec government history program' by invoking the story of Famine Irish immigrants as excluded predecessors to help students challenge and question their curriculum.

More specifically, the teacher adverts to Montreal's Black Rock Famine Memorial as a catalyst to prompt discussion about their own curricular omission as a minority community whose 'collective pasts get left out'. They are given a tough lesson about why they cannot see themselves or their ancestors in the official history programme. The teacher's claim 'that Montreal's greatest single tragedy is forgotten' occasions reflection not only about whose past is prioritised in the Quebec curriculum but also how curriculum itself is created. This questioning of its 'values, beliefs, and understandings' is certainly not teaching for the Quebec History secondary four exam, which is a compulsory requirement for a high school degree and often taught in an instrumental fashion.[56] The Black Rock Famine Monument thus becomes a vehicle for students' self-recognition that they are often misconstrued as descendants of the conqueror and foils for 'French-speaking political aspirations'. They are confronted with the devastating self-realisation 'that their community is not valued in the program and hence in Quebec'.[57]

Yet Zanazanian does not quote this teacher's testimonial simply to express dissatisfaction with the Quebec history curriculum. Rather, he seeks to help 'English-speaking students produce personal narratives of belonging' and 'to make curricular space for these excluded groups from the program'. Indeed, in developing a narrative template toolkit, his intent is to complement Quebec's official history programme and not replace it.[58] 'The creation of such collective templates would help promote awareness of English-speakers' diverse historical experiences', he suggests, 'and thus help dispel negative historic stereotypes that emerge from the province's traditional master narrative'.[59] 'In a more practical vein, these experiential templates would offer culturally diverse English-speaking youth guiding frameworks for developing their own stories of integration', Zanazanian observes. As English-speaking students, teachers, and community leaders attest, they want to find common ground with the French-speaking majority without relinquishing their distinct cultural and linguistic identity, both within the classroom and in Quebec society as a whole.[60]

Most recently, Zanazanian has worked with his doctoral student Robert Harris (who is also an English sector history teacher at North Star Academy in the Greater Montreal Area) to find 'rupture points' that prompt critical reflection about curricular exclusion in an Irish historical context. Like the aforementioned Montreal teacher, they regard the Black Rock as a potential pedagogical resource. Indeed, Harris acknowledged in a Zoom interview on 4 February 2023 that he himself is a descendant from Famine Irish emigrants whose ancestor, James Harris, sailed from Dublin in 1847 to escape the Great Hunger. Harris makes a point of sharing his Famine Irish ancestry with his students in framing an early genealogical assignment about their own family origins to help them realise that history is never confined to a singular perspective. His Irish ancestry provides an impetus for students to explore their own cultural backgrounds that otherwise receive little coverage in the course.

Harris also emphasises that mention of the Black Rock can become a rupture point or jumping-off point to break away from curriculum and consider the challenges of preserving minority identities. As he contends, 'it is the last beacon of Irish historical memory in Montreal [...] The Black Rock is the last marker of Irish public history and historical consciousness.'[61] More to the point, the Black Rock is not simply a 'beacon of Irish historical memory', Harris states, but a potentially rich repository of intercommunal stories about French and English civic and ecclesiastical authorities as well as ordinary people working together to care for disease-stricken Irish emigrants on the very site that it marks.

Indeed, the Black Rock is not only a physical monument but also a narrative marker of French and English caregivers' heroic self-sacrifice and compassion for immigrants that counterbalances storylines of host society accommodation and migrant integration in both historically specific and comparative and generalisable ways. Furthermore, numerous French and English language primary sources include eyewitness accounts of what transpired in Montreal's fever sheds that the Black Rock marks. These texts provide historical evidence and a readily available educational resource for students and community members to recover and, in some instances, recreate in their own 'personal narratives of belonging' as protagonists in their own story.[62] In short, such Famine Irish 'figures of memory'[63] can be readily incorporated into a narrative template toolkit and inspire students and teachers to campaign for a more inclusive curriculum.

Conclusion

The low-key presence of Ireland's Great Famine and the Famine diaspora to Canada in textbooks, and teaching practices in Ontario and Quebec can be explained in various ways. Past religious and ethnic tensions between the Irish Famine generation and Ontario's Anglo-Saxon, Protestant majority might account for the limited coverage of their traumatic historical experiences and that of the province's Irish Catholic minority. The Famine itself is often represented as a chapter in the history of British economic politics with little consideration of its victims. The Famine migration of 1847 does feature in Quebec history textbooks, but not the integration of Irish emigrants into its English-speaking and French-speaking communities that followed. Quebec's sensitivity to language politics has relegated them, as a mainly Catholic but largely English-speaking minority, into the background after their arrival in the mid-1840s. And yet, these Irish immigrants did also integrate in sizable numbers into French-speaking communities, as epitomised by the widespread cultural memory of Famine orphan adoptions into French-Canadian families. Indeed, Thomas Quinn's repudiation of Regulation 17 aligned his legacy with generations of Franco-Ontarian students who regarded its repeal as pivotal in defining their community.

There is a stark contrast between these limited textbook representations of Famine Irish emigrants and their prospective mobilisation as exemplary predecessors in narratives of integration within a broader narrative template (as theorised by Zanazanian) by Quebec's English-speaking students and teachers who often feel excluded from its history curriculum. This tension is elicited in teacher accounts of Montreal's Black Rock Famine Monument with its potential to provide rupture points that break away from curriculum in classroom discussion as a beacon of memory and marker of omitted minority histories. It both elucidates curricular limitations and encapsulates migrant stories of reception and integration.

The challenge is to equip students to both recognise these limitations and maintain respect for their cultural heritage while still meeting course requirements. This is not a case of special pleading for more coverage of a particular migrant or minority ethnic group, but rather more emphasis on its historical experiences of integration as interpreted from its perspective. Famine Irish immigrants stand out because they were Quebec's first sizeable minority that was not a part of its British Protestant and French Canadian majorities or Indigenous communities. Their calamitous arrival but not their role in helping shape Quebec society is what is currently taught in the history curriculum. By contrast, the Ontario textbook *Many Gifts* frames the Great Irish Famine and its Canadian diaspora in relation to broader themes such as 'World Health' and 'Disaster Relief' as an example of an early global crisis, while generating empathy with the fate of the Irish as refugees, although it reaches a much smaller segment of the student population.

The Irish hunger crisis and its victims, as well as its emigrants, remain underexplored in Quebec and Ontario teaching and textbook representations. This is becoming increasingly apparent in the light of recent campaigns to enhance the curricular presence of the Ukrainian famine (1932–33), also called Holodomor, in Ontario and further west, through efforts made by Ukrainian-Canadian communities. There is no mention of Ukrainian communities or Holodomor in the Quebec history curriculum. The focus on the period after 1914 in history teaching in Ontario might have made it easier to claim attention for this famine and its diaspora, but the strong network among Ukrainian-Canadian citizens has been a powerful force in getting Holodomor on teaching agendas as well.[64] It is important not to overstate the success of these Ukrainian-Canadian educational initiatives that have had little impact in Quebec and achieved nothing comparable as of yet to the designation in 1996 of Grosse Île and the Irish Memorial as a National Historic Site of Canada (which itself was created as a result of grassroots Irish-Canadian political pressure).[65] But they do provide a salutary reminder that curriculum is not created in a vacuum and remains amenable to the inclusion of underrepresented groups, which beacons an educational future worth striving for.

Notes

1 Mark G. McGowan, *It's Our Turn: Carrying on the Work of the Pioneers of Catholic Education in Ontario* (Toronto: Novalis, 2019), 46.
2 Carmel Roofe and Christopher Bezzina, 'Introduction', in *Intercultural Studies of Curriculum Theory, Policy and Practice* (London: Palgrave, 2018), 2.
3 See Marguérite Corporaal, *Relocated Memories: The Famine in Irish and Diaspora Fiction, 1846*–70 (Syracuse, NY: Syracuse UP, 2017); and Jason King, 'The Remembrance of Irish Famine Migrants in the Fever Sheds of Montreal', in Marguérite Corporaal et al., eds., *Global Legacies of the Great Irish Famine: Transnational and Interdisciplinary Perspectives* (Oxford: Peter Lang, 2014), 245–67.
4 See https://www.canadairelandfoundation.com/irish-in-canada/, accessed 16 September 2022.
5 See https://www.canadairelandfoundation.com/grasettpark/, accessed 16 September 2022. Also see https://www.irishfaminestories.ca/en, accessed 5 February 2023.
6 Emily Moriarty, 'Hibernia News: Bones Found in Montreal Linked to Famine Victims', *Irish America*, https://www.irishamerica.com/2022/12/hibernia-news-bones-found-in-montreal-linked-to-famine-victims/, accessed 5 February 2023. The cultural and historical significance of Montreal's Black Rock Famine memorial is discussed in Colin McMahon, 'Montreal's Ship Fever Monument: An Irish Famine Memorial in the Making', *Canadian Journal of Irish Studies* 33, no. 1 (2007): 48–60; Colin McMahon, 'Recrimination and Reconciliation: Great Famine memory in Liverpool and Montreal at the Turn of the Twentieth Century', *Atlantic Studies* 11, no. 3 (2014): 344–64; Jason King, 'Montreal's Grey Nuns: The Great Hunger Migration and the Miracle of Rose's Marble', in Christine Kinealy, Jason King, Gerard Moran, eds., *Heroes of Ireland's Great Hunger* (Cork and Hamden, Connecticut: Cork University Press and Quinnipiac University Press, 2021), 205–20; Jason King, 'Staging Famine Irish Memories of Migration and National Performance in Ireland and Quebec', *CLCWeb Comparative Literature and Culture* 18, no. 4 (2016): 1–8. https://docs.lib.purdue.edu/clcweb/vol18/iss4/6/, accessed 6 February 2023.
7 Chau Vu, 'Representation of World War II in Vietnam, China, and the USA: Political Ideologies in Secondary History Textbooks', in Carmel Roofe and Christopher Bezzina, eds., *Intercultural Studies of Curriculum* (Basingstoke: Palgrave, 2018), 169–70.

8 For the term, see James V. Wertsch, *Voices of Collective Remembering* (New York: Cambridge University Press, 2002), 9.

9 Sylvain Fortin, Dominique Lapointe, Rémi Lavoie, Alain Parent, *Reflections.qc.ca, 1840 to Our Times: History of Québec and Canada, Secondary IV. Student Textbook.* Trans. Gwendolyn Schulman, Natasha De Cruz (Montreal: Chenelière Éducation, 2016), 28, 74.

10 Paul Zanazanian and Nathalie Popa, 'Using a Narrative Tool to Help Quebec English-Speaking Students Produce Personal Histories of Belonging', *LEARNing Landscapes* 11, no. 2 (2018): 365–79.

11 Daniel Murphy, *A History of Irish Emigrant and Missionary Education* (Dublin: Four Courts, 2000), 281.

12 McGowan, *It's Our Turn*, 20.

13 Ibid.

14 Ibid., 24.

15 Stéphane Lévesque and Jean-Philippe Croteau, *Beyond History for Historical Consciousness: Students, Narrative, and Memory* (Toronto: University of Toronto Press, 2020), 37.

16 Jason King, '"Une Voix d'Irlande": Integration, Migration, and Travelling Nationalism Between Famine Ireland and Quebec', in Ciarán Reilly, ed., *The Famine Irish: Emigration and the Great Hunger* (Dublin: The History Press Ireland, 2016), 194.

17 Thomas Quinn's legacy is more fully examined in Jason King, '"Une Voix d'Irlande", and Jason King, '"Remember Your Soul and Your Liberty": Childhood Memories of the Tighe and the Quinn Famine Orphans', in Christine Kinealy, Jason King, Mark G. McGowan, eds., *Hunger & Hope: The Irish Famine Migration from Strokestown, Roscommon in 1847* (Hamden, CT: Quinnipiac University Press & Cork: Cork University Press, 2023), 101–20.

18 Ibid., 229. Thomas Quinn's original French language text reads: 'C'était en 1847. Une famine plus terrible que celle qui l'avait précédée menaçait le peuple irlandais d'une extermination complète. Le spectacle le plus étonnant n'était pas de voir mourir les gens, mais de les voir vivre, tant la détresse était grande [...] Spectres ambulants, ils s'en allèrent en pleurant, demander l'hospitalité à des pays plus fortunés'.

19 Ibid., 230. Quinn's original French language text reads: 'Mes parents adoptifs, pour me permettre de conserver la langue de ma famille, m'avait placé, tout enfant, dans une école anglaise, tenue par deux vieilles institutrices, imbues du plus étroit fanatisme. Un jour que le Saint Sacrement passait dans la rue, porté par un prêtre, je voulus me mettre à genoux, suivant la coutume catholique. Ma maîtresse me relève violemment, avec une apostrophe que je ne vous redirai pas. J'obéis, en vertu de la loi du plus fort; mais, c'était pour sortir de l'école et n'y plus revenir. Mon cours d'anglais était fini. Ce n'était pas la langue de mon âme ni de ma liberté!'

20 King, '"Une Voix d'Irlande"', 196.

21 Murphy, *A History of Irish Emigrant and Missionary Education*, 296–303.

22 McGowan, *It's Our Turn*, 39–43.

23 Mary Cairo and Luci Soncin, *Many Gifts: Social Studies for Catholic Schools* (Toronto: Nelson, 2015), 131.

24 W.J. Robertson, *Public School History of England & Canada.* Authorized by the Education Department of Ontario (Toronto: The Copp, Clark Company, 1892), 182.

25 Arabella Buckley & W.J. Robertson, *High School History* of *England & Canada* (Toronto: The Copp, Clark Company, 1891), 302.

26 T.K. Derry, C.H.C. Blown & T.L. Jarman, *Great Britain: Its History to 1901* (Toronto: Oxford UP, 1960), 356.

27 Cairo and Soncin, *Many Gifts*, 130.
28 George W. Brown, *Building the Canadian Nation* (Toronto & Vancouver: J.M. Dent & Sons, 1942), 194.
29 Ibid., 195.
30 J. Bradley Cruxton and W. Douglas Wilson, *Flashback Canada* (Toronto: Oxford UP, 2000), 36.
31 Cairo and Soncin, *Many Gifts*, 130.
32 Brown et al., *Notre Histoire* (Toronto: Copp Clark, 1952), 228–31.
33 Ibid., 235. The French-language text reads: 'Il est impossible de décrire notre misère. Le cholera se répand rapidement et onze personnes sont mortes en moins d'une semaine'
34 Jacques Lacoursière, *Notre Histoire: Quebec-Canada* (Montréal: Éditions Format, 1971), 505. The French text reads: 'L'été de 1847 est assombri par la mort de plusieurs milliers, d'immigrants irlandais pour la plupart. Lé typhus ne cause pas seulement ses ravages chez les immigrants, mais aussi chez la population canadienne. Mais l'épidémie est moins grave que celle de 1832'.
35 John Alexander Dickinson. *Diverse Pasts: A History of Quebec and Canada, 2nd edition.* (Toronto: Copp Clark, 1995), 197.
36 Ibid., 199.
37 For instance, although not a textbook, *Une histoire du Canada* (2009), a French translation of Robert Bothwell's *Penguin History of Canada*, mentions 1,400 Irish immigrants who fell victim to typhus after having escaped the Famine in their homeland, but mainly focuses on the infected host population of Canada East: 'Les commerçants de fourrure et, par la suite, les bateaux à vapeur qui remontent les grandes rivières des plaines contribuent à la propagation à l'intérieur du continent des maladies d'origine européenne qui continuent de décimer la population autochtone'. See Robert Bothwell, *Une histoire du Canada* (Québec: Presses de l'Université Laval, 2009), 174.
38 Danielle Dion-McKinnon and Pierre Lalongé, *Notre Histoire* (Montréal: Éditions du Renouveau Pédagogique, 1984), 93. The French text reads: 'Ceux-ci sont de citoyenneté canadienne, car ils sont nés au pays. Ils fréquentent l'école française du village. En bons catholiques, ils refusent d'aller à l'école anglaise protestante'.
39 Francis Campeau, Rémi Lavoie, Sylvain Fortin, Alain Parent, *Reflections.qc.ca, Origins to 1840: History of Québec and Canada, Secondary III*, trans. Gwendolyn Schulman, Natasha De Cruz (Montréal: Chenelière Éducation, 2016), 208–9.
40 Ibid., 208.
41 Ibid., 209.
42 Fortin et al., *Reflections.qc.ca, 1840 to Our Times*, 74.
43 The supplemental *Teaching Resources Guide* for *Reflections.qc.ca* also makes reference to 'the threat of the Fenians, a group of Irish nationalists based in the United States who resorted to violence to fight British domination', and recommends Jane Urquhart's novel *Away* which 'traces one family's past, from the harsh northern Irish coast in the 1840s to Canada' that is exposed to the Fenian threat, as a student resource. Ibid., 479, 507.
44 Ibid., 477.
45 Ibid., 625.
46 Among his many publications, see in particular Simon Jolivet, *Le vert et le bleu: Identité québécoise et identité irlandaise au tournant du xxe siècle* (Montréal: Les Presses de l'Université de Montréal, 2011).
47 See *Précision des apprentissages au secondaire: Monde contemporain, 5e secondaire* (Québec: Éducation, Loisir et Sport, Québec, 2013), 6.

48 Marie McAndrew, *Fragile Majorities and Education: Belgium, Catalonia, Northern Ireland, and Quebec*, trans. Michael O'Hearn (Montreal & Kingston: McGill-Queens University Press, 2013), 98, 97.
49 Ibid., 70, 69.
50 Marie McAndrew, *Exploring Collective Memory: Rencontre à Grosse-Île* (Montréal: GREAPE, 2003), https://youtu.be/JWB0C8JSBSU, last accessed 5 February 2023.
51 Lévesque and Croteau, *Beyond History for Historical Consciousness*, 23, 22.
52 Ibid., 48.
53 Ibid., 103.
54 Zanazanian and Popa, 'Using a Narrative Tool', 370.
55 Zanazanian, 'Presentation to Irish Famine Summer School Online', 29 May 2021.
56 Carmel Roofe and Christopher Bezzina, 'Introduction', 2.
57 Zanazanian quoting Montreal teacher, 'Presentation to Irish Famine Summer School Online', 29 May 2021.
58 Zanazanian and Popa, 'Using a Narrative Tool', 369–70.
59 Zanazanian, 'History Teaching and Narrative Tools: Towards Integrating English-Speaking Youth into Quebec's Social Fabric', *Minorités linguistiques et société / Linguistic Minorities and Society* 7 (2016): 91.
60 More broadly, Zanazanian has examined English-speaking community leaders' testimonials to help refine these templates and enhance their role in facilitating civic engagement and communal vitality beyond the Quebec history curriculum. In doing so, he 'selectively picked the emerging narrative threads that were the most conducive to fostering a positive sense of self and living together with Francophones'. '*The diversification through immigration* thread as a thematic undercurrent of participants' narratives and the smaller theme of *Working together with Francophones to build a common civic project* were favored over *Group duality* representing a history of two homogenous entities in constant competition', he contends. Paul Zanazanian, 'Teaching History for Narrative Space and Vitality: Historical Consciousness, Templates, and English-Speaking Quebec', in Henrik Åström Elmersjö, Anna Clark, and Monika Vinterek, eds., *International Perspectives on Teaching Rival Histories: Pedagogical Responses to Contested Narratives and the History Wars* (London: Palgrave Macmillan, 2017), 124.
61 Also see Matthew Barlow, *Griffintown: Identity and Memory in an Irish Diaspora Neighbourhood* (Vancouver: University of British Columbia Press, 2017), 224.
62 See Jason King, *Irish Famine Archive*, 2015, http://faminearchive.nuigalway.ie, accessed 6 February 2023.
63 Jan Assmann, 'Collective Memory and Cultural Identity', *New German Critique* 65 (1995): 129.
64 The National Holodomor Education Committee collaborates with local branches of the Ukrainian Canadian Congress to promote the inclusion of 'the Holodomor in provincial curricula across Canada'. See https://www.ucc.ca/about-ucc/committees/national-holodomor-education-committee/, last accessed 6 February 2023. This campaign has been particularly successful in Ontario, where curricular applications have been developed to integrate the Holodomor under the umbrella subject of human rights, next to the Armenian genocide and Holocaust, and where the famine is commemorated as part of the 'April Genocide Remembrance, Condemnation and Prevention Month' in schools. See https://www.ucc.ca/2022/04/14/april-genocide-remembrance-condemnation-prevention-and-education-month/, accessed 6 February 2023. Learning resources were developed by HREC Education in Edmonton and Toronto, under the leadership of Valentina Kuryliw. For these resources, see https://education.holodomor.ca/teaching-materials/background/, accessed 7 February 2023. The Holodomor National Awareness Tour, a mobile classroom which

visits schools across the country, has further enhanced its educational outreach, especially through its creation of learning materials in both English and French. See https://holodomortour.ca/, accessed 7 February 2023.

65 See Michael Quigley, 'Languages of Memory: Jeremiah Gallagher and the Grosse Île Famine Monument', in Ciarán Reilly, ed., *The Famine Irish: Emigration and the Great Hunger* (Dublin: The History Press Ireland, 2016), 218–22.

References

Assmann, Jan, 'Collective Memory and Cultural Identity', *New German Critique*, 65 (1995): 125–33.

Barlow, Matthew, *Griffintown: Identity and Memory in an Irish Diaspora Neighbourhood*. Vancouver: University of British Columbia Press, 2017.

Bothwell, Robert, *Une histoire du Canada*. Quebec: Presses de l'Université Laval, 2009.

Brown, George W., *Building the Canadian Nation*. Toronto & Vancouver: J.M. Dent & Sons, 1942.

Brown, George W., et al., *Notre Histoire*. Toronto: Copp Clark, 1952.

Buckley, Arabella and W.J. Robertson, *High School History of England & Canada*. Toronto: The Copp, Clark Company, 1891.

Cairo, Mary and Luci Soncin, *Many Gifts: Social Studies for Catholic Schools*. Toronto: Nelson, 2015.

Campeau, Francis, et al., *Reflections.qc.ca, Origins to 1840: History of Québec and Canada, Secondary III*, trans. Gwendolyn Schulman and Natasha De Cruz. Montréal: Chenelière Éducation, 2016.

Canada Ireland Foundation, https://www.canadairelandfoundation.com/. 2022.

Canada Ireland Foundation, https://www.irishfaminestories.ca/en. 2023.

Corporaal, Marguérite, *Relocated Memories: The Famine in Irish and Diaspora Fiction, 1846–70*. Syracuse, NY: Syracuse UP, 2017.

Cruxton, J. Bradley and W. Douglas Wilson, *Flashback Canada*. Toronto: Oxford UP, 2000.

Derry, T.K., C.H.C. Blown and T.L. Jarman, *Great Britain: Its History to 1901*. Toronto: Oxford UP, 1960.

Dickinson, John Alexander. *Diverse Pasts: A History of Quebec and Canada*, 2nd edition. Toronto: Copp Clark, 1995.

Dion-McKinnon, Danielle and Pierre Lalongé, *Notre Histoire*. Montreeal: Éditions du Renouveau Pédagogique, 1984.

Fortin, Sylvain, et al., eds., *Reflections.qc.ca, 1840 to Our Times: History of Québec and Canada, Secondary IV. Student Textbook*, trans. Gwendolyn Schulman, Natasha De Cruz. Montreal: Chenelière Éducation, 2016.

Holodomor National Awareness Tour. https://holodomortour.ca/.

HREC. https://education.holodomor.ca/teaching-materials/background/.

King, Jason, 'The Remembrance of Irish Famine Migrants in the Fever Sheds of Montreal'. In Corporaal et al., eds, 245–67. *Global Legacies of the Great Irish Famine: Transnational and Interdisciplinary Perspectives*. Oxford: Peter Lang, 2014.

King, Jason, *Irish Famine Archive*. 2015. http://faminearchive.nuigalway.ie.

King, Jason, 'Staging Famine Irish Memories of Migration and National Performance in Ireland and Quebec'. *CLCWeb Comparative Literature and Culture* 18, no. 4 (2016): 1–8. https://docs.lib.purdue.edu/clcweb/vol18/iss4/6/.

King, Jason, '"Une Voix d'Irlande": Integration, Migration, and Travelling Nationalism Between Famine Ireland and Quebec'. In Ciarán Reilly, ed., 193–208. *The Famine Irish: Emigration and the Great Hunger*. Dublin: The History Press Ireland, 2016.

King, Jason, 'Montreal's Grey Nuns: The Great Hunger Migration and the Miracle of Rose's Marble'. In Christine Kinealy, Jason King, Gerard Moran, eds., 205–20. *Heroes of Ireland's Great Hunger*. Cork and Hamden, CT: Cork University Press and Quinnipiac University Press, 2021.

King, Jason, '"Remember your soul and your liberty": Childhood Memories of the Tighe and the Quinn Famine Orphans'. In Christine Kinealy, Jason King, Mark G. McGowan, eds., 101–20. *Hunger & Hope: The Irish Famine Migration from Strokestown, Roscommon in 1847*. Hamden, CT: Quinnipiac University Press & Cork: Cork University Press, 2023.

Lacoursière, Jacques, *Notre Histoire: Quebec-Canada*. Montréal: Éditions Format, 1971.

Lévesque, Stéphane and Jean-Philippe Croteau, *Beyond History for Historical Consciousness: Students, Narrative, and Memory*. Toronto: University of Toronto Press, 2020.

McAndrew, Marie, *Exploring Collective Memory: Rencontre à Grosse-Île*. Montréal: GREAPE, 2003. https://youtu.be/JWB0C8JSBSU.

McAndrew, Marie, *Fragile Majorities and Education: Belgium, Catalonia, Northern Ireland, and Quebec*, trans. Michael O'Hearn. Montreal & Kingston: McGill-Queens University Press, 2013.

McGowan, Mark G., *It's Our Turn: Carrying on the Work of the Pioneers of Catholic Education in Ontario*. Toronto: Novalis, 2019.

McMahon, Colin, 'Montreal's Ship Fever Monument: An Irish Famine Memorial in the Making'. *Canadian Journal of Irish Studies* 33, no. 1 (2007): 48–60.

McMahon, Colin, 'Recrimination and reconciliation: Great Famine memory in Liverpool and Montreal at the turn of the twentieth century'. *Atlantic Studies* 11, no. 3 (2014): 344–64.

Moriarty, Emily, 'Hibernia News: Bones Found in Montreal Linked to Famine Victims'. *Irish America*. https://www.irishamerica.com/2022/12/hibernia-news-bones-found-in-montreal-linked-to-famine-victims/. December 2022.

Murphy, Daniel, *A History of Irish Emigrant and Missionary Education*. Dublin: Four Courts, 2000.

Précision des apprentissages au secondaire: Monde contemporain, 5e secondaire. Quebec: Éducation, Loisir et Sport, Québec, 2013.

Quigley, Michael, 'Languages of Memory: Jeremiah Gallagher and the Grosse Île Famine Monument'. In Ciarán Reilly, ed., 218–22. *The Famine Irish: Emigration and the Great Hunger*. Dublin: The History Press Ireland, 2016.

Robertson, W.J., *Public School History of England & Canada. Authorized by the Education Department of Ontario*. Toronto: The Copp, Clark Company, 1892.

Roofe, Carmel and Christopher Bezzina, 'Introduction'. In Roofe and Bezzina, eds., 1–7. *Intercultural Studies of Curriculum Theory, Policy and Practice*. London: Palgrave, 2018.

Ukrainian Canadian Congress. https://www.ucc.ca/about-ucc/committees/national-holodomor-education-committee/.

Vu, Chau, 'Representation of World War II in Vietnam, China, and the USA: Political Ideologies in Secondary History Textbooks'. In Carmel Roofe and Christopher Bezzina, eds., 165–90. *Intercultural Studies of Curriculum*. Basingstoke: Palgrave, 2018.

Wertsch, James V., *Voices of Collective Remembering*. New York: Cambridge University Press, 2002.

Zanazanian, Paul, 'History Teaching and Narrative Tools: Towards Integrating English-Speaking Youth into Quebec's Social Fabric'. *Minorités linguistiques et société/Linguistic Minorities and Society*, 7 (2016): 70–96.

Zanazanian, Paul, 'Teaching History for Narrative Space and Vitality: Historical Consciousness, Templates, and English-Speaking Quebec'. In Henrik Åström Elmersjö et al., 107–32. *International Perspectives on Teaching Rival Histories: Pedagogical Responses to Contested Narratives and the History Wars*. London: Palgrave Macmillan, 2017.

Zanazanian, Paul, 'Presentation to Irish Famine Summer School Online'. 29 May 2021.

Zanazanian, Paul and Nathalie Popa, 'Using a Narrative Tool to Help Quebec English-Speaking Students Produce Personal Histories of Belonging'. *LEARNing Landscapes* 11, no. 2 (2018): 365–79.

PART II

Memory and commemoration

4

RELATIVE ABSENCE

Dutch memory culture and monuments of the Hunger Winter of 1944–45

Ingrid de Zwarte and Lotte Jensen

On 4 May 1981, the national day of Remembrance of the Dead of the Second World War in the Netherlands, a bronze statue of a female cyclist was revealed in the Prinsentuin, a public park in the Frisian capital city of Leeuwarden. The commemorative act was performed by three sisters—Ali, Gré, and Gelfke Haanstra—who had been actively involved in the resistance movement during the war. All three had transported food on their bicycles to people in hiding. Their resistance activities intensified during the harsh winter of 1944–45.[1] The bronze figure on the bicycle symbolises the many women who went searching for food during the final months of the German occupation. In a wider sense, it has also been interpreted as a tribute to all those couriers who carried out their work clandestinely during the war (Image 4.1).[2]

The female cyclist statue is part of a vast memorial culture of the Dutch famine, popularly known as the 'Hunger Winter' of 1944–45. The famine resulted from the culmination of several transportation and distribution difficulties after the Allied liberation of the south of the Netherlands in the autumn of 1944, causing severe problems with the food and fuel supply. At least 20,000 people died as a result of the famine, which mostly affected the population in the large cities in the western Netherlands.[3] Today, every Dutch child is still taught about this important phase of the Second World War at school, as the Hunger Winter forms an integral part of the 'historical canon' of the Netherlands.[4] In addition to receiving extensive coverage in educational materials, the Hunger Winter features prominently in museum exhibitions, documentaries, novels, and children's books. Most Dutch people become familiar with the Hunger Winter via the children's book *Oorlogswinter* (1972), by Jan Terlouw, which remains popular to this day and was made into a feature film in 2008.

DOI: 10.4324/9781003391524-7

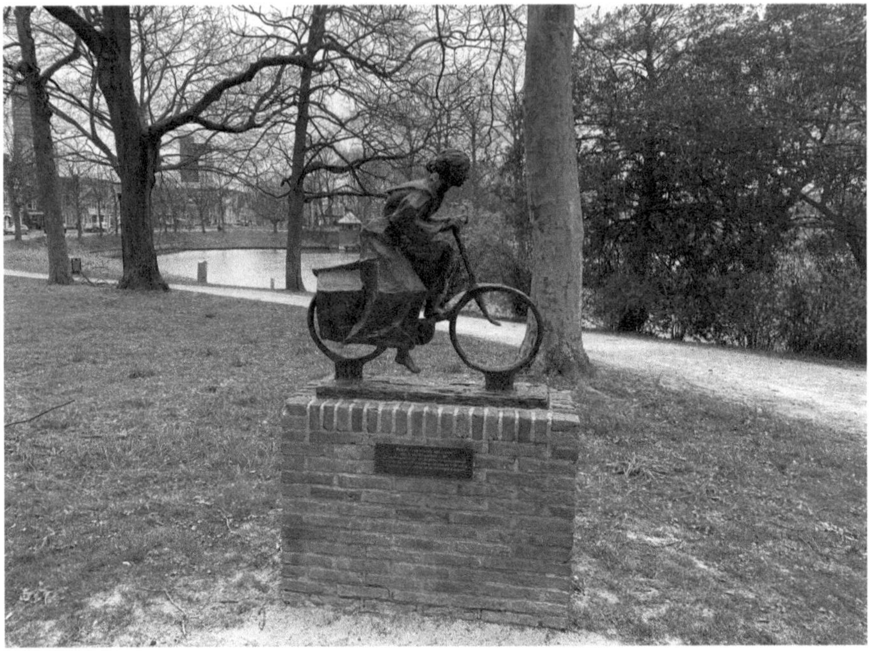

IMAGE 4.1 'The Courier' by Tineke Bot (1981), Leeuwarden. Photograph by Ingrid de Zwarte.

Yet, contrary to the ample attention devoted to the Dutch Hunger Winter in education and popular culture, nowadays only a few inconspicuous monuments—plaques, memorial stones, sculptures, and public artworks—scattered across the Netherlands commemorate the Hunger Winter. The statue of the young woman on the bicycle in Leeuwarden is, in fact, exceptional. Indeed, while almost every Dutch person is familiar with this episode of history, hardly anyone will be able to name or place a single monument—defined as 'the material objects, sculptures and installations used to memorialize a person or thing'[5]—dedicated to the Hunger Winter. This 'relative absence' of Hunger Winter monuments stands in stark contrast with the visual memorialisation of many other European famines, in particular the many monuments in both Europe and North America dedicated to the Great Irish Famine of 1845–50 and the Ukrainian 'Holodomor' of 1932–33.[6] It also diverges significantly from the material memorialisation of other Dutch disasters, such as the Dutch North Sea Flood of 1953, which is kept alive in public remembrance in the Netherlands through at least 150 monuments.[7] Neither does it align with the Dutch memorialisation of the Second World War in general, which finds expression in c. 4,000 monuments across the country.[8]

This chapter raises the question of why the Dutch Hunger Winter has left relatively few material objects of commemoration in the Dutch landscape, while it seems to be abundantly present in, for instance, formal educational practices and popular culture. In this chapter, we are the first to investigate the seventeen known Hunger Winter monuments that have been erected between the end of the war in 1945 and today. Our study is based on extensive fieldwork, supplemented by historical newspaper articles that reveal the social, cultural, and political contexts in which these sites of memory were developed.

We investigate our research question by situating the memorialisation of the Hunger Winter within the broader context of Dutch memory culture and comparing and contrasting the memorial culture of the Dutch famine with that of other European famines. We argue that the relative absence of famine monuments in the Netherlands stems from a combination of several factors, including the absence of a tradition of representing famines in the Dutch public sphere; Dutch post-war memory politics; and the absence of actively engaged diasporic communities. These factors may help explain material 'presence' and 'absence' in other famine heritage contexts as well.

Dutch memorial culture

To understand why famine monuments are relatively absent in the Dutch public sphere nowadays, it is necessary to adopt a wider historical perspective and establish how Dutch memorial culture took shape in the nineteenth century. In many respects, the Dutch developments align with international patterns, yet certain aspects can be considered characteristic for the Netherlands. What, how, and why individuals and communities remember reveals how the past lives on in present-day society, thus forging personal and communal identities.[9] Memory scholars have convincingly shown that this process of remembering is never neutral but can be seen as a performative act. As Jay Winter puts it, 'When individuals and groups express or embody or interpret or repeat a script about the past, they galvanize the ties that bind groups together and deposit additional memory traces about the past in their own minds'.[10]

Celebrating the national past and emphasising shared victimisation have played a crucial role in processes of national identity formation since the early nineteenth century. The arts—paintings, music, literature, architecture, and sculptures—were important instruments in nation-building, as were historiographical, educational, and philological writings. By representing the past as a continuous story of oppression and liberation, and by creating national myths that celebrated glorious victories, visual and textual media contributed to the constitution of certain interpretations and coherent national historical narratives.[11] Leaving out certain less favourable and painful episodes, however, was (and still is) just as constitutive. In his famous lecture '*Qu'est-ce q'une nation*' (1882), the French philosopher Ernest Renan already stressed the importance of collective amnesia with regard to nation-building:

'the essence of a nation is that all of its individual members have a great deal in common and also that they have all forgotten many things'.[12]

As in other European countries, in the Netherlands, the celebration of the national past peaked in the nineteenth century. Artists singled out stories of revolt and liberation, such as the Batavian revolt against the Romans (69–70) and the Eighty Years War against Spain (1568–1648), while celebrating the so-called Golden Age, in which Dutch economy and culture flourished at the cost of colonised peoples.[13] Shared victimisation contributed to the shaping of patriotic feelings: the war against Spain was also represented as a period during which the Dutch suffered severely. They showed their resilience by overcoming the brutalities and violence inflicted by the Spanish enemy. Most Dutch national heroes—and only a very few heroines—who were canonised in history, came from that period, such as the 'founding father' of the Netherlands, William of Orange, naval hero Michiel de Ruyter, painter Rembrandt van Rijn, and poet Joost van den Vondel. The creation of a coherent, nationally unifying story excluded many other important events that were more inconvenient to remember, such as the 'Martyrs of Gorkum' (the hanging of a group of Catholics by militant Calvinists, 1572), the brutal murder of the Dutch statesmen Johan van Oldenbarnevelt (1619) and the brothers Cornelis and Johan de Witt (1672), or the massacres in the Netherlands East Indies (1621, 1740).

The erection of monuments added to this (selective) image of the Dutch national past. However, as Marita Mathijsen has also noted, unlike in France and England, a thriving memorial culture in the form of monuments remained largely absent in the Netherlands.[14] From the 1840s onwards, several naval heroes, poets, painters, and statesmen who fitted the dominant national self-image were honoured with a statue, but compared to other European countries, the number of memorial objects was rather modest. The relatively few monuments in Dutch memorial culture could possibly be explained as a consequence of the dominance of Protestant culture, which renounced the worshipping of saints' statues in churches. Furthermore, contrary to many other European countries, the Dutch state was hardly ever involved in commissioning or funding these monuments. Most monuments from the nineteenth and twentieth centuries were realised through fundraising by private initiatives or civilian committees in collaboration with local governments.[15] The success of these monuments thus depended largely on local efforts, as was, for example, the case with monuments erected for the nineteenth-century female author A.L.G. Bosboom-Toussaint (1912, Alkmaar), Suriname resistance fighter Anton de Kom (2006, Amsterdam), and the first Dutch female physician, Aletta Jacobs (2019, The Hague). Such local initiatives were usually motivated by emancipatory ambitions to make forgotten people and events in Dutch history visible again.

Besides paying tribute to the memory of important persons, the majority of Dutch monuments have been commissioned in response to traumatic events and disasters, such as floods and wars. Famines, however, have traditionally not left any traces in Dutch memorial culture. Indeed, while the European-wide potato failure in the mid-nineteenth century—which caused the Great Irish Famine (1845–50)—also significantly affected the Netherlands and Flanders in terms of famine-related excess mortality,[16] there are no monuments that commemorate this event.

By contrast, the physical commemoration of floods in the Netherlands is vastly different, including many statues, plaques, and sculptures. Floods are commemorated in countless places, including the St. Elisabeth's Flood of 1421, the Christmas Flood of 1717, the Storm Surge of 1825, and the Flood of 1916. The North Sea Flood of 1953, however, surpasses all other floods in Dutch memorial culture.[17] Generally speaking, monuments to the North Sea Flood of 1953 can be divided into two categories. The first group visualises traumatic losses by portraying vulnerable people, often employing the victim mother and child trope. The second group represents heroic rescue activities and the rebuilding and reconstruction of the landscape after the calamity, portraying fishermen skippering boats with refugees and dike workers. The visual representation of this catastrophe thus runs emphatically along gender lines.[18]

Of all traumatic events, the Second World War has left by far the most visible traces in the Dutch landscape. In the first years after the war, commemoration of the German occupation period and its victims aligned with traditional political and religious beliefs of continuity and progress. Based on 'grand narratives' and national sentiments, memorials of the war were focused on national restoration and moving into the future.[19] The National Monument on Dam Square in Amsterdam (1956), which had already become the place of the annual commemoration, represents this post-war dominant narrative, which revolved around stories of national suffering, endurance, courage, and sacrifice.[20]

In the mid-1960s, these traditional views became challenged through social and political change, including countercultural movements, which undermined these dominant representations of national unity and continuity. Renewed attention for the atrocities committed against the Jewish population, through publications and television series, brought about a new, pluralistic view on the war, which created space for differentiating between victim groups. Consequently, 'counter monuments' dedicated to commemorating the war's violation of morality and humanity were erected throughout the Netherlands. These include the Jewish monument (Groningen, 1969), the National Monument at former concentration camp Westerbork (Westerbork, 1970), the Gypsy Monument (Amsterdam, 1978), and the Never Again Auschwitz Monument (Amsterdam, 1977).[21]

A second shift in the Dutch memorial culture of the war took place in the mid-1990s, around the 50th commemoration of the end of the war. This period has been referred to as the 1990s 'memory boom' also in other European countries. Under the influence of European integration and globalisation processes, the dominant black-and-white narrative of the war in terms of 'good' and 'evil' and of 'victims' and 'perpetrators' was abandoned in favour of monuments that carried universal messages related to human rights, freedom, and peace.[22] In addition to national memorials, throughout the post-war decades, nearly every city and village in the Netherlands created WWII monuments and commemorative sites, which are visual reminders of the many various groups and individuals who lost their lives during the German occupation.[23]

The abundance of monuments of, among other traumatic events, the North Sea Flood of 1953 and the Second World War, raises the question why the Hunger Winter has left so few visual objects of commemoration. Before suggesting possible explanations for this paradoxical absence, it is necessary to take a closer look at the few monuments of the Hunger Winter that are present in the Dutch landscape: what or who is represented, how did these monuments come into being, and what commemorative functions do they have today?

Monuments of the Dutch Hunger Winter

While they have remained largely unknown to the wider public, in the direct post-war years, five small monuments were erected which were dedicated to commemorating the Hunger Winter. Without exception, these monuments came about through local initiatives, financed privately through fundraising. Although vastly different in material form, these early post-war monuments share two common themes: relief and national solidarity, both strongly tied to Christian symbolism. As mentioned in the previous section, there was hardly any attention for individual victim groups in the immediate post-war year. The dominant political discourse emphasised shared victimhood, as this would benefit a swift reconstruction of the Dutch state and identity. As a result, these early monuments were mostly about overcoming victimhood rather than about the suffering during the famine.

The first of these Hunger Winter monuments, revealed in July 1947, was cemented into the wall of the Oosterkerk, a large Reformed church in Amsterdam. The stone relief was made by the famous Dutch sculptor Hildo Krop and financed by the 'nickels and dimes' of local inhabitants.[24] The small relief shows a male figure carrying a sack of wheat next to a boat, with a female figure and two children on the other side of the river, and was meant as a display of gratitude towards the Interdenominational Committee, which provided food aid and evacuated malnourished children during the Hunger

Winter. The rhyming accompanying text states: 'What love brought together in the year of dire distress, saved many parents and children from starvation. This monument represents the gratitude of the entire neighbourhood. Gratefulness which lasts forever in the heart of God'.[25] Around the same time, another memorial stone (undated) dedicated to famine relief efforts was cemented into a brick wall in Holwerd (Frisia), donated by inhabitants from the town of Diemen (North Holland): 'During the last winter of the Second World War, famine in Holland threatened many lives. Holwerd then opened its home and heart lovingly for our children and sent us food. This way, Frisian selflessness generosity offered invaluable help and obliged us to gratitude'. The monument was signed in stone by Diemen's mayor, two local physicians, the local head of school, reformed ministers of two Protestant denominations, and a Catholic priest, thus reinforcing the dominant post-war narrative of national unity.

Other Hunger Winter monuments from the same period similarly represent these dynamics between relief, resistance, and national unity. For example, in the small village of Lollum, in 1947, a sundial pillar made by sculptor Frits Sieger was unveiled by Nel 'the courier' in the presence of 'several authorities' and former resistance fighters.[26] The monument was commissioned by inhabitants of the Amsterdam Watergraafsmeer neighbourhood to express their gratitude for the relief offered by the Frisian resistance and population. The pillar shows the Frisian coat of arms, a pelican—the Christian symbol of self-sacrifice—and a young man with a grain shuffle surrounded by loaves of bread, symbolising food aid. Christian symbolism to commemorate the famine is also part of the Gouda (South Holland) monument 'Saint George and the Dragon' (Ludwig Oswald Wenkebach, 1948), which refers to the battle between Good and Evil: 'When the water was up to our necks, God gave us liberation'.[27] The stone relief installed on the exterior wall of a large church mentions Hunger Winter victims—'when mortality rose threefold'—together with victims from the resistance, prisons and concentration camps, bombardments of cities, and deported Jewish citizens.[28]

The memorial windows in Kamerik (Utrecht, 1955),[29] one of which is dedicated to the Hunger Winter, also demonstrate how nationalist stories of sacrifice and redemption were interwoven with Christian symbolism after the war. The stained glass window shows a boat sailing under the Frisian flag and lighthouse, signifying the light that guides the way to Christian redemption. Below is a figure of the Grim Reaper, dressed in Nazi uniform, whipping a defenseless young woman at his feet. The bottom of the window shows a man bent over his handcart in the snow with two other figures in the distance, referring to the so-called hunger journeys (*hongertochten*) as the embodiment of suffering and endurance during the famine. Indeed, the Kamerik memorial window is the only Dutch monument that conveys suffering during the Hunger Winter rather than emphasising a narrative of overcoming victimhood.

As the descriptions above demonstrate, all of these early monuments were predominantly inspired by a traditional and Christian repertoire of representations, which includes familiar tropes such as doves, lions, broken chains, flags, and olive branches, as well as Christian figures such as the Good Samaritan and the merciful mother figure. Defenseless victims cast to the ground by Nazi oppression and victorious, strong male and female figures represent the battle between good and evil and the story of national trial and resurrection.[30] These tropes show that Hunger Winter monuments were, to a large extent, 'premediated' by a familiar representative repertoire,[31] which had already been part of Dutch memorial cultural prior to the war.

As mentioned in the previous section, the interconnectedness of the troubled past with social and political aspirations—the dominant nationalistic and ideological representations in which unity and continuity prevailed—began to shift in the 1960s. New, pluralistic perspectives created space for new groups of victims in the memorialisation of the war besides resistance fighters, soldiers, and political prisoners—in particular, Jews, Roma, Sinti, and other victims of Nazi persecution. The dominant view of the war was therefore no longer in line with that of historical continuity and national resurrection. Instead, it positioned the Second World War, and the Holocaust in particular, as a definitive breaking point in history.[32] Still, during these decades in which Dutch memorial culture rapidly found new expressions, hardly any new monuments dedicated to the Hunger Winter were erected.

The two main exceptions were the monuments 'Almost Free' (1970) and 'The Courier' (1981)—the sculpture of the young woman on the bicycle mentioned in the introduction of this chapter (Image 4.1). 'Almost Free' is located in Achterveld (Gelderland), in front of a school building in which important negotiations between Dutch, Allied, and German authorities took place in April 1945. These conversations determined the terms of Allied food relief for the starving western Netherlands. The sculpture represents a young girl with a dove in her hand about to spread its wings, symbolising peace, hope, and freedom. What sets the monument apart from previous memorial objects of the Hunger Winter is that it was made by a female artist, Willy Albers Pistorius-Fokkelman. The fact that the unveiling was also done by a woman, Mrs. Beernink, wife of the Dutch minister of Internal Affairs, is indicative of changing gender relations, and perhaps even feminist agendas, in Dutch memorialisation practices in the 1970s.

The same is true for the sculpture of the young woman on the bicycle mentioned earlier (Image 4.1), which was made by artist Tineke Bot and financed anonymously by someone who had been in hiding during the war. The precise meaning of the monument remains rather ambiguous, with some calling the sculpture 'The Courier', as it allegedly expressed the important role of female couriers in the Dutch resistance, while others referred to it as 'Woman on Food Journey' or 'The Food Bringer'. Based on the earliest mentions of the monument in newspapers, the sculpture seems to have been intended to symbolise all women who ventured out to search for food during the final year of the war.[33] While the monument shows continuity with early post-war memorials in that it focuses on resistance and resilience, it significantly diverges from the previously described monuments as the only memorial object of the Hunger Winter without any obvious Christian symbolism. The fact that the statue attained a broader interpretation beyond the Hunger Winter and was scripted into the more popular resistance narrative, however, also demonstrates an important continuity with monuments of the early post-war decades.

Victims of the famine are only mentioned in two monuments dating from the period of 1955 to 1995. The first is a plaque on the outer wall of the Zuiderkerk (undated), a large Protestant church in the city centre of Amsterdam. In restrained words, the small and hardly noticeable plaque states: 'From February until August 1945 this church was the Municipal Morgue. Through deprivation, hunger and German violence more people died in Amsterdam during the final year of war then could be buried. This was their temporary resting place'. The other mention of Hunger Winter victims is on The Hague Resistance and Liberation Monument (1992). This large monument, overlooking the Peace Palace, consists of four pillars, representing four socio-denominational groups of Dutch society: Roman Catholic, Protestant, Jewish, and non-religious people. It was initiated by the Foundation for National Commemoration The Hague (*Stichting Nationale Herdenkingen 's-Gravenhage*), which consisted of former resistance fighters and representatives of the Interdenominational Committee, and designed by the well-known Jewish artist Appie Drielsma, who had been in hiding during the war as a child.[34] Although the text on the monument explicitly mentions the Hunger Winter, it remains very much grounded in the religious and political ideology that had dominated memorialisation of WWII since 1945, in the sense that it intends to commemorate *all* those who died during the war, without distinguishing between victim groups.

As in many other European countries, the mid-1990s marked a turning point in the Dutch commemoration of the war. Under the influence of European integration and globalisation processes, patriotic sentiments and Christian symbolism slowly gave way to the reconceptualisation of war experiences in relation to broader global issues of human rights, mass violence, and racism.[35] These new, globalised commemoration and memorialisation practices were reflected in new monuments connected to the Hunger Winter, which began to be focused almost exclusively on Allied relief efforts. Commemorative years proved especially important for the erection of these new Hunger Winter monuments. In particular, these monuments commemorated the Allied food drops—Operation Manna/Chowhound—which took place in the western Netherlands between 29 April and 8 May 1945 and which became symbolic for the liberation of the Netherlands.[36] Again, by focusing on relief efforts, visual representations of suffering during the famine remained notably absent.

The first of these monuments was a plaque unveiled on 30 April 1995—50 years after Operation Manna/Chowhound—at horse track Duindigt (South Holland), which was one of the designated zones for the Allied food drops. The plaque was commissioned by the 'Foundation Food and Freedom', which organised the unveiling in the presence of British and American veterans who had been involved in the actual food drops. The plaque shows two mirrored bombers releasing food parcels, accompanied by text in both Dutch and English: 'In grateful commemoration of the food drop operations, 29 April–8 May 1945'. Ten years later, on 30 April 2005, a similar plaque was unveiled in front of the town hall of Vlaardingen (South Holland), again in the presence of British and American war veterans. The plaque, entitled 'Food from heaven', as a reference to the Jewish and Christian legend of manna (Exodus 16), shows a remarkably similar image of a bomber releasing parcels. The text on the plaque briefly explains the historical background of the food drops, concluding: 'With operation "Manna", the Allies saved many lives in April and May 1945. After 60 free years, Vlaardingen says once again: "Thank you for coming!" [final sentence in English].'

The largest monument dedicated to Operation Manna—and to the Hunger Winter in general—was unveiled on 28 April 2006 by Secretary of State of Defense Cees van der Knaap. Built on top of a sound wall along the A20 highway in Rotterdam, the monument overviews the Terbregge neighbourhood, another designated zone for the food drops. The driving force behind the monument was local citizen Hendrik Dijkxhoorn, who spent eleven years gaining support for the monument through fundraising and negotiations with local administrators until finally Ruud Reutelingsperger of the artistic group Observatorium was commissioned to design it.[37] The monument is constructed from metal crash barriers, resembling the fuselage of a bomber plane, with yellow steel constructions in its hold that represent stacked parcels featuring symbols related to the food drops: bombers, houses, and windmills. Opposite the main installation is a metal column, below a flag pole, with the same yellow symbols. On the one side, the column includes a quote from one of the bomber pilots: 'For five years we spread death and destruction and in the last week we saved thousands from starving'. The other side lists all co-financers, including a neighbourhood committee, several families from the Netherlands and the USA, the local football club, the Centre of Visual Arts Rotterdam, and multiple other local foundations and companies. The footpath leading past the monument has been renamed 'Air Commodore Geddes Path', after the senior Royal Air Force officer Andrew James Wray Geddes who led Operation Manna from the British side. As such, the monument demonstrates how Hunger Winter memorials function as connecting vectors between local, national, and transnational commemorations of the war.

The same can be said of a small plaque on the IJssel bridge (2005), which connects the cities of Hattem (Gelderland) and Zwolle (Overijssel). The bridge was an important crossing for people from the western Netherlands who ventured into the northeast of the country in search of food during the Hunger Winter. The commemorative functions of the bridge since 2005—aptly renamed 'Bridge between fear and hope'—are, however, much more layered than the simple and sober commemorative plaque suggests. In 2007, a local commemoration committee organised a 'hunger journey' with veterans and famine survivors from various countries who walked from Rotterdam to Zwolle in multiple legs of 25 kilometres to commemorate the suffering during the Hunger Winter. Nowadays, the bridge is part of the bicycle route 'Oorlogswinter', named after the famous children's book by Jan Terlouw. These commemorative performances show the inherent fluidity of famine memory, travelling beyond time and space.[38]

Another monument that manages to combine different levels of commemoration is 'Manna' (2020) in Amsterdam, a pop art memorial object designed by Dutch-Israeli sculptor and graphic designer Ram Katzir (Image 4.2). The

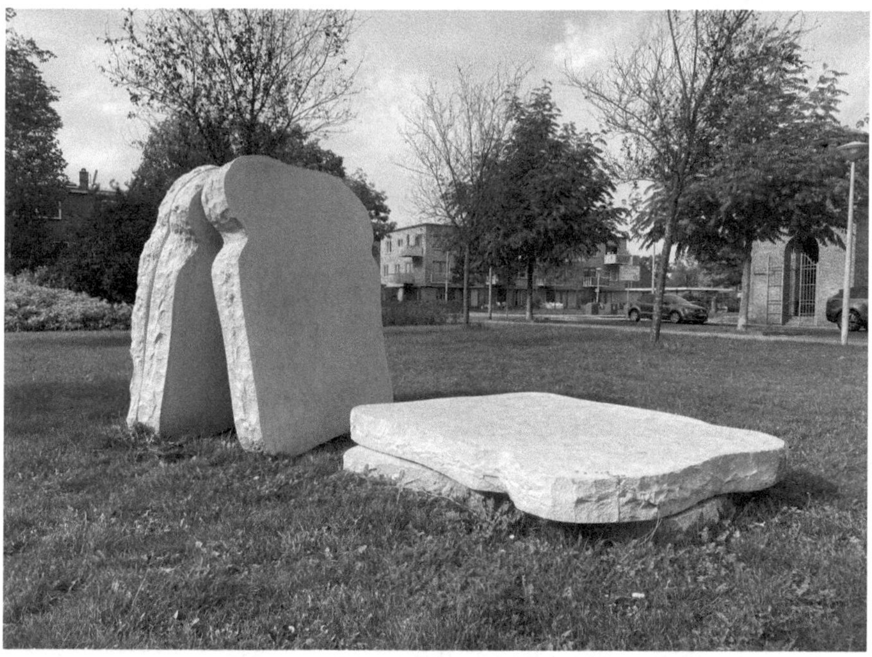

IMAGE 4.2 'Manna' by Ram Katzir (2020), Amsterdam. Photograph by Ingrid de Zwarte.

artwork consists of five large slices of white bread, three standing up and two laid down, and is situated in a public park. The name refers to Operation Manna, while the artwork itself symbolises the Swedish white bread that was baked using Swedish Red Cross relief shipments during the Hunger Winter (and thus not from Allied relief).[39] Official photographs of the artwork show children playing between and on top of the bread slices, turning it into an active performative object. Katzir's design was selected by the municipality and local residents because it expressed 'gratitude' and 'commemoration', while potentially becoming a connecting factor in the multicultural neighbourhood Sloterdijk: 'Bread plays an important role in multiple cultures and brings people together. The artwork is designed as a meeting place for the neighbourhood'.[40] To facilitate cultural exchange, the municipality of Amsterdam intends to organise near the monument one of its many annual 'freedom meals', part of the 5 May Celebration, 'where people can bring food from their own culture to share with each other'.[41]

With 'Manna', we see how the effects of globalisation and migration make Dutch famine heritage part of a 'global memory culture'.[42] At the same time, 'Manna' is the first Hunger Winter monument that functions 'multidirectionally',[43] by placing the Dutch famine in dialogue with other events. In this case, these are the possibly manifold hunger experiences of migrant newcomers in the Netherlands. As such, 'Manna' can be seen as an attempt to 'bridge the gap between famine legacies and today's communities in multicultural societies', and is a good example of how 'famine monuments can be inclusive of new groups of Europeans in heritage practices', including migrants and refugees.[44]

In an entirely different way, the significance of the famine past for the social and political present also became evident through a temporary Hunger Winter monument: the 'Ferry-pontoon bridge' across the River IJ in Amsterdam (2015–16), constructed to commemorate the seventieth anniversary of the original bridge. It was commissioned by the municipality of Amsterdam and designed by its 4–5 May Commemoration Committee, which, unfortunately, produced several persistent myths about the bridge, suggesting that it was the 'last lifeline' for people during the Hunger Winter searching for food: 'Many did not survive the harsh cold during this journey'.[45] However, the bridge opened in April 1945, after the winter, and not to facilitate the hunger journeys but as a practical solution for the fuel shortage that prevented ferries from running.[46] In part, these misconceptions seem to have resulted from memory politics: probably not incidentally, the temporary monument coincided with the presentations of plans by the municipality to open a permanent bridge across the River IJ, thus showing the politically mediated nature of the famine past in the present.

Although we can see a clear shift after the 1990s memory boom from a local to a global orientation in famine monuments, some recent monuments demonstrate continuity with early post-war memorialisation practices. For example, in 2017, former child evacuee Dirk van Reenen initiated the planting of a commemorative tree in Ruinen (Drenthe) to commemorate local efforts to foster malnourished children from the western Netherlands. Similarly, in 2021, football players from Ajax (Amsterdam) offered a plaque to football club VV Heerenveen to commemorate the aid they supplied, evacuating 12- to 14-year-old football players from Ajax and fostering them in Frisia during the Hunger Winter.[47]

The still highly localised commemorative function of Hunger Winter monuments is also demonstrated by the fact that, from 2010 onwards, many were 'adopted' by local primary schools, which symbolically take care of these monuments, as a way to connect new generations with the war experience. Furthermore, many of these monuments function as memorial sites for the annual Remembrance of the Dead on 4 May, as is, for example, the case with the monuments in Lollum, Gouda, Rotterdam, and The Hague. A national famine monument remains absent in the Dutch memorial landscape until today.

Explaining relative absence

Although there are clearly some physical traces of the Hunger Winter left in the Dutch memorial landscape, these stand in stark contrast to the numerous visual objects of, for example, the Great Irish Famine and the Ukrainian Holodomor. Why is this the case? Part of the answer to this question may lie in the difficulty of representing hunger and famine through monuments. Contrary to floods, famines are longer term disasters, making it more difficult to represent them in a single shape or form: there is often no clear beginning, middle, or end, nor are there specific geographical locations associated with famines. Famines are so-called slow-onset disasters, silent killers, which emerge gradually over time and with long-lasting social consequences. In this respect, the 'plot' is far more complicated than is the case with floods, where the narrative pattern is instantly 'ready to use' and entails identified individual victims, survivors, and known heroes and heroines.[48]

Furthermore, as has been explained earlier, there had previously not been a tradition of memorialising historical famines in the Netherlands. This can be understood in terms of what Ann Rigney has referred to as 'representational scarcity', in this case, the limited cultural forms at our disposal for remembering famines.[49] Rigney has also referred to this scarcity in the context of 'differential memorability', meaning that 'not all events are equally memorable because they do not equally lend themselves to the scarce number of cultural forms we have for talking about them'.[50]

However, representational scarcity fails to explain why other countries did manage to find representational forms to commemorate famines. Most notably, the trope of female and child victims has become globally connected to what Margaret Kelleher calls the 'inexpressible reality of famine', as women and children are 'figures that already occupy an ambiguous boundary between culture and nature'.[51] These female and child figures 'not only furnish easier objects for compassion and pity but may also seem to secure an a priori distance from the cultivated spectator'.[52] As such images can easily travel beyond their national contexts, mother and child victims are perhaps the most frequently used representative forms for famine monuments across the world.[53] Thus, while representational scarcity may help explain why hardly any famine monuments were erected in the Netherlands in the early post-war decades, it fails to explain why none were developed after the 1990s 'memory boom', which did witness a sharp increase in monuments of, for example, the Great Irish Famine.

A second part of the explanation seems to be connected to Dutch post-war memory politics. As mentioned, after the war, the political and social climate in the war-torn Netherlands focused on the restoration of national unity. Some parallels can be drawn with famine memory politics surrounding the Siege of Leningrad. As Lisa Kirschenbaum explains, monuments of the Siege only commemorated resistance and the collective heroism of those who survived the blockade, thus perpetuating the image of a united Soviet people rather than allowing space for victimhood and personal trauma suffered during the famine.[54] The main difference between both cases is, of course, that the Dutch famine was not 'silenced' in any way but found manifold expressions in media, museums, and educational practices, which allowed space for personal stories of trauma and victimhood.

In this sense, the Dutch case seems to fit with Andrew Newby's call for nuancing the alleged 'silencing' of the Great Finnish Famine of the 1860s. In Finland as well, large national monuments are absent, while the famine is commemorated locally with a wide variety of relatively small famine memorials and is also covered in popular writing and children's books. Newby therefore proposes a shift from the concept of 'amnesia' to the idea of 'relative silence'.[55] He explains the absence of national Finnish famine monuments by stressing that the Finnish government, albeit officially under Russian rule, had a high degree of self-governance and was therefore responsible for its own economic and political administration during the famine. This made it inconvenient to stress national trauma resulting from famine, as this could interfere with national identity formation.[56] Similar observations about the inconvenience of stressing national trauma and suffering because of famine can be made for the Spanish Hunger Years (1939–52), which took place under Franco's regime and was not only suppressed top-down as a result of political oppression and censorship but also did not serve as a unifying story after Franco's death because it was accompanied by feelings of shame. Rather than dwelling on the past, old

Francoist parties and a new generation of politicians sought to work towards rebuilding the future.[57]

Some of these factors explaining absence and 'silence', or 'relative silence', related to the Finnish and Spanish famines can also be connected to the Dutch case, in particular the focus on national unity and progression towards the future instead of dwelling on the past. However, there is one vital difference: in the Netherlands, there was no political inconvenience in remembering the famine. On the contrary, already shortly after the war, the Hunger Winter became a symbol for the national suffering among all Dutch people throughout the occupation years 1940–45.[58] Instead of enforced forgetting, remembering the Hunger Winter through monuments could have potentially served an important role in nation-building processes in Dutch post-WWII society.

That is why we argue that there is one final variable that helps explain the relative absence of famine monuments in the Dutch public space while being abundantly present in other forms of memorialisation, namely the absence of engaged diasporic communities. Previous studies convincingly show that diasporic communities have played a crucial role in transmitting and instigating European famine heritage.[59] As Mark-FitzGerald has argued in her study of famine monuments in both Ireland and North America, memorialisation of the Great Irish Famine even became a 'foundational myth of immigrant nations', mythologising the 'emigrant experience'.[60] The significance of diasporic communities is also demonstrated by the physical erection of Ukrainian famine heritage, both in the form of financing monuments as well as by developing famine education.[61] The Netherlands, by contrast, does not have such strong ties with diasporic communities related to the Dutch Hunger Winter. Combined with the absence of a tradition of famine memorialisation and a disengaged Dutch state when it comes to commissioning monuments, this most likely explains why there are no national monuments to the Hunger Winter, while local famine monuments remain largely unknown to the wider public.

Concluding remarks

The few Hunger Winter monuments that have been erected after 1945 all reflect contemporary societal preoccupations and changing memorial practices of the war. While early monuments were inspired by Christian tradition and reinforced the opposition between good and evil forces, religious symbolism gradually disappeared from the 1960s onwards. Instead, following broader societal and political processes, more room was created for the role of women and Allied relief efforts during the famine. The most recent monuments combine different levels of local, national, and transnational commemoration and respond to broader issues, such as globalisation and migration. Significantly, almost all Dutch famine monuments are about overcoming victimhood rather than suffering, which is very different from the material memorialisation of other European famines.

Explaining the relative absence of famine monuments in the Netherlands requires a long-term cultural-historical and comparative international perspective. History shows that the shaping of a Dutch national self-image has been primarily focused on memorialising flood disasters and wars, while a tradition of commemorating famines was notably absent. Furthermore, the Dutch state has traditionally never been involved in commissioning monuments, leaving their erection largely to private initiatives and local fundraising. This, in combination with post-war memory politics, which focused on the restoration of national unity and the absence of engaged diasporic communities, likely explains the relative absence of monuments from the Dutch Hunger Winter and may also help explain the presence and absence of memorialisation in other comparative famine contexts.

Notes

1 The unveiling of the monument, which was donated by an anonymous person to the city's council and made by the artist Tineke Bot, is described in *Leeuwarder Courant* (4 May 1981).
2 See the different interpretations in *Leeuwarder Courant* (4 May 1981), *Trouw* (12 August 1982) and *De Telegraaf* (12 August 1982).
3 See Ingrid de Zwarte, *The Hunger Winter: Fighting Famine in the Occupied Netherlands, 1944–1945* (Cambridge: Cambridge University Press, 2020).
4 The Canon of the Netherlands is used in primary and secondary schools. See *De Canon van Nederland. Vijftig vernieuwde vensters voor onze tijd* (Amsterdam: Amsterdam University Press, 2020), 93. See also https://www.canonvannederland.nl/en/tweedewereldoorlog, last consulted 2 September 2022.
5 James Young, *The Texture of Memory: Holocaust Memorials and Meanings* (New Haven: Yale University Press, 1993), 4. According to Young, the memorial encompasses the entire field of commemorative forms and practices that also include the monument, making monuments into a 'subset of memorials', while a memorial 'may be a day, a conference, a space, but it need not be a monument'. Ibid.
6 See Emily Mark-FitzGerald, *Commemorating the Irish Famine: Memory and the Monument* (Liverpool: Liverpool University Press, 2013); Wiktoria Kudela-Swiatek, *Eternal Memory: Monuments and Memorials of the Holodomor* (Toronto: Canadian Institute for Ukrainian Studies, 2021).
7 An inventory of the monuments of the North Sea Flood of 1953 was made by Marijke van Hamelsveld, Piet van der Have, Simon van der Haagen. See *De monumenten van de watersnood 1953. Supplement.* (Ouwerkerk: Watersnoodmuseum, 2010), and the supplement: Marijke van Hamelsveld, Piet van der Have, Simon van der Haagen, *De monumenten van de watersnood 1953* (Ouwerkerk: Watersnoodmuseum, 2016).
8 See the inventory on: https://www.4en5mei.nl/oorlogsmonumenten.
9 See, for example, Jan Assmann, 'Collective Memory and Cultural Identity', *New German Critique* 65 (1995): 125–33; and Aleida Assmann, 'Four Formats of Memory: From Individual to Collective Constructions of the Past', in Christian Emden and David Migley, eds., *Cultural Memory and Historical Consciousness in the German-Speaking World Since 1500* (Oxford: Peter Lang, 2004), 19–37.

10 Jay Winter, 'The performance of the past: Memory history, identity', in Karin Tilmans, Frank van Vree, Jay Winter, eds., *Performing the Past: Memory, History and Identity in Modern Europe* (Amsterdam: Amsterdam University Press, 2010), 11–23.
11 Lotte Jensen, Joep Leerssen and Marita Mathijsen, eds., *Free Access to the Past. Romanticism, Cultural Heritage and the Nation* (Leiden and Boston: Brill 2010). The shaping of national self-images by celebrating the past had older roots. See Lotte Jensen, ed., *The Roots of Nationalism: National Identity Formation in Early Modern Europe, 1600–1815* (Amsterdam: Amsterdam University Press, 2016).
12 'L'essence d'une nation est que tous les individus aient beaucoup de choses en commun, et aussi que tous aient oublié bien des choses'. Ernest Renan, *Qu'est-ce q'une nation?* (Paris: Ancienne Maison Michel Lévy Frères, 1882), 3. The translation used here is by Ethan Rundell, accessed at http://ucparis.fr/files/9313/6549/9943/What_is_a_Nation.pdf.
13 Lotte Jensen, *De verheerlijking van het verleden: Helden, literatuur en natievorming in de negentiende eeuw* (Nijmegen: Vantilt, 2008). This glorifying of the national past emerged in the seventeenth century. See Lotte Jensen, *Celebrating Peace. The Emergence of Dutch Identity, 1648–1815* (Nijmegen: Vantilt, 2017).
14 Marita Mathijsen, *Historiezucht. De obsessie met het verleden in de negentiende eeuw* (Nijmegen: Vantilt, 2013), 390–2.
15 Exceptions to this rule are, notably, two monuments of persons who played an important role in the colonial past as governor-general of the Dutch East Indies: J.P. Coen (1587–1629, realised in 1893) and J.B. van Heutz (1851–1924, realised in 1935). See *Het Vaderland* 25 (1893): 96; and see Vilan van de Loo, '"Tot het einde toe op den ingeslagen weg blijven voortgaan": Het testosteronproza van generaal J.B. van Heutz', *Indische letteren* 33 (2018): 405–16.
16 Daniel Curtis et al., 'Low Countries', in Guido Alfani and Cormac Ó Gráda, eds., *Famine in European History* (Cambridge: Cambridge University Press, 2017), 123–33.
17 Lotte Jensen, *Water: A Dutch Cultural History* (NIjmegen: Radboud University Press, 2024).
18 Ibid., 233–7.
19 The concept 'grand narrative' was developed by Jean-François Lyotard in *La condition postmoderne: rapport sur le savoir* (Paris: Menuit, 1979).
20 Frank van Vree, 'De dynamiek van de herinnering: Nederland en de Tweede Wereldoorlog in een internationale context', in Frank van Vree and Rob van der Laarse, eds., *De dynamiek van de herinnering: Nederland en de Tweede Wereldoorlog in een internationale context* (Amsterdam: Bakker: 2009), 21–2.
21 Ibid., 32–7.
22 Ibid., 39–40.
23 For a complete overview of all Dutch monuments of the Second World War, see: https://www.4en5mei.nl/oorlogsmonumenten, last consulted 2 September 2022.
24 *Weekblad Kerknieuws* (5 July 1947). For more on food relief and child evacuations during the Hunger Winter, see Ingrid de Zwarte, 'Coordinating Hunger: The Evacuation of Children during the Dutch Food Crisis, 1945', *War & Society* 35, no. 2 (2016): 132–49; And Ingrid de Zwarte, 'Fighting Vulnerability: Child Feeding Initiatives during the Dutch Hunger Winter', in Tatjana Tönsmeyer et al., eds., *Coping with Hunger and Shortage under German Occupation in World War II* (London: Palgrave Macmillan, 2018), 293–310.
25 All translation of Dutch quotes are ours.
26 *Friesch Dagblad* (20 November 1947).
27 'Toen het water tot de lippen was gerezen gaf God ons de bevrijding'.

28 Already in late May 1945, the church's minister Dubois and Gouda's mayor had decided that a future war monument should commemorate 'all those who had fallen' during the war, asking for donations in August of that year. See *De Vrije Pers* (31 May 1945); *Trouw* (15 August 1945).
29 *Het Parool* (24 September 1955).
30 Van Vree, 'De dynamiek van de herinnering', 24–5.
31 Ann Rigney, 'Plenitude, Scarcity and the Circulation of Cultural Memory', *Journal of European Studies* 35, no. 1 (2005): 15; Astrid Erll, 'Remembering across Time, Space, and Cultures: Premediation, Remediation and the 'Indian Mutiny'', in Astrid Erll and Ann Rigney, eds., *Mediation, Remediation and the Dynamics of Cultural Memory* (New York: Walter de Gruyter, 2009), 109–38.
32 Van Vree, 'De dynamiek van de herinnering', 32–4.
33 *Leeuwarder Courant* (4 May 1981); (10 August 1982); (12 August 1982); (2 May 1986).
34 *Limburgs Dagblad* (6 July 1991). Drielsma, among other things, also designed the Mauthausen Monument (1986).
35 Van Vree, 'De dynamiek van de herinnering', 39–40.
36 De Zwarte, *The Hunger Winter*, 141–56.
37 *Reformatorisch Dagblad* (28 April 2006).
38 Astrid Erll, 'From "district six" to district 9 and back: The plurimedial production of travelling schemata', in Chiara de Cesari and Ann Rigney, *Transnational Memory: Circulation, Articulation, Scales* (Berlin and New York: Walter de Gruyter, 2014), 29–50.
39 *Het Parool* (6 July 2020).
40 Ibid.
41 Ibid.
42 Mark-Fitzgerald, *Commemorating the Irish Famine*, 155.
43 Michael Rothberg, *Multidirectional Memory: Recollecting the Holocaust in the Age of Decolonization* (Stanford: Stanford University Press, 2009), 7.
44 Mark-FitzGerald, *Commemorating the Irish Famine*, 213; Marguérite Corporaal and Ingrid de Zwarte, 'Heritages of hunger: European famine legacies in current academic debates', *International Journal of Heritage Studies* 28, no. 1 (2022): 41.
45 *Het Parool* (7 March 2015); (2 April 2015).
46 Ingrid de Zwarte, 'Brug over het IJ speelde geen rol in Hongerwinter', *Het Parool* (22 April 2015).
47 The initiative came from Janneke Lenstra, daughter of Frisian football hero Abe Lenstra, who also fostered and trained evacuated children during the famine. See *Het Parool* (16 October 2021).
48 Lotte Jensen, 'Floods as shapers of Dutch cultural identity: Media, theories, practices', *Water History* 13, no. 2 (2021) 217–33.
49 Rigney, 'Plenitude, scarcity and the circulation of cultural memory', 16.
50 Ann Rigney, 'Remembering Hope: Transnational Activism beyond the Traumatic', *Memory Studies* 11, no. 3 (2018): 371.
51 See Margaret Kelleher, *The Feminization of Famine: Expressions of the Inexpressible?* (Durham: Duke University Press, 1997).
52 David Lloyd, 'The Indigent Sublime: Specters of Irish famine', *Representations* 92, no. 1 (2005): 163.
53 See Erll, 'The plurimedial production of travelling schemata'.
54 Lisa Kirschenbaum, *The Legacy of the Siege of Leningrad, 1941-1995: Myth, Memories, and Monuments* (Cambridge: Cambridge University Press, 2006), 113–50.
55 Andrew Newby, 'Finland's 'Great Hunger Years' Memorials: A Sesquicentennial Report', *Collegium* 22 (2016): 173–214.
56 Ibid., 178.

57 Miguel Ángel del Arco Blanco and Peter Anderson, 'Introduction: Famine, Not Hunger?' in *Franco's Famine: Malnutrition, Disease and Starvation in Post-Civil War Spain*, (London: Bloomsbury, 2022), 2–5; Claudio Hernández Bugos and Gloria Román Ruiz, 'Remembering the Spanish Famine: Official Discourse and the Popular Memory of Hunger during Francoism', in Miguel Ángel del Arco Blanco and Peter Anderson, eds., *Franco's Famine: Malnutrition, Disease and Starvation in Post-Civil War Spain* (London: Bloomsbury, 2022), 205–24.
58 De Zwarte, *The Hunger Winter*, 257.
59 Corporaal and De Zwarte, 'Heritages of Hunger', 35–6.
60 Mark-Fitzgerald, *Commemorating the Irish Famine*, 275.
61 See Kudela-Swiatek, *Eternal Memory*; educational materials have been developed by the Holodomor Research and Education Consortium.

References

Assmann, Aleida, 'Four Formats of Memory: From Individual to Collective Constructions of the Past'. In Christian Emden and David Migley, eds., *Cultural Memory and Historical Consciousness in the German-Speaking World Since 1500*, 19–37. Oxford: Peter Lang, 2004.

Assmann, Jan, 'Collective Memory and Cultural Identity'. *New German Critique* 65 (1995): 125–33.

Arco Blanco, Miguel Ángel del and Peter Anderson, 'Introduction: Famine, not Hunger?' In *Franco's Famine: Malnutrition, Disease and Starvation in Post-Civil War Spain*, 1–18. London: Bloomsbury, 2022.

Corporaal, Marguérite and Ingrid de Zwarte, 'Heritages of Hunger: European Famine Legacies in Current Academic Debates'. *International Journal of Heritage Studies* 28, no. 1 (2022): 30–43.

De Canon van Nederland. Vijftig vernieuwde vensters voor onze tijd. Amsterdam: Amsterdam University Press, 2020.

Curtis, Daniel, et al., 'Low Countries'. In Guido Alfani and Cormac Ó Gráda, eds., *Famine in European History*, 123–33. Cambridge: Cambridge University Press, 2017.

Erll, Astrid and Ann Rigney, eds., *Mediation, Remediation and the Dynamics of Cultural Memory*, 109–38. New York: Walter de Gruyter, 2009.

Erll, Astrid, 'From "District Six" to District 9 and Back: The Plurimedial Production of Travelling Schemata'. In Chiara de Cesari and Ann Rigney, eds., *Transnational Memory: Circulation, Articulation, Scales*, 29–50. Berlin and New York: Walter de Gruyter, 2014.

Hamelsveld, Marijke van, Piet van der Have, Simon van der Haagen, *De monumenten van de watersnood 1953*. Ouwerkerk: Watersnoodmuseum, 2010.

Hamelsveld, Marijke van, Piet van der Have, Simon van der Haagen, *De monumenten van de watersnood 1953. Supplement*. Ouwerkerk: Watersnoodmuseum, 2016.

Hernández Bugos, Claudio and Gloria Román Ruiz, 'Remembering the Spanish Famine: Official Discourse and the Popular Memory of Hunger during Francoism'. In Miguel Ángel del Arco Blanco and Peter Anderson, eds., *Franco's Famine: Malnutrition, Disease and Starvation in Post-Civil War Spain*, 205–24. London: Bloomsbury, 2022.

Jensen, Lotte, *De verheerlijking van het verleden: Helden, literatuur en natievorming in de negentiende eeuw*. Nijmegen: Vantilt, 2008.

Jensen, Lotte, ed., *The Roots of Nationalism: National Identity Formation in Early Modern Europe, 1600–1815*. Amsterdam: Amsterdam University Press, 2016.

Jensen, Lotte, *Celebrating Peace. The Emergence of Dutch Identity, 1648–1815*. Nijmegen: Vantilt, 2017.

Jensen, Lotte, 'Floods as Shapers of Dutch Cultural Identity: Media, Theories, Practices'. *Water History* 13, no. 2 (2021): 217–33.
Jensen, Lotte, *Water: A Dutch Cultural History*. Nijmegen: Radboud University Press, 2024.
Jensen, Lotte, Joep Leerssen and Marita Mathijsen, eds., *Free Access to the Past. Romanticism, Cultural Heritage and the Nation*. Leiden and Boston: Brill 2010.
Kelleher, Margaret, *The Feminization of Famine: Expressions of the Inexpressible?*. Durham: Duke University Press, 1997.
Kirschenbaum, Lisa, *The Legacy of the Siege of Leningrad, 1941–1995: Myth, Memories, and Monuments*. Cambridge: Cambridge University Press, 2006.
Kudela-Swiatek, Wiktoria, *Eternal Memory: Monuments and Memorials of the Holodomor*. Toronto: Canadian Institute for Ukrainian Studies, 2021.
Lloyd, David, 'The Indigent Sublime: Specters of Irish famine', *Representations* 92, no. 1 (2005): 152–85.
Loo, Vilan van de, '"Tot het einde toe op den ingeslagen weg blijven voortgaan": Het testosteronproza van generaal J.B. van Heutz'. *Indische letteren* 33 (2018): 405–16.
Lyotard, Jean-François, *La condition postmoderne: rapport sur le savoir*. Paris: Menuit, 1979.
Mark-FitzGerald, Emily, *Commemorating the Irish Famine: Memory and the Monument*. Liverpool: Liverpool University Press, 2013.
Mathijsen, Marita, *Historiezucht. De obsessie met het verleden in de negentiende eeuw*. Nijmegen: Vantilt, 2013.
Newby, Andrew, "Finland's 'Great Hunger Years' Memorials: A Sesquicentennial Report." *Collegium* 22 (2016): 173–214.
Renan, Ernest, *Qu'est-ce q'une nation?* Paris: Ancienne Maison Michel Lévy Frères, 1882.
Rigney, Ann, 'Plenitude, Scarcity and the Circulation of Cultural Memory'. *Journal of European Studies* 35, no. 1 (2005): 11–28.
Rigney, Ann, 'Remembering Hope: Transnational Activism beyond the Traumatic'. *Memory Studies* 11, no. 3 (2018): 368–80.
Rothberg, Michael, *Multidirectional Memory: Recollecting the Holocaust in the Age of Decolonization*. Stanford: Stanford University Press, 2009.
Vree, Frank van, 'De dynamiek van de herinnering: Nederland en de Tweede Wereldoorlog in een internationale context'. In Frank van Vree and Rob van der Laarse, eds, *De dynamiek van de herinnering: Nederland en de Tweede Wereldoorlog in een internationale context*, 17–40. Amsterdam: Bakker: 2009.
Winter, Jay, 'The Performance of the Past: Memory History, Identity'. In Karin Tilmans, Frank van Vree, Jay Winter, eds., *Performing the Past: Memory, History and Identity in Modern Europe*, 11–23. Amsterdam: Amsterdam University Press, 2010.
Young, James, *The Texture of Memory: Holocaust Memorials and Meanings*. New Haven: Yale University Press, 1993.
Zwarte, Ingrid de, 'Coordinating Hunger: The Evacuation of Children during the Dutch Food Crisis, 1945'. *War & Society* 35, no. 2 (2016): 132–49.
Zwarte, Ingrid de, 'Brug over het IJ speelde geen rol in Hongerwinter' *Het Parool* (22 April 2015).
Zwarte, Ingrid de, 'Fighting Vulnerability: Child Feeding Initiatives during the Dutch Hunger Winter'. In Tatjana Tönsmeyer et al., eds., *Coping with Hunger and Shortage under German Occupation in World War II*, 293–310. London: Palgrave Macmillan, 2018.
Zwarte, Ingrid de, *The Hunger Winter: Fighting Famine in the Occupied Netherlands, 1944–1945*. Cambridge: Cambridge University Press, 2020.

5

'WE WENT THROUGH A LOT THAT ... CANNOT BE DISCUSSED, CANNOT BE WRITTEN'[1]

Remembering the Greek Famine of the early 1940s

Violetta Hionidou

There has been a slowly growing literature on European famine memory.[2] This chapter investigates the memory of the Greek Famine of the early 1940s within Greece, a less researched case study. Greece was occupied in April 1941 by Germany and soon after by Italy and Bulgaria. Different parts of the country were allocated to each of the occupying forces. A serious food crisis started soon after the occupation, if not before, and the winter of 1941–42 saw a full-blown famine with widespread increased mortality.[3]

The famine had attracted limited interest, and the official collective narrative of its causes attributed almost all responsibility for its outbreak to the Axis occupation.[4] During the years of occupation, the responsibility for the food crisis was attributed to—among other reasons—the black-marketers, an interpretation that suited all parties. Thus, the Greek occupation government of Athens transferred its inability to contain the situation to some rogue individuals. The occupation forces transferred any responsibility to members of the Greek population. At the same time, EAM (National Liberation Front)—the main, communist-led resistance organisation—framed the black-marketers as collaborators and self-interested enemies of the starving population.[5]

This chapter ascertains three strands of Greek famine memory: the national official historical narrative which has become the national collective memory (thereafter referred to mostly as official collective memory), the local, and the individual. These strands are distinct, though overlapping, and, at times, very different from one another. The soft 'silence' identified as prevalent at the national level between 1950 and 2009, changed with the start of the Greek economic crisis in the same year.[6]

DOI: 10.4324/9781003391524-8

The chapter therefore will also address the re-affirmation of the official collective narrative and its use in the public discourse since 2009, both of which consolidated the identification of Germany as bearing the prime responsibility for the famine. In fact, the occupation—and famine—came back into focus because of the crisis, and Germany's perceived responsibility for the crisis further enhanced the official collective memory, sometimes at the expense of individual ones.

The famine and its memory

During Greece's hunger crisis, local variations were very important, with neighbouring areas having different experiences of the crisis, as indeed were the experiences of the members of the various classes.[7] For example, the food crisis turned into famine on Mykonos when the pre-war mortality increased nine-fold from November 1941 to June 1942. In neighbouring Syros, the famine lasted significantly longer, from August 1941 to December 1942, with a six-fold increase occurring in this period.[8] Moreover, on Syros, there was a secondary famine of a lesser magnitude from January to July 1944. In such cases, not only did the experiences of individual communities vary significantly, but also those of individuals within the same community. Such differences were due to many reasons, for example, whether a family had access to land, whether the individual was a civil servant (which usually meant a guaranteed monetary income and privileged access to any available food), whether an individual had access to tangible wealth that would be exchanged for food, or whether the individual's occupation offered them access to food (e.g., bakery workers).[9]

As in all famines, the causes are confounded. Food availability declined immediately upon the occupation, if not before, partly because food was hoarded by everyone on the expectation of a food crisis. A naval blockade was imposed by the Allies, and therefore no food imports could be made. Stored foodstuffs were confiscated by the German authorities. The country was broken down into small units, and movement of food was strictly prohibited from place to place. The central government imposed strict regulation of food prices though it was impossible to actually enforce the regulations, and therefore, the black market dominated the markets throughout the years of occupation.[10] But despite the severity of the famine, the perseverance of the food crisis throughout the years of occupation and its gradual embracing of all aspects of life and all social classes and regions of Greece, historiography in the pre-crisis years presented the famine as a rather peripheral theme, certainly in comparison to the themes of resistance, civil war, and foreign intervention.

Up until 2009, the widely accepted official narrative was short and poignant, outlining why the famine happened (due to the occupation), who bore responsibility for it (the Germans) and who suffered the most (particularly the Athenians in 1941–42).[11] While during and immediately after the end of the occupation, the Italians were also imputed with some responsibility for the famine; by 1949, this was almost exclusively attributed to the Germans.[12] This became the official collective memory and was never disputed in public thereafter. It has been regularly rekindled at and around the annual national anniversary of the start of the Second World War (WWII) for Greece on 28 October, firmly embedding this narrative into the collective memory of young and old. However, public speeches and commemorative services that took place around that date referred to the occupation in general and not to the famine specifically. It would be the media that would refer, occasionally and usually in passing, to the famine, repeating the official collective narrative.

This 'official' history of the immediate post-war years was shaped and maintained by the governing Right and, sometimes, ultra-Right with little room left for dialogue up until the mid-1970s.[13] In the 1980s and in reference to the redefined resistance—by the then Socialist Prime Minister Andreas Papandreou—the official history of the occupation years was reshaped, aiming at 'reconciliation'.[14] The Left did not challenge the official collective memory of the famine at any point in time. However, the Left claimed for itself aspects of the famine, such as the virtually exclusive 'background' running of the soup kitchens in Athens/Piraeus.[15] This resistance-influenced false memory has been included in the national curriculum since the mid-1980s and subsequently absorbed into national and individual understandings of the famine, especially by the younger generations.[16]

The lack of contention between Left and Right in apportioning the blame for the famine exclusively to the Germans, at a time when Left and Right did not concede in much else, may explain to a degree the lack of discourse or any public discussions on the famine prior to 2000. In 2006 and 2009, two public exhibitions took place in Athens focusing wholly or partially on the famine. Both utilised rich visual material such as photographs and a film.[17] Both refrained from offering explicit commentary on the famine. While neither had an ideological stance, both largely reproduced the official collective memory as they focused on Athens in 1941–42. As these exhibitions happened before the financial crisis, both referred to the occupation but did not explicitly attribute responsibility to anyone.

The official collective memory has been annually re-iterated and frequently reproduced in popular culture.[18] This top-down-formulated official collective memory softly imposed a culture of 'silence' onto those who had their own firsthand memories. The silence did not mean forgetting. The famine's extraordinary importance in the people's psyche tentatively surfaces when someone comes to realise that the word *Katohe* (literally meaning occupation) for Greeks has come to be equated with hunger and extreme living conditions.

Local memory

The unifying holistic (hi)story of the famine coming from above sharply contrasts the multiplicity and variability of local famine (hi)stories. Such multiplicities are the result of numerous factors: the plurality of occupying forces; the varying agendas of each occupying force from place to place; the different practices and reactions of the local authorities; the isolation of the localities due to the lack of transport and the restrictions in movement; and the level of local food production, to name a few.[19] Comparing, for example, the famine memory on the islands of Hios and Syros, it was established that one of the strongest memories on Hios was the departure of a large number of the population to Turkey in order to escape the famine.[20] This was remembered by all who experienced the famine, both those who left and those who stayed, simply because it changed life for all, thus shaping their memory of the famine.[21] On Syros, where there was a long-standing antagonism between Greek Catholics and Orthodox islanders, all remembrance of the famine was centred around that relationship. For example, while the common motive throughout Greece was that urbanites were stealing produce from the peasants and were punished when caught, on Syros, this was interpreted as the Greek-Catholic peasants being unusually cruel to the Orthodox urbanites. Again on Syros, the number of deaths was hugely exaggerated in the memorial that was erected in 1984, and that was dedicated to the dead of the famine, claiming that 8,000 people died in (Orthodox) Hermoupolis, more than double the number that in fact did.[22] This, not noticeable to outsiders but obvious to locals, proportionately diminishes the famine death toll number of the Catholics.[23]

In comparing the two localities of Hios and Syros, it becomes clear that while both communities reacted to similar events in a similar manner, the local collective memories were shaped quite differently between the two.[24] They were shaped around the pre-famine past of each locality and independently of the national historical representation, which has not addressed issues that lie outside its main preoccupations. Thus, the local, long-standing religious rivalry on Syros proved very significant in shaping the local memory there and hence produced diverging ways of 'remembering' the same theme among the populations on Hios and Hermoupolis. This conclusion does not preclude that the remembering may well have been 'real' in both cases. That is, the acclaimed 'cruelty' shown at the time by the Catholic farmers may have been such because of the rivalry of the two religious groups, though there is evidence that they were also 'cruel' to Catholic 'thieves'.[25] Still, judging from all the sources consulted, especially the oral histories, it looks much more probable that the situation was similar at the time of the famine between Hios and Syros in terms of thefts and punishments.[26] What seems to differ is the subsequent local interpretation of the past.

Individual memories and everyday memory

For those who experienced the famine as adolescents or adults, beyond the local collective memory, there were a rich variety of individual memories. These were articulated during the interviews conducted by the author in 1999–2000, when the famine had not yet been publicly discussed to a significant extent. Individual memories articulated the everyday 'non-significant' issues that were not necessary to process in the public sphere. The autonomous existence of these individual memories speaks to the enormous significance and tremendous consequences that these personal experiences had for those who lived through this period. On a personal level, the famine was a significant traumatic event.[27]

> My wife's siblings died of hunger … they were wasted slowly slowly slowly slowly, her father … her brother and her two sisters died of hunger. They were truly victims of hunger … slowly slowly … they were lying [in bed], they could not even walk … slowly they died like that.[28]

These individual memories do not necessarily fit existing 'cultural scripts or mental templates', nor do they represent a shared collective group memory.[29] Rather, they represent the very exceptional lived experiences of the interviewed persons. The existence of individual memories, independent of the official collective narrative, is demonstrated by the diverging positions of the informants in relation to some of the main 'positions' of the official collective memory of the famine, such as the agricultural production during the famine years or their understanding of who was the black marketer. The individual memories challenge the official position of a massive decline in production during all the occupation years, a claim that was unknown to the informants, as it is one of the lesser known claims of the famine historiography. The informants asserted that their own production was very or exceptionally good from 1942 onwards.[30] In defining who was the black marketer, with the exception of two who admitted that they themselves were, each of the informants described the opposite of 'self'.[31] For example, a farmer and an unemployed worker identified the merchants and the grocers as black marketers. A different unemployed worker believed that the farmers and the grocers were the black marketers. For the civil servants, the black marketers were the workers, the boatmen, the Italians, the merchants, and private sector employees, 'but not civil servants'.[32] Individual memories challenged the official collective memory and that of the Left that the few 'real' black marketers were collaborators who enriched themselves at the expense of all the others. Rather, they demonstrated that everyone was involved in the black market, as there was not a 'white one'.[33]

While there are individual and local collective memories of the famine, the existing national collective memory is the simple reproduction of official collective memory. The official collective memory contrasts some of the individual and local memories of those who experienced the famine, leading to their silencing. The official collective memory of the famine has not been challenged or enriched by the individual and local memories of the population. Individuals and local societies see their memories as additional dimensions to the official collective memory and not as challenges to it, even if at times their memories inadvertently challenge some parts of the official collective memory's narrative.

Evolving memory: The economic crisis

The harsh economic crisis that started in Greece in 2009 resulted in the rapid impoverishment of Greeks, especially the Athenians. Hunger emerged as an issue, and soup kitchens and food handouts cropped up for homeless people and for families that had previously coped well.[34] The International Monetary Fund and European Union, especially Germany, shaped Greece's economic future during the crisis through the imposition of strict economic controls and painful austerity measures. Germany, for the Greek populace, once again became the main 'enemy' imposing its economic vision onto Greece, and leaving Greeks in abject poverty.

When Angela Merkel visited Athens in early October 2012, a large protest took place objecting to her presence in the country. Many of the protesters invoked Nazi symbols, linking Merkel's presence with that of the Nazis in 1940s Greece. The small number of protesters who were dressed in Nazi-style uniforms and using the Nazi salute were warmly cheered by the rest of the protesters who thus demonstrated their approval of this comparison.[35] Others carried a placard of Merkel with a Hitler-type moustache drawn on her face.[36] The focus on Germany's role in the economic crisis, projected onto and personified by Angela Merkel, continued through most of the crisis years. The extreme conditions of poverty on the ground, especially in Athens, brought the famine and the years of occupation to the fore, linking the crisis with the past hardships endured under the Germans in the 1940s.[37]

Only a few days after Merkel's visit and just a few days before the anniversary of the start of WWII for Greece, Alexis Tsipras, leader of the Left-wing opposition, made a statement that struck a chord with the Greek public and explicitly linked the 2012 situation and the 1940s famine, claiming that the 'oncoming winter will be worse than that of 1941.'[38] As expected, the oncoming winter of 2012–13, as harsh as it may have been, did not resemble that of 1941–42. However, anti-German sentiment remained present and strong. This political manipulation by Tsipras renewed interest in the famine and propelled its regular discussion in the media.[39] Moreover, in 2013, discussions had already begun in Greece about the WWII reparations that Greece claimed Germany owed her.[40] By 2016, a parliamentary commission estimated the value of these reparation costs and, in 2019, the Greek parliament officially asked Germany to enter negotiations in relation to the reparations.[41] Germany's rejection to such demands and the continuation of such demands by Greece in the last few years have propelled the mainstream media's fascination with the occupation years and the famine, exclusively focusing on Germany.[42] This angry public focus on Germany was impactful in a discernible, if not measurable, manner. It was certainly visible in everyday life as the following personal incident demonstrates.

While in Santorini in the summer of 2015, I was waiting for the bus at the island capital's bus depot. I overheard a 50-year-old man 'explaining' loudly to two approximately 80-year-old acquaintances of his that the Germans were responsible for the famine on Santorini as they were for the whole of Greece and therefore they had to pay reparations.[43] It was the behaviour of the two elderly people that fascinated me: they did not say a word. Neither did they give any sign as to whether they agreed or not with the speaker. Their silence and absence of spontaneous agreement suggested to me that they knew—because they were alive at the time—that the famine occurred during the Italian occupation in Santorini, not during the German one. However, they did not challenge the speaker. Possibly, they did not want to discuss the topic in public, as the loud conversation was heard by everyone in the vicinity, including myself. Or perhaps the speaker's loud and public confidence wiped out any potential 'opposition' to the prevailing position of the time, which follows the narrative that the Germans were responsible for the famine across the country. Similar comments were made to me in passing in the late 2010s by acquaintances in their late 50s on Mykonos about the German responsibility for the famine there, a claim that is not true.[44] It appears that the younger generations have adopted the national official collective memory and during the crisis have developed a confidence to assert this to the few surviving elders, even when the memories of the older generations differ from this official collective memory. The younger generations, therefore, reflect Halbwachs's assertion that individuals 'adopt' the collective (and in this case, official) memory, so then their accounts reflect such a collective memory.[45]

In short, the effects of the economic crisis and its association with the occupation and the famine further enhanced the official collective narrative, namely its focus on Germany's responsibility and the suffering of Athens in 1941–42. A recent effort to enrich the famine-teaching in the state-controlled curriculum involved an oral history project focused on the German occupation of Greece through the prepared lesson on 'Everyday life—Hunger'.[46] The project features 98 interviews from around Greece, some of which refer to the famine. In the devised lesson plan, two interviews were chosen, both from Athens, both with middle-class informants, both of whom explained that they went hungry but did not starve. The lesson reinforces the official collective memory, with one of the informants declaring that beyond mid-1942 they did not go hungry. This is correct for many middle-class Athenians but is not true for the rest of the population. Nevertheless, this project and its lessons never reached the pupils: some historians, including Giorgos Margaritis, the National Council claiming German reparations (ESDOGE), and many politicians vilified the programme because it had been partially funded by the German government and therefore it could not be possibly permitted to influence the understanding of history of the occupation of the younger Greek generations.[47] Thus, the sparse teaching of the famine continues to endorse the official collective memory, as did the occupation-focused discourses surrounding the economic crisis.

Discussion and conclusions

This chapter has sketched the Greek famine's memory evolution within Greece. It has demonstrated the existence of three different modes of remembering: the official national collective memory, the local collective memory, and individual recollections. I have argued that, for several historical reasons, the national collective memory has been that of the official historical narrative, which removed the possibility of apportioning any responsibility for the famine or for its handling to the Greek people and to the Allies. This official historical narrative softly imposed a culture of 'silence' during the twentieth century, that is, an absence of a public dialogue. This was not contested by the population as people themselves were not keen to delve into these issues as they were traumatic at the individual and community level too.[48]

Apportioning full responsibility to the occupiers meant that painful histories did not need to be further discussed or revealed. And such histories certainly do exist. Even informants who extensively spoke about their famine experiences with me made it clear that some of their famine experiences were too difficult to discuss for them to allow me to write about them:

H. We went through a lot that are …
W. These are … cannot be discussed, cannot be written. Cannot be written.[49]

The 'silence' surrounding the finer details of the famine is not exceptional, rather it represented the rule for most aspects of social history of the occupation years up to the mid-1970s. Among historians, it was Mazower's 1993 *Inside Hitler's Greece* that brought social history to the fore while also drawing attention to resistance. However, his treatment of the famine did not explicitly divert from the official narrative. Only after 2009, with the economic crisis, did the occupation and consequently the famine assume a centrality in the public discourse. The effect of the crisis and the subsequent public discourse have helped only to enhance the official collective memory and to further focus the blame on Germany. However, some changes have also quietly taken place. Though the black market has not been an integral part of the official collective memory, it has been part of the version promoted by the Left. While a small number of Leftist historians continue to advocate that a small number of major Greek black marketeers did bear responsibility for the famine, the overwhelming majority of historians—as well as lay authors writing in the public domain at all levels—have shifted quietly but decisively towards an understanding of the black market as something that all people engaged with through sheer necessity, showing that most people participated both as sellers and buyers.[50]

At the local level and where no long-term strong antipathies existed between local groups, a consensus and a compromise were reached by the year 2000 on the major local issues that emerged as a result of the famine. Events, at times, have further enhanced the local collective famine memory, such as the arrival of thousands of refugees on Hios from Syria from 2015 onwards. These arrivals rekindled the local famine collective memory on Hios, reminding the local population that among their parents and grandparents, some became refugees because of the famine, while many among them found refuge in Syria.[51] In localities where antipathies pre-dated the famine, the local collective memory was shaped by long-term local rivalries, which infiltrated or even promoted its construction. Syros provides such an example where the food thefts during the famine were interpreted through the local Orthodox–Catholic antagonism. Significant divergences between local collective memories and national official collective narrative are nothing new to Greece.[52]

Individual memories of the famine—among the ordinary people who experienced it—in the pre-crisis years remained vivid and full of challenges to the widely accepted academic writings that reflected the official collective memory. Some individual memories explored topics for which informants had no direct knowledge of their official historical representation and thus had no qualms in voicing and discussing those memories. It was the lack of public discourse and the 'silence' that surrounded the famine in the twentieth century that was, to a large degree, responsible for such lack of knowledge among the individuals. One such example is the level of agricultural production in the years of occupation. For other memories, the cultural uneasiness of the topic prevented many from discussing them at all or extensively. Here, an example would be sex exchanged for food.[53] Yet again, events that go against the national patriotic narrative are strictly not discussed, especially by those who perceive them as wrong. Such an example is that (Catholic) young men from Ano Syros voluntarily went to Germany to work during the occupation to survive the famine. Interestingly, it was the (Orthodox) informants from Hermoupolis who were silent about this, implying their very strong disapproval, rather than the (Catholic) informants from Ano Syros who saw it as a pure famine survival strategy and thus discussed it without hesitation.[54] Yet another such example is the understanding of the operation of the black market, a notion that was challenged in the pre-crisis years by the use of oral histories. The evidence provided by the informants has been used by historians to argue that the population was more universally involved in the black market.[55] This interpretation has become increasingly accepted by historians and the wider public. The official narrative 'orthodoxy' has been challenged by historians through the use of individual memories and not directly by the individuals. What is clear in all cases is that individual memories, experienced firsthand and sustained within familial and intimate social circles, were readily available and used by historians to elucidate our understanding of the years of occupation and to challenge prevailing 'orthodoxies' of the official collective narrative and national historical representation.[56]

Individual memories of the famine discussed beyond intimate social circles along with relevant local publications that led to further discussions within the local society, contributed to the construction of the local collective memory. Here, local allegiances and antagonisms also helped shape these primarily oral local collective memories. This corresponds to what Jan Assmann called the everyday/communicative collective memory, one that is intrinsically linked with oral communication and lasts while those who experienced the event are still alive.[57] As the numbers of those who had firsthand experience of the Greek famine and are capable of providing an interview dwindles—and will be virtually nullified by the end of the 2020s—the timing of the re-enforcement of the official collective memory is, most probably, not a co-incidence. It is the increasing absence of individuals with firsthand experience of the events that enable the advocates of the official collective memory to further strengthen it.

Here the official collective memory can be equated with what Assmann identified as cultural collective memory: the long-term collective memory is maintained and reproduced through cultural mechanisms, such as institutional communications and monuments.[58] This memory, in the case of Greece, is exemplified through school lessons, the annual remembering of the 1940s war and occupation around its 28 October anniversary and the main existing memorial to the famine, one out of the three that exist in the country.[59] It is displayed in the main, most prestigious, Athenian cemetery, depicting a dead, emaciated mother and her still living baby trying to suckle her breast.[60] The statue contradicts the historical knowledge in all possible ways: it depicts a woman and a child, when adult men and the elderly were the main famine casualties, and it is situated in Athens, when other localities suffered more than the capital. The statue, though in a public space, is discreetly placed and difficult to notice, and so accurately reflects the memory of the famine in the pre-crisis years: present and existing, but simultaneously inaccurate and inconspicuous.

Notes

1 No. 15 Hios. Interview conducted by the author in 1999 on the island of Hios with an elderly couple. Numbers rather than names have been used in order to retain anonymity. Thematically organised extracts of all the interviews cited in the chapter are available in Violetta Hionidou, *Η κατοχική πείνα μέσα από προφορικές μαρτυρίες: Η περίπτωση της Χίου, της Σύρου και της Μυκόνου* (Athens: Patakis, 2020). This chapter relies heavily on Violetta Hionidou, '"Καλά που ήρθες Μάριε, να τα επιβεβαιώνεις, γιατί δεν θα τα πίστευε"': Μνήμη, Λήθη και πολιτισμικό τραύμα του κατοχικού Λιμού'. In Nikos Demertzis, Eleni Paschaloudi and Giorgos Antoniou, eds., *Εμφύλιος. Πολιτισμικό Τραύμα* (Athens: Alexandreia, 2013), 289–322.

2 See, for example, Christian Noack, Lindsay Janssen and Vincent Comerford, eds., *Holodomor and Gorta Mór: Histories, Memories and Representations of Famine in Ukraine and Ireland* (London: Anthem Press, 2012); and Felix Wemheuer, 'Regime Changes of Memory: Creating the Official History of the Ukrainian and Chinese Famines Under State Socialism and after the Cold War', *Kritika* 10, no. 1 (2009): 31–59.

3 Violetta Hionidou, *Famine and Death in Occupied Greece, 1941-44. Cambridge Studies in Population, Economy, and Society in Past Times* Series (Cambridge: Cambridge University Press, 2006), Chapter 9.

4 Hionidou, 'Καλά που ήρθες Μάριε'; Hionidou, *Η κατοχική πείνα*, 9–50.

5 Giorgos Margarites, *Από την ήττα στην εξέγερση Ελλάδα: Άνοιξη 1941-Φθινόπωρο 1942* (Athens: Polites, 1993), 24; Mark Mazower, *Inside Hitler's Greece: The Experience of Occupation, 1941–44* (New Haven, CT: Yale University Press, 1993), 62–63. See also, for example *Προλετάριος*, 3 January 1943; *Κυκλαδική Φωνή*, 18, 12 August 1945; *Κυκλαδική Φωνή*, 23, 16 September 1945; *Παγχιακή*, 3490, 7 Oct. 1941; *Πρόοδος*, 4185, 20 April 1944. The same pattern of thinking, accusatory of the few black marketer traders, was reproduced by academics in the 1980s and beyond. See Stavros Thomadakis, 'Black Market, inflation and force in the economy of Occupied Greece'. In John Iatrides, ed., *Greece in the 1940s: A Nation in Crisis* (Hanover, NH: University Press of New England, 1981), 61–80. This position was articulated for the first time during the occupation in September 1942 in EAM's first proclamation. For further details, see Dimitris Glinos, 'What is the National Liberation Front [EAM] and what does it want?', in Richard Clogg, ed., *Greece 1940–1949: A documentary History* (Basingstoke: Palgrave, 2002), 76–91.

6 Hionidou, 'Καλά που ήρθες Μάριε'; Hionidou, *Η κατοχική πείνα*, 9–50.

7 Hionidou, *Famine*, 159–62.

8 Ibid., 159.

9 Ibid., 159–60, Chapter 11.

10 See Hionidou, *Famine*; see also Violetta Hionidou, '"Ποιός έφταιγε; Ποιός; Άραγε, μόνο οι Γερμανοί": Η επισιτιστική κατάσταση της Ελλάδας, Οκτώβριος 1940-Απρίλιος 1941'. In Stratos Dordanas and Nikos Papanastasiou, eds., *Ο «μακρύς» ελληνογερμανικός εικοστός αιώνας: Οι μαύρες σκιές στην ιστορία των διμερών σχέσεων* (Thessaloniki: Epikentro, 2018), 199–226.

11 This is reproduced even in non-historical academic works. See, for example, Cleo Gougoulis, 'Working Class Children's Toys in Times of War and Famine. Play, Work and the Agency of Children in Piraeus Neighbourhoods during the German Occupation of Greece', in Luísa Magalhães and Jeffrey Goldstein, eds., *Toys and Communication* (Basingstoke: Palgrave Macmillan, 2017), 171–96. Most historians have focused exclusively on investigating Athens in 1941–42. See, for instance, Eugenia Bournova, 'Θάνατοι από πείνα: Η Αθήνα το χειμώνα του 1941–1942', *Arheiotaxio* 7 (2005): 52–73. However, few did venture beyond the 1941–42 timeframe or Athens. Examples are Ypakoe Hatzemehael, *Τα δημογραφικά της*

Αθήνας κατά την περίοδο 1940–45, MA dissertation, University of Crete, 2000; Maria Kavalla, *Η Θεσσαλονίκη στην Γερμανική κατοχή (1941–1944)*, University of Crete, unpublished PhD thesis, 2009.

12 Anon., *Η Πείνα: Το προμελετημένο σχέδιο του Άξονος για τη φυλετική μας Εξόντωση* (Athens: Elleniko Aima, 1943); Konstantinos A. Doxiadis, *The sacrifices of Greece in the Second World War* (Athens: Ministry of Reconstruction, 1946); Demetrios I. Magkriotes, *Θυσίαι της Ελλάδος και Εγκλήματα κατοχής, 1941–1944* (Athens: Formigx, 1996), originally published in 1949. Magkriotes also attributes a small part of the responsibility to the Italians; see 182–4.

13 David Close, referring to these years, discusses the 'prevailing habit of distorting the past'. See David Close, 'The Road to Reconciliation? The Greek Civil War and the politics of Memory in the 1980s,' in Philip Carabott and Thanasis D. Sfikas, eds., *The Greek Civil War. Essays on a Conflict of Exceptionalism and Silences* (Aldershot: Ashgate, 2004), 258.

14 Mark Mazower, 'The Cold War and the Appropriation of Memory: Greece after Liberation', *East European Politics and Societies* 9, no. 2 (1995): 289–90. Marantzides suggests that this reconciliatory 'memory' became 'an official national state ideology'. See Nikos Marantzides, *Yasasin Millet: Zeto to Ethnos* (Erakleio: University of Crete, 2001), 242.

15 Andreas Kedros, *Η Ελληνική αντίσταση 1940–1944* (Athens: Themelio, 1976), first edition 1966. This claim is false; see Hionidou, *Famine*, Chapter 7; Violetta Hionidou, 'Relief and Politics in Occupied Greece, 1941–1944', *Journal of Contemporary History* 48, no. 4 (2013): 761–83.

16 V. Skoulatou, N. Demakopoulou and S. Konde, *Ιστορία νεότερη και σύγχρονη*, vol. 2 (Athens: OEDV, 2005), 268–74. This is a textbook taught in the final year of High School from the mid-1980s to, at least, the mid-2000s. Its narrative focuses on the 'terrible winter of 1941-42' with the hunger having affected 'Greece', while all primary sources and photos utilised referred only to Athens. The school text mentions all three occupiers but it is the Germans that are associated with the famine consistently, though in two instances the Italians are also mentioned. Only one of the four sources used for teaching the famine is not ideologically shaped by resistance rhetoric.

17 The first was the exhibition referring to the work of the photographer Voula Papaioannou (Fannie Konstantinou and Olga Hardalia, 'Η φωτογράφος Βούλα Παπαϊωάννου (1898–1990)' (The photographer Voula Papaioannou), *Benaki Museum*, 4 October–3 December 2006. https://www.benaki.org/index.php?option=com_events&view=event&type=&id=1993&lang=en). One of the exhibition themes was 'The Hunger, 1941–1942'. The second exhibition was essentially a booth showing in a loop a short film of a famished man: Giorgos Hatzimehales, 'Η πείνα στην Αθήνα τον Χειμώνα του 1941–1942 (*The hunger in Athens in the winter of 1941–1942*)', *National Museum of Contemporary Art,* 18 January–15 March 2009.

18 See, for example, the film by director Dinos Katsouridis, *Τι έκανες στο πόλεμο Θανάση* (Athens: Dinos Katsouridis, 1971).

19 Hionidou, *Famine*, Chapter 2.

20 The discussion of local and individual memory heavily draws on 44 oral histories from Hios and Syros, collected by the author in 1999–2000. Background information concerning the informants can be found in Hionidou, *Η κατοχική πείνα*, Appendix.

21 On the remembering of the famine on Hios see Hionidou, '"Καλά που ήρθες Μάριε"'. See also Violetta Hionidou, '"If we hadn't left … we would have all died": Escaping Famine from the Greek Island of Chios, 1941–44', *Journal of Refugee Studies* 34, no. 1 (2021): 1101–20.

22 Violetta Hionidou, '"Send us either food or coffins": The 1941-43 famine on the Aegean island of Syros,' in Tim Dyson and Cormac O' Gráda, eds. *Famine Demography. Perspectives from the Past and Present* (Oxford: Oxford University Press, 2002) 181–203; Sheila Lecoeur, *Το νησί του Μουσολίνι: Φασισμός και Ιταλική κατοχή στη Σύρο* (Athens: Alexandreia, 2013), 143–50. The figure of 8,000 is regularly used in local journalism. See Anon., 'Σύρος: Η κατοχή και η λιμοκτονία στον Β Παγκόσμιο πόλεμο', *Cyclades24.gr*, 28 Oct. 2021. Σύρος: Η κατοχή και η λιμοκτονία στο Β΄ Παγκόσμιο Πόλεμο | Cyclades24 (all web links in this chapter were accessed in March 2023); Georgios N. Poussaios, ' "Το νησί που ερωτεύτηκε ο Θάνατος": Όταν ο μύθος διδάσκει ιστορία …', 25 August 2014. http://booksyros.blogspot.com/2014/08/blog-post_25.html.

23 Hionidou, '"Καλά που ήρθες Μάριε"'.

24 Ibid.

25 See, for example, No. 3, Syros, male, born in 1932 in Ano Syros (Syros), lived in Ano Syros, working class background. The informant was interviewed by the author in Ano Syros in 2000; Hionidou, '"Καλά που ήρθες Μάριε"'.

26 Hionidou, *Famine*, 237–8; Hionidou, *Η κατοχική πείνα*, 148–88.

27 Hionidou, '"Καλά που ήρθες Μάριε"', 312–18.

28 No. 5, Syros, male, born in 1924 in Hermoupolis (Syros), lived in Hermoupolis, occupation civil servant, middle class. The informant was interviewed by the author in Hermoupolis in 2000.

29 Much of the memory literature focuses on how individual remembering is negotiated, articulated, and shaped by the social and political environment. That led to posing the question as to whether individual memories are at all significant or not. See Anna Green, 'Individual Remembering and "Collective Memory": Theoretical Presuppositions and Contemporary Debates', *Oral History* (2004): 35–7. Portelli convincingly argued that these individual memories are important, even when they are not historically accurate. See Alessandro Portelli, 'The Peculiarities of Oral History', *History Workshop* 12 (1981): 96–107.

30 Hionidou, *Famine*, Chapter 5.

31 Ibid., 98–104.

32 Ibid.

33 Ibid., *Famine*, Chapter 6; Hionidou, *Η κατοχική πείνα*, Chapter 4.

34 Hionidou, 'Greece: History Repeating Itself?', *History Workshop online, Histories of the Present*, January 2012, Greece: History Repeating Itself? | History Workshop.

35 Rachel Donadio and Nicholas Kulish, 'Official Warmth and Public Rage for Merkel in Athens', *New York Times*, 9 October 2012. https://www.nytimes.com/2012/10/10/world/europe/angela-merkel-greece-visit.html.

36 Katy Barnato, 'Merkel Should Bury Euro During Greece Visit: Economist', *CNBC*, 8 October 2012. https://www.cnbc.com/2012/10/08/merkel-should-bury-euro-during-greece-visit-economist.html.

37 Hionidou, 'Greece'. Such explicit connections are also made in Daniel Knight, *History, Time, and Economic Crisis in Central Greece* (London: Palgrave Mcmillan, 2015); and, Anon., 'Κατοχική πείνα. Η Γερμανοαγγλική γενοκτονία του ελληνικού πληθυσμού', 3 September 2012. http://pluton22.blogspot.com/2012/09/blog-post_3.html.

38 Anon., 'Τσίπρας: " Έρχεται χειμώνας χειρότερος από αυτόν του 1941"', *Ta Nea*, 21 Oct. 2012. 'Τσίπρας: «Ερχεται χειμώνας χειρότερος από αυτόν του 1941"', TA NEA (tanea.gr); Violetta Hionidou, '"Remembering" the Greek famine of the early 1940s: Oral Histories, individual memories and collective memory', paper presented at the *Famine Stories and Survival Legends: Legacies to the Following Generations* Workshop organised by COMPOT, Uppsala University, Sweden, 2017; Hionidou, *Η κατοχική πείνα.*

39 Demetres Damaskenos, 'Η φωτογραφία-ντοκουμέντο ως πράξη αντίστασης κατά της γερμανοιταλικής κατοχής (1941–1944)', *Haniotika Nea*, 8 March 2014. https://www.haniotika-nea.gr/fotografia-ntokoumento-os-praxi-antistasis-kata-tis-germanoitalikis-katochis-1941-1944/; Maria Sampatakaki, 'Η εκτέλεση, τα συσσίτια και η 20th century Fox', *Proto Thema*, 24 February 2019, https://www.protothema.gr/city-stories/article/867751/i-ektelesi-ta-sussitia-kai-i-20th-century-fox/.

40 Ilias Sourdis, 'Greece's Unsettled WWII German Reparations: A Stain in the International Legal System', *HUFFPOST*, 21 March 2013. https://www.huffpost.com/entry/greeces-unsettled-wwii-german-reparations_b_2857143; Vassilis Paipais, 'The politics of the German war reparations to Greece', *LSE*, 8 May 2013. https://blogs.lse.ac.uk/eurocrisispress/2013/05/08/the-politics-of-the-german-war-reparations-to-greece/. The famine was by far the deadliest element of the occupation. All other deaths put together make up only a fraction of the famine deaths. While the figures have been disputed, the proportional significance of the famine has not. See Violetta Hionidou, 'Πόσοι πέθαναν εξαιτίας του κατοχικού λιμού; Ένα ερώτημα και η αναζήτηση μιας απάντησης', in Stratos Dordanas and Menelaos Charalambides, eds., *Ανθρώπινες απώλειες και υλικές καταστροφές στην Ελλάδα κατά τη διάρκεια της τριπλής κατοχής (Γερμανικής, Ιταλικής, Βουλγαρικής), 1941–1944* (Athens: Alexandreia, 2024), forthcoming.

41 Renee Maltezou and George Georgiopoulos, 'Greek parliament calls on Germany to pay WW2 reparations', *Reuters*, 17 April 2019. https://www.reuters.com/article/us-greece-germany-reparations-idUSKCN1RT1PL.

42 For example, 'Ο λιμός της Αθήνας', *Η Μηχανή του Χρόνου*, *CosmoteHistory*, 24 January 2022. https://www.youtube.com/watch?v=IeGTN3bU_vg; Anon., 'Οι ταινίες που ενόχλησαν τους Γερμανούς – Το αποκαλυπτικό βιβλίο "Γκιαβόλ!" του Γιώργου Χαρβαλιά', *Olympia*, 11 Mar. 2023. https://www.olympia.gr/1533647/viral/oi-tainies-poy-enochlisan-toys-germanoys-to-apokalyptiko-vivlio-giavol-toy-giorgoy-charvalia/; Elene Mpellou, 'Μάνος Ιωαννίδης: Οι συνεταιρισμοί αλληλεγγύης έσωσαν την Ελλάδα στην Κατοχή', *TVXS*, 18 August 2014. https://tvxs.gr/news/prosopa/m-ioannidis-oi-synaiterismoi-allileggyis-esosan-tin-ellada-stin-katoxi&dr=tvxsmrstvxs. The latter article utilises an interview conducted on the television programme *Ρεπορτάζ χωρίς Σύνορα* in 2012. Historical fiction also tried to fill 'the knowledge gap' of those years: see Panos Amyras, *Ο λιμός* (Athens: Dioptra, 2018), and his interview with Hristina Kanatake, 'Λιμός-Βιβλίο/Πάνος Αμυράς', 2019. https://www.youtube.com/watch?v=n6fQ5FXx1PE.

43 Hionidou, *Η κατοχική πείνα*, 9–10.

44 As in Santorini, it was the Italians who occupied the island during the famine. The oral histories of those who experienced the famine are explicit in apportioning responsibility to the Italian occupation and not the German one. See Hionidou, *Η κατοχική πείνα*.

45 Maurice Halbwachs, *The Collective Memory* (New York, NY: Harper & Row, 1980), 24, Chapter 1.

46 Μνήμες από την Κατοχή στην Ελλάδα-MOG. https://www.occupation-memories.org/deutsche-okkupation/ergebnisse-des-terrors/index.html.

47 Giorgos Sahinis, 'Γ. Μαργαρίτης: Ξαναγράφοντας την ιστορία της κατοχής για να την αλλάξουν', 7 December 2020. https://www.radio984.gr/post/g-margaritis-xanagrafontas-tin-istoria-tis-katochis-gia-na-tin-allaxoyn/; ESDOGE, 'Διαμαρτυρία του Εθνικού Συμβουλίου Διεκδίκησης των οφειλών της Γερμανίας προς την Ελλάδα για την διαδικτυακή ημερίδα του χρηματοδοτουμένου από το Υπουργείο Εξωτερικών (MOG Μνήμες από την Κατοχή στην Ελλάδα)', Greek Parliament, no. 2541, Report, 3rd Session, 18th period, 3 June 2022, submitted by the MP Alexandros Vasileios Kegkeroglou,. See *Μέσα Κοινοβουλευτικού Ελέγχου*, www.hellenicparliament.gr.

48 Hionidou '"Καλά που ήρθες Μάριε"'.
49 No. 15 Hios. H. stands for husband, W. for wife. The husband was born in 1922, born and lived in Vrontados (Hios), and was working class. The informant was interviewed by the author in Vrontados in 1999.
50 Such Leftist historians are: Giorgos Margarites, 'Ομιλία του κ. Γιώργου Μαργαρίτη στην Ημερίδα στο Κορωπί', *Mesogianews.gr*, 26 October 2016. https://www.youtube.com/watch?v=V-rQJjSPKV0; and Tasos Kostopoulos, 'Το φάντασμα του μαυραγορίτη', *efsyn.gr*, 23 October 2016. https://www.efsyn.gr/arheio/fantasma-tis-istorias/87233_fantasma-toy-mayragoriti. On recent public perceptions of the black marketers, see Yiannou, Vassiliki, 'Surviving Under Pressure: Famine in Greece', https://historiana.eu/historical-content/viewpoints/surviving-under-pressure-famine-in-greece; Manoles Ntaloukas, 'Και όμως υπήρχαν και καλοί μαυραγορίτες!', *ogdoo.gr*, 28 October 2017. https://www.ogdoo.gr/erevna/thema/kai-omos-ypirxan-kai-kaloi-mavragorites.
51 Hionidou, '"If we hadn't left ... we would have all died"'.
52 See, for example, Van Boeschoten's work on Ziaka where she found her informants challenging the new 'official' history of the resistance imposed from 'above' in the 1980s. Riki Van Boeschoten, *Ανάποδα χρόνια. Συλλογική μνήμη και ιστορία στο Ζιάκα Γρεβενών (1900–1950)* (Athens: Plethron, 1997), 223. The same informants had refused to accept the 'old' 'official' history of the resistance as this was imposed from above before the 1980s, though I can only assume that at the time their refusal was less vocal. See also Doumanis' work on the Italian Occupation of the Dodecanese islands. Nicholas Doumanis, *Myth and memory in the Mediterranean: Remembering Fascism's Empire* (London: Macmillan, 1997, 1–13).
53 Lecoeur, *Το νησί*, 266–70; Hionidou, *Famine*, 98, 237.
54 Hionidou, *Famine*, 156, no. 2 (Syros, male, born in 1924 in Ano Syros (Syros), lived in Ano Syros, working class background. The informant was interviewed by the author in Ano Syros in 2000), no. 3, Syros.
55 Hionidou, *Famine*, 35–44, Chapter 6.
56 Violetta Hionidou, 'Famine in Occupied Greece: "Choosing" between children and the elderly', in Tatjana Tönsmeyer, ed., *Coping with Hunger and Shortage under German Occupation in World War II* (Basingstoke: Palgrave Macmillan, 2018), 203–22.
57 Jan Assmann & John Czaplicka, 'Collective memory and cultural identity', *New German Critique* 65 (1995): 125–33.
58 Ibid.
59 The three memorials are situated in Hermoupolis on Syros, in Skado on Naxos, and in Athens in the 1st cemetery. I am extremely grateful to Charles Stewart who alerted me to the existence of the Skado memorial.
60 Kostas Valsames, 'Η Μάνα της Κατοχής (The Mother of the Occupation)'. For more on the sculptor see Leuteres Xanthopoulos, 'Κώστας Βαλσάμης', *Periskopio* (1989). https://www.ert-archives.gr/0000069909/.

Newspapers

Κυκλαδική Φωνή 18, 12 August 1945.
Κυκλαδική Φωνή 23, 16 September 1945.
Παγχιακή 3490, 7 October 1941.
Προλετάριος, 3 January 1943.
Πρόοδος 4185, 20 April 1944.

References

Amyras, Panos, *Ο λιμός*. Athens: Dioptra, 2018.
Anon., 'Κατοχική πείνα. Η Γερμανοαγγλική γενοκτονία του ελληνικού πληθυσμού', 3 September 2012. http://pluton22.blogspot.com/2012/09/blog-post_3.html.
Anon., 'Ο λιμός της Αθήνας', *Η Μηχανή του Χρόνου*, *CosmoteHistory*, 24 January 2022. https://www.youtube.com/watch?v=IeGTN3bU_vg.
Anon., 'Οι ταινίες που ενόχλησαν τους Γερμανούς – Το αποκαλυπτικό βιβλίο "Γκιαβόλ!" του Γιώργου Χαρβαλιά', *Olympia*, 11 March 2023. https://www.olympia.gr/1533647/viral/oi-tainies-poy-enochlisan-toys-germanoys-to-apokalyptiko-vivlio-giavol-toy-giorgoy-charvalia/.
Anon., 'Σύρος: Η κατοχή και η λιμοκτονία στον Β Παγκόσμιο πόλεμο', *Cyclades24.gr*, 28 Oct. 2021. Σύρος: Η κατοχή και η λιμοκτονία στο Β΄ Παγκόσμιο Πόλεμο | Cyclades24.
Anon., 'Τσίπρας: " Έρχεται χειμώνας χειρότερος από αυτόν του 1941"', *Ta Nea,* 21 Oct. 2012.
Anon., *Η Πείνα. Το προμελετημένο σχέδιο του Άξονος για τη φυλετική μας Εξόντωση*. Athens: Elleniko Aima, 1943.
Assmann, Jan & John Czaplicka, 'Collective memory and cultural identity', *New German Critique*, 65 (1995): 125–33
Barnato, Katy, 'Merkel Should Bury Euro During Greece Visit: Economist', *CNBC*, 8 October 2012. https://www.cnbc.com/2012/10/08/merkel-should-bury-euro-during-greece-visit-economist.html.
Bournova, Eugenia, 'Θάνατοι από πείνα: Η Αθήνα το χειμώνα του 1941-1942', *Arheiotaxio*, 7 (2005): 52–73.
Close, David, 'The Road to Reconciliation? The Greek Civil War and the Politics of Memory in the 1980s'. In Philip Carabott and Thanasis D. Sfikas, eds., 257–80, *The Greek Civil War. Essays on a Conflict of Exceptionalism and Silences*. Aldershot: Ashgate, 2004.
Damaskenos, Demetres, 'Η φωτογραφία-ντοκουμέντο ως πράξη αντίστασης κατά της γερμανοιταλικής κατοχής (1941–1944)', *Haniotika Nea,* 8 March 2014. https://www.haniotika-nea.gr/fotografia-ntokoumento-os-praxi-antistasis-kata-tis-germanoitalikis-katochis-1941-1944/.
Donadio, Rachel and Nicholas Kulish, 'Official Warmth and Public Rage for Merkel in Athens', *New York Times*, 9 October 2012. https://www.nytimes.com/2012/10/10/world/europe/angela-merkel-greece-visit.html.
Doumanis, Nicholas, *Myth and Memory in the Mediterranean. Remembering Fascism's Empire*. London: Macmillan, 1997.
Doxiadis, Konstantinos A., *The Sacrifices of Greece in the Second World War*. Athens: Ministry of Reconstruction, 1946.
ESDOGE, 'Διαμαρτυρία του Εθνικού Συμβουλίου Διεκδίκησης των οφειλών της Γερμανίας προς την Ελλάδα για την διαδικτυακή ημερίδα του χρηματοδοτουμένου από το Υπουργείο Εξωτερικών (MOG Μνήμες από την Κατοχή στην Ελλάδα)', Greek Parliament, no 2541, Report, 3rd Session, 18th period, 3 June 2022, submitted by the MP Alexandros Vasileios Kegkeroglou. Μέσα Κοινοβουλευτικού Ελέγχου (hellenicparliament.gr).
Glinos, Dimitris, 'What is the National Liberation Front [EAM] and what does it want?' In Richard Clogg, ed., 76–91, *Greece 1940–1949: A documentary History*. Basingstoke: Palgrave, 2002.
Gougoulis, Cleo, 'Working Class Children's Toys in Times of War and Famine. Play, Work and the Agency of Children in Piraeus Neighbourhoods during the German Occupation of Greece'. In Luísa Magalhães and Jeffrey Goldstein, eds., 171–96, *Toys and Communication*. Basingstoke: Palgrave Macmillan, 2017.

Green, Anna, 'Individual Remembering and "Collective Memory": Theoretical presuppositions and Contemporary Debates', *Oral History* 32, no. 2 (2004): 35–44

Hatzemehael, Ypakoe, *Τα δημογραφικά της Αθήνας κατά την περίοδο 1940–45*. MA dissertation, University of Crete, 2000.

Hatzemihales, Giorgos, 'Η πείνα στην Αθήνα τον Χειμώνα του 1941–1942 (The hunger in Athens in the winter of 1941–1942)', *National Museum of Contemporary Art*, 18 January–15 March 2009.

Halbwachs, Maurice, *The Collective Memory*. New York, NY: Harper & Row, 1980.

Hionidou, Violetta, 'Πόσοι πέθαναν εξαιτίας του κατοχικού λιμού; Ένα ερώτημα και η αναζήτηση μιας απάντησης'. In Stratos Dordanas and Menelaos Charalambides, eds., forthcoming, *Ανθρώπινες απώλειες και υλικές καταστροφές στην Ελλάδα κατά τη διάρκεια της τριπλής κατοχής (Γερμανικής, Ιταλικής, Βουλγαρικής)*, 1941–1944. Athens: Alexandreia, 2024.

Hionidou, Violetta, '"If we hadn't left … we would have all died": Escaping Famine from the Greek Island of Chios, 1941-44', *Journal of Refugee Studies* 34, no. 1 (2021): 1101–20.

Hionidou, Violetta, *Η κατοχική πείνα μέσα από προφορικές μαρτυρίες. Η περίπτωση της Χίου, της Σύρου και της Μυκόνου*. Athens: Patakis, 2020.

Hionidou, Violetta, 'Famine in Occupied Greece: "Choosing" between Children and the Elderly'. In Tatjana Tönsmeyer, ed., 203–22, *Coping with Hunger and Shortage under German Occupation in World War II*. Basingstoke: Palgrave Macmillan, 2018.

Hionidou, Violetta, '"Ποιός έφταιγε; Ποιός; Άραγε, μόνο οι Γερμανοί": Η επισιτιστική κατάσταση της Ελλάδας, Οκτώβριος 1940-Απρίλιος 1941'. In Stratos Dordanas and Nikos Papanastasiou, eds., 199–226, *Ο «μακρύς» ελληνογερμανικός εικοστός αιώνας: Οι μαύρες σκιές στην ιστορία των διμερών σχέσεων*. Thessaloniki: Epikentro, 2018.

Hionidou, Violetta, "'Remembering' the Greek famine of the early 1940s: Oral Histories, individual memories and collective memory", paper presented at the *Famine Stories and Survival Legends: Legacies to the Following Generations*. Workshop organised by COMPOT, Uppsala University, Sweden, 2017.

Hionidou, Violetta, '"Καλά που ήρθες Μάριε, να τα επιβεβαιώνεις, γιατί δεν θα τα πίστευε". Μνήμη, Λήθη και πολιτισμικό τραύμα του κατοχικού Λιμού'. In Nikos Demertzis, Eleni Paschaloudi and Giorgos Antoniou, eds., 289–322, *Εμφύλιος: Πολιτισμικό Τραύμα*. Athens: Alexandreia, 2013.

Hionidou, Violetta, 'Relief and Politics in Occupied Greece, 1941–1944', *Journal of Contemporary History* 48, no. 4 (2013): 761–83.

Hionidou, Violetta, 'Greece: History Repeating Itself?', *History Workshop Online, Histories of the Present*, January 2012, Greece: History Repeating Itself? | History Workshop.

Hionidou, Violetta, *Famine and Death in Occupied Greece, 1941–44. Cambridge Studies in Population, Economy, and Society in Past Times Series*, Cambridge: Cambridge University Press, 2006.

Hionidou, Violetta, '"Send us either food or coffins": The 1941-43 famine on the Aegean island of Syros'. In Tim Dyson and Cormac O' Gráda, eds., 181–203, *Famine Demography. Perspectives from the Past and Present*. Oxford: Oxford University Press, 2002.

Hodgkin, Katharine and Susannah Radstone, 'Feature: Rethinking Memory', *History Workshop Journal* 59 (2005): 129–33.

Kanatake, Hristina, 'Λιμός-Βιβλίο/Πάνος Αμυράς', 2019. https://www.youtube.com/watch?v=n6fQ5FXx1PE.

Katsouridis, Dinos, dir., *Τι έκανες στο πόλεμο Θανάση*. Athens: Dinos Katsouridis, 1971.

Kavalla, Maria, *Η Θεσσαλονίκη στην Γερμανική κατοχή (1941–1944)*. PhD Thesis, University of Crete, 2009.
Kedros, Andreas, *Η Ελληνική αντίσταση 1940–1944. 1966*. Athens: Themelio, 1976.
Knight, Daniel, *History, Time, and Economic Crisis in Central Greece*. London: Palgrave Macmillan, 2015.
Konstantinou, Fannie and Olga Hardalia, 'Η φωτογράφος Βούλα Παπαϊωάννου (1898–1990) (The photographer Voula Papaioannou)', *Benaki Museum*, 4 October–3 December 2006. https://www.benaki.org/index.php?option=com_events&view=event&type=&id=1993&lang=en.
Kostopoulos, Tasos, 'Το φάντασμα του μαυραγορίτη', *efsyn.gr*, 23 October 2016. https://www.efsyn.gr/arheio/fantasma-tis-istorias/87233_fantasma-toy-mayragoriti.
Lecoeur, Sheila, *Το νησί του Μουσολίνι. Φασισμός και Ιταλική κατοχή στη Σύρο*. Athens: Alexandreia, 2013.
Magkriotes, Demetrios I., *Θυσίαι της Ελλάδος και Εγκλήματα κατοχής, 1941–1944*. Athens: Formigx, 1996.
Maltezou, Renee and George Georgiopoulos, 'Greek parliament calls on Germany to pay WW2 reparations', *Reuters*, 17 April 2019. https://www.reuters.com/article/us-greece-germany-reparations-idUSKCN1RT1PL.
Marantzides, Nikos, *Yasasin Millet. Zeto to Ethnos*. Erakleio: University of Crete Press, 2001.
Margarites, Giorgos, 'Ομιλία του κ. Γιώργου Μαργαρίτη στην Ημερίδα στο Κορωπί', *Mesogianews.gr*, 26 October 2016. https://www.youtube.com/watch?v=V-rQJjSPKV0.
Margarites, Giorgos, *Από την ήττα στην εξέγερση. Ελλάδα: Άνοιξη 1941–Φθινόπωρο 1942*. Athens: Polites, 1993.
Mazower, Mark, 'The Cold War and the Appropriation of Memory: Greece after Liberation', *East European Politics and Societies* 9, no. 2 (1995): 212–32.
Mazower, Mark, *Inside Hitler's Greece: The Experience of Occupation, 1941–44*. New Haven: Yale University Press, 1993.
MOG, Μνήμες από την Κατοχή στην Ελλάδα-MOG. https://www.occupation-memories.org/deutsche-okkupation/ergebnisse-des-terrors/index.html.
Mpellou, Elene, 'Μάνος Ιωαννίδης: Οι συνεταιρισμοί αλληλεγγύης έσωσαν την Ελλάδα στην Κατοχή', *TVXS*, 18 Aug. 2014. https://tvxs.gr/news/prosopa/m-ioannidis-oi-synaiterismoi-allileggyis-esosan-tin-ellada-stin-katoxi&dr=tvxsmrstvxs.
Noack, Christian, Lindsay Janssen and Vincent Comerford, eds., *Holodomor and Gorta Mór: Histories, Memories and Representations of Famine in Ukraine and Ireland*. London: Anthem Press, 2012.
Ntaloukas, Manoles, 'Και όμως υπήρχαν και καλοί μαυραγορίτες!', *ogdoo.gr*, 28 October 2017. https://www.ogdoo.gr/erevna/thema/kai-omos-ypirxan-kai-kaloi-mavragorites.
Paipais, Vassilis, 'The politics of the German war reparations to Greece', *LSE*, 8 May 2013. https://blogs.lse.ac.uk/eurocrisispress/2013/05/08/the-politics-of-the-german-war-reparations-to-greece/.
Panselinos, Asimakis, *Τότε που ζούσαμε. 1974*. Athens: Kedros, 1997.
Portelli, Alessandro, 'The Peculiarities of Oral History', *History Workshop*, 12 (1981): 96–107.
Poussaios, Georgios N., '"Το νησί που ερωτεύτηκε ο Θάνατος": Όταν ο μύθος διδάσκει ιστορία …', 25 August 2014. http://booksyros.blogspot.com/2014/08/blog-post_25.html.
Sahinis, Giorgos, 'Γ. Μαργαρίτης: Ξαναγράφοντας την ιστορία της κατοχής για να την αλλάξουν', 7 December 2020, https://www.radio984.gr/post/g-margaritis-xanagrafontas-tin-istoria-tis-katochis-gia-na-tin-allaxoyn/.

Sampatakaki, Maria, 'Η εκτέλεση, τα συσσίτια και η 20th century Fox', *Proto Thema*, 24 February 2019. https://www.protothema.gr/city-stories/article/867751/i-ektelesi-ta-sussitia-kai-i-20th-century-fox/.
Skoulatou, V., N. Demakopoulou and S. Konde, *Ιστορία νεότερη και σύγχρονη*, vol. 2. Athens: OEDV, 2005.
Sourdis, Ilias, 'Greece's Unsettled WWII German reparations: A stain in the international legal system', *HUFFPOST*, 21 March 2013. https://www.huffpost.com/entry/greeces-unsettled-wwii-german-reparations_b_2857143.
Thomadakis, Stavros, 'Black Market, inflation and force in the economy of Occupied Greece'. In John Iatrides, ed., 61–80, *Greece in the 1940s: A Nation in Crisis*. Hanover, NH: University Press of New England, 1981.
Van Boeschoten, Riki, *Ανάποδα χρόνια. Συλλογική μνήμη και ιστορία στο Ζιάκα Γρεβενών (1900-1950)*. Athens: Plethron, 1997.
Wemheuer, Felix, 'Regime Changes of Memory: Creating the Official History of the Ukrainian and Chinese Famines Under State Socialism and after the Cold War', *Kritika* 10, no. 1 (2009): 31–59.
Xanthopoulos, Leuteres, 'Κώστας Βαλσάμης', *Periskopio*, 1989. https://www.ert-archives.gr/0000069909/.
Yiannou, Vassiliki, 'Surviving Under Pressure: Famine in Greece'. https://historiana.eu/historical-content/viewpoints/surviving-under-pressure-famine-in-greece.

6

HOLODOMOR MONUMENTS ON THE BATTLEFIELD

Monuments and memorials of the Great Famine (1932–33) in post-Maidan Ukraine

Wiktoria Kudela-Świątek

In *Memorylands: Heritage and Identity in Europe Today* (2013) Sharon Macdonald identifies processes of memorialisation as both 'complex' and involving a form of 'assemblage'.[1] She views memory practices as forming a kind of 'entity' which is made up of constituent inter-related parts—practices, affects, and materialisations—that then have effects of their own.[2] Holodomor memory practices can also be seen as an assemblage of practices, affects, and physical objects, which are accompanied by memorial services, nostalgia, and sometimes even historical artefacts. As three-dimensional compositions, they mirror social memory as a process of signification and change under the influence of political and social factors.

This chapter aims to explore how the re-enactment of the Holodomor past through monuments and the ways in which they are framed have changed over time, including under the influence of the current situation in Ukraine. What story about the Holodomor do monuments and memorials tell? And do they suggest any interesting mode of representing the past in a more persuasive and effective way in the present time because of the Russian war in Ukraine? My research orientation is methodological pluralism, which means that I will combine linear analytical work with ethnographic descriptions and case studies.[3] To begin, the first 23 years of Holodomor memory culture formation in independent Ukraine (1991–2014) will be analysed. Subsequently, changes in the Holodomor memory culture over the last eight years (2015–date) will be investigated: a period marked by Russia's occupation of the Crimean and Donbas regions, followed by full-scale warfare in Ukraine in 2022.

In so doing, I will focus on two case studies: significant Kyiv 'places of memory', which are an example of how Holodomor memory culture in independent Ukraine has changed over the last two decades on the level of state memory

DOI: 10.4324/9781003391524-9

politics. The first is a monument that was unveiled in 1993 in one of the pedestrian zones in the city centre of the Ukrainian capital. It was created as an embodiment of the policy of memory in the first years of independence. However, its urban surroundings still undergo significant changes and, as such, complement the symbolism in the original design of the monument. The second is a Holodomor memorial called 'Candle of Memory', conceived as part of a national Holodomor mourning site in 2008. The construction of it and the adjoining museum has been going on and off from 2008 to the present, due to the political and economic situation in the country. The date on which construction works will be completed is still uncertain due to the ongoing war in Ukraine. In my considerations, I will discuss these memory sites in chronological order with regard to their construction and evolution.

Holodomor and memory in independent Ukraine: A brief introduction

For years, the Ukrainian Great Famine of 1932–33, better known as the Holodomor, has played a significant role in Ukraine's heritage practices and societal debates. For Camilla Orjuela, the Great Famine of 1932–33 in Soviet Ukraine, during which Stalin's collectivisation efforts and large-scale grain requisitions killed an estimated four million people, is central to Ukraine's nation-building project. She emphasises that the official narrative erases complexities by picturing all Ukrainians as victims and by silencing the role of local people who were implicated in the requisitions.[4] In Ukraine's case, history was also instrumentalised in international politics. 'Ukraine remembers, the world recognises' is the slogan of a still ongoing state-led campaign to gain international recognition of the famine as a genocide against Ukrainians, a campaign that has been more successful since Russia's invasion.[5]

'Holodomor' comes from *'holod'*, meaning hunger, and *'moryty'*, meaning to exhaust or waste. The term Holodomor was first used by Ukrainians in Czechoslovakia in the 1930s, and after World War II, it took root in the Ukrainian diaspora in North America.[6] As an event, the Great Famine of 1932–33 already appeared in the statements and writings of the communist opposition in Soviet Ukraine after the mid-1980s, and from that moment, the term Holodomor was also used interchangeably (often written in lower case).

During the presidency of Leonid Kuchma (1994–2005), the term Holodomor was extended to include other experiences of famine in Soviet Ukraine, namely the famine of the 1920s and the post-war famine of 1946–48. During the 2000s, The Great Famine of 1932–33 was often combined with the Great Terror (1937) to denote a longer period of oppression of the population of Soviet Ukraine, without emphasis on the famine's artificial and planned nature as a genocide. Roman Serbyn notes that, to Ukrainians, the meaning of the term Holodomor has gained similar connotations of genocide as the word Holocaust.[7] Under the name Holodomor, the hunger crisis was transformed into a key element in discourses and processes of Ukrainian identity formation.

The politics of memory concerning the Holodomor were realised by the national democratic camp, with the support of politically like-minded media. The presidential decree issued by Leonid Kravchuk in March 1993 on the occasion of the Great Famine's 60th anniversary set the parameters for a whole range of top-down initiatives. To mark this anniversary, various monuments were erected. Monuments to the victims of the Holodomor were unveiled in virtually all larger cities in Ukraine—in the centre of Kyiv, in Kherson and Kharkov, in Chervonohrad in the Lviv Oblast, in the Luhansk Oblast, and in Odesa, in the Vinnytsia and Chernihiv oblasts, as well as in Lubny (on the Zazhura hill). The cemeteries of most towns and villages were tidied up, and efforts were made to identify the graves (whether real or symbolic) of the famine victims.[8]

The first monument was built in the centre of the capital of the newly independent country in 1993, in close proximity to places that are symbols referring the viewer to Kyivan Rus and the beginnings of statehood in the Ukrainian lands in the Middle Ages. The monument was designed to create a new space of memory for a post-Soviet Ukrainian state keen to stress its separation from Soviet heritage, not just as a site to commemorate the events of 1932–33. The official unveiling of the first monument was tied to the commemorations of the 60th anniversary of the Holodomor. The commemorations began in the square in front of St. Sophia's Cathedral with a sombre march that proceeded towards St. Michael's Cathedral, where the monument was to be unveiled.

The ceremonies were attended by then President Kravchuk, who emphasised in his speech that it was the first time Ukrainians could ceremoniously and publicly pay tribute to the memory of the Holodomor's victims: 'The Holodomor's anniversary is being nationally observed for the first time, established to honour the eternal memory of the murdered millions of innocent Ukrainian farmers and to draw the attention of the world's community to this event'.[9] As Catherine Wanner noticed, in many other speeches during the commemoration of the 60th anniversary of the Holodomor in Kyiv, it was said that it was the colonial policy of the Russian-Soviet authorities that had caused the death of a million victims among the Ukrainians. Thus, in the newly emerged post-USSR Ukrainian memory politics concerning Holodomor, Russia was positioned as the dreaded Other threatening the Ukrainian nation.[10]

Yet, the celebration of the 60th anniversary of this event in 1993 was followed by years of ambivalence about the Holodomor. The famine was not ignored, but it was on the peripheries of the main historical narrative. Oleksandr Hrytsenko notes in his research on Ukrainian presidents Leonid Kuchma, Viktor Yushchenko, and Viktor Yanukovych that in each of these cases, the theme of the 1933 Great Famine served an important role in their policies of memory.[11] On 26 November 1998, Kuchma signed a resolution establishing the fourth Saturday of every November as the Day of the Victims of the Great Famine in Ukraine, proposing that flowers be laid in 'places of memory' on the occasion.[12] For the anniversary in 1999, the President assigned tasks related to the Holodomor's commemoration to specific ministries, and in February 2003 parliament declared the Great Famine of 1932–33 (Holodomor) an act of genocide. In the same year, a new social ritual was created—the 'Light a Candle' campaign.[13] To that purpose, the cultural landscape of post-Soviet Ukraine was filled with more monuments and recognition of mass burial sites. In post-communist Ukraine, these Holodomor memorials coexisted with the previously built Soviet monuments for many years.[14]

However, more serious efforts to anchor the Holodomor in Ukrainian national identity were undertaken after 2005, under President Viktor Yushchenko. The president established the Institute of National Remembrance as the institutional home for the study of and communication about the Holodomor and ran an awareness campaign that intensified as the 75th anniversary of the famine approached.[15] In addition to its entrenchment in the state apparatus and legislation, the Holodomor effectively became a key element of the politics of memory (The Holodomor Law in 2006). Under Yushchenko, official commemoration ceremonies such as nation-wide candle-lighting memorials and discourses of the Holodomor as a defining national tragedy were sacralised. The National Museum of Holodomor-genocide, known at the time as the Memorial in Commemoration of Famines' Victims in Ukraine, is a prime example. In 2008, an estimated 457 monuments and mass graves in Ukraine commemorated the Holodomor, with the largest number found in the Poltava, Kyiv, and Vinnytsia oblasts. Ukraine's eastern regions have been less active; less than ten monuments honouring Holodomor victims had been unveiled in the Dnipropetrovsk Oblast, but none in the Russian-speaking Donetsk and Zaporizhzhia oblasts.[16]

Early in his term, the pro-Russian President Viktor Yanukovych (2010–14) attempted to make the Holodomor vanish from public discourse, but he eventually only gave up on insisting on its genocidal nature.[17] As Georgi Kasyanov emphasises, the refusal of the 'genocidal' version of the Holodomor was a necessary symbolic gesture for Yanukovych, relieving tension in one of the aspects of his relations with Russia. All other components of the Holodomor and related memorial practices remained unchanged because it was already a de facto part of the official historical policy and an essential component of the national founding myth. On 26 November 2010, on the Memorial Day of Holodomor victims, an address appeared on the president's website, in which Yanukovych called the Great Famine of 1932–33 some kind of disaster (initially he used the term 'Armageddon'), spoke out against speculations about the number of dead, and urged to speak the truth about Holodomor.[18]

The overthrow of Yanukovych took place in February 2014. The accompanying dramatic challenges to the integrity of Ukraine's borders, the annexation of Crimea, and the declaration of self-proclaimed republics in the east of the country pushed Holodomor commemoration initiatives to the background. Following Russia's military aggression on Ukraine in 2014, Russian and pro-Russian-Ukrainian voices from politics and the media have accused Ukraine of genocide, with the purpose of demonising the perceived enemy, mobilising internal support, and gaining interpretative authority over events. Ukraine has responded by intensifying its historical discourse of genocide, framing Putin's policies as a direct follow-up to Stalin's policies of destroying Ukraine.[19] At the beginning of the war in 2014, the Russian aggression against Ukraine led to an increase in nationalist and anti-Russian sentiments that affected the interpretation of the famine, which many Ukrainians see as Russia's planned extermination of the Ukrainians.

As to the politics of memory under President Petro Poroshenko (2014–19), the Holodomor was further embedded in the Ukrainian politics of memory as evidence that Russia is Ukraine's eternal enemy.[20] Already in his role as president on the anniversary of the Holodomor in 2014, Poroshenko called those in the lead of the self-proclaimed Luhansk People's Republic and Donetsk People's Republic the descendants of the organisers of the Great Famine of 1932–33, stressing that the famine was a consequence of the absence of the Ukrainian state and army.[21] The following year, he reused this thesis but modified it, noting that the lack of unity among Ukrainians was another prerequisite for the tragedy. That is exactly what happened in 2017, when, during the 84th commemoration of the Holodomor, President Poroshenko called on Russian authorities to finally 'repent' for the famine that their regime had caused.[22] In this period, the Holodomor was called an escalation of the centuries-old hybrid war that Russia was waging against Ukraine. Specific innovations within the canonical discourse were being introduced at the Ukrainian Institute of National Remembrance.

It is also worth noting that the policy of memory in the context of the Holodomor in the case of the current President Volodymyr Zelensky is a reference to both the positively assessed initiatives from the policy of his last two predecessors: drawing attention from the international arena to the subject of the Holodomor (Yushchenko) and strengthening memory through educational and social actions such as the construction of a museum in Kyiv (Poroshenko). In 2019, as President Zelensky and Israeli Prime Minister Benjamin Netanyahu prepared to honour the victims of the Holocaust on 19 August in Kyiv, Ukraine's leader called on Israel via Twitter: 'In commemorating the eternal memory of the victims of the Holocaust, which killed over 2 million Ukrainian Jews, Ukraine appeals to Israel to also recognise the Holodomor as an act of genocide against the Ukrainian people'. Twelve years earlier, President Yushchenko had made a similar appeal to the Israeli authorities.[23] Although Israel still does not recognise the genocidal nature of Holodomor, as of July 2023, 34 countries as well as the European Parliament identify the Holodomor as a genocide.[24]

Zelensky also invested in national Holodomor heritage: in 2020, he proclaimed that the project of the National Museum of the Holodomor Genocide was significant for Ukraine and promised that the second part of the museum construction would be completed by the autumn of 2023,[25] on the occasion of the state celebrations of the 90th Anniversary of the Holodomor.[26] However, this promise will not be fulfilled as long as the Russo-Ukrainian war continues. On 13 July 2023, the Parliament supported the allocation of the funds to reconstruct the first stage and commission a second stage of the museum. Former Culture Minister Oleksandr Tkachenko defended these policies, saying they played a key role in winning the international recognition of Holodomor as a genocide. Tkachenko was, however, criticised for the decision to relocate funds, prompting calls for a more sensible use of the state's budget during wartime, and the Parliament finally dismissed him on 27 July 2023. Subsequently, Zelensky vetoed the bill allocating Hr 573.9 million (approximately $15.6 million) to finish the construction of the National Museum of the Holodomor-Genocide.[27] This demonstrates that the Holodomor is currently an essential but not the most important element of the symbolic canon that shapes Ukrainian national identity in wartime.

The question also arises in what ways the full-scale aggression of the Russian Federation in Ukraine since 2022 has demanded a further reassessment of Holodomor heritage and its existing commemorative sites, such as monuments. For Christoph Mick, the Russian aggressor targets specifically those parts of the Ukrainian heritage incompatible with the version of history dominant in Russia and that could support a distinct Ukrainian nation. For example, several museums or monuments concerning the Ukrainian national poet Taras Shevchenko have been destroyed. Similarly, monuments commemorating victims of Soviet terror, Holocaust memorials, and the Holodomor Monument in Mariupol, dedicated to victims of the Holodomor, were demolished by war violence. Russian authorities deny the genocidal nature of the famine of 1932–33 in Soviet Ukraine, preferring to refer to it as a 'tragedy' which also affected Russians and other ethnic groups.[28] We are also witnessing how, under the influence of the ongoing war, the image of the Holodomor changes into the most important symbol of the steadfastness of the Ukrainian nation. The main message is that the memory of Holodomor should be cultivated as a warning that the once unpunished evil may always return in a new form. This marks the beginning of a new stage in Holodomor memory culture, the effects of which we will be able to appreciate in some time.

A shared symbolic space of memory: The 1993 monument

Now that we have examined transformations in the instrumentalisation of Holodomor memory in Ukraine, it is time to look more closely at two Kyiv memorials. The first monument commemorating the Holodomor was unveiled in Kyiv in 1993 and was located near St. Michael's Golden-Domed Orthodox

Monastery. It has the shape of a square stele made of grey granite. A cross was cut out in the stone slab, inside of which a female figure (made of metal) was placed. This structure, in turn, contains the figure of a child with outstretched arms. According to the official interpretation, the female figure, alluding to Orthodox iconography, is supposed to 'symbolise (...) a woman-mother with outstretched arms and a dead child in her womb'.[29] Both figures were placed in the middle of the cross to emphasise that they died as martyrs. The monument was co-designed by Mykola Kysly and Vasyl Perevalsky. Memory scholar James Young has drawn attention to the significance of the space around monuments:

> A monument becomes a point of reference amid other parts of the landscape, one node among others in a topographical matrix that orients the rememberer and creates meaning in both the land and our recollections. For, like a narrative, which places events in chronological order, the memorial places events in some cognitive order. [...] It is still perceived in the midst of its geography, in some relation to other nearby landmarks.[30]

The location of this monument in the centre of Kyiv is, therefore, fundamentally important for investing it with symbolic content. For one thing, it stands between the two most important Orthodox temples, which reference the historical figure of Kievan Rus. The first one is St. Michael's Golden-Domed Monastery, which was initially built by Sviatopolk II in 1108–13, destroyed by the Soviets in 1935–36 but rebuilt in 1999 through funding by the Kyiv city council and Orthodox Metropolitan Filaret. The second one is the medieval St. Sophia Cathedral, on the walls of which there is a painting of Our Lady Oranta, similar to the one used by the artists in the monument design.

When the Holodomor Monument was erected after the state-sponsored 60th anniversary commemorations in 1993, St. Michael's Cathedral was in ruins. In the mid-1930s, after the transfer of the Ukrainian capital from Kharkiv to Kyiv, a decision was made to demolish the cathedral and build administrative buildings in its place. Considering the atheistic nature of the Soviet state, in order to obtain space for the development of substantial modernist public utility buildings, the city authorities decided to demolish a number of sacral buildings from the early Middle Ages, which were unique monuments of sacred art and architecture from the times of Kyivan Rus and, in fact, lent splendour to Kyiv as the capital. Historic church interiors were plundered or placed in primarily Russian museums, and most were never returned (Image 6.1).[31]

In the Kyiv Holodomor Monument (1993), the central image of a mother and child offers a perspective for interpreting the political and Holodomor memory culture issue in post-communist Ukraine. On the pre-iconographic

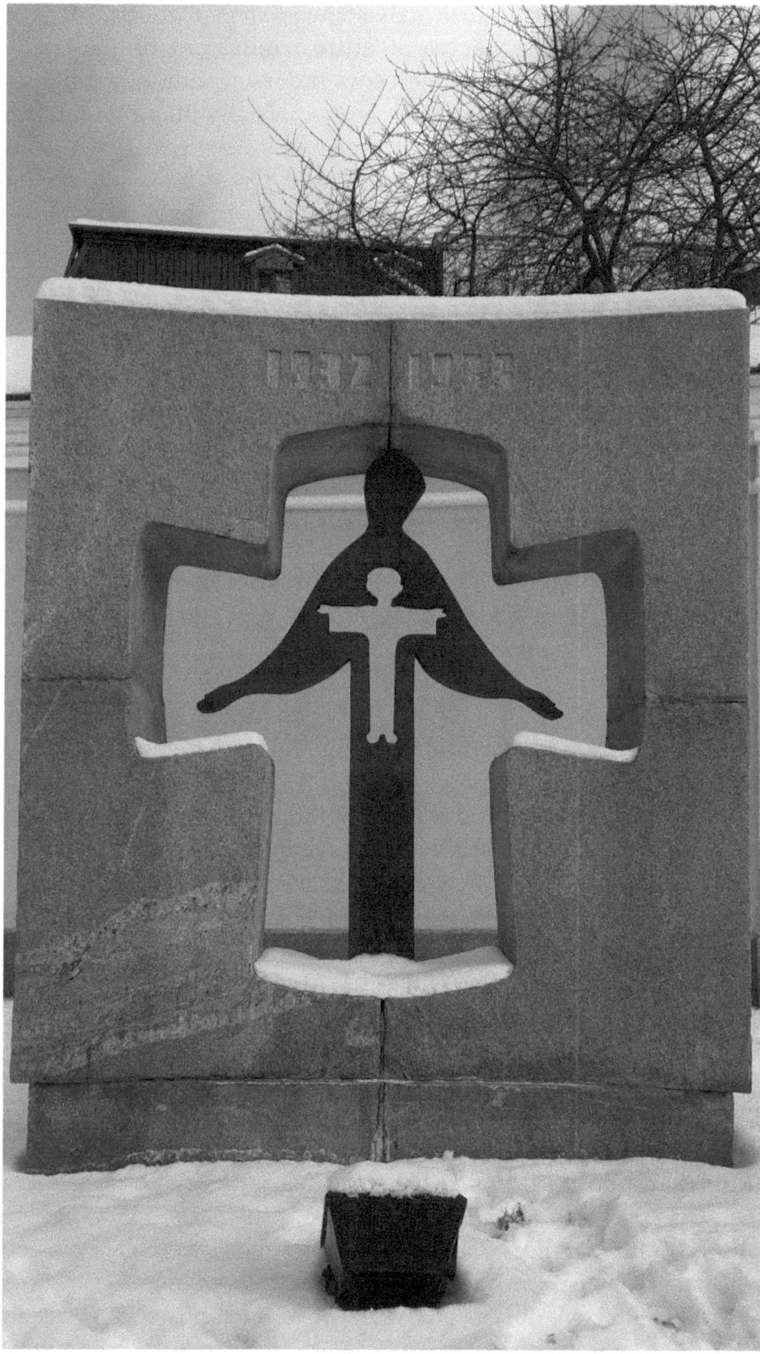

IMAGE 6.1 The Holodomor Monument in Kyiv (1993). Photograph by the author.

level, we observe a figure with delicately etched female features, suggested by the shape of the head, the sleeves of attire reminiscent of the traditional clothing of married Ukrainian women, and the inscription of a child's figure within it. Both figures appear within a cross, partially filling its interior. On an iconographic level, we note that the female form recalls two canonical representations of the Virgin Mary: The Virgin Orans icon and the Icon of the Protection. The first refers to representations of the Virgin Mary in a praying pose with raised and outstretched arms that represent a redeemed soul in Christian iconography. The image is deeply rooted in Ukrainian culture. What is more, Vasyl Perevalsky confirms that this Orthodox icon was an inspiration for him in designing the monument.[32] Despite its similarity to the image of the Orthodox Marian Iconography, this depiction should not be considered a religious masterpiece. The design put forth by Perevalsky and Kysly references religious themes from a secular perspective, which would become a characteristic feature of Holodomor remembrance in early independent Ukraine.

The soil on which the Holodomor Monument was erected in 1993 had been brought in from all regions of Ukraine but also from the Autonomous Republic of Crimea.[33] From a symbolic point of view, this is a significant step in creating a culture of memory that would bind together all communities in the newly independent Ukraine, even those that were not part of Soviet Ukraine at the time of the Holodomor. As a reminder, the Great Famine of 1932–33 took place in Soviet Ukraine, which did not yet include Crimea and Western Ukrainian areas belonging to the Second Polish Republic in the interwar period. Commemoration of the 60th anniversary was not restricted to the official part, with the unveiling of the monument. Visitors from almost every oblast in Ukraine placed wreaths at the memorial. Some individuals from the centre and east provinces affected by famine in 1932–33 brought soil from the famine victims' mass graves for the monument's official unveiling event. Others brought clay pots and still capsules filled with black earth as symbols of fertility and abundance of food. Representatives of western Ukraine brought documents to show the efforts they had made at the time to lessen the suffering in the stricken areas.[34]

Two issues are important regarding the original design: firstly, the imagery contained at the iconographic stage of the monument itself and the symbolic grave heaped around it; secondly, the iconological interpretation of how the Holodomor is presented at this site of memory. In her erudite study on the political life of dead bodies, Katherine Verdery came to the conclusion that improper burials, which we deal with in the case of mass crimes against humanity, also disturb the social order on a metaphysical level. As she explains, this belief is especially strong in Eastern Europe.[35] Exhumation and proper burial are thus not only common, but also locally saturated symbolic activities aimed at overturning the 'right world order'—one where bodies are literally rooted in a specific (religiously dedicated) place. When, however, in the case of commemoration of the victims of the Holodomor, it was not always possible to organise a 'proper' burial, initiatives were taken to make the interment in mass graves more appropriate through symbolic religious services (*panakhyda*) for the dead souls and to create places of symbolic burial in consecrated spaces on the parish cemetery.[36] Placing the monument near an important Orthodox temple, ruined in the 1930s by the communist authorities, reinforced the message about 'overturning the right world order'.

In post-Soviet Ukraine, the religious character of commemoration was to meet a broad spectrum of social needs, ranging from detachment from the communist past, national revival, and the creation of new social rituals to the establishment of a new pantheon of heroes and victims of history.[37] The reconstruction of the church and the construction of the monument under its walls in the first decades of Ukraine's independence, therefore, had great symbolic significance and, at the same time, reflected the social and political conditions of post-communist society. In fact, the monument is relatively small, but the rebuilding of St. Michael's (finished in May 1999) means that it occupies one of the city's central spaces.[38]

During the beginning of Leonid Kuchma's presidency (1994–2004), the Holodomor monument was relocated to one of Kyiv's parks during the reconstruction of St. Michael's Golden-Domed Monastery. It stood there merely as an adornment in the park at the time, which speaks to the relative indifference of society towards the Holodomor before the Orange Revolution (2004).[39] While interest in the topic of commemorating the Holodomor was waning at the end of Leonid Kuchma's second term of office, around the 70th anniversary of the Holodomor (2003), the monument did not regain its original symbolical social and political meaning. President Yushchenko decided to create the national memorial of the Holodomor in Kyiv (The Candle of Memory), which was unveiled in 2008 on his initiative and personal participation.[40]

Meanwhile, famine commemoration also attained a different meaning in public city space. A museum room was created in the Candle of Memory, the purpose of which was to commemorate. Over time, another goal was added to this memorial, namely educational activity. When the Candle of Memory was assigned this purpose, the 1993 Holodomor Monument in front of St. Michael's Golden-Domed Monastery ceased to function as the national monument. Nonetheless, it continues to play an impressive but completely different social role in the culture of memory. For years, it has become one of the world's most recognisable images of the Holodomor. Its eclecticism and mixture of religious symbolism and secular understanding of the suffering of people experiencing famine caused it to be used as graphics on books, bouquets, posters, and other monuments or commemorative plaques (Images 6.2 and 6.3).

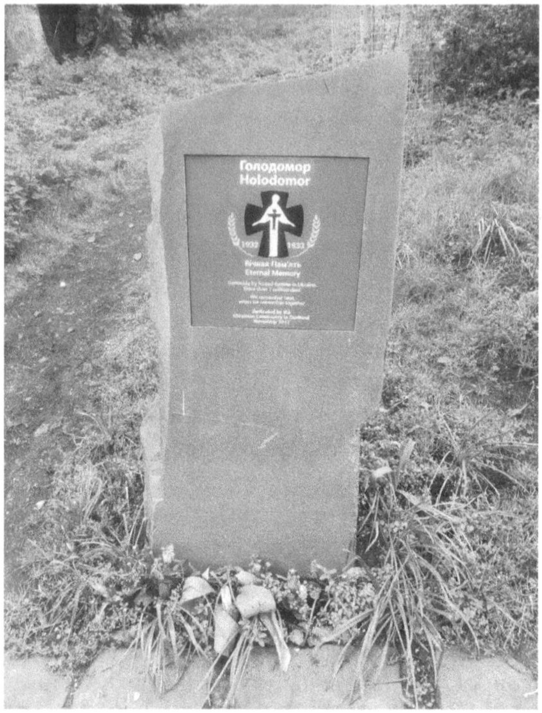

IMAGE 6.2 The Holodomor Monument in Edinburgh, Scotland (2017). Photograph by the author.

During the Revolution of Dignity (2013–14), this monument became a site marked by dramatic events, and from that moment on, it has become integrated into the cultural memory of Maidan. In fact, St. Michael's Golden-Domed Monastery was one of the central places during protests in Kyiv. On the night of 11 December 2013, the bells of the monastery rang for the first time in eight centuries. The last time this had happened was in 1240 during the Mongol invasion. Thanks to the sound of the bells, many people from Kyiv gathered in the centre of the capital, and the attempt to clear the Euromaidan by employees of the superior unit 'Berkut' and military personnel of the Internal Forces of the Ministry of Internal Affairs turned out to be unsuccessful. From that moment, the monastery began to become a symbol of the struggle for democracy.[41]

As a sign of this, on the other of the monastery's external walls bordering the square, The Wall of Remembrance of the Fallen for Ukraine, a Russian-Ukrainian War memorial has come into existence, honouring those who defended Ukrainian Statehood.[42] When this site became inaugurated in 2014, symbolically, the legacies of the heroes of the revolution and those of the victims of the Stalinist famine merged. Since May 2022, the site around the

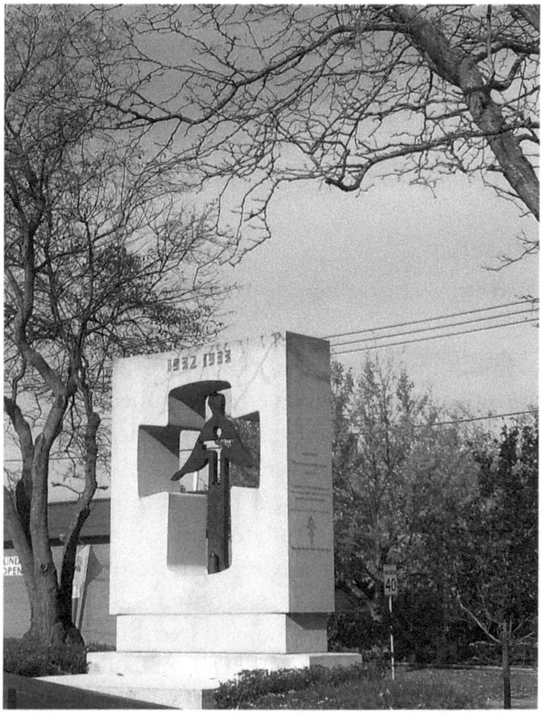

IMAGE 6.3 The Holodomor Monument at St. Demetrius parish in Toronto, Canada (2018). Photograph by the author.

monastery has hosted an exhibition that features Russian military equipment captured and destroyed during the 2022 Russian invasion of Ukraine.[43] In this way, the Holodomor Monument found itself at the epicentre of Ukrainian national memory: behind its back are the victims of the Heavenly Hundred, and in front of it is the testimony of the ongoing war in Ukraine. In September 2022, Zelensky promised that the exhibition on Mykhailivska Square would become part of the exposition of the National Military Historical Museum of Ukraine.[44] The pedestrian area would be cleared, and the Holodomor Monument would be in the centre of Square again.

As Marguérite Corporaal and Ingrid de Zwarte conclude, famine heritage is often 'multidirectional memory' in that it is often placed in dialogue with commemorations of other events. Famine monuments and museums are sites of practice that are social, embodied, and generative, for example, by invoking other cultural memories and by eliciting the creation of other heritage sites related to different pasts.[45] Upon a visit to Mykhailivska Square now, one can get the impression that it is a memorial site for both the Holodomor and today's Ukrainian war victims. Since the Russian annexation of Crimea, the monument, which contains a piece of now occupied land, also reminds us of this recent loss. As such, this place resembles a three-dimensional collage of Ukrainian national memory and mourning. In social rituals surrounding the 1993 monument, we see that the centre of gravity has shifted from the sacrifices made by the nation to the individual sacrifices made by innocently murdered war. Furthermore, this place continues to accumulate new (hi)stories that reinforce its identification as an assemblage of memory.

Changing presidents, changing memory cultures: The 2008 National Memorial

The National Holodomor Memorial (2008), better known as The Candle of Memory, is the product of many years of collective effort on the part of academics, social activists, and various political powers, and has been inspired by perceptions and knowledge of the historical events surrounding the Holodomor. The idea of creating a Holodomor memorial and museum as a 'national place of memory' came to fruition in 2002, when the former presidents Kravchuk and Kuchma asserted that a Holodomor Museum must be built in the Ukrainian capital. It was only in 2004, however, that the idea for its construction gained an influential patron in the form of President Yushchenko, who put a stop to earlier attempts and embarked on an entirely new commemorative undertaking, which was to be the epitome of his politics of memory. A competition for the best design was announced in the spring of 2006 and attracted entries from 17 artistic teams from all over Ukraine.[46] The winning design was by a team headed by a Kyiv architect, Anatoliy Haydamaka.[47] In its initial variant, the monument resembled more of a bell tower, a chapel of memory, which may have been dictated by the proximity of the monument's location to Pechersk Lavra—the most important centre of Orthodox pilgrimage in Ukraine. Its decorative elements were exclusively Christian in their symbolism, without the use of any pagan symbols, characteristic of Ukrainian folk culture. At the time, it was still a monument refined in its simplicity, its task being to recall an important event in the history of Ukraine.

Museum construction was split into two distinct stages: the erection of the monument and the building the museum. By 2017, due to a lack of public funds, only the first part of the plan had been realised, which included the sculptures of the mourning angels and the little girl with ears of wheat, the querns of history, the Candle of Memory monument, and 'the black plaques' behind it, the Hall of Memory (located underground), as well as the Viburnum Grove. The Candle of Memory seals the historical policy of the Yushchenko presidency in a way, functioning as a kind of manifesto that stands out in the context of his other undertakings in the realm of memory politics and the 'de-Sovietisation' of Ukrainian national identity. The degree of the president's involvement in the work on this memorial is well known and included concrete suggestions for symbolic solutions and a rejection of those ideas that did not align with his vision. The monument has therefore often been analysed as a key point for the Ukrainian memory policy of Yushchenko and as a place of national memory of Ukrainians in the period before the Revolution of Dignity.[48]

The design of the museum itself was based on the most recognisable iconography of suffering from the cultural repertoire of Ukrainian martyrology and centres around the concept of earth. The architectonic compositions are fundamentally individualised but also fit together with the common denominator of a 'memorial to Holodomor victims'. The stony path leading from the angels to the Candle of Memory is bumpy and is described by the guides as the 'dominion of memory'; it is intended to symbolise the Ukrainian *chernozems* (areas of fertile black Earth). Around the halfway point to the entrance underneath the memorial, one encounters a little square surrounded by round, flat stones resembling querns. In the centre of this symbolic stone circle stands a sculpture of a little girl with ears of wheat, officially entitled *Bitter Memories of Childhood.* The monument's makers also decided to inscribe the plinth with the title of Taras Shevchenko's poem, '*I mertvym, i zhyvym, i nenarodzhenym zemliakam moim v Ukraini i ne v Ukraini moie druzhnieie poslaniie*' (To my fellow-countrymen, in Ukraine and not in Ukraine, living, dead, and as yet unborn my friendly epistle) in gold lettering.[49] The fragment should be understood as a warning and a reminder for future generations of Ukrainians. Notably, visitors at the monument often leave sweets and candy rather than flowers. This custom of taking food to cemeteries in order to leave it on the graves of dead relatives is an established part of the Orthodox tradition[50] (Image 6.4).

Behind the girl's statue looms an imposing white monument resembling the shape of a candle, commonly known as the Candle of Memory. The body of the monument rises to a height of over 30 metres, with its surface made to look like the traditional Ukrainian fabrics, *rushnyks*, known for their cross-stitch pattern, as a symbol of Ukrainian indigenous traditions. The first museum exhibition was located in a symbolic way beneath the Candle of Memory, as the names of numerous victims of the Holodomor were projected onto the wall, and lived memories of the survivors were used. On the wall in the background of this diverse scenery, a document about the Great Famine is used interchangeably with the names of Holodomor victims. The light in all the rooms is dimmed. This first exhibition also accentuates the contrast between the world 'before' and 'after' the Holodomor. Before the visitors enter into the main hall, they can look at a display of old family photographs of Ukrainian peasants in festive costume (which has aroused much controversies, given the lack of a historical context). The display of various agricultural tools around the room is likely meant to symbolise the

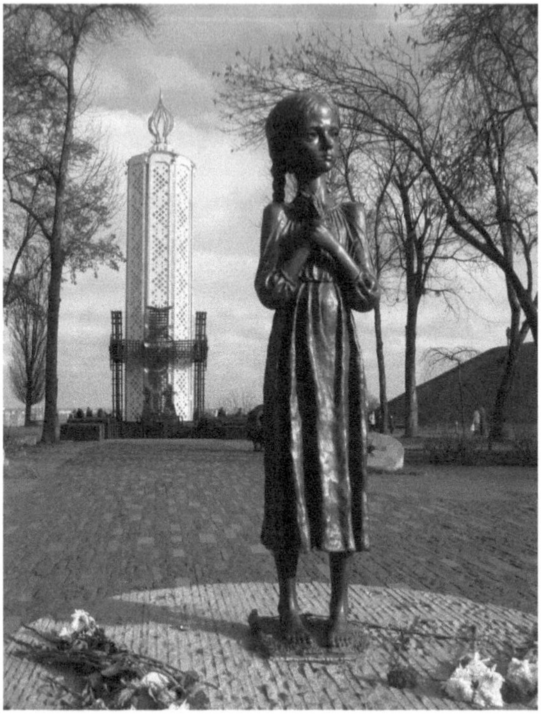

IMAGE 6.4 The Candle of Memory and sculpture *Bitter recollections of childhood* in Kyiv, Ukraine (2008). Photograph by the author.

agricultural character of Ukrainian culture and traditional forms of work among Ukrainian peasants.

In the centre of the hall is an altar in the shape of a glass coffin filled with grain, around which stone columns adorned with an image of the 'Tree of Life' have been placed. Significantly, the images are not identical representations of this common Ukrainian pagan symbol. Above the altar, a pagan straw protection doll hangs to ward off evil spirits from the hearth. This is not the result of artistic indecisiveness. It is instead a question of having such an extensive mix of symbols of 'authentic' Ukrainian culture and sacral symbols in one place that leads to confusion (Image 6.5).

On leaving the hall, visitors can once again look at the photographs displayed in the entry way; this time in the form of their negatives, as a symbol of a lost world registered by the camera, but not 'developed' into a future. Notably, while the steps leading to the main entrance go down into the depths of the Earth, as if 'into the land of the dead', at the end of the exhibition, en route to the 'black plaques', the staircase leads visitors upwards, from darkness into the light of day. This metaphor of passage, some kind of cleansing through immersion in the suffering of forebearers and

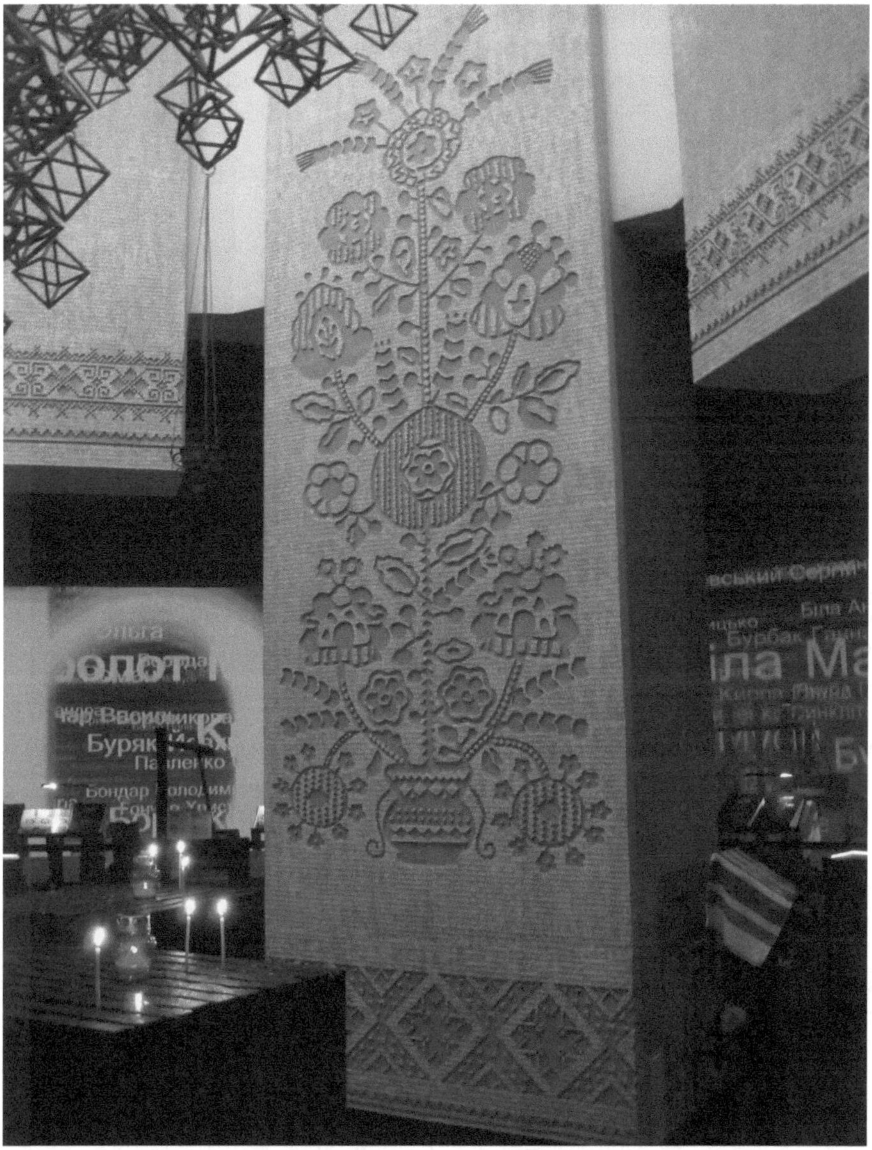

IMAGE 6.5 A part of installation 'The Tree of Life' in the National Museum of the Holodomor-Genocide. Photograph by the author.

learning the truth about the nation's past, may be helpful to properly understand the Holodomor's significance for the current Ukrainian national identity.

The Viburnum Grove part of the complex is also worth noting founded by Yushchenko as a symbol of national rebirth and hope for better times.

Initially, important dignitaries planted trees there on the occasion of various events, but at present, new trees are planted infrequently. The majority of guides finish the tour of the site with a moment of silence for those who died in the Holodomor. Foreign guests, including official delegations from other countries, also observe a minute of silence.

During the first years of its existence, the museum hall inside the Candle of Memory stressed allegiances to the soil, work on the land, and Ukrainian victimhood under Russian rule. The composition is a complete mix of folk and Christian symbols. The latter appears to be used in a more artistic and symbolic fashion rather than as unequivocal references to Orthodoxy, the faith of most Holodomor victims. It is a refined symbolism, emptied of religious meaning; the monument's makers utilised the Christian treasure trove of symbols, just as they did folk and pagan ones, to make specific meanings and compositional assumptions understandable to the broadest possible circle of recipients to stimulate empathy for the victims of the Holodomor.

Yushchenko's project of the national Holodomor Memorial, the museum complex to be built in the memorial's shadow was blocked for years by Yanukovych. However, due to the beginning of the war in Eastern Ukraine in 2014, Poroshenko returned to the topic of building a museum as the so-called second part of the Candle of Memory. In November 2016, a parliamentary committee was set up to this end, and a state-owned company was created to oversee the museum's construction.[51] An architectural design for the museum was developed by a group of Ukrainian architects from the company 'Project Systems' (Kyiv, Ukraine; Chief Architect Andrii Myrhorodsky), in cooperation with a leading European studio, 'Nizio Design International' (Warsaw, Poland), along with Haley Sharpe Design Ltd. (Great Britain).[52] For this new team of architects, the starting challenge was to take into account the tectonics and landscape of the slopes of the Dnipro Valley in the vicinity of Kyivan Cave Monastery, a place of exceptional significance in the history of Ukraine.

The new museum building is on an imaginary axis connecting the Candle of Memory monument and the observation deck along the Dnieper Descent. It will be possible to enter the museum building with the exhibition from both sides: the Candle of Memory and the observation deck by the bridge. In front of the entrance to the museum building, the square for ceremonies will be located. The monumental entrance from the side of Candle of Memory symbolises an open door to the dungeon, where the truth about the Holodomor is hidden.[53] The dual symbolism of the Ukrainian land—fertile but also concealing the graves of Holodomor victims—is the leitmotif appearing in the entire artistic concept of the building and the exhibition. Its narrative, contained in a script developed by experts from the Holodomor Museum, is intended to provoke reflection. It is intended to help find an answer to the question of why the Holodomor took place and what can be done to avoid such suffering in the future.[54] The museum plan also provides a separate exhibition space for temporary thematic exhibitions, a conference hall, a room for educational projects, a library, as well as archival and research centres.[55] Due to the war, the construction was initially suspended but then resumed, giving the completion of the museum a new symbolic meaning.

The concept of the exhibition is based on the contrast between light and darkness. Full and bright light will dominate the exhibition's initial spaces, which present the history of Ukrainian culture and the evolution of Ukrainian identity before 1932. The narrative of the formation of the mechanism of Soviet power that led to the mass murder will be accompanied by a deepening darkness in the central galleries depicting the course of the Holodomor crimes. Flashes of light will gradually begin to return with the story of witnesses to history and people who fought in Ukraine and around the world to remember the victims. The light will be entirely on again in the final gallery speaking of the victory of truth.[56] The very carefully directed play of light and dark in the sequences of rooms aims to have a strong psychological impact on the visitor. The light is undoubtedly associated with a candle, or rather with the Candle of Memory, which is located in the immediate vicinity of the museum in construction.

In this sense, not surprisingly, the designer Mirosław Nizio considers his project as a kind of artwork of museology. In one of his interviews, he says:

> In the same way, a poet uses words, I work with forms to create a narrative in many ways; designing a museum is similar to creating a sculpture. Simplicity, aesthetics, form, shape, architecture, structure, texture and context—these are what are important to me. [...] I like to work directly with the structure of a narrative, moving my thoughts like an actor to explore and explain history.[57]

Nizio skilfully uses terms such as the void, emptiness, labyrinth, or trauma; terms that have been used in memory studies for years. Nizio's museum design successfully meets the challenge of reincorporating the Ukrainian past into the history of modern Ukraine. The above interpretation of Holodomor Museum design demonstrates that, despite its deconstructive form of representing the past, the view of history it expresses is rather monumental counterhistory. It is a project that meets the expectations of the Ukrainian memory policies of the last few years, reinforcing the most important aspects of the contemporary message about the Holodomor as an unsettled crime from the past and reinforcing the conviction that the victims of the Holodomor are impeccable people of exceptional strength of spirit. In Nizio Studio projects, emotions are the most important, which help to understand the past through empathy and stimulate reflection on it. In line with this, the Holodomor Museum is conceived as a memory space that should be visited more than once. The museum is envisaged as a meaningful void that gives expression to loss and death,[58] while at the same time addressing histories that were previously silenced by Soviet governments.

Meanwhile, the museum is an unfinished project: its construction was exposed to several suspensions during the days of Yanukovych, due to numerous reconceptualisations of the exhibition narrative of the museum itself, the COVID-19 pandemic, and, since 2022, Russia's full-scale military aggression. Especially Russia's invasion of Ukraine has had a significant impact, both on the process of implementing the museum project and on its present-day meaning. Despite the outbreak of war, construction works on the museum continue, and people still feel the urge to visit the 2008 memorial. As the acting director of the Memorial, Lesya Hasydzhak, states:

> But we were probably one of the first in Kyiv to open the memorial hall for visitors on August 4, 2022. Even though there was shelling, we believed that we had to work. We still worked despite the difficult autumn, turning off the electricity supply. Of course, compared to 2019, we have fewer visitors today, as in every museum. But I think there are a lot of them. […] Moreover, we have increased the number of individual excursions. If earlier there were many groups of schoolchildren, students, tourists, now these are families, friends, two or three people. What does this indicate? This shows that people want to know the truth and history. […] Of course, the exhibition will present a parallel between genocide then and crimes with signs of genocide now, with the understanding that evil that has not been condemned (because there was never a tribunal over communism) returns and repeats itself.[59]

Hasydzhak's observations illustrate the fact that the monument and museum have gained significance among Ukrainians because they see parallels between Russia's implication in the Holodomor and its current occupation and destruction of their country. Nizio himself made a similar claim in an interview from July 2023, asserting that, 'the need to talk about this event and liberate oneself from trauma and tell the story of people who were annihilated in an artificially induced famine is growing stronger'.[60] The 2008 Holodomor Memorial, which has been gradually changing the way of talking about the Holodomor since the Revolution of Dignity, has become a symbol of the 'stout heartedness' of Ukrainians as a nation in the currently implemented project after the full-scale invasion of the territory of Ukraine.

Conclusions

From the 1990s, famine heritage proved useful for some Ukrainian political leaders wishing to formulate national unity around famine trauma and seeking to instrumentalise famine history for their politics. As this chapter has revealed, the development of the two famine memorials in Kyiv has been impacted by the successive government of Ukrainian Prime Ministers, as well as by the Maidan Revolution and Russian-Ukrainian warfare. This memorialisation of the Holodomor has evolved, despite the blurred lines between victims and victimisers that have complicated Holodomor legacies.

Since the full-scale Russian invasion of Ukraine in 2022, the memorialisation of Holodomor has come to be seen as an important way to create awareness of new Russian mass atrocities in Ukraine. Memories of current war trauma are no obstacle to memorialising the famine; in fact, in the case of the Holodomor, they fuel it because present atrocities are committed by the same perpetrator. Moreover, from 2022, it is possible to construct a narrative of past famine that no longer stresses collective victimhood but contrasts it to the 'stout heartedness' of Ukrainians as a post-famine genocide nation. We can observe leaders and activists who can compose a story of national pride and resilience in the face of famine and thus find strategies to overcome the new Russian-Ukrainian war trauma. In many other cases of memorialisation of complex heritage, war heroes tend to be commemorated or held sacred, and those violated by hunger are publicly mourned. However, in Ukrainian memory culture, famine victims and Maidan or war heroes are memorialised similarly to some sort of secular martyrs in the same 'spaces of memory'.

Notes

1 Sharon Macdonald, *Memorylands: Heritage and Identity in Europe Today* (London: Routledge, 2013), 5–6.
2 Ibid.
3 Pamela A. Moss and Edward H. Haertel, 'Engaging Methodological Pluralism', in *Handbook of Research on Teaching*, eds. Drew Gitomer and Courtney Bell (Washington, DC: AERA, 2016), 127–247.
4 Camilla Orjuela. 'Remembering/Forgetting Hunger: Towards an Understanding of Famine Memorialisation'. *Third World Quarterly* 45, no. 2 (2024): 259–76. Online pre-publication. doi: 10.1080/01436597.2023.2200928.
5 Ibid.
6 Anne Applebaum, *Red Famine: Stalin's War on Ukraine* (New York: Doubleday, 2017), 363.
7 Roman Serbyn, 'The Holodomor: Genocide Against the Ukrainians', in *Holodomor: Reflections on the Great Famine of 1932–1933 in Soviet Ukraine,* eds. Lubomyr Y. Luciuk and Lisa Grekul (Kingston, ON: The Kashtan Press, 2008), 61–6.
8 Kudela-Świątek, *Eternal Memory*, 191–2.
9 Mykola Miroshnychenko, 'Smertiu smert' podolavshy', *Literaturna Ukraïna* (16 September 1993): 2.
10 Catherine Wanner, *Burden of Dreams: History and Identity in Post-Soviet Ukraine* (University Park, PA: The Pennsylvania State University Press, 2008), 156.
11 Oleksandr Hrytsenko, *Prezydenty i pam'iat': Polityka pam'iati prezydentiv Ukraïny* (Kyiv: K.I.S., 2017).
12 'Pro vstanovlennia Dnia pam'iati zhertv holodomoriv. Ukaz Prezydenta Ukraïny vid 26 lystopada 1998 roku № 1310/98', *Uriadovyi kur'ier* (28 November 1998): 4.

13 Georgij Kas'ianov, *Rozryta Mohyla: Holod 1932–1933 rokiv u politytsi, pam'iati ta istorii (1980-ti – 2000-ni)* (Kharkiv: Folio, 2019), 66, 233.
14 Simone A. Bellezza, 'Building Memory: National Identities and Monuments in Post–Soviet Ukraine', in *Ukraine Twenty Years After Independence: Assessments, Perspectives, Challenges,* eds Giovanna Brogi, Marta Dyczok, Oxana Pachlovska, and Giovanna Siedina (Rome: Aracne editrice S.r.l., 2015), 241–64.
15 Georgii Kas'ianov, 'The Holodomor and the Building of a Nation', *Russian Politics & Law* 48, no. 5 (2010): 25–47.
16 'Holodomor monuments in Ukraine', The Ukrainian Canadian Research & Documentation Centre, at http://www.holodomor-monuments.org/, last accessed 25 July 2023.
17 Kas'ianov, *Rozryta Mohyla*, 70–1.
18 Ibid., 71.
19 Nicolas Dreyer, 'Genocide, *Holodomor* and Holocaust Discourse as Echo of Historical Injury and as Rhetorical Radicalization in the Russian-Ukrainian Conflict of 2013–18', *Journal of Genocide Research* 20, no. 4 (2018): 545–64.
20 Kas'ianov, *Rozryta Mohyla*, 73.
21 'Ukraine: Poroshenko Compares Holodomor with War in East', Radio Free Europe/Radio Liberty, 22 November 2014, https://www.refworld.org/docid/548ea90b3b3.html, last accessed 10 August 2023.
22 'Ukraine's Poroshenko Calls on Russia to "Repent" for Holodomor', RFE/RL's Ukrainian Service, 25 Noveember 2017, https://www.rferl.org/a/ukraine-holodomor-poroshenko-commemoration/28876715.html, last accessed 18 May 2023.
23 Josef Zisels and Halyna Kharaz, 'Will Holodomor Receive the Same Status as the Holocaust?', Human Rights in Ukraine. The Information Portal of the Kharkiv Human Rights Protection Group, 15 November 2007, https://khpg.org/en/1195083066, last accessed 12 August 2023.
24 'Global Holodomor Recognition', HREC, https://holodomor.ca/resources/memorialization/global-holodomor-recognition/, last accessed 12 August 2023.
25 'The Holodomor Museum is of Paramount Importance for Ukraine and Will Definitely Be Completed – President at the Holodomor Victims Remembrance Ceremony', President of Ukraine Volodymyr Zelensky Official Website, 28 November 2020, https://www.president.gov.ua/en/news/muzej-golodomoru-ye-nadvazhlivim-dlya-ukrayini-j-obovyazkovo-65321, last accessed 12 August 2023.
26 Elina Kent, 'The Road for Truth campaign seeks to expand Holodomor Museum in Kyiv', US.-Ukraine Business Council, 20 November 2019, https://www.usubc.org/site/recent-news/the-road-for-truth-campaign-seeks-to-expand-holodomor-museum-in-kyiv, last accessed 12 August 2023.
27 Martin Fornusek, 'Zelensky Vetoes Bill Allocating almost $16 Million to Holodomor Museum', *The Kyiv Independent*, 28 July 2023, https://kyivindependent.com/zelensky-vetoes/, last accessed 12 August 2023.
28 Christoph Mick, 'The Fight for the Past: Contested Heritage and the Russian Invasion of Ukraine', *The Historic Environment: Policy & Practice* 14, no. 2 (2023): 147–48.
29 Miroshnychenko, 'Smertiu smert' podolavshy', 1.
30 James E. Young, *The Texture of Memory: Holocaust Memorials and Meaning* (New Haven and London: Yale University Press, 1993), 7.
31 Olena Buniak, 'Heneral'nyi plan rekonstruktsii mista Kyïva 1935 r. (za materialamy periodychnykh vydan)', *Naukovyi visnyk Natsional'noho muzeiu istorii Ukraïny* 1, no. 1 (2017): 192–6, https://visnyk.nmiu.org/index.php/nv/article/view/36, last accessed 18 May 2023.
32 Siksana Lysenko, 'Cherkashchanyn Vasyl' Pereval's'kyi stvoryv usesvitn'ovidomyi symvol Holodomoru', Uman' info, 20 November 2012, http://uman.info/

ua/news/cherkashchanyn-vasyl-perevalskyy-stvoryv-usesvitnovidomyy-symvol-golodomoru–1540.html, last accessed 18 May 2023.

33 Oleksandra Veselova, 'Pam'iatni znaky i pam'iatnyky zhertvam Holodu-henotsydu 1932–1933 rr. v Ukraïni', *Problemy istoriï Ukraïny: Fakty, sudzhennia, poshuky*, 13 (2005): 434.

34 Wanner, *Burden of Dreams*, 157.

35 Katherine Verdery, *The Political Lives of Dead Bodies: Reburial and Postsocialist Change* (New York: Columbia University Press, 1999), 29–33.

36 Vitalii Ogiienko, 'The Memorial Topography of the Holodomor Between Cumulative and Cultural Trauma: A Genealogical Approach', in *Image, History and Memory: Central and Eastern Europe in a Comparative Perspective*, eds. Michal Haake and Piotr Juszkiewicz (London and New York: Routledge, 2022), 133–50.

37 Uilleam Blacker, 'Martyrdom, Spectacle, and Public Space: Ukraine's National Martyrology from Shevchenko to the Maidan', *Journal of Soviet and Post-Soviet Politics and Society* 1, no. 2 (2015): 257–92.

38 Wilson, *The Ukrainians*, 227.

39 Veselova, 'Pam'atni znaky', 434–41.

40 Hrytsenko, *Prezydenty i pam'iat'*, 638–95.

41 Olga Dudar, 'Heritage Burnt, Heritage Born – Paradox of "Space of Memory" in Conflicts: Ukraine's Experience Reconsidered', in *Instrumentalizing the Past: The Impact of History on Contemporary International Conflicts*, eds. Jan Rydel and Stefan Troebst (Berlin and Boston: De Gruyter Oldenbourg, 2022), 71–8.

42 Dudar, 'Heritage Burnt, Heritage Born', 71–8.

43 'Exhibition of Destroyed Russian Military Equipment Opens in Kyiv', *Euronews*, 28 May 2022, https://www.euronews.com/video/2022/05/28/exhibition-of-destroyed-russian-military-equipment-opens-in-kyiv, last accessed 18 May 2023.

44 Brendan Cole, 'Ukraine Military Shares Display of Destroyed Russian Equipment in Kyiv', *Newsweek*, 20 August 2022, https://www.newsweek.com/russia-kyiv-ukraine-tanks-destroyed-independence-moscow-1735398, last accessed 18 May 2023.

45 Marguérite Corporaal and Ingrid de Zwarte, 'Heritages of Hunger: European Famine Legacies in Current Academic Debates'. International Journal of Heritage Studies 28, no. 1 (2022): 30–43.

46 'Anatolii Haidamaka: "U muzeï khochu pokazaty «chervonyi terror» proty Ukraïny za sto rokiv', *Ukraïna moloda*, 126 (20 November 2018), https://www.umoloda.kiev.ua/number/3388/188/128184/, last accessed 18 May 2023.

47 Vitalij Ohiienko, 'Vizual'na kul'tura pam'iatnykiv zhertvam holodomoru v Ukraïni', *Hileia: Naukovyi visnyk* 65 (2012): 114–19.

48 Kudela-Świątek, *Eternal Memory*, 278.

49 See Taras Shevchenko, '*Song out of Darkness*': *Selected Poems*, trans. Vera Rich (London: Mitre Press, 1961), 74–80.

50 Natalia Havryl'iuk, 'The Structure and Function of Funeral Rituals and Customs in Ukraine', *Folklorica, Journal of the Slavic, East European, and Eurasian Folkore Association* 8, no. 2 (2003): 7–23.

51 Mariia Ivashchuk, 'Proekt muzeiu Holodomoru', *The Village*, 1 August 2017, at http://www.the-village.com.ua/village/city/city-news/260765-proekt-muzeyu-golodomoru, last accessed 30 July 2020.

52 'Mirosław Nizio projektuje Muzeum Ofiar Wielkiego Głodu w Kijowie', InfoArchitekta, 4 December 2018, https://www.infoarchitekta.pl/artykuly:4-projekty:17748-miroslaw-nizio-projektuje-muzeum-ofiar-wielkiego-glodu-w-kijowie.html, last accessed 31 March 2019; and see 'Arkhitekturnyi projekt muzeiu', Holodomor Museum, at https://holodomormuseum.org.ua/arkhitekturnyj-proekt-muzeiu/, last accessed 18 May 2023.

53 'Architectural Project of the Museum', Holodomor Museum, https://holodomormuseum.org.ua/en/architectural-project-of-the-museum/, last accessed 18 May 2023.

54 Pawel Łoza, 'To będzie podróż w poszukiwaniu prawdy', *Nashe slovo* 2 (5 January 2022), https://nasze-slowo.pl/to-bedzie-podroz-w-poszukiwaniu-prawdy/, last accessed 18 May 2023.
55 See 'The Project of the Second Part of the National Museum "Holodomor Victims Memorial" Was Presented to President of Ukraine Petro Poroshenko', Holodomor Museum, 23 November 2018, https://holodomormuseum.org.ua/en/news/the-project-of-the-second-part-of-the-national-museum-quot-holodomor-victims-memorial-quot-was-presented-to-president-of-ukraine-petro-poroshenko/, last accessed 30 July 2020.
56 'Meeting with the Supervisory Board of the Holodomor Museum Foundation', *Nizio Design International*, 21 April 2023, https://nizio.com.pl/en/meeting-with-the-supervisory-board-of-the-holodomor-museum-foundation/, last accessed 18 May 2023.
57 Alex Webber, 'A museum isn't just for tourists. It a place for interaction with history', *The First News*, 23 Dec. 2020, https://www.thefirstnews.com/article/a-museum-isnt-just-for-tourists-it-a-place-for-interaction-with-history-18645, last accessed 12 August 2023.
58 Anna Khotsianivs'ka, 'Sribna lozhka – za shmatok chornoho khliba: v Natsional'nomu muzeï Holodomoru predstavyly novi pokhmuri eksponaty', *TSN*, 7 September 2021, https://tsn.ua/exclusive/sribna-lozhka-za-shmatok-chornogo-hliba-v-nacionalnomu-muzeyi-golodomoru-predstavili-novi-pohmuri-eksponati-1862269.html, last accessed 18 May 2023.
59 Mariia Kabatsii, '"Za roky nezalezhnosti my zbuduvaly 10 muzeïv": Kerivnytsia Muzeiu Holodomoru – pro te, chomu dobuduvaty ioho s'ohodni vazhlyvishe, nizh zdaiet'sia', *Ukraïns'ka pravda*, 21 July 2023, https://life.pravda.com.ua/culture/2023/07/21/255506/, last accessed 12 August 2023.
60 Sołomiewicz, 'Mirosław Nizio o tworzeniu'.

References

'Anatolii Haidamaka: "U muzeï khochu pokazaty «chervonyi terror» proty Ukraïny za storokiv'. *Ukraïna moloda* 126 (20 November 2018). https://www.umoloda.kiev.ua/number/3388/188/128184/

Applebaum, Anne, *Red Famine: Stalin's War on Ukraine*. New York: Doubleday, 2017.

'Architectural Project of the Museum'. Holodomor Museum. https://holodomormuseum.org.ua/en/architectural-%20%20project-of-the-museum/

'Arkhitekturnyi projekt muzeiu'. Holodomor Museum. https://holodomormuseum.org.ua/arkhitekturnyj-proekt-muzeiu/

Avdokushyn, Pavel, '#14. Budivnytsvo II cherhy Natsional'noho muzeiu Holodomoru henotsydu: Shcho zminylos'ia za rik?'. YouTube. 1 February 2023. https://www.youtube.com/watch?v=3M_8O13z2eE.

Bellezza, Simone A., 'Building Memory: National Identities and Monuments in Post–Soviet Ukraine'. In Giovanna Brogi, Marta Dyczok, Oxana Pachlovska, and Giovanna Siedina, eds., 241–64, *Ukraine Twenty Years After Independence: Assessments, Perspectives, Challenges*. Rome: Aracne editrice S.r.l., 2015.

Blacker, Uilleam, 'Martyrdom, Spectacle, and Public Space: Ukraine's National Martyrology from Shevchenko to the Maidan'. *Journal of Soviet and Post-Soviet Politics and Society* 1, no. 2 (2015): 257–92.

Buniak, Olena, 'Heneral'nyi plan rekonstruktsiï mista Kyïva 1935 r. (za materialamy periodychnykh vydan"'. *Naukovyi visnyk Natsional'noho muzeiu istoriï Ukraïny* 1, no. 1 (2017): 192–6. https://visnyk.nmiu.org/index.php/nv/article/view/36

Cole, Brendan. 'Ukraine Military Shares Display of Destroyed Russian Equipment in Kyiv'. *Newsweek*. 20 August 2022. https://www.newsweek.com/russia-kyiv-ukraine-tanksdestroyedindependence-moscow-1735398.

Corporaal, Marguérite and Ingrid de Zwarte, 'Heritages of Hunger: European Famine Legacies in Current Academic Debates'. *International Journal of Heritage Studies* 28, no. 1 (2022): 30–43.

'Dity – naivrazlyvishi zhertvy henotsydu: UINP rozpochav informkampaniiu do 88-kh rokovyn Holodomoru'. Ukraïns'kyi instytut natsional'noï pam'iati. https://uinp.gov.ua/pres-centr/novyny/dity-nayvrazlyvishi-zhertvy-genocydu-uinprozpochavinformkampaniyu-do-88-h-rokovyn-golodomoru, last accessed 15 November 2021.

Dreyer, Nicolas, 'Genocide, *Holodomor* and Holocaust Discourse as Echo of Historical Injury and as Rhetorical Radicalization in the Russian-Ukrainian Conflict of 2013–18'. *Journal of Genocide Research* 20, no. 4 (2018): 545–564.

Dudar, Olga, 'Heritage Burnt, Heritage Born – Paradox of "Space of Memory" in Conflicts: Ukraine's Experience Reconsidered'. In Jan Rydel and Stefan Troebst, eds., 71–8, *Instrumentalising the Past: The Impact of History on Contemporary International Conflicts*. Berlin and Boston: De Gruyter Oldenbourg, 2022.

'Exhibition of Destroyed Russian Military Equipment Opens in Kyiv'. Euronews. 28 May 2022. https://www.euronews.com/video/2022/05/28/exhibition-of-destroyed-russian-military-equipment-opens-in-kyiv.

Fornusek Martin, 'Zelensky Vetoes Bill Allocating Almost $16 Million to Holodomor Museum'. *The Kyiv Independent*, 28 July 2023. https://kyivindependent.com/zelensky-vetoes/.

'Global Holodomor Recognition'. HREC. https://holodomor.ca/resources/memorialization/global-holodomor-recognition/

Havryl'iuk, Natalia, 'The Structure and Function of Funeral Rituals and Customs in Ukraine'. *Folklorica, Journal of the Slavic, East European, and Eurasian Folkore Association* 8, no. 2 (2003): 7–23.

'Holodomor monuments in Ukraine'. *The Ukrainian Canadian Research & Documentation Centre*. http://www.holodomor-monuments.org/.

'The Holodomor Museum is of Paramount Importance for Ukraine and Will Definitely Be Completed – President at the Holodomor Victims Remembrance Ceremony'. *President of Ukraine Volodymyr Zelenskyy Official Website*. 28 November 2020. https://www.president.gov.ua/en/news/muzej-golodomoru-ye-nadvazhlivim-dlya-ukrayini-jobovyazkovo-65321

Hrytsenko, Oleksandr, *Prezydenty i pam'iat'. Polityka pam'iati prezydentiv Ukraïny*. Kyiv: K.I.S., 2017.

Ivashchuk, Mariia, 'Proekt muzeiu Holodomoru'. *The Village*, 1 August 2017. http://www.thevillage.com.ua/village/city/city-news/260765-proekt-muzeyu-golodomoru.

Kabatsii, Mariia, '"Za roky nezalezhnosti my zbuduvaly 10 muzeïv". Kerivnytsia Muzeiu Holodomoru – pro te, chomu dobuduvaty ioho s'ohodni vazhlyvishe, nizh zdaiet'sia'. *Ukraïns'ka Pravda*, 21 July 2023. https://life.pravda.com.ua/culture/2023/07/21/255506/

Kas'ianov, Georgi, *Rozryta Mohyla: Holod 1932–1933 rokiv u politytsi, pam'iati ta istoriï (1980-ti – 2000-ni)*. Kharkiv: Folio, 2019.

Kas'ianov, Georgii, 'The Holodomor and the Building of a Nation'. *Russian Politics & Law* 48, no. 5 (2010): 25–47.

Kent, Elina, 'The Road for Truth campaign seeks to expand Holodomor Museum in Kyiv'. U.S.-Ukraine Business Council, 20 November 2019. https://www.usubc.org/site/recent-news/the road-for-truth-campaign-seeks-to-expand-holodomor-museum-in-kyiv.

Khotsianivs'ka, A., 'Sribna lozhka – za shmatok chornoho khliba: v Natsional'nomu muzeï Holodomoru predstavyly novi pokhmuri eksponaty'. TSN, 7 September 2021. https://tsn.ua/exclusive/sribna-lozhka-za-shmatok-chornogo-hliba-v-nacionalnomu-muzeyigolodomoru-predstavili-novi-pohmuri-eksponati-1862269.html.

Kudela-Świątek, Wiktoria, *Eternal Memory: Monuments and Memorials of the Holodomor*. Translated by G. R. Torr, introd. Frank E. Sysyn. Edmonton, Toronto, Cracow: University of Alberta, University of Toronto and Księgarnia Akademicka, 2021.

Lysenko, Siksana. 'Cherkashchanyn Vasyl' Pereval's'kyi stvoryv usesvitn'ovidomyi symvol Holodomoru', Uman' info. 20 November 2012. http://uman.info/ua/news/cherkashchanyn-vasylperevalskyy-stvoryv-usesvitnovidomyy-symvol-golodomoru–1540.html

Łoza, Pawel. 'To będzie podróż w poszukiwaniu prawdy'. *Nashe slovo 2*. 5 January 2022. https://nasze-slowo.pl/to-bedzie-podroz-w-poszukiwaniu-prawdy/.

Macdonald, Sharon. *Memorylands: Heritage and Identity in Europe Today*. London: Routledge, 2013.

Marples, David R. *Ukraine in Conflict: An Analytical Chronicle*. Bristol: E-International Relations, 2017.

'Meeting with the Supervisory Board of the Holodomor Museum Foundation'. Nizio Design International, 21 April 2023. https://nizio.com.pl/en/meeting-with-the-supervisory-board-ofthe-holodomor-museum-foundation/.

Mick, Christoph, 'The Fight for the Past: Contested Heritage and the Russian Invasion of Ukraine'. *The Historic Environment: Policy & Practice* 14, no. 2 (2023): 135–53.

Miroshnychenko, Mykola, 'Smertiu smert' podolavshy'. *Literaturna Ukraïna* (1993): 1–2.

'Mirosław Nizio projektuje Muzeum Ofiar Wielkiego Głodu w Kijowie'. InfoArchitekta, 4 December 2018. https://www.infoarchitekta.pl/artykuly:4-projekty:17748-miroslaw-nizioprojektuje-muzeum-ofiar-wielkiego-glodu-w-kijowie.html.

Moss, Pamela A. and Edward H. Haertel, 'Engaging methodological pluralism'. In Drew Gitomer and Courtney Bell, eds., 127–47, *Handbook of Research on Teaching*. Washington, DC: AERA, 2016.

'Muzeum Ofiar Wielkego Głodu w Kijowie: trwa realizacja Narodowego Muzeum Hołodomoru według projektu Nizio Design International'. Architektura Murator, 4 December 2018. https://architektura.muratorplus.pl/projekty/muzeum-ofiar-wielkiego-glodu-w-kijowiezaprojektowali-polacy_9276.html.

Nijakowski, Lech M., 'Monument Wars and the Pursuit of Symbolic Dominion over a Territory: Analysis Based on the Case of Germans in Poland'. *International Journal of Sociology* 36, no. 4 (2006): 27–44.

'Novyi holova Instytutu natspam'iati kazhe, shcho bude ne rozvorot, a "kut nakhylu"'. *Ukraïns'ka pravda*, 27 December 2019. https://www.pravda.com.ua/news/2019/12/27/7235964/.

Ogiienko, Vitalii. 'The Memorial Topography of the Holodomor Between Cumulative and Cultural Trauma: A Genealogical Approach'. In Michal Haake and Piotr Juszkiewicz, eds., 133–50, *Image, History and Memory: Central and Eastern Europe in a Comparative Perspective*. London and New York: Routledge, 2022.

Ohiienko, Vitalii, 'Vizual'na kul'tura pam'iatnykiv zhertvam holodomoru v Ukraïni'. *Hileia: Naukovyi visnyk* 65 (2012): 114–19.

Orjuela, Camilla. 'Remembering/Forgetting Hunger: Towards an Understanding of Famine Memorialisation'. *Third World Quarterly* 45, no. 2 (2024): 259-276.

'Pro vstanovlennia Dnia pam'iati zhertv holodomoriv. Ukaz Prezydenta Ukraïny vid 26 lystopada 1998 roku № 1310/98'. *Uriadovyi kur'ier* (1998): 4.

'The Project of the Second Part of the National Museum "Holodomor Victims Memorial" Was Presented to President of Ukraine Petro Poroshenko'. Holodomor Museum. 23 November 2018. https://holodomormuseum.org.ua/en/news/the-project-of-the-second-part-ofthenationalmuseum-quot-holodomor-victims-memorial-quot-was-presented-to-president-of-ukraine-petro-poroshenko/.

Serbyn, Roman, 'The Holodomor: Genocide Against the Ukrainians'. In Lubomyr Y. Luciuk and Lisa Grekul, eds., 61–6, *Holodomor: Reflections on the Great Famine of 1932–1933 in Soviet Ukraine*. Kingston, ON: The Kashtan Press, 2008.

Shevchenko, Taras, *"Song out of Darkness": Selected Poems*. Trans. Vera Rich. London: Mitre Press, 1961.

Sołomiewicz, Anna, 'Mirosław Nizio o tworzeniu architektury pamięci'. *Property Design*, 19 July 2023. https://www.propertydesign.pl/wywiady/109/miroslaw_nizio_o_tworzeniu_architektury_pamieci,44164.html.

Sontag, Susan, 'The Aesthetics of Silence'. *Aspen* 5+6, item 3 (1967). https://www.kim-cohen.com/Assets/CourseAssets/Texts/Sontag_The%20Aesthetics%20of%20Silence.pdf

'Take part in the Annual Observances of the Holodomor-Genocide'. Ukrainian World Congress, 22 November 2022. https://www.ukrainianworldcongress.org/take-part-in-the-annualobservances-of-the-holodomor-genocide/

'Ukraine's Poroshenko Calls on Russia to "Repent" for Holodomor'. RFE/RL's Ukrainian Service, 25 November 2017. https://www.rferl.org/a/ukraine-holodomor-poroshenkocommemoration/28876715.html.

'Ukraine: Poroshenko Compares Holodomor with War in East'. Radio Free Europe/Radio Liberty, 22 November 2014. https://www.refworld.org/docid/548ea90b3b3.html.

'Ukraine's Great Famine Memories Fuel Resentment of Kremlin'. BBC, 12 February 2022. https://www.bbc.com/news/world-europe-60353677.

Verdery, Katherine, *The Political Lives of Dead Bodies: Reburial and Postsocialist Change*. New York: Columbia University Press, 1999.

Veselova, Oleksandra, 'Pam'iatni znaky i pam'iatnyky zhertvam Holodu-henotsydu 1932 1933 rr. v Ukraïni', *Problemy istoriï Ukraïny: Fakty, sudzhennia, poshuky* 13 (2005): 434–41.

Veselova, Oleksandra, *Z istoriï stvorennia i diial'nosti Asotsiatsiï doslidnykiv holodomoru v Ukraïni (ADHU) 1933: monohrafiia*. Kyiv: ADHU, 2007.

Vidomosti Verkhovnoï Rady Ukraïny (VVR), no. 51 (2002).

Wanner, Catherine, *Burden of Dreams: History and Identity in Post-Soviet Ukraine*. University Park, PA: The Pennsylvania State University Press, 2008.

Webber, Alex, 'A museum isn't just for tourists. It a place for interaction with history'. *The First News*, 23 December 2020. https://www.thefirstnews.com/article/a-museum-isnt-just-for tourists-it-a-place-for-interaction-with-history-18645.

Wilson, Andrew, *The Ukrainians: Unexpected Nation*. New Haven, CT: Yale University, 2015.

Young, James E., *The Texture of Memory: Holocaust Memorials and Meaning*. New Haven, CT, and London: Yale University Press, 1993.

'"Zberezhy pam'iat'. Zberezhy pravdu": UINP rozpochynaie informatsiinu kampaniiu do 87- ykh rokovyn Holodomoru'. Ukraïns'kyi instytut natsional'noï pam'iati, 17 November 2020. https://uinp.gov.ua/pres-centr/novyny/zberezhy-pamyat-zberezhy-pravdu-uinp-rozpochynayeinformaciynu-kampaniyu-do-87-yh-rokovyn-golodomoru.

Zisels, Josef and Halyna Kharaz, 'Will Holodomor receive the same status as the Holocaust?' *Human Rights in Ukraine*. The Information Portal of the Kharkiv Human Rights Protection Group, 15 November 2007. https://khpg.org/en/1195083066.

PART III
Musealisation

7

FAMINE CLEARANCES IN THE SCOTTISH HIGHLANDS

The musealisation of the past and the socio-political function of museums

Laurence Gouriévidis

> So it was that with increasing poverty, the ever-pressing threat of eviction, the small size and infertility of their holdings, the crofters were forced into complete dependence on the potato. In 1846 this led to appalling disaster. The potato crop was hit by blight. How ironic that most people have heard of the Battle of Culloden in 1746, whilst few know of the disastrous famine of 1846! The Famine destroyed and distorted people's lives as the cause of the Bonnie Prince never did.

Thus, does the National Museum of Rural Life (NMoRL) in West Kilbride inform the visitor about the potato blight and the famine that the Highlands and Islands of Scotland experienced between 1846 and the early 1850s in the video *Clansman to crofter* shown next to its display on the Highland Clearances. Yet the NMoRL is not representative of the Scottish museum world, as attention is seldom brought to the potato famine in venues, whether national or local, independent or state-run. Overall, the crisis seems more like a comma within the long narrative of increased vulnerability, dispossession, and emigration encapsulated by the Highland Clearances (1750–1886). As opposed to Ireland which, in the 1990s, experienced an upsurge of famine memorialisation triggered by the sesquicentenary of the Great Famine, be it through commemorative monuments or exhibitions—temporary or permanent—hardly any heritage initiative revisited this aspect of the past in the Highland and Island region, let alone Scotland.

The Irish and Highland famines were caused by the same pathogen—the potato blight or *phytophthora infestans* and occurred at roughly the same time, from the mid-1840s to the early 1850s. The pestilence affected areas inhabited by an increasing population heavily reliant on a single crop, the potato, as a means

DOI: 10.4324/9781003391524-11

of subsistence.[1] In terms of scale and demographic consequences, however, the effects of famine in both countries were extremely different. While in Ireland, they were cataclysmic with over one million deaths and two million Irish fleeing the country to overseas destinations, in Scotland, the Famine was not associated with a protracted mortality crisis and was circumscribed to the Highland and Island region, mostly the Inner and Outer Hebrides and certain western parishes of the mainland, notably western Inverness and Wester Ross.[2] Significantly, the region was no stranger to food scarcities and subsistence crises:

> The frequency and scale of these crises were such as to ensure that most Highlanders and Hebrideans living before the mid-nineteenth century would have experienced the realities of famine more than once in their lives.[3]

Prior to the Great Highland potato Famine (GHF) of 1846–47, years of scarcity were severe enough to alarm the government in 1782, 1816–17, and more acutely in 1836–37, which heralded what was to follow ten years later.[4] Food insecurity and destitution were facts of life for the majority of the population and the clearing process which intensified after the Napoleonic Wars exacerbated an already critical situation.

The aim of this chapter is to explore the ways in which Scottish museums have addressed the GHF. It will argue that the Famine is but a subsidiary theme in many museum narratives due to the fact that not only is it subsumed within the much broader and notorious Clearances period, but also because museums privilege the politics of the land over the politics of food within their interpretive framework, a position reflective of contemporary concerns in Scotland. The argument first places the emergence of museums tackling the Clearances within broader museological developments. It then concentrates on museum choices as regards the representation of famine and more widely endemic poverty: the interpretation of material culture, in particular folk material culture, of famine relief and its artefacts and, finally, the dominant discourse of the politics of the land and its implications.

Museological developments and the history of Famine clearances in Scottish museums

The analysis of the way the GHF is addressed in Scottish museums dovetails with the way museums have evolved since the mid-twentieth century. The musealisation of the period of the Clearances, like many other social history subjects focusing on marginalised or peripheral topics, was long discounted and started from the late 1960s, gaining greater currency from the 1980s and 1990s, most specifically in Highland and Island Scotland.[5] It coincided with the advent of New Museology leading to the re-definition and -design of older museums and, most of all, the emergence of new types of venues which grew exponentially from then on. These were envisioned in contrast to models born out of Enlightenment thinking, critiqued because of their tendency to 'petrif[y] and decontextualiz[e] living traditions, alienat[e] people from their past, disseminat[e] hegemonic national narratives and ideologically instrumentaliz[e] bodies of knowledge as part of new disciplines of power'.[6] New Museologists viewed museums not simply as repositories of objects, but above all as deeply political and ideological institutions with legitimising power. Their ultimate goal was to transform museums into more democratic and inclusive spaces and move away from exhibitions that hinged on collections organised in order to bolster master narratives of progress, social control, and cultural imperialism, meant to consolidate nation-building and colonial projects.[7] Museums have since then been regarded as implicated with issues of power, citizenship, and democracy and tasked with making visible and audible the heritage, views and concerns of formerly neglected and silenced groups, such as minority, subaltern, or vulnerable populations.[8]

Their approach to their source communities and audiences was equally re-appraised, with emphasis laid on fostering relationships between museums and their communities through outreach programmes and participatory practices to enhance community agency and control over the narratives projected. Strongly linked with notions of empowerment and identity construction or rehabilitation, such an approach was to serve as a conduit for the restoration of self-esteem in peripheral areas—be they rural or urban. As such, the promotion of local heritage also served objectives of socio-economic regeneration, as was the case with many Highland venues.[9] With the exception of two national museums, the Museum of Scotland and the NMoRL, respectively, opened in 1998 and 2001, and two council-run museums, the Highland Folk Museum administered by the Council from 1996 and Museum nan Eilean (MnE) opened in its present form in 2016, the museums that feature the Clearances are independently managed, either by trusts or individual owners.[10] In the Outer Hebrides, in particular, MnE collaborates closely with *Comainn Eachdraidh* (historical societies) which, from the 1980s, appeared as part of a grass-root movement to defend and promote Gaelic language and heritage and respond to the descendants of Scottish emigrants' interest in genealogy. Crucially, the function of these societies and the venues they oversee is not only to preserve and transmit local history, but also to act as repositories of local collective memories, through their collection of photographs, recording of individual stories and accounts and, importantly, the preservation of intangible heritage.[11]

Under the influence of new museology, the role of museums in the public sphere has continued to be probed. They have become envisaged as agents of social change, to be enlisted in the promotion of a more tolerant, equitable and inclusive society.[12] The socially engaged museum does not simply aim to reflect society's diversity, but actively seeks to transform ways of thinking and perceptions of others. Gradually, the idea has also been introduced that museums' agency and role as consciousness raisers and civic resources could be enlisted to actively promote alternative ideologies, discourses, and practices in light of contemporary pressing concerns, such as climate change, environmental challenges, human rights issues, socio-economic inequalities, and the detrimental effects of rampant consumerism, to name but a few.[13] As will be seen later, in the case of Highland museums and the experience of the Clearances, some museum professionals have embraced 'activism' in terms of goal and practice.

While the agency of museums is increasingly accepted, they are also above all reflective of the age in which they are produced and the narratives they construct mirror current concerns, priorities, and values. 'As such, they are also always tied to the broader category or genre of 'history' as well as the everyday ordinary as well as spectacular ways in which histories are understood, represented, commemorated—and contested.'[14] In popular imaginaries, the small peasants of the Highlands and Islands rank among the archetypal victims of the great social and economic upheaval of eighteenth- and nineteenth-century Scotland, and notions of injustice and moral responsibility underpin interpretations and pepper contemporary and modern discourses of the events.[15] Karl Marx, in *Das Kapital* (1867), famously featured the Highland Clearances as part of his argument against the ravages of private property on traditional communal rights, by presenting the crofters as the casualty of the rise of the capitalist ethos. The Marxist interpretation has, in fact, been influential in Clearance historiography and is also one which chimes in with popular memory.[16]

One of the latest developments in Clearances historiography has been to place this experience of rural transformation within a broader national perspective.[17] Tom Devine, who is also the author of an exhaustive analysis of the GHF, has applied the notions of Clearance and dispossession to the whole of rural Scotland, thus bringing out similarities and differences in the changes that both the Highlands and the Lowlands underwent and, in terms of periodisation, extending the chronology as, in the Lowlands, the process commenced earlier.

Devine's approach demonstrates that the society—most notably as a result of alterations in the pattern of landholding—and landscape of rural Scotland were radically transformed, with the destabilising consequences this entailed at an individual and collective level. Yet, it still emphasises the distinctiveness of the Highland and Island experience of dispossession in socio-economic, environmental, and cultural terms—not least the meaning and values, or the residual structure of feeling,[18] that the Gaels had forged over time and that were still vibrant amongst the peasantry at the time of the Clearances. This structure of feeling was ignored by the dominant culture, such as the right of access to land and elite protection or military service in return for land granted for fixed periods.[19]

This distinctiveness largely accounts for the acrimony and pain that attended dispossession and subsequently its resonance in popular consciousness, in contrast with the process in the Lowlands 'that has for the most part been ignored and forgotten except by a few scholars'.[20] Not only were removals more extensive, widespread, and disruptive in the Highlands, but also the social engineering orchestrated by landlords through the creation of the crofting system has been another specific feature of the region. The crofts, where some of the displaced were relocated, were established all too often on marginal land and made deliberately small; they were never devised to support a family without additional earning, but instead were meant to retain a peasant population on the land and, at the same time, force it to engage in the new industries that proprietors were promoting, fishing, and kelping in particular—changes part of the doctrine of Improvement. As a result, the famine, due to potato blight, which struck the region—at a time when kelp manufacture as an additional resource had collapsed after the Napoleonic Wars—also distinguishes the Highland and Island experience on the national scene, as does the brutal wave of clearances which followed. It was felt most acutely in the areas where the population had been encouraged to increase in order to boost the labour force and where crofters eked out a pitiful living on miserable plots in overcrowded settlements: the western isles and mainland coastal seaboard.[21]

This may well explain why the GHF, confined to structurally, environmentally, and socio-culturally specific areas, has been widely neglected in national and regional tangible heritage and, as opposed to the Irish Famine in Ireland, is not used as a foundational event or defining moment in the national narrative. Furthermore, the choice to include the Clearances, and more precisely Famine clearances, in museum displays and narratives stems from a variety of reasons. As much as this choice is related to their function in the national or more localised master narratives—in turn partly conditioned by historiographical shifts and, partly, by socio-political conditions—it is also influenced by the nature, specificity, and location of the museum concerned. As Desvallées and Mairesse have stated: 'As a tool of social life, museums demand that endless choices are made to determine the use to which they will be put'.[22] Of particular significance are museum collections and the availability of suitable artefacts through which the period is mediated and interpreted. Which object, if any, is featured? What storyline is the period woven in? What thematic and conceptual framework is privileged? As a concept, famine is many-faceted and can be approached from a wealth of themes and artefacts: through potato cultivation and diet, poverty and vulnerability, relocation on marginal land, provision of relief, local initiatives, and emigration, to name but a few.

Famine clearances and the polysemy of objects in museum narratives

In regional and local museums, situated in areas where the GHF was most strongly felt, it is through the Clearances, the land war, and subsequent land reform that a sense of place, past, and ultimately identity is articulated. The GHF is represented as a phase, however harrowing, in a protracted process of impoverishment and expulsion. The GHF often enters a narrative surreptitiously, sketchily revealed in a label or a historical background—a few brief words easily missed by visitors. A case in point is Ullapool Museum, whose new exhibition opened in 2013; next to photographs of a hunting party and modern-day crofters is a short context devoted to the Clearances period with the following few lines: 'By the 1850s large areas across the inland of Lochbroom had been cleared for sheep farms. Life became much harder. Overpopulation and famine caused widespread poverty'.

In all museums, a sense of this past is rarely mediated through objects, but through textual panels.[23] The assumption is that, as the displaced vanished from their places of abode and their dwellings—when not purposefully razed or burnt to the ground—gradually tumbled down, became recycled, or buried under moss or forest plantation, their material culture disappeared. That the clearing process had left 'no surviving objects' was underscored by Calder in her discussion of the choices made by the developers of the Scotland galleries of the National Museum of Scotland when they were being conceived.[24] Significantly, in the museum's narrative, the Clearances are not a key theme but an adjunct, presented in a section entitled 'Scotland and the world' which charts the movement of Scots to various parts of the globe. Information on the subject is impressionistic, fragmented and has to be gleaned from various sources and areas. Interestingly, on display are artefacts related to the Clearances, such as the silver teapot belonging to Rev. Donald Sage, who was minister in Sutherland during some of the most notorious evictions of the early nineteenth century. Yet, despite being very loosely related to the migratory process, all the objects are re-contextualised within a meta-narrative of emigration, and the GHF is omitted. It would therefore take a visitor well versed in the history of Northern Scotland to build a full picture of the complexity of the experience out of those sparse clues. The choice operated illustrates another point made by Calder: 'every object had potential to be featured in more than one context, to tell more than one story'.[25] Objects, whether authentic or replicas, whether used as relics or traces of a past, whether unique or seriated, have multiple layers of meaning and will be made to speak in accordance with the environment in which they are placed and the questions they are made to answer.

In the representation of the GHF, the NMoR provides an illustration of some of the alternatives chosen to broach the topic in its display. It is first cursorily mentioned in connection with wax models of potato breeds in the

'Land gallery' which presents the transformation of the Scottish landscape, notably through the role of improvers initiating new farming methods and crops, amongst which the potato that came to replace grain in many parts of Scotland. Initially potato cultivation warded off food shortage in bad seasons, but in the 1840s, it provoked it. Therefore, potatoes, as a theme or artefact, are an emblematic signal of famine experience and can act as a marker of exposure to scarcity, as is the case on the Isle of Skye at the Museum of the Isles. There, the visitor can read in a part entitled 'Oats and Potatoes':

> Any failure of the crop had a devastating effect. Blight led to a series of bad harvests culminating in the potato famine of the late 1840s and early 1850s. 1846 was known as *a'bliadhna a dh'fhaibh an buntata* – the year the potato went away. By then landlords were less keen to support what they saw as a population surplus to requirements.

At the NMoRL, however, the wax potato models do not signify vulnerability and hardship, but scientific proficiency, innovation, and economic progress: 'Many old varieties of potato were wiped out during the potato disease years of 1845–50. This led to the breeding of new disease-resistant ones. Models like these showed what the new breeds looked like'. It is in the 'People gallery', where the video *Clansman to Crofter* is shown and the Clearances are a major social theme, that potato, in the textual panel, is associated with hardship and hunger:

> The plight of the crofters worsened in 1845 when a devastating potato blight reached the western Highlands from Ireland. Starvation was narrowly avoided by help from the Lowlands. While the population struggled against famine, a minority of Lairds attempted to help, but their efforts left them financially ruined. Many landlords continued to carry out evictions.

The choice made at the NMoRL is to interpret the Clearances in terms of their national resonance, and the Famine starkly differentiates the Lowland and Highland experiences.[26] Nevertheless, importantly, within this perspective, even though the GHF stands for regional disparity, it is also used to symbolise national solidarity—although the Highlanders were berated in the racial discourse peddled by Lowland newspapers.

The artefact featured is the *cas chrom*, or foot plough commonly used in the North West Highlands (Image 7.1). Isabel F. Grant, founder of the Highland Folk Museum and author of many publications on the Highlands, explains the continued existence of such a 'primitive and laborious implement' because of its 'special suitability for the tiny holdings and the difficult

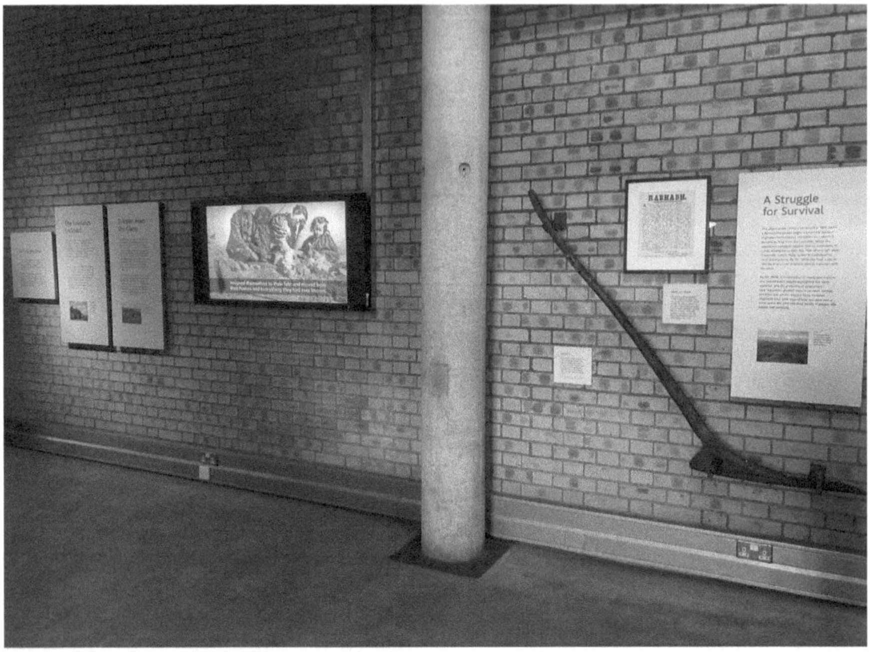

IMAGE 7.1 NMoRL—'An Emptying Land' (2022), copyright Laurence Gouriévidis.

terrain of the west'.[27] Here it is used as a prop to demonstrate the 'struggle for survival' and 'marginal character of many crofts', a narrative not commonly found in other museums, as will shortly be argued.

Museal theories have insisted on the polysemic nature of objects and their ability to be made to speak in a plurality of locations or contexts and within a multiplicity of discourses and narratives. As compellingly argued by Eilean Hooper-Greenhill:

> Objects have the capacity to carry meanings, and these meanings can be attributed from a number of perspectives. Objects, therefore, have the capacity to be polysemic, to bear multiple meanings [...] When the physicality of the object is identified, its meaning will depend on the narrative framework into which it is placed. Narratives are constructed by interpreting subjects; the reading and the significance of the materiality of the objects is variable according to who is reading.[28]

This emphasis on the 'framework of intelligibility', conditioning the meaning ascribed to objects at a given time and place by curators or other agents, partakes of an important moment in time in the history of museological thinking: the reassessment of the colonial gaze. It had conditioned the acquisition, display, and interpretation of many collections within a variety of museums and underpins many of the examples used in Hooper-Greenhill's analysis. In a kindred vein, questions could be raised as regards another type of subaltern culture: that of the poor and marginalised, and the lack of visibility of their experiences in material terms, given the fact that museum collections were, traditionally, heavily mortgaged to dominant voices and cultures.

Folk material culture and the representation of poverty in Highland and Island museums

To what extent are folk life collections, frequently encapsulating past practices and patterns of life in rural areas, made to speak about vulnerability, destitution, and dispossession? In the process of exhibiting folk material culture, the line distinguishing adaptability to an inhospitable environment from penury could arguably be said to be tenuous. However, it can reasonably be asserted that rarely do local museums succeed in conveying a sense of the inhabitants' precarious standard of living and existence.[29] The most successful might be the small 'idiosyncratic' folk museums, such as Colbost Croft Museum on the Isle of Skye, an independently owned museum opened in 1969, whose owner used traditional skills and techniques to reconstruct a croft house (Image 7.2).[30] With the smoke of

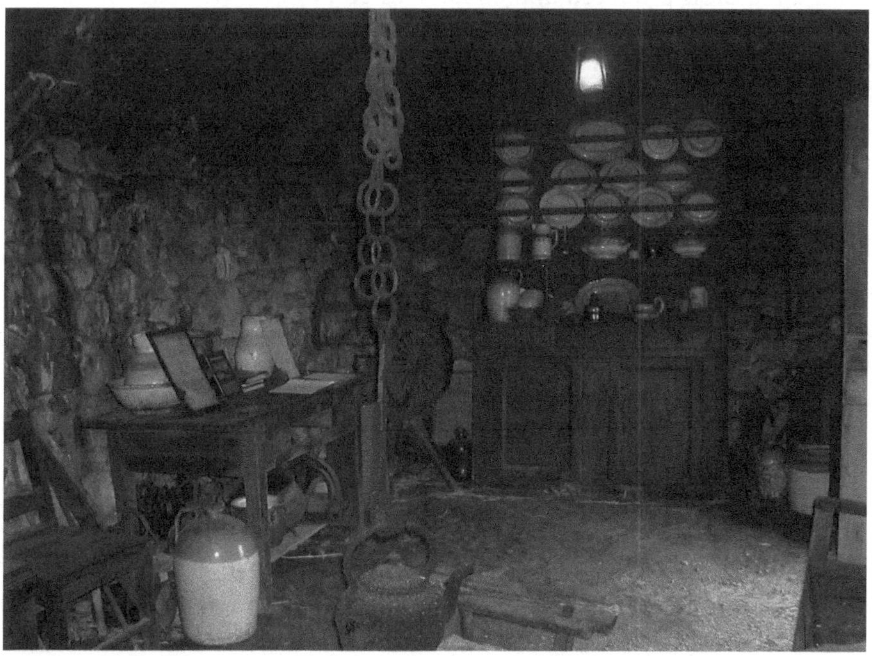

IMAGE 7.2 Colbost Croft Museum (2009), copyright Laurence Gouriévidis.

its peat fire winding its way through the thatch, its soot-stained furnishings, and its exposed location on the coast—particularly if visited on a windy and damp day—this typical, cold and draughty, black house does convey some sense of the constraints of the local environment, but does it signal poverty and vulnerability?

Like the museums previously mentioned, the folk museums that do tackle the Clearances period ultimately rely on more than the mobilisation of artefacts to tell the story of dispossession, destitution, crofting, and agrarian unrest. The Skye Museum of Island Life is a perfect illustration, as its exhibition is effectively dichotomised between two separate storylines and spaces: one of pastoral tranquillity and comfort built around a wealth of artefacts amassed over time and staged in various dwellings, some with stuffed mannequins—a croft house (kitchen and bedroom), a barn, a smithy and a weaver's workshop. The second is presented separately in 'the ceilidh house' where a conventionally styled historical narrative recounts the history of crofting. Advertised as offering 'a unique experience and a true insight into island life 100 years ago',[31] the visitor might be forgiven for imagining that crofters, in the past (a broad non-specific time period), had a distinct penchant for ornaments and clutter, so packed is the croft kitchen with china and decorations. When gauged as a marker of material standard and socio-economic integration, this collection tends to signal inhabitants who had acquired mass-produced and commoditised objects, were part of market networks and were trying to better their material standard of living. It does little to convey hardship and vulnerability. This could be said of most Highland and Island museal practices, where folk material culture forms a mainstay, notably through the reconstruction of croft interiors and the display of tools, often organised around such taxonomic groupings as domestic life—with a ubiquitous dresser displaying china—agricultural activities, fishing, crafts, and trades (Images 7.3 and 7.4).

In Highland and Island museums, material heritage is seldom interpreted within the perspective of a vulnerable lifestyle, but rather as multi-skilled craftsmanship, resourcefulness, and adaptability which, of course, was also the case. Implements and furnishings are displayed as 'typical' of a region or locality and of a loose time period—'old things' conjuring up a pre-mechanised age and drawing attention to the cultural and environmental specificity of a place. If social vulnerability or economic hardship percolate, it is through surrounding textual panels.

Grant's observation as an early museum developer is edifying with respect to the experience of poverty, its perception, and the emotions it triggered retrospectively. She was a precursor in the British folk museum movement and scoured the Highlands and Islands to build the collection for the first folk museum in Scotland.[32] In her recollection of her collecting forays, she remembers the obstacles she faced and the reluctance that a sense of shame

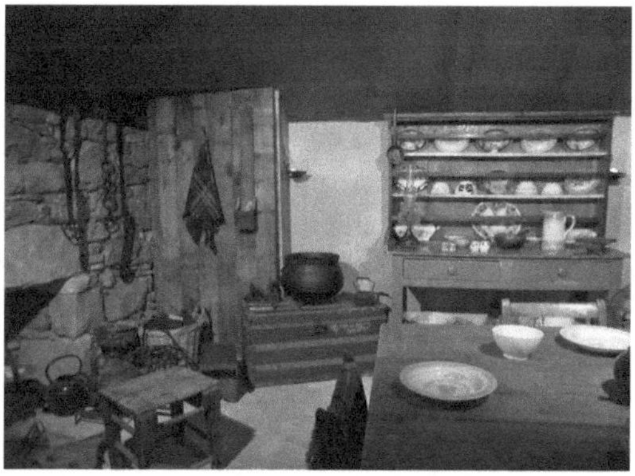

IMAGE 7.3 Gairloch Museum—Croft house interior (2022), copyright Laurence Gouriévidis.

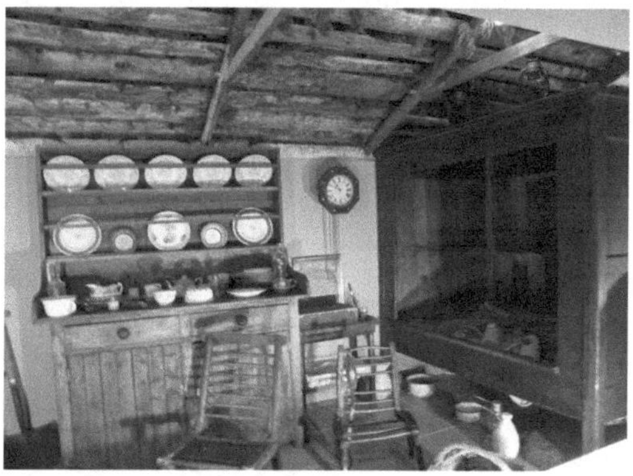

IMAGE 7.4 Timespan—Croft house interior (2022), copyright Laurence Gouriévidis.

about the poor living conditions and primitive farming methods of their forebears induced in the country people she encountered:

> [A]s I was to find over and over again in collecting, their attitude was an ambivalent one. They had a rightful pride in their race. They could reel off their own family pedigrees and that of their neighbours, but they were reticent about the primitive ways of tilling the land and of living and the poverty of the old Highlanders. I was becoming all too familiar with this attitude.[33]

This hindered her own collecting endeavours, as people held on to objects long abandoned in attics and barns:

> In collecting, I was to discover that some people were not only indifferent to relics of the past, but were ashamed of having them. I have no doubt

> that their feeling was derived from the days when children were beaten for speaking Gaelic in school and when Highlanders were despised by the Lowlanders for their poverty and different way of life.[34]

Such objects, as intimated by Grant, carry enormous emotional meaning beyond their functional characteristics. Their interpretive potential also stems from the frameworks of intelligibility and sensitivity in which they had long been inscribed, in this case, self-deprecation born out of past experiences and discourses, yet this does not percolate in their museal biography on display.

Material culture and the conundrum of famine relief

Another sensitive issue is famine relief, through which the GHF is at times approached, more specifically the home industries that were promoted through local relief initiatives spearheaded by the landed classes. In some cases, not only are the products of these home industries still successfully marketed today, but also they have entered museum collections. However, the discourses that accompany their presentation do not necessarily connect them with the GHF.

As highlighted by Devine, several landowners were praised by government officials for their efforts and initiatives, notably the Duke of Sutherland, James Matheson (Lewis), Lady Mackenzie of Gairloch, and Lady Dunmore (Harris).[35] Yet, their contribution during the famine can be elided in relation to the showcasing of famine-related local craft production, even in museums with a socio-historical remit. The choices made by museum staff ultimately depend on the local environment, the discursive structure in which the artefact is inserted, and the identity which the museum is seeking to develop within its own socio-cultural milieu and local environment. Selection and interpretation are also reflective of the significance of the clearing process in local imaginaries, notably in relation to landowning power and personalities.

In Gairloch Museum (Wester Ross), the famine period is a major aspect of the museum narrative, appearing in two parts of the exhibition.[36] The gallery entitled 'our land, our people' maps the estate and introduces the visitors to its owners, the Mackenzies, and their benevolent approach to the transformation and reorganisation of their land in the nineteenth century, insisting on their concern for the welfare of their tenants during the Famine period: 'On other estates in the parish, landowners were removing families from their land to create sheep farms. However, the Mackenzies of Gairloch believed that both landlords and tenants could benefit from agricultural reform without emigration or eviction'. Details are provided of the actions undertaken locally to help people during the GHF, namely the initiative of Lady Mackenzie encouraging women to learn to spin wool and knit stockings along with the stretches of road, known as Destitution roads, funded with government loans for which she lobbied the Destitution Board. The latter are featured through a photograph and the recording in Gaelic of a local man speaking about his grandfather's work on one of those roads—between Gairloch and Ullapool.

In another section of the exhibition entitled 'A walk through time', where various rooms are recreated, the GHF percolates briefly through the narrative contextualising an iconic artefact: 'the famous Gairloch stockings' whose origins are traced back to the famine period (Image 7.5). With the Gairloch stockings, the famine is inserted in a narrative not only underscoring the relief initiative of the local owner but also, most strikingly, celebrating the craftsmanship, creativity, and success over time of a female industry. The artefact was given accrued visibility as a result of the pandemic, during which 14 museums and heritage centres across the Highlands decided to join forces to create an online exhibition focusing on clothing through the ages. 'Highland Thread' was launched on 1 April 2021, and the Gairloch pattern socks were the artefact selected by Gairloch Museum.[37]

The Gairloch estate contrasts with many other Highland and Island properties. It did not undergo major clearances and, as a result, its management is not associated with contentious and grievous memories. The exhibition, in terms of artefacts and themes, was devised with community consultation over a period of time.[38] By bringing to light the more benign nature of the local landed class, whilst still conveying the development of

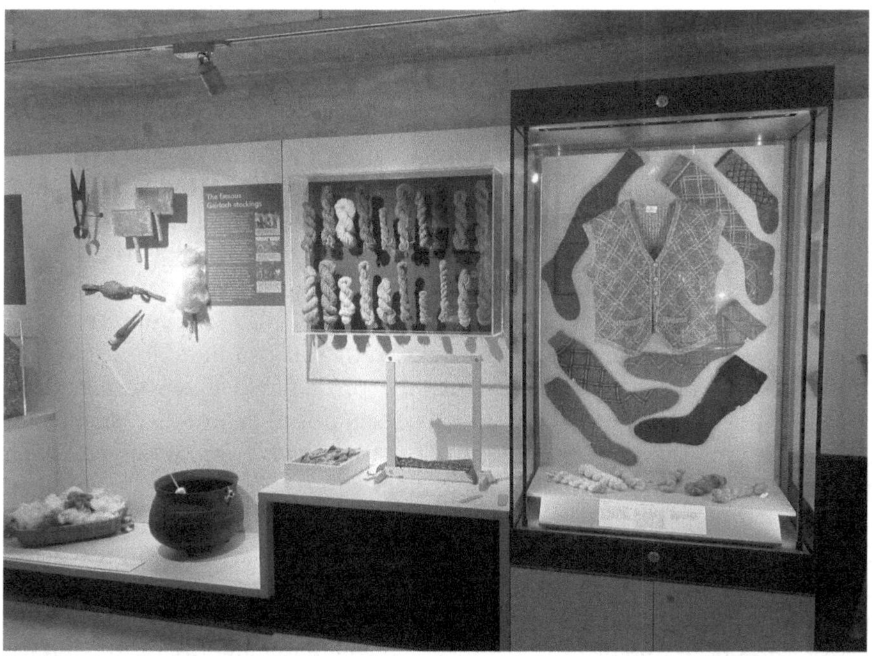

IMAGE 7.5 Gairloch Museum—Gairloch pattern (2022). Copyright Laurence Gouriévidis.

crofting in the area and its difficulties, it underscores its singularity within the Highland and Island region, most strikingly through the use of artefacts and recollections linked with the Famine period.

In Stornoway's Museum nan Eilean (MnE), located on the island of Lewis which, at the time of the GHF, was owned by the immensely rich Sir James Matheson who was knighted for his relief initiatives, nothing is said about the famine.[39] MnE's permanent exhibition has a wide geographical remit as it is dedicated to presenting the history, culture, and heritage of the whole of the Outer Hebrides, and how life 'on the edge' has shaped the identity of islanders. It is divided into three galleries: the film 'A sense of place', 'the Islanders' with its many recordings of present-day island voices, and the main gallery 'A taste of the Islands'. The latter is structured around six themes with display cases—'land', 'sea', 'the Lewis Chessmen', 'working life', 'community life', and 'on the threshold', most of which, apart from the Lewis chess pieces and the future-oriented 'threshold', cover a wide timeframe. Although the land section historicises people's relationship to the land with the Clearances, the land war and subsequent land reform, the famine era is not deciphered.

The same silence surrounds the museum's building, a modern extension appended to Lews Castle, built by James Matheson. As *An Suileachan*, the work of public art initiated by the Bhaltos community Trust in Western Lewis and unveiled in 2013, symbolises eloquently, the long-lasting legacy of Matheson in popular memory, in spite of his generosity during the Famine, is not one of munificence but of coercion, forcing removals and emigration on a population reluctant to leave in the 1850s.[40] The words that welcome visitors to MnE's exhibition set the tone of the overall narrative and message: 'These islands and our people are one. We have a strong and lasting bond. Wherever we may be in the world, the islands remain our home'. In the land section, while the relation between tenants and landlords dominates the narrative, it is presented in generic terms: 'whoever controls the land controls the people' and emphasis is laid on the present outcome of past events and tensions: community buyouts and management of the land since 1998, a collective right enshrined in the 2003 Land Reform Act. Matheson is a notable casualty of this discursive approach. Furthermore, the prominence given to islanders' initiative and enterprise colours the representation of another significant home industry in the section 'working life'—the Harris tweed industry, which was developed as a means of alleviating distress by the Dunmore family, then proprietors of Harris.[41] The samples of material, trainer, and high heel shoes showcased are not historically contextualised in the surrounding texts, but appear as one of the many luxury goods, which 'we once survived on' and have found their way to 'the catwalks of New York'.

MnE's zooms in on key aspects that encapsulate the identity of the islands, their environment and their people, foregrounding the significance of land for the community, notably the issue of 'control of the land', landownership, and the conflicts they have generated. Taking centre stage in the 'land' display case, are the artistic drawings by Will Maclean of two of the cairns that he designed and were erected on Lewis in the 1990s; these monuments anchor in the landscape the memory of 'the bitter fight to protect the land rights of islanders', through land raids and other desperate acts of defiance.[42] At MnE, pride of place is given to the people's perception of the past and their memorialisation of foundational moments, the politics of the land overshadowing the politics of food.

The politics of the land, the politics of food, and museum activism

Landed power, inequality, and oppression have long featured in Highland and Island museums, most specifically in micromuseums, which project the personal vision and experience of their owners, and where the Clearances period has had a distinct political resonance.[43] The politics of the land—landownership, private property rights and practices, and their ethics and validity against collective ownership—have seeped into many museum narratives drawing from present concerns and priorities. As François Hartog argued, heritagisation 'will remain a distinctive feature of the moment in which we are living or have just lived: a certain relation of the present and an expression of presentism'.[44] The growth of museum activism has given added impetus to this discursive mode, the best example of which in the Highlands and Islands being Timespan, in Helmsdale on the east coast of Sutherland—where some of the most infamous clearances pre-dating the GHF took place. Since its refurbishment and reopening as a major and innovative cultural venue in 2008, it has embraced this ethical turn, as reflected in its self-definition:

> Timespan is a cultural organisation in Helmsdale, a village [...] with local, global and planetary ambitions to *weaponise culture for social change* [my italics]. Timespan is a place for art, research, heritage, local history, future propositions and action. We believe that cultural institutions are a political and public space which belong to society, and as such, have a responsibility to shape a brighter new world based on principles of equality, emancipation and inclusion.[45]

Over the past decade, Timespan has indeed 'weaponised' the land question and people's forced displacement to engage with contemporary issues of social justice, poverty, and hunger. In 2013, the 200th anniversary of the Kildonan evictions was commemorated by a year of events, among which a seminar entitled 'History Repeating? Land Grabs and the Highland Clearances', held in support of the campaign ran by Enough Food for Everyone IF.[46] Although it did not specifically tackle Famine periods in Sutherland, the seminar teased out parallels between the Highland Clearances, land rights, and modern-day 'land grabs' in developing countries, which affect the poorest and are a major cause of hunger. Timespan's identity as a museum is one that purposefully engages with current issues with a view to raising questions relevant to the future. Its exhibition is in the process of being redeveloped and rethought, and its narrative will be recalibrated in order to open vistas into questions of climate change, landownership and soil exploitation, colonialism, and biodiversity. It will 'reconfigure our local history in a global context and imagine a brighter future'.[47] Within this approach, the reinterpretation of past Famines and the disease that started the process has much to offer a programmatic perspective giving insight into the politics of food related as they are to: food supply, security, and aid; plant genetics and export; intervention on the part of governments or non-governmental organisations; discourses surrounding policies and actions; and relations of power inevitably at work in times of crisis. Timespan illustrates compellingly that museums, as knowledge-based and knowledge-shaping venues, are ideally placed to make connections between past, present, *and* future, reflecting on past choices, highlighting current challenges, and endorsing a mission, informed by ethical values and thinking.

Conclusion

The inclusion of the GHF in museum exhibitions in Scotland is subject to many factors. Some are linked to the nature of individual museums; national museums tend to emphasise themes relevant to the whole of Scotland, a posture partly accounted for by constraints of space or balance within their overall narrative. In object-based exhibitions, the availability of artefacts is not necessarily a major issue, since artefacts can be re-contextualised and ultimately depend on the framework of intelligibility in which they are placed, as the *cas chrom* used at the NMoRL highlights. In this respect, folk material culture is rarely interpreted to convey a sense of vulnerability, precariousness and want, but local colour, craftmanship, and adaptability. Although these readings are not mutually exclusive, object biographies and textual panels seldom signal the darker undertones of this tangible culture.

It is in local and regional museums, whose expansion coincided with the development of 'New Museology' and the democratisation of museum voices, that the most exhaustive treatments of the Clearances are found with few providing details regarding the GHF. However, depending on local circumstances, notably the role of the local landed elite, such key aspects as proprietorial involvement in relief operations may be foregrounded. Ultimately, what dominates Highland and Island museum narratives is the discourse surrounding the politics of the land and its significance in modern-day devolved Scotland, whose newly appointed parliament granted communities the right to collective ownership. Local museums, notably those privately owned, acted as public platforms for relaying community views in the decades preceding devolution and the 2003 Land Reform Act. More recently, the ethical turn which has been promoted by many in the museum world may well herald a form of normalisation of the role that museums play in activism and political engagement with a view to the future—a model fully endorsed by Timespan. In this context, famines and the politics of food are ideally suited to address current environmental as well as geo-political concerns and issues.

Notes

1 L.M. Cullen and T.C. Smout, *Comparative Aspects of Scottish and Irish Economic and Social History, 1600–1900* (Edinburgh: John Donald, 1977), Cormac Ó Gráda, Richard Paping, Eric Vanhaute, eds., *When the Potato Failed. Causes and Effects of the Last European Subsistence Crisis, 1845–1850* (Turnhout: Brepols, 2007).
2 Thomas M. Devine, *The Great Highland Famine* (Edinburgh: John Donald, 1988), 79–80.
3 Robert A. Dodgshon, 'Coping with Risk: Subsistence Crises in the Scottish Highlands and Islands, 1600–1800', *Rural History* 15 (2004): 1.
4 John MacAskill, 'It Is Truly, in the Expressive Language of Burke, a Nation Crying for Bread': The Public Response to the Highland Famine of 1836-7', *The Innes Review* 61, no. 2 (2010): 170.
5 Laurence Gouriévidis, *The Dynamics of Heritage: History, Memory and the Highland Clearances* (London: Routledge, 2010), xix–xxi and 45–60.
6 Silke Arnold-de Simine, *Mediating Memory in the Museum: Trauma, Empathy, Nostalgia* (Basingstoke: Palgrave Macmillan, 2013), 7.
7 Gouriévidis, *Dynamics* 10-11; Tony Bennett, *The Birth of the Museum: History, Theory, Politics* (London: Routledge, 1995); Kylie Message, 'Afterword: Making History in Contested Times', *Museum International* 70, no. 3–4 (2018): 136–45.
8 Kylie Message and Andrea Witcomb, 'Introduction. Museum Theory: An Expanded Field', in *Museum Theory*, eds. Kylie Message and Andrea Witcomb (Chichester: John Wiley & Sons, 2020), xxxv–Ixiii.
9 Gouriévidis, *Dynamics*, 139–55.
10 Ibid., xvi–xviii and 45–60.
11 Màiri Robertson, '*Àite Dachaidh*: Re-connecting people with place—island landscapes and intangible heritage', *International Journal of Heritage Studies* 15, no. 2–3 (2009): 153–62.
12 Richard Sandell, *Museums, Prejudice and the Reframing of Difference* (London: Routledge, 2007); Karen Brown and François Mairesse. 'The Definition of the Museum through its Social Role', *Curator: The Museum Journal* 61, no. 4 (2018): 525–39.
13 Kylie Message, *Museums and Social Activism: Engaged Protest* (London: Routledge, 2014), Robert J. Janes and Richard Sandell, *Museum Activism* (London: Routledge, 2019).
14 Kylie Message, 'Afterword. Making History in Contested Times', *Museum International* 70, no. 3–4 (2018): 137.
15 Gouriévidis, *Dynamics,* 19–44.
16 Ibid., 40–1.
17 Thomas M. Devine, *The Scottish Clearances: A History of the Dispossessed* (London: Penguin Books, 2019). See also P. Aitchison and A. Cassell, *The Lowland Clearances: Scotland's Silent Revolution 1760–1830* (East Linton: Tuckwell, 2003).

18 This notion is borrowed from Raymond Williams: 'certain experiences, meanings and values which cannot be expressed or substantially verified in terms of dominant culture, are nevertheless lived and practised on the basis of the residue—cultural as well as social—of some previous social and cultural institution or formation'. See *Marxism and Literature* (Oxford: Oxford University Press, 1977), 122.
19 Devine, *The Scottish Clearances*, 356.
20 Ibid., 12.
21 Ibid., 306–31; Devine, *Great Highland Famine.*
22 André Desvallées and François Mairesse, *Key Concepts of Museology* (Paris: Armand Colin, 2010), 34.
23 Gouriévidis, *Dynamics,* 124–35.
24 Jenni Calder, 'From Artefacts to Audience: Strategy for Display and Interpretation', in *Heritage and Museums: Shaping National Identity*, ed. J. Magnus Fladmark (Shaftesbury: Donhead Publishing, 2000), 43.
25 Ibid., 4. See also Hugh Cheape, 'Objects as Evidence: The Evaluation of Material Culture', in *Heritage and Museums: Shaping National Identity*, ed. J. MagnusFladmark (Shaftesbury: Donhead Publishing, 2000), 61–76.
26 Originally the display only focused on the Highland Clearances but, in 2006, it was modified to include the Lowland Clearances 'to offer a late 20th-century explanation by historians of the wider implication of agricultural 'improvement'. See personal correspondence with museum Curator, 27 February 2009.
27 Isabel F. Grant, *The Making of Am Fasgadh: An Account of the Origins of the Highland Folk Museum by Its Founder* (Edinburgh: National Museums Scotland, 2007), 103.
28 Eilean Hooper-Greenhill, *Museums and the Interpretation of Visual Culture* (London: Routledge, 2000), 111 and 114.
29 Gouriévidis, *The Dynamics of Heritage*, 103–7.
30 Ibid, 124–9. In my 2010 study, I used the term 'idiosyncratic' to describe independent, small-scale and single-subject museums. These museums come under the definition of micromuseology, as defined by Fiona Candlin in *Micromuseology. An Analysis of Small Independent Museums* (London: Routledge, 2015).
31 http://www.skyemuseum.co.uk, last accessed 20 August 2023.
32 She established the Highland Folk Museum single-handedly in 1935 on the Hebridean Island of Iona. See Gouriévidis, *The Dynamics of Heritage*, 119–24.
33 Grant, *The Making of Am Fasgadh*, 17.
34 Ibid., 60.
35 Devine, *Great Highland Famine*, 89–90.
36 Gairloch Museum, first opened in 1977, was recently relocated and revamped—its new exhibition launched in July 2019. In contrast with its previous version, which focused on the recreation of rooms (classroom, shop, etc.), it now addresses the GHF—and the Clearances.
37 https://highlandthreads.co.uk, last accessed 12 December 2022. Highland Thread was run by Museums and Heritage Highland and funded by the National Lottery Heritage Fund. The Gairloch socks featured were knitted in the 1970s.
38 Online interview (27/04/2022) with Dr Karen Buchanan who helped develop the 'new' Gairloch Museum and was its curator until early 2023.
39 Devine, *Great Highland Famine*, 89.
40 Bill Lawson, *Lewis the West Coast in History and Legend* (Edinburgh: Birlinn, 2008), 193–6.
41 Bill Lawson, *Harris in History and Legend* (Edinburgh: John Donald Publishers, 2002), 61–3.

42 For studies of the Lewis Cairns and their memorialisation of the past, see Iain Robertson and Tim Hall. 'Memory, Identity and the Memorialisation of Conflict in the Scottish Highlands', in *Heritage, Memory and the Politics of Identity: New Perspectives on the Cultural Landscape*, eds. Niamh Moore and Yvonne Whelan (Farnham: Ashgate, 2007), 19–37. See also Laurence Gouriévidis, 'Le present du passé: La commemoration de l'histoire des *crofters* sur l'île de Lewis', *Études Écossaises,* 11 (2008): 175–92. Significantly the cairn drawings are the artefacts that were chosen by museum staff to feature in a BBC radio 4 programme, 'The Museums That Make Us': https://www.bbc.co.uk/programmes/m00154py, last accessed 18 August 2023.

43 Gouriévidis, *Dynamics*, 171.

44 François Hartog, 'Time and Heritage', *Museum International* 57, no. 3 (2005): 15

45 https://timespan.org.uk/about/, last accessed 20 August 2023.

46 Organised in 2013 at the time of the G8 meeting held in Britain, the 'Enough food for everyone … IF' campaign brought together over 100 organisations across the UK, amongst which OXFAM. The campaign underlined four 'ifs' that, if implemented, could help relieve hunger and bring food security. https://oxfamapps.org/scotland/2013/03/05/2013-03-scottish-past-linked-to-modern-land-grabs/, last accessed 15 December 2022.

47 https://timespan.org.uk/museum/, last accessed 20 August 2023.

References

Aitchison P. and A. Cassell, *The Lowland Clearances: Scotland's Silent Revolution 1760–1830*. East Linton: Tuckwell, 2003.

Arnold-de Simine, Silke, *Mediating Memory in the Museum: Trauma, Empathy, Nostalgia*. Basingstoke: Palgrave Macmillan, 2013.

Bennett, Tony, *The Birth of the Museum: History, Theory, Politics*. London: Routledge, 1995.

Brown, Karen and François Mairesse, 'The Definition of the Museum through its Social Role'. *Curator: The Museum Journal* 61, no. 4 (2018): 525–39.

Calder, Jenni, 'From Artefacts to Audience: Strategy for Display and Interpretation'. In J. Magnus Fladmark, ed., 41–52, *Heritage and Museums: Shaping National Identity*. Shaftesbury: Donhead Publishing, 2000.

Candlin, Fiona, *Micromuseology. An Analysis of Small Independent Museums*. London: Bloombury, 2015.

Cheape, Hugh, 'Objects as Evidence: The Evaluation of Material Culture'. In J. Magnus Fladmark, ed., 61–76, *Heritage and Museums: Shaping National Identity*. Shaftesbury: Donhead Publishing, 2000.

Cullen L.M. and T.C. Smout, *Comparative Aspects of Scottish and Irish Economic and Social History, 1600–1900*. Edinburgh: John Donald, 1977.

Daly, Mary, *The Famine in Ireland*. Dundalk: Dundalgan Press, 1986.

Desvallées, André and François Mairesse, *Key Concepts of Museology*. Paris: Armand Colin, 2010.

Devine, Thomas M., *The Great Highland Famine*. Edinburgh: John Donald, 1988.

Devine, Thomas M., *The Scottish Clearances. A History of the Dispossessed*. London: Penguin Books, 2019.

Dodgshon, Robert A., 'Coping with Risk: Subsistence Crises in the Scottish Highlands and Islands, 1600–1800'. *Rural History* 15 (2004): 1–25.

Gouriévidis, Laurence, 'Le present du passé: La commemoration de l'histoire des *crofters* sur l'île de Lewis'. *Études Écossaises*, 11 (2008): 175–92.

Gouriévidis, Laurence, *The Dynamics of Heritage: History, Memory and the Highland Clearances*. Farnham: Ashgate, 2010.

Gouriévidis, Laurence, 'Commemorating Irish and Scottish Famine Migrants in Glasgow: Migration, Community Memories and the Social Uses of Heritage'. *History & Memory* 35, no. 2 (2023): 143–68.

Grant, Isabel F., *The Making of Am Fasgadh. An Account of the Origins of the Highland Folk Museum by its Founder*. Edinburgh: National Museums Scotland, 2007.

Hartog, François, 'Time and Heritage'. *Museum International* 57, no. 3 (2005): 7–18.

Hooper-Greenhill, Eilean, *Museums and the Interpretation of Visual Culture*. London: Routledge, 2000.

Janes, Robert J. and Richard Sandell, *Museum Activism*. London: Routledge, 2019

Lawson, Bill, *Lewis the West Coast in History and Legend*. Edinburgh: Birlinn, 2008.

Lawson, Bill, *Harris in History and Legend*. Edinburgh: John Donald Publishers, 2002.

MacAskill John, 'It Is Truly, in the Expressive Language of Burke, a Nation Crying for Bread': The Public Response to the Highland Famine of 1836-7'. *The Innes Review* 61, no. 2 (2010): 169–206.

Message, Kylie, *Museums and Social Activism: Engaged Protest*. London: Routledge, 2014.

Message, Kylie, 'Afterword: Making History in Contested Times'. *Museum International* 70, no. 3–4 (2018): 136–45.

Message, Kylie and Andrea Witcomb, 'Introduction. Museum Theory: An Expanded Field'. In Kylie Message and Andrea Witcomb, eds., *Museum Theory*. Chichester: John Wiley & Sons, 2020, xxxv–Ixiii

National Museum of Rural Life. *Clansman to Crofter*. Video.

Ó Gráda, Cormac, Richard Paping, Eric Vanhaute, eds. *When the Potato Failed. Causes and Effects of the Last European Subsistence Crisis, 1845–1850*. Turnhout: Brepols, 2007

Robertson Iain and Tim Hall, 'Memory, Identity and the Memorialisation of Conflict in the Scottish Highlands'. In Niamh Moore and Yvonne Whelan, eds., 19–37. *Heritage, Memory and the Politics of Identity. New Perspectives on the Cultural Landscape*. Farnham: Ashgate, 2007.

Robertson Màiri, '*Àite Dachaidh*: Re-connecting People with Place—Island Landscapes and Intangible Heritage', *International Journal of Heritage Studies* 15, no. 2–3 (2009), 153–62.

Sandell, Richard, *Museums, Prejudice and the Reframing of Difference*. London: Routledge, 2007.

Williams, Raymond, *Marxism and Literature*. Oxford: Oxford University Press, 1977.

8

FAMINE LANDSCAPES

Finland's 'Skeleton Track' in memorials and museums

Charley Boerman

11 September 2020 marked the 150th anniversary of the completion of the Riihimäki–St. Petersburg railway.[1] This anniversary was celebrated and commemorated with several exhibitions in Finland. As elsewhere in the world, the development of the Finnish railway network, and particularly this international track, is lauded for the boost it gave the Finnish economy and state-building.[2] However, the Riihimäki–St. Petersburg connection is also known as the 'Hunger Track' [*nälkärata*] or 'Skeleton Track' [*luurata*]. Built between 1867 and 1870 as a public relief work to combat hunger and poverty during the famine that afflicted Finland in the late 1860s, the harsh working conditions and spread of epidemic diseases at the railway construction sites led to a spike in local mortality rates. The resulting mass burial sites along the tracks were often unmarked 'non-places' that were neglected, until nearly a century later, local initiatives erected memorials and turned these rural sites into heritage.

The harshest years of the famine were 1867–68, and it is estimated that in total, around 8% of the population died due to starvation and related diseases.[3] While characterised as 'Europe's second-to-last major peacetime subsistence crisis' and notwithstanding its exceptionally high percentage of population loss, the 'Great Hunger Years' [*Suuret Nälkävuodet*] have often been said to be a 'forgotten famine'.[4] Unlike, for example, how Ireland has memorialised the Great Famine (1845–50), Finland does not have major monuments, memorials, or museums dedicated to its famine.[5] At a local level, however, a different approach to commemorating the Great Hunger Years presents itself: there are over a hundred local memorials to remember the famine and its victims.[6] One of the most significant concentrations of these memorials is found along the Riihimäki–St. Petersburg 'Skeleton Track'.

DOI: 10.4324/9781003391524-12

Previous research has discussed the railway from a historical perspective or engaged with it when discussing the memorialisation and cultural memory of the famine years in Finland.[7] However, there has been no discussion of the railway and burial sites exclusively, nor any analysis of how this past is exhibited and musealised in Finland.

In this chapter, I will analyse how the Skeleton Track is understood and memorialised through heritage interventions—such as interpretive signs, plaques, and markers—at burial sites, and how this past is curated in recent exhibitions engaged with the railway. The sites along the railway that will be analysed are the largest memorials dedicated to the relief work, namely the Lahti (1953–54), Kärkölä (1967), and Uusikylä (1990) memorials. The exhibitions that this chapter examines include those in the Finnish Railway Museum in Hyvinkää (2020–21), the National Workers' House Museum in Riihimäki (2020–21), and the railway workers exhibition curated by the Werstas museum in Tampere (2022).

As Laurajane Smith argues, heritage and heritage sites are 'used to construct, reconstruct and negotiate a range of identities and social and cultural values and meanings in the present'.[8] When investigating famine sites in general and the memorial sites of the Skeleton Track specifically, initiatives to conserve and manage these previously derelict sites imbue them with meaning and construct them as 'heritage'. The initial neglect and unmarked character of these famine sites and later processes of heritage making thus reflect a societal interest in these famine pasts at the local level and not a 'discovery' of an innate value. Ultimately, I will argue that these memorials and exhibitions tend to reflect a dominant interpretation of Finland's famine past. In this narrative, the famine is framed as a burden equally shared between all classes and a 'Divine test' for a developing nation.[9] The railway functions as an emblem for Finland's progression, modernity, and perseverance—much like how railways symbolise modernity in the Western cultural imagination generally.[10] Yet, the famine sites scattered along the tracks contain the possibility for an alternative and critical reading of Finland's famine past.

Before discussing the memorials and exhibitions, this chapter will first provide necessary historical context of the famine, Finnish–Russian relations, as well as the use of relief works both in Finland and Europe. The chapter will then engage with the three significant famine sites, after which it will proceed to analyse recent exhibitions that include the Skeleton Track. The main aims of this chapter are two-fold: firstly, to offer further insight into the heritagisation practices and musealisation of the famine broadly, and secondly, to illuminate the role of the railway in the cultural memory of the famine specifically. As such, the chapter will offer two contributions to the understanding of the famine in Finnish cultural memory broadly and the railway specifically.

'Erected on behalf of our nameless fallen'

After being part of the Swedish empire for nearly seven centuries, in 1809, Finland became a Grand Duchy of the Russian Empire when Sweden lost the Finnish War (1808–09). As part of the Tsarist Russian Empire, Finland had enjoyed a degree of cultural and political autonomy not given to other parts of the empire, to the point that in the 1860s, civil servants working under the Senate's control held most of the power in the country.[11] During the worst famine years (1867–68), Tsar Alexander II was in a position of 'decisive power'; however, in practice, the Finnish Senate was in charge of most crucial decisions—including how to alleviate the famine.[12] Significantly, no food aid from Russia was accepted, as the nationalist Finnish Fennoman movement not only emphasised the distinctive Finnish language, but also 'character traits such as self-sufficiency, forbearance, and sedulity'.[13] Instead, the famine was managed independently by the Finnish authorities through public work schemes such as the railway.[14]

In 1862, the construction of an inland track between Helsinki and Hämeenlinna was completed. This project was not considered to be a relief work scheme, but as Andrew Newby argues, a 'demonstration of Finland's national maturity and adherence to European norms of modernity'.[15] In 1867, the Finnish Diet received plans to expand the Finnish railway network, from Riihimäki (a stop on the Hämeenlinna-Helsinki route) via Viipuri to St. Petersburg. In Finland's fragile economy, the construction of a narrow-gauge track was preferable, as this cost two-third of the Russian Empire's wide-gauge track. However, Russian imperial demands for a railway system compatible with its western Grand Duchy overrode Finnish national considerations—with the result that until this day Finland's railway network is not compatible with Central Europe or Scandinavia.[16] To accommodate the difference in cost of the two gauge sizes, the Russian Empire lent the Finnish state ten million marks. Responses were mixed: Secretary of the Finnish Treasury J. V. Snellman, who 'was a supporter of local relief models instead of centralized working sites', feared that the public work would draw impoverished individuals and their families to the site and spread diseases.[17] At the same time, proponents saw the railway as a necessary intervention to limit the strain on public spending as the famine grew worse and provide a potential boost to the Finnish economy in the long term.[18]

When the construction work started in February 1868, many hungry people flocked to work sites along the route in hope of finding food and work. No housing was provided, working conditions were terrible, wages were too low to feed a single man, let alone his family, and the sites were too crowded to feed everyone. In these conditions, epidemic diseases such as typhoid fever, dysentery, and typhus could spread rapidly.[19] Kalle Kallio estimates that of the 10,000 people working on the track in 1868, 700–800 track builders died in that year alone.[20] However, since only the deaths of workers were recorded and not deaths among vagrants or the unemployed who came to the route in hopes of finding food, it is hard to say how many died exactly.[21] As the number of deaths exceeded the burial capacity of local parishes, mass burial sites were constructed along the tracks.

Despite these conditions, the construction proceeded rapidly and traffic from St. Petersburg to Helsinki officially started on 11 September 1870. Due to the low wages offered to the railway workers, the railway works were completed below budget: approximately 27.5 million instead of the estimated 30 million marks. Pleased with this result, Tsar Alexander II rewarded the railway's board of directors with a significant bonus. This reward provoked fierce criticism at the time, which inspired the notion of the 'Hunger Track', as the Skeleton Track is also known.[22] Although the completion was celebrated soberly due to the massive number of casualties involved in its construction, in 1892, leader of the Finnish Fennoman party, Agathon Meurman, argued that no monument in remembrance of the deceased track builders was needed. Instead, he claimed that: 'Our people could not have had a more valuable memorial than the Riihimäki–St. Petersburg railway, erected on behalf of our nameless fallen'.[23] Indeed, those who died were seen as a 'manifestation of the people's spiritual progress towards nationhood', and their deaths considered a noble sacrifice for this purpose.[24]

It was not uncommon in the nineteenth century for public works to be deployed as anti-famine and anti-poverty measures, in accordance with the principles of classical economics, which advocated minimal governmental interference in order not to upset the free market and prevent the poor from becoming dependent on government support.[25] Finland's autonomous administration thus followed a general practice to ensure that money or food were only given in return for labour. Rather than being remembered in the context of a colonial and oppressive 'other' (in Finland's case, imperial Russia), in Finland, the relief works were incorporated into a conception of Finnish national identity, composed of self-sacrifice and forbearance.[26] This interpretation was crystalised in Meurman's book *Nälkävuodet 1860-luvulla* ('The famine years of the 1860s', 1892), in which he developed the hegemonic narrative of the famine as the 'the birth pangs of a nation'—a burden that was carried equally by all.[27]

By contrast, when anti-capitalist and socialist voices ('the Reds') emerged in Finland prior to the Finnish Civil War (1918), the railway featured in accounts of capitalist inhumanity and 'callous bourgeois attitudes towards the proletariat'.[28] However, with the loss of the socialist Red Guards to the conservative White Guards, supported by the German Empire and Sweden, these narratives all but disappeared.[29] As the next sections will demonstrate, the railway became embedded in the cultural imagery of modernisation and progress, yet the famine sites scattered along the track remind us of its human cost. In these negotiations and configurations of 'Finnishness' and the famine past, modernity, and the nation, the mass burial sites scattered around the Skeleton Track resist total integration into the hegemonic Fennoman narrative of the railway.

Memorialising the Skeleton Track

In folk memory and early literature on the Skeleton Track, it was often said that railway workers were buried under the tracks themselves.[30] While this is commonly understood as a metaphor, the mass burial sites in close proximity to the track indeed contain the remains of unknown and unnamed workers and vagrants. The exact numbers of people buried there are unknown, yet they are thought to comprise thousands of bodies.[31] Nevertheless, these places soon began to fall into disuse, as they were located outside of parishes and their cemeteries. Seven of such sites have since been identified, marked, and heritagised. In this section, I will analyse three of these in depth: the memorials near Lahti (1953–54), Kärkölä (1967), and Uusikylä (1990).[32]

The memorials erected at these sites were the result of local initiatives. In 1910, for example, an individual going by the initials 'l-r-o' complained in a letter to the newspaper *Uusi Rautatielehti* ('Railway Gazette') that the burial site in Lahti had 'no sign of any kind' and was used by local youth for 'purposes that are not suitable for a cemetery'; a situation altogether unacceptable.[33] Similar sentiments were expressed in a 1913 letter by a railway worker to the *Suomalainen* newspaper concerning the burial site in Kärkölä: this 'Rautatieläinen' ('Railway man') expressed discontent with the almost unnoticeable marking of the site and argued that such a site should be a place for 'quiet reflection and contemplation of one's ancestors', in an act of 'compassion and gratitude' for those buried there.[34] In both cases, it would take several decades before the requested memorials were established.

In 1950, the Lahti Society petitioned the town to ensure that the unattended 'Hunger Years Graveyard' should be 'protected and equipped with the appropriate symbols of a cemetery'.[35] In support of their argument, the society provided a history of the town and famine years, concluding that the railway had contributed greatly to the development of the town. Hence, those who gave their lives should be given recognition.[36] Money was raised locally, and in 1953, the monument was erected. More than 50 years after the 'Rautatieläinen' had written to the press, a joint effort of the town and parish of Kärkölä led to the memorial for the 100th anniversary of the start of the railway's construction in 1967. After the establishment of both monuments, in 1988, someone called Seppa Ahonen complained in a letter written to a local newspaper that while the historical significance of the mass grave sites in Lahti and Kärkölä was recognised, 'the neglect of the Uusikylä mass grave just continues ...'[37] Action was taken quickly, and in 1990—marking the

120th anniversary of the completion of the railway—a memorial was unveiled there too.

The letters request that these sites are turned into formal cemeteries by marking them and including recognisable signage and symbols in line with dominant heritage practices. In doing so, the authors of these letters (perhaps unknowingly) point to a distinction between cemeteries and burial sites that is based on 'both form and content': cemeteries are symbolically formalised places where the dead are named, whereas burial sites are 'defined by a lack of certainty over who is interred' there and are not symbolised according to a common pattern.[38] This uncertainty—both regarding who is interned there as well as the symbolic meaning of these sites—marks the difference between the mass grave as a burial *site* and the cemetery as a *place*. Whereas a place is contained and demarcated, a site is without a clear boundary (both geographically and temporally) and 'suggests a location being between other places, a liminal space at once incomplete and in transition (as in "grave site")'.[39]

The letters written to local newspapers, which voice complaints about the absence of demarcation and the inappropriate use of these sites, thus seem to refer exactly to this difference between 'site' and 'place': asking, as it were, that the non-placeness of these burial mounds be turned into 'places' that are marked and demarcated. Emily Mark-FitzGerald analyses a similar process with regard to the mass burial sites and workhouses of the Irish famine, where heritage and monumental interventions convert these 'mass gravesites into respectful zones of remembrance'.[40] The derelict and wild landscapes of these burial sites were thus 'civilised' through processes of heritage making. As a result, they can become part of the practices and behaviour associated with places of mourning, such as laying wreaths, contemplation, and maintenance.

Both sites in Lahti and Kärkölä are now encircled by fences, which demarcate and contain the mass grave and surrounding area. While in Kärkölä, the fence is made of wood, in Lahti, it is made of railway tracks in the shape of Finnish croft fences (see Image 8.1). The tracks function as a material testimony and an indexical trace of the railway and its workers, while the croft-style fences are reminiscent of Finnish agriculture and its collapse during the famine. In the middle of the fenced-off area stands a large two-metre stone slab with the inscription: 'During the 1867–1868 Great Hunger Years, were buried in this place railway builders who died of hunger and disease from Hollola parish, the villages of Lahti and Järvenpää, and from other places. Monument erected by Lahti Parish, 1953'.[41] As in the fence surrounding the Lahti site, the use of track in the construction of these memorials recurs in Kärkölä and Uusikylä. There, the material is employed to form a memorial cross rather than a fence. Re-using part of the railway track to construct these memorial sites—while forming a material trace—also paradoxically recalls Meurman's statement that the Finnish people 'could not have had a more valuable memorial than the Riihimäki–St. Petersburg

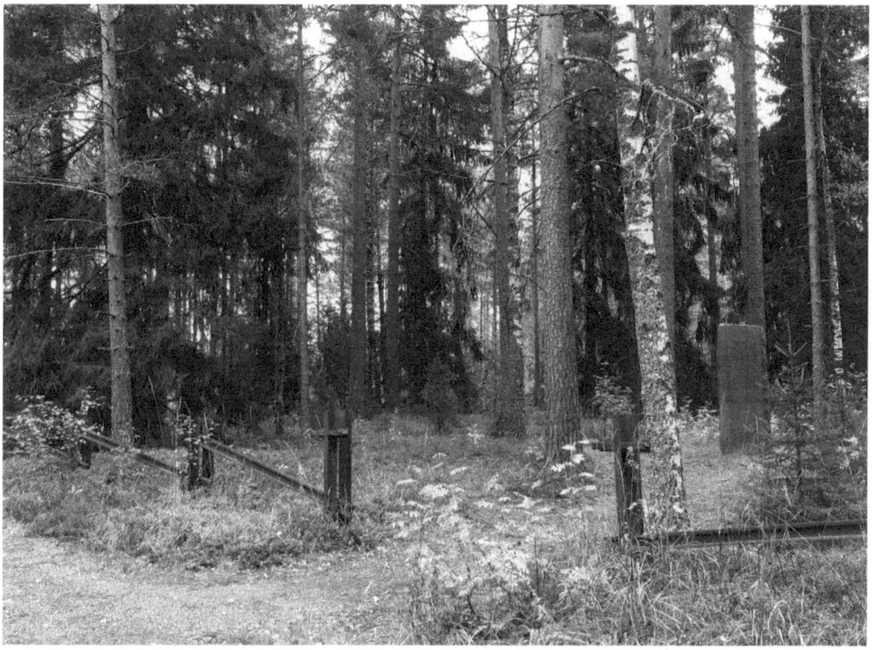

IMAGE 8.1 The croft-style fence and granite slab in Lahti. 19 September 2021. Photograph by the author.

railway'.[42] Ultimately, the crosses and fences adhere to established regimes of commemoration and the construction of the cemetery and thus turn these sites into designated places.

In Kärkölä, moreover, part of demarcating the site included the instalment of an interpretive board. This constructs the site not only as a memorial, but also as a heritage site with historical significance. The text—only in Finnish and thus addressing a national audience—gives a detailed account of the relationship between the famine and the railway as a public relief work to alleviate unemployment. The spread of diseases and mortality due to hunger, poor housing, and hygiene, as well as the subsequent construction of emergency hospitals and special burial sites (such as the one in Kärkölä), are also discussed. Although no one is blamed for these conditions, the casualties as a result of the relief work are also not obfuscated by embedding them in a narrative of Finnish national progress. Rather, the starkness of the relief work is emphasised by the explanation that it is unknown who is buried at the site. The text ends with the rather poetic sentence: 'It remains a mystery … who were destined to find their final resting place in this pine grove'.[43] Aside from constructing the site as a national tourist destination, it also lays bare more than any other memorial site the terrible working conditions at the construction site.

Despite being marked, demarcated, and given a status as heritage, the peripheral locations of these sites prevent them from becoming the 'respectful zones of remembrance' that they were likely intended to become.[44] Similar to what Mark-FitzGerald has argued about Irish workhouses during the Great Irish Famine, 'these places powerfully convey the desolation and starkness of the Famine, their peripheral locations mirroring the stigmatized status of the workhouse, as well as the inability of society to contain the scale of death and suffering within normative boundaries'.[45] In the Finnish case, the spatial division between the mass burial sites and centres of towns reflects the mnemonic division between the railway as the centre of Finnish modernity and the absence of the deceased in this narrative.[46] In Lahti and Uusikylä, this division and a sense of 'otherworldliness' is further provoked by the proximity of these sites to the motorway and railway, respectively.

Unlike in Lahti and Kärkölä, part of the double memorial in Uusikylä is not fenced off. This memorial was erected in 1990 and consists of two parts: a large stone close to the road and a cross close to the railway. The memorial stone contains the inscription 'To the memory of the dead builders of the Riihimäki–St. Petersburg railway, 1868–1870. Nastola Council and Parish, 1990'.[47] Next to the stone memorial is an old, moss-covered stone wall (see Image 8.2). The wall was thought, both popularly and academically, to have been constructed by locals as well as by women and children from elsewhere as part of the relief work and, as shall be analysed in the next section, was invoked in the Finnish Railway Museum exhibition to show that work was provided even for the weak. However, Kallio argues that the wall was built after the famine as a fire hazard safety measure; not as a relief work.[48] The accompanying cross is made of steel rails with the simple engraving '1868–70'. The cross is on a mound—which might or might not cover the bodies of railway workers—next to the actual railway, with no fence to separate the two (see Image 8.3). The absence of a fence around the cross or between the cross and the tracks provides a different landscape from the ones in Lahti and Kärkölä: there is no separation between the site of mourning and its surroundings: most prominently the railway, which was indirectly responsible for the deaths of victims possibly buried here.

The lack of spatial demarcation enhances the sense of this site as a liminal space, where past and present are not clearly separated but intertwined. When standing near the mound and cross, VR or Allegro trains (the Finnish railway service and high-speed Helsinki–St. Petersburg service, respectively) run past. From within the train carriage, movement is likely too fast for the cross to be anything but a blur. Yet, from the burial site, it is as if time stands still, as the tracks and train cut through the landscape from one destination to the other. In Lahti, the burial site is surrounded by a fence and trees but enclosed by the motorway that runs around the site. At the site, the monotonous noise of traffic can be heard, but one cannot see beyond the trees. This creates the

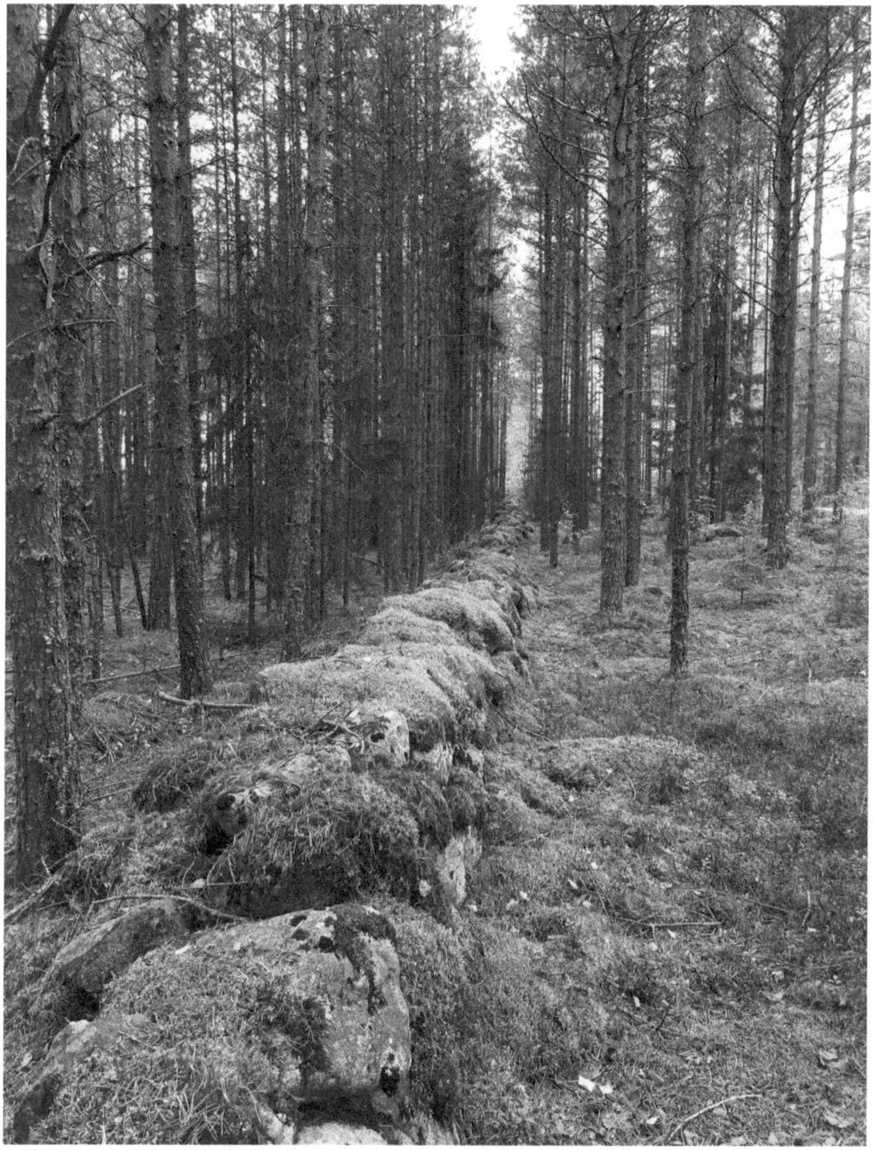

IMAGE 8.2 The stone wall. 19 September 2021. Photograph by the author.

impression that the burial site is part of another world, separated and sealed off from the fast-moving present and the temporality of modernity that the railway helped create.

Writing about monumental interventions in the landscape, Trigg describes their effects as not only interrupting the landscape spatially and symbolically, but also illuminating 'the irreducibility of the past, taken at the limits of its

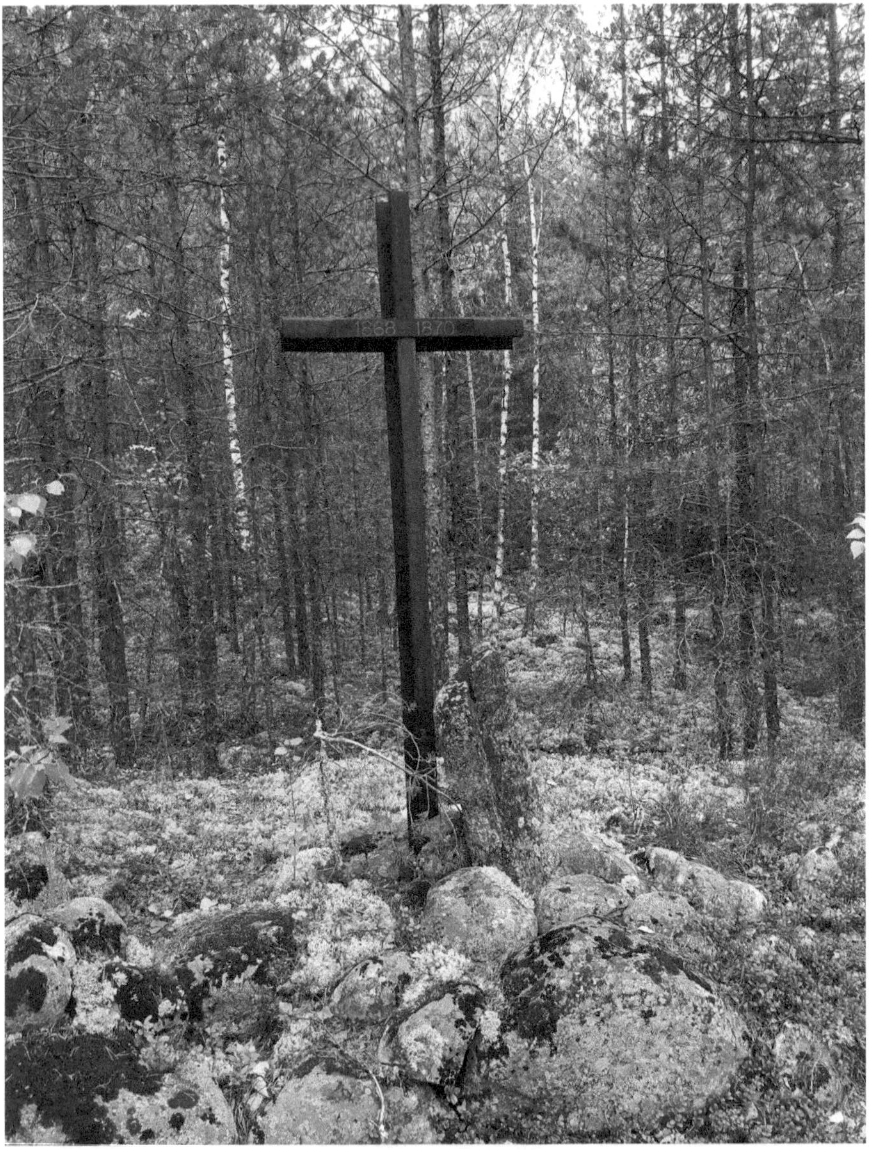

IMAGE 8.3 The cross made from railway tracks, on a mound next to the railway. 19 September 2021. Photograph by the author.

materiality'. As such, 'closure is usurped by the legacy of an event that exceeds the spatiotemporally of the present [...] the certainty masking the historical past is met with radical uncertainty'.[49] Similarly, the presence of these peripheral sites along the track 'speak back' and rupture the progressive, linear temporality of modernity associated with the railway. In his work on famine ruins in the Irish landscape, David Lloyd argues that if the temporality of modernity is 'to naturalize progress as the self-evident form of human time', these sites function as a reminder of the 'continuing violence or ruination that afflicts at once the present and the unsubsumed remnants of the past'.[50] The liminality of the famine sites scattered along the Finnish part of the railway as well as their peripheral locations speak to the societal stigmatisation and collapse of funerary customs associated with this period of destitution.[51] They thus contain within them a critique of the narrative of Finland's supposedly completed modernisation by reminding the spectator of the failure that is part of the origin of this celebrated railway.

Exhibiting the Skeleton Track

Heritage sites and museums, their collections, exhibitions, and curatorial practices are inextricably bound up with constructions of collective identity as well as state- and nation-building. As Kelly reminds us, they 'broker personal and collective identity formations typically cued from viewing displayed collections'.[52] While this is perhaps more evident for ethnographic and history museums, science and technology museums are also concerned with power and nation-building.[53] Transport museums, such as the Finnish Railway Museum, fall somewhere between technological and historical museums and project 'deep-rooted myths about transport and its role in shaping the societies in which we live', while 'narratives about the past are usually presented as absolute truths'.[54] In terms of exhibitions on the history of transport, such as the railway, this is particularly relevant as 'modernity was rendered imaginatively through the materials of technology'.[55] The railway became modernity's most prominent emblem in the Western cultural imagination.[56] When exhibiting railways, then, the social history of the railway as well as critical questions like 'what is progress?' and 'progress for *whom*?' are often left out in favour of simplistic, linear, and progressive narratives.[57] It can be complex to intervene in such narratives and established curatorial practices, particularly when it comes to histories of destitution. As Marguérite Corporaal and Ingrid de Zwarte note in their comprehensive review of contemporary famine heritage practices, it is exactly the lack of material traces and oral history which makes these famine pasts complicated to exhibit.[58] The three exhibitions discussed here are no exception to these trends.

Due to the COVID-19 pandemic, many physical exhibitions in celebration of the 150th anniversary were moved to the summer of 2021. The Finnish Railway Museum in Hyvinkää curated a physical exhibition in 2021 based on their online exhibition published on 11 September 2020. The online exhibition is only available in Finnish, whereas the physical exhibition is both in Finnish and Russian.[59] The Finnish Railway Museum has been in existence since 1898, albeit in a smaller place and as the 'Finnish Railway Officials Association' in

Helsinki. In 1974, the museum moved to larger premises in Hyvinkää, where the locomotives and wagons could be exhibited. Since 1997, it has been a national museum, operating under the name 'Finnish Railway Museum', abbreviated as FRM.[60] The museum is divided over many different buildings: three exhibition halls, a locomotive shed, a station, and barracks.

The smaller exhibition space of the museum engages with the social history of the railway and provides longer descriptions and historical context in a guide book to interpret the objects and mannequins in historical dress. Yet, in the main exhibition hall, the locomotives are left to 'speak for themselves', and interpretive signs focus on technological developments. In this manner, the permanent exhibition is similar to many transport museum exhibitions discussed by Divall and Scott, who argue that 'these object-centered and minimally-interpreted transport exhibitions are heirs to the celebratory and progressivist legacies of the nineteenth-century museum'.[61] Transport museums in general and the FRM in specific structure narratives in a linear fashion, progressing from the early development of the railway and rolling stock to the present day. As such, the museum emphasises the connection between national identity and technological progress to 'sustain a sense of national identity based upon industrial excellence', termed the 'patriotic view of technology' by Alan Morton.[62] It is within this context of progress, linearity, and the railway as emblem of modernity that the FRM anniversary exhibition was curated.

The virtual component of the anniversary exhibition uses a great amount of text and highlights various aspects of the railway through a plethora of articles: its history, use, context of construction, and development. The same themes were present in the physical exhibition, but with less extensive texts. The museum's website announced the exhibition by stating that much happened on the track during its history: 'it was built during a famine, it has been at the centre of wars' [...] it has used to transport huge quantities of goods', and became Finland's 'most important foreign trade route'.[63] The connection between the famine and the railway is mentioned; however, it is embedded in a progressive narrative that glosses over the terrible labour conditions on the railway as part of famine relief work. The exhibition, housed in the main locomotive hall, consisted of graphic panels on the hall's wall with photographs, text, and a few objects. The multitude of photographs of identical stations along the route construct it as something quintessentially 'Finnish', while the images of endless tracks, celebratory occasions, and well-kept train interiors evoke a well-established visual repertoire of train travel that sparks fantasies of adventure, boundlessness, and progress. Both in the website announcement and in the exhibition itself, the famine and relief work are but a sidenote in the origin story of the Finnish state and nation-building through tracks.

The textual section in the physical exhibition on the famine is brief: it explains that in 1867, Tsar Alexander II ordered the building of the track, and that due to the famine, many people sought work and bread at the construction site, often with their entire family. It mentions how jobs were created 'even for the weakest', such as women and children who were enlisted to build the stone protective wall between Uudenkyluä and Kausala. While it is mentioned in a later section that the railway was finished below budget, this is attributed to easier working conditions than expected—not to cheap labour. No mention is made of the bonuses handed out by the Tsar in appreciation for the completion of the project below budget, nor of the ample critique these bonuses received at the time and since then.[64] Furthermore, the text makes no mention of the high death rate and mass graves along the track, nor of the harsh working conditions and spread of diseases.

The exhibition text thus provides a sanitised version of the railway as a public relief project and avoids discussion of the controversy that has surrounded the railway since its construction. When 'reading' the exhibition (both text and images) together, it represents the railway as an impetus for modernisation and state-building in Finland, borne out of a poor (but neglectable) past.[65] However, when reading the exhibition 'against the grain', internal inconsistencies become apparent, such as the absence of any discussion on rampant diseases, high mortality rates, wages that were too low for workers to sustain themselves and their families, and the inclusion of women and children in the relief work scheme.[66] The terrible working conditions as well as the requirement that women and children work in exchange for bread illuminate the harsh contemporaneous attitudes towards charity and poor relief, which would surely be criticised in the welfare state that is present-day Finland. Scott and Divall argue that even when transport museums host exhibitions that engage with social history, these 'rarely offer visitors the cognitive and other resources needed to engage critically with the myths of collective memory'.[67] Similarly, in the anniversary exhibition in the FRM, the Riihimäki–St. Petersburg railway is discussed in terms of the dominant interpretation of the period of the famine, and counternarratives or alternative readings are erased. However, in the other exhibitions, a focus on labour provides the possibility for a more critical reading of the railway.

For example, labour conditions are central to the anniversary exhibition organised by the National Workers' House Museum, located in Riihimäki. This museum, a small-scale initiative that nonetheless bears the 'national' status, opened its doors in 1969 and is only open to visitors on Sundays during the summer. It is run by volunteers and houses a small collection, mainly focused on the history of the labour movement in Finland. The anniversary exhibition consisted of text (only in Finnish) and photographs printed on A4 sheets tacked to panels, as well as a glass display with photographs of burial and memorial sites in honour of the railway workers. Due to the lack of objects in the collection, the exhibition was a 'book-on-the-wall' type. In so doing, it focused much more on the specifics of working conditions than the exhibition at the FRM: it discussed the spread of diseases, how 14 hospitals were built, how 20% of the workforce was ill during the worst stages of the project, and the need for mass burial sites along the tracks. Furthermore, as the 150th anniversary of the railway coincided with the 60th anniversary of Riihimäki's acquisition of city rights, part of the exhibition focused on how the railway connection changed the town itself. The railway and its connection to Riihimäki are still presented as a narrative of progress—understandably so, as Riihimäki was barely a settlement before the railway passed through it. However, the emphasis in the exhibition is on labour conditions and high mortality rates, and the inclusion of the memorialisation of the railway workers burial sites gesture towards an alternative and critical reading of the origin of the railway—one which is not embedded in a linear narrative of national progress.

A different critique is visible in the 2022 *Ratajätkät* ('Railway Builders') exhibition curated by Werstas, the Finnish Labour Museum located in the industrial city of Tampere. The museum operates under the same 'special national museum' status as the Finnish Railway Museum. The exhibition, based on museum director Kalle Kallio's research and recently published book on the subject, explores the history and experiences of railway labourers in Finland.[68] The introduction text on the museum's website remarks that while 'the railway revolutionised mobility, spread civilisation and laid the foundations for a modern, prosperous world', very little attention is paid to the railway workers, 'sons of these poor rural families'.[69] While relying on the motif of the railway as the emblem of modernisation, the exhibition text highlights the absence of human history in this imagination. The exhibition itself consists of multiple panels that contain photographs and texts, each highlighting a different period and aspect of railway workers' experience. Unlike in the other museums, the texts are presented in Finnish, Swedish, and English and contain fictional accounts of historical people—a trend more commonly observed in exhibitions dealing with histories of famine and destitution where oral histories are lacking and therefore replaced by fictionalised accounts.[70]

The panel which mentions the famine features an 1870 photograph that shows the construction of the railway bridge over the frozen Kymijoki lake. The text is written from the perspective of Gustaf Theodor Ahlgren, the engineer of the railway. It is a satirical take on the railway as a 'national' achievement: 'Just to think that a couple of years ago local residents were starving to death, but now my bridge will complete a rail link to St. Petersburg, ensuring year-round crop deliveries. I am sure this feat will be touted as a Finnish achievement, even though the bridge is made of English pig iron, paid for with Russian roubles, and it was designed by me, a Swedish-born engineer'. Although the panel provides little historical or contextual information on the building of the railway or the famine (nor do the other panels for their respective time periods), it does critique the notion of the railway as a product or symbol of 'Finnishness' or a national achievement. In this sense, it negates the 'patriotic view of technology' maintained in the FRM. While Ahlgren's position on nationalism is unknown, the curator Kalle Kallio used the engineer's 'voice' to remind ordinary visitors of the transnational scale of transportation and transport technologies.[71]

Conclusion

The transformation of the railway into heritage through the erection of memorials, interpretive signs and curating of museum exhibitions can be seen to fall largely within the hegemonic narrative of the famine as the 'birth pangs' of a modernising nation.[72] Hence, the losses associated with the construction of the railway are framed as expressions of the national spirit and heroic sacrifice and legitimised in terms of the modernisation processes that were necessary for Finland to come to fruition as a nation-state. However, the presence of a possible 'Red' narrative can be seen in certain iterations of the railway: the subtle critique aimed at the understanding of the railway as a 'Finnish feat' as expressed in the Werstas exhibition, or through the explicit focus on the conditions of the railway workers and memorialisation of the burial sites in the National Workers' House anniversary exhibition. It is perhaps unsurprising that the FRM maintains a hegemonic narrative, whereas the museums in Riihimäki and Tampere provide critical reflections on the railway, based on their regional focus (in the case of Riihimäki) and attention to the labour movement and labour relations in these museum's mandates (for both). Ultimately, however, it is the burial sites themselves and their material testimony to the past that complicate the teleology of this hegemonic narrative of progress: their peripheral locations remind us of the societal stigmatisation and disturb the temporality of modernity. Their transformation from sites into places through conservation and heritage practices has not deluded and even emphasised this disturbance.

It is, however, not only the past that speaks to the present of the railway. As mentioned earlier, the gauge of the tracks was chosen to connect Helsinki to the Russian Empire rather than to Central Europe or other Scandinavian countries. As a result, trade between Finland and Russia was made easy, but overland connections between Finland and the rest of Europe were less so. Since 2010, the Allegro train (that runs swiftly past the cross in Uusikylä) ran twice daily between Helsinki and St. Petersburg in less than 3.5 hours. The 150th anniversary exhibition in the FRM emphasised the past and present connection between Finland and Russia. However, on 28 March 2022, the connection was discontinued after being the last remaining land connection between Europe and Russia. As a result of sanctions imposed on the Russian Federation following its invasion of Ukraine on 24 February 2022, most airspace and most land borders in Europe were closed to Russians and Russian aircraft. Before the connection was discontinued, many who fled Russia would have passed by the cross and burial mound, most likely unaware of their significance. These tracks, built with the same gauge as those in Russia—built to connect yet built on hunger—are now closed off for international traffic to and from Russia, which did not even happen during the Cold War. After what was almost exclusively a celebratory anniversary, with a large emphasis on the positive international relations between Russia and Finland materialised through this railway, it will be instructive to see how this new phase of Finnish–Russian bilateral relations is inscribed onto the Skeleton Track.

Notes

1 The author would like to express her gratitude to Andrew G. Newby for his generosity and time in showing her the memorials discussed in this chapter, as well as the insightful conversations during the many hours on the road, that have all contributed to this chapter.
2 See, for example, Fred Singleton and Anthony Frederick Upton, *A Short History of Finland*, 2nd edn. (Cambridge: Cambridge University Press, 1998), 85; Seppo Zetterberg, *Getting There Together: 150 Years of VR*, trans. Andrew Fisher (Helsinki: WSOY, 2012), 8–10.
3 Kari Pitkänen, *Deprivation and Disease: Mortality During the Great Finnish Famine of the 1860's* (Helsinki: Finnish Demographic Society, 1993).
4 Cormac Ó Gráda, *Eating People Is Wrong, and Other Essays on Famine, Its Past, and Its Future* (Princeton: Princeton University Press, 2015), 107.
5 By contrast, Ireland has a national monument to the famine in Murrisk (1997) and the National Famine Museum in Strokestown.
6 Andrew G. Newby, *Finland's 'Great Hunger Years' Memorials: A Sesquicentennial Report* (Helsinki: Helsinki Collegium for Advanced Studies, 2017).
7 See, for example Henrik Mikael Forsberg, 'Masculine Submission: National Narratives of the Last Great Famine, c. 1868–1920', *Journal of Finnish Studies* 20, no. 1 (2017); Andrew G. Newby, *Finland's Great Famine, 1856–68* (Basingstoke: Palgrave Macmillan, 2023); Eliza Kraatari and Andrew G. Newby, 'Memory of the Great Hunger Years Revisited – Finland's 1860s Famine Memorials, Mass Graves and a Commemorative Craft Initiative', *Thanatos* 7, no. 2 (2019); Antti Häkkinen, Kari Pitkänen, and Hannu Soikkanen, *Kan Halla Nälän Tuskan Toi* [When the Cold Brought the Pain of Hunger] (Helsinki: WSOY, 1991).
8 Laurajane Smith, *Uses of Heritage* (London: Routledge, 2006), 3.
9 Andrew G. Newby, 'Overcoming Amnesia? Memorializing Finland's "Great Hunger Years"', in *The Great Irish Famine: Visual and Material Culture*, eds. Marguérite Corporaal, Oona Frawley, and Emily Mark-FitzGerald (Liverpool: Liverpool University Press, 2018); Declan Curran, Lubomyr Y. Luciuk, and Andrew G. Newby, eds., *Famines in European Economic History: the Last Great European Famines Reconsidered* (London: Routledge, 2015), 9–10. For research on the regional and economic divisions of the famine, see Miikka Voutilainen, 'Feeding the famine: Social vulnerability and dislocation during the Finnish famine of the 1860s', in *Famines in European Economic History: the Last Great European Famines Reconsidered*, Declan Curran, Lubomyr Y. Luciuk, and Andrew G. Newby (London: Routledge, 2015), 124–44.

10 Marian Aguiar, 'Making Modernity: Inside the Technological Space of the Railway', *Cultural Critique* 68 (2008): 71; Matthew Beaumont and Michael J. Freeman, 'Introduction', in *The Railway and Modernity: Time, Space, and the Machine Ensemble*, eds. Beaumont and Freeman (Oxford: Peter Lang, 2007), 13; Newby, 'Overcoming Amnesia?'
11 Antti Häkkinen and Henrik Mikael Forsberg, 'Finland's Famine Years of the 1860s: A Nineteenth-century Perspective', in *Famines in European Economic History: The Last Great European Famines Reconsidered*, eds. Declan Curran, Lubomyr Y. Luciuk, and Andrew G. Newby (London: Routledge, 2015), 100; Singleton and Upton, *A Short History of Finland*, 63.
12 Häkkinen and Forsberg, 'Finland's Famine Years of the 1860s: A Nineteenth-Century Perspective', 107.
13 Newby, 'Overcoming Amnesia?', 184.
14 Ibid., 185.
15 Newby, *Finland's Great Famine, 1856–68*, 215.
16 Ibid., 215–16. Eduard J. Alvarez-Palau and Jordi Martí-Henneberg, 'Shaping the Common Ground: State-Building, the Railway Network, and Regional Development in Finland', *Journal of Interdisciplinary History* 51, no. 2 (2020): 267–96.
17 Lari Rantanen, 'A Pitfall on a Nation's Path of Politics?,' *Jahrbücher für Geschichte Osteuropas* 67, no. 2 (2019): 227.
18 Newby, *Finland's Great Famine, 1856–68*, 215.
19 Antti Häkkinen, 'On Attitudes and Living Strategies in the Finnish Countryside in the Years of Famine 1867–68,' in *Just a Sack of Potatoes?: Crisis Experiences in European Societies, Past and Present*, ed. Antti Häkkinen (Helsinki: Societas Historica Finlandiae, 1992), 159; Kalle Kallio, *Ratajätkät — Rautatienrakentajien kokemukset 1857–1939* (Helsinki: SKS Kirjat, 2022), 136.
20 Kallio, *Ratajätkät — Rautatienrakentajien kokemukset 1857–1939*, 136–7.
21 Newby, *Finland's Great Famine, 1856–68*, 220.
22 Kallio, *Ratajätkät — Rautatienrakentajien kokemukset 1857–1939*, 137; Häkkinen, Pitkänen, and Soikkanen, *Kan Halla Nälän Tuskan Toi*; Forsberg, 'Masculine Submission', 46. Novels that expressed critique were K. A. Tavastjernan's *Hårda Tider* ('Hard Times', 1891) and Frans Emil Sillanpää's *Hurskas kurjuus* ('Meek Heritage', 1919).
23 Translated and quoted by Andrew G. Newby and Timo Myllyntaus, '"The Terrible Visitation": Famine in Finland and Ireland, 1845 to 1868', in *Famines in European Economic History: The Last Great European Famines Reconsidered*, eds. Declan Curran, Lubomyr Y. Luciuk, and Andrew G. Newby (London: Routledge, 2015), 157–58.
24 Forsberg, 'Masculine Submission', 47.
25 For more information on public work schemes in the nineteenth century, see Peter Gray, 'Famine Relief Policy in Comparative Perspective: Ireland, Scotland, and Northwestern Europe, 1845–1849', *Éire-Ireland* 1 (1996): 86–108. See also James S. Donnelly, *The Great Irish Potato Famine* (New York: History Press, 2012), particularly Chapter 3; Tom Devine, *The Great Highland Famine: Hunger, Emigration and the Scottish Highlands in the Nineteenth Century* (Edinburgh: Birlinn Ltd., 2021), particularly Chapter 5.
26 Newby, *Finland's Great Famine, 1856–68*, 223.
27 Declan Curran, Lubomyr Luciuk, and Andrew Newby, 'Introduction', in *Famines in European Economic History*, 11; Newby, 'Overcoming Amnesia?', 186.
28 Newby, *Finland's Great Famine, 1856–68*, 223.
29 Kraatari and Newby, 'Memory of the Great Hunger Years Revisited,' 99.
30 Häkkinen, Pitkänen, and Soikkanen, *Kan Halla Nälän Tuskan Toi*, 130–3.
31 Newby, *Finland's Great Famine, 1856–68*, 220.

32 The other memorial sites are interpretive boards placed near a mass grave by Elimäki Parish (2018), a memorial stone in Hausjärvi (likely contemporary), a memorial stone in Kouvola (1987), and a contemporary stone in Hausjärvi with an interpretive plaque that was added in 1988. For more information, see www.katovuodet1860.wordpress.com/tag/luurata/. An eighth memorial site can be found in Riihimäki, where in 1970, a sculpture dedicated to the railway workers was erected. However, this memorial is not located at a burial site and dedicated to the moment when the workers finished their work and could stand upright. As such, it is not included in this chapter.
33 Quoted and translated in Kraatari and Newby, 'Memory of the Great Hunger Years Revisited', 98.
34 Ibid.
35 Translation by Andrew G. Newby. See Andrew G. Newby, 'Radanrakentajien', *Finland's 'Great Hunger Years' Memorials*, 2019, www.katovuodet1860.wordpress.com/tag/radanrakentajien/, last accessed 14 August 2023.
36 Andrew G. Newby, 'Lahti', *Finland's 'Great Hunger Years' Memorials, WordPress*, 2019, www.katovuodet1860.wordpress.com/tag/lahti/.
37 Andrew G. Newby, 'Uusikylä (Arola) [Nastola],' *Finland's 'Great Hunger Years' Memorials*, 2018, www.katovuodet1860.wordpress.com/2018/08/05/uusikyla-nastola/.
38 Niamh Ann Kelly, *Imagining the Great Irish Famine: Representing Dispossession in Visual Culture* (London: I.B. Tauris & Co., 2018), 148.
39 Dylan Trigg, 'The place of trauma: Memory, hauntings, and the temporality of ruins,' *Memory Studies* 2, no. 1 (2009): 89.
40 Emily Mark-FitzGerald, *Commemorating the Irish Famine: Memory and the Monument* (Liverpool University Press, 2013), 106.
41 The original reads: 'Vuosien 1867–1868 Suurina nälkävuosina haudattiin tähan paikkaan nälkään ja kulkutauteihin kuolleita Hollolan Pitäjän Lahden ja jarvenpään kylistä seka muualta kotoisin olleita Riihimäen-Pietarin radan rakentajia. Patsaan pystytti Lahden seurakunta 1955'. Translation by Andrew G. Newby.
42 Newby and Myllyntaus, 'The terrible visitation', 157–8.
43 The original reads: 'Historian kätkemäksi arvoitukseksi jää keitä varmuudella olivat ne katovuosien radanrakennustyömaalle ajamat, joiden kohtalona oli saada viimeinen leposijansa tässä männikössä'.
44 Mark-FitzGerald, *Commemorating the Irish Famine*, 106.
45 Ibid.
46 See, for example, Anika Walke, 'Split Memory', *Slavic Review* 77, no. 1 (2018): 174–97.
47 The original reads: 'Vuosina 1868–1870 kuolleiden Riihimäki-Pietarin Radanpakentajien muistolle. Nastolan neuvosto ja seurakunta, 1990'. Translated by Andrew G. Newby.
48 Kallio, *Ratajätkät—Rautatienrakentajien kokemukset 1857–1939*, 137.
49 Dylan Trigg, *The Memory of Place: A Phenomenology of the Uncanny* (Athens, OH: Ohio University Press, 2012), 97.
50 David Lloyd, *Irish Times: Temporalities of Modernity* (Dublin: Field Day Publications in Association with the Keough-Naughton Institute for Irish Studies at the University of Notre Dame, 2008), 4.
51 Most of the burial sites can be found along the track between Riihimäki and Lahti. For a map with the approximate location of the sites, see Andrew G. Newby, 'Hikiä [Hausjärvi]', *Finland's 'Great Hunger Years' Memorials, WordPress*, 7 December, 2018, www.katovuodet1860.wordpress.com/2018/07/30/hikia-hausjarvi/.
52 Kelly, *Imagining the Great Irish Famine*, 92.
53 Sharon Macdonald, 'Introduction', in *The Politics of Display: Museums, Science, Culture* (London: Routledge, 1998), xii–xiii.

54 Colin Divall and Andrew Scott, *Making Histories in Transport Museums* (London: Leicester University Press, 2001), 29.
55 Aguiar, 'Making Modernity', 71.
56 Ibidem; Beaumont and Freeman, *The Railway and Modernity*, 13.
57 Divall and Scott, *Making Histories in Transport Museums*, 62–4.
58 Marguérite Corporaal and Ingrid De Zwarte, 'Heritages of Hunger: European Famine Legacies in Current Academic Debates', *International Journal of Heritage Studies* 28, no. 1 (2021): 35–8.
59 Normally the Finnish Railway Museum provides scripts in Finnish, Russian and English, but due to COVID-19 restrictions and the limited travel possible, it was decided to focus on the many Russians still visiting Finland.
60 Finland has three national museums (all located in Helsinki) and 16 (+1) 'National Special Museums', one of which is the Finnish Railway Museum. For more information, see Janne Vilkuna, 'The Development of Finnish Museums over the Last Forty Years', *Nordic Museology* 1 (2018): 96–103.
61 Divall and Scott, *Making Histories in Transport Museums*, 39.
62 Ibid., 68.
63 'Erikois- Ja Verkkonäyttelyt', Suomen Rautatiemuseo, 2020, www.rautatiemuseo.fi/fi/erikois-ja-verkkonayttelyt, accessed 5 September 2022. Translation provided with DeepL, last accessed 5 September 2022.
64 See endnote 20 for literature on this critique.
65 For an explanation of a textual approach to museum studies, see Rihannon Mason, 'Cultural Theory and Museum Studies', in *A Companion to Museum Studies*, ed. Sharon Macdonald (Malden: Blackwell Publishing, 2006), 26–9.
66 Graeme Turner, *British Cultural Studies: An Introduction*, 3rd ed. (London: Routledge, 2003), 71–108.
67 Divall and Scott, *Making Histories in Transport Museums*, 78.
68 See Kallio, *Ratajätkät*.
69 'Rautatienrakentajien kokemuksia Suomessa', Työväenmuseo Werstas, 2022, www.tyovaenmuseo.fi/nayttelyt/juuri-nyt/ratajatkat/, accessed 5 September 2022. Translated with DeepL.
70 Corporaal and De Zwarte, 'Heritages of Hunger', 31–2.
71 Kalle Kallio, 2022. Personal communication. Email.
72 Curran, Luciuk, and Newby, 'Introduction', 11.

References

Aguiar, Marian, 'Making Modernity: Inside the Technological Space of the Railway'. *Cultural Critique* 68 (2008): 66–85.

Alvarez-Palau, Eduard J., and Jordi Martí-Henneberg, 'Shaping the Common Ground: State Building, the Railway Network, and Regional Development in Finland'. *Journal of Interdisciplinary History* 51, no. 2 (2020): 267–96.

Beaumont, Matthew, and Michael J. Freeman, eds., *The Railway and Modernity: Time, Space, and the Machine Ensemble*. Oxford: Peter Lang, 2007.

Corporaal, Marguérite, and Ingrid De Zwarte, 'Heritages of Hunger: European Famine Legacies in Current Academic Debates'. *International Journal of Heritage Studies* 28, no. 1 (2021): 30–43.

Curran, Declan, Lubomyr Y. Luciuk, and Andrew G. Newby, eds., *Famines in European Economic History: The Last Great European Famines Reconsidered*. London: Routledge, 2015.

Devine, Tom, *The Great Highland Famine: Hunger, Emigration and the Scottish Highlands in the Nineteenth Century*. Edinburgh: Birlinn Ltd., 2021.

Divall, Colin, and Andrew Scott, *Making Histories in Transport Museums*. London: Leicester University Press, 2001.
Donnelly, James S., *The Great Irish Potato Famine*. New York: History Press, 2012.
'Erikois- Ja Verkkonäyttelyt'. Suomen Rautatiemuseo, 2020. www.rautatiemuseo.fi/fi/erikois-ja-verkkonayttelyt.
Forsberg, Henrik Mikael, 'Masculine Submission: National Narratives of the Last Great Famine, c. 1868–1920', *Journal of Finnish Studies* 20, no. 1 (2017): 38–64.
Gray, Peter, 'Famine Relief Policy in Comparative Perspective: Ireland, Scotland, and Northwestern Europe, 1845–1849', *Éire-Ireland* 1 (1996): 86–108.
Häkkinen, Antti, 'On Attitudes and Living Strategies in the Finnish Countryside in the Yearsof Famine 1867-68'. In Antti Häkkinen, ed., 149–65, *Just a Sack of Potatoes?: Crisis Experiences in European Societies, Past and Present*. Helsinki: Societas Historica Finlandiae, 1992.
Häkkinen, Antti, and Henrik Mikael Forsberg, 'Finland's Famine Years of the 1860s: A Nineteenth-Century Perspective'. In Declan Curran, Lubomyr Y. Luciuk and Andrew G. Newby, eds., 99–123, *Famines in European Economic History: The Last Great European Famines Reconsidered*. London: Routledge, 2015.
Häkkinen, Antti, Kari Pitkänen, and Hannu Soikkanen, *Kan Halla Nälän Tuskan Toi*. Helsinki: WSOY, 1991.
Kallio, Kalle, *Ratajätkät — Rautatienrakentajien Kokemukset 1857–1939*. Helsinki: SKS Kirjat, 2022.
Kelly, Niamh Ann, *Imagining the Great Irish Famine: Representing Dispossession in Visual Culture*. London: I.B. Tauris & Co, 2018.
Kraatari, Eliza, and Andrew G. Newby, 'Memory of the Great Hunger Years Revisited—Finland's 1860s Famine Memorials, Mass Graves and a Commemorative Craft Initiative'. *Thanatos* 7, no. 2 (2019): 90–126.
Lloyd, David, *Irish Times: Temporalities of Modernity*. Dublin: Field Day Publications in Association with the Keough-Naughton Institute for Irish Studies at the University of Notre Dame, 2008.
Macdonald, Sharon, ed., *The Politics of Display: Museums, Science, Culture*. London: Routledge, 1998.
Mark-FitzGerald, Emily, *Commemorating the Irish Famine: Memory and the Monument*. Liverpool University Press, 2013.
Mason, Rihannon, 'Cultural Theory and Museum Studies'. In Sharon Macdonald, ed., 17–32, *A Companion to Museum Studies*. Malden: Blackwell Publishing, 2006.
Newby, Andrew G, *Finland's Great Famine, 1856–68*. Basingstoke: Palgrave Macmillan, 2023.
Newby, Andrew G, *Finland's 'Great Hunger Years' Memorials: A Sesquicentennial Report*. Helsinki: Helsinki Collegium for Advanced Studies, 2017.
Newby, Andrew G, 'Hikiä [Hausjärvi]'. *Finland's 'Great Hunger Years' Memorials*. 7 December, 2018, www.katovuodet1860.wordpress.com/2018/07/30/hikia-hausjarvi/.
Newby, Andrew G, 'Lahti'. *Finland's 'Great Hunger Years' Memorials*. 2019, www.katovuodet1860.wordpress.com/tag/lahti/.
Newby, Andrew G, 'Overcoming Amnesia? Memorializing Finland's "Great Hunger Years"'. In Marguérite Corporaal, Oona Frawley and Emily Mark-FitzGerald, eds., 183–206, *The Great Irish Famine: Visual and Material Culture*. Liverpool: Liverpool University Press, 2018.
Newby, Andrew G, 'Radanrakentajien'. *Finland's 'Great Hunger Years' Memorials*. 2019. www.katovuodet1860.wordpress.com/tag/radanrakentajien/.
Newby, Andrew G, 'Uusikylä (Arola) [Nastola]', *Finland's 'Great Hunger Years' Memorials*. 8 May 2018. www.katovuodet1860.wordpress.com/2018/08/05/uusikyla-nastola/.

Newby, Andrew G., and Timo Myllyntaus, *'"The Terrible Visitation": Famine in Finland and Ireland, 1845 to 1868'*. In Declan Curran, Lubomyr Y. Luciuk and Andrew G. Newby, eds., Famines in European Economic History: The Last Great European Famines Reconsidered, 145–65. London: Routledge, 2015.
Ó Gráda, Cormac, *Eating People Is Wrong, and Other Essays on Famine, Its Past, and Its Future*. Princeton: Princeton University Press, 2015.
Pitkänen, Kari, *Deprivation and Disease: Mortality During the Great Finnish Famine of the 1860's*. Helsinki: Finnish Demographic Society, 1993.
Rantanen, Lari, 'A Pitfall on a Nation's Path of Politics?'. *Jahrbücher für Geschichte Osteuropas* 67, no. 2 (2019): 206–38.
'Rautatienrakentajien Kokemuksia Suomessa'. Työväenmuseo Werstas. 2022, www.tyovaenmuseo.fi/nayttelyt/juuri-nyt/ratajatkat/.
Singleton, Fred, and Anthony Frederick Upton, *A Short History of Finland*. 2nd ed. Cambridge: Cambridge University Press, 1998.
Smith, Laurajane. *Uses of Heritage*. London: Routledge, 2006.
Trigg, Dylan, *The Memory of Place: A Phenomenology of the Uncanny*. Athens, OH: Ohio University Press, 2012.
Trigg, Dylan, 'The Place of Trauma: Memory, Hauntings, and the Temporality of Ruins', *Memory Studies* 2, no. 1 (2009): 87–101.
Turner, Graeme, *British Cultural Studies: An Introduction*. 3rd ed. London: Routledge, 2003.
Vilkuna, Janne, 'The Development of Finnish Museums over the Last Forty Years', *Nordic Museology* 1 (2018): 96–103.
Voutilainen, Miikka, 'Feeding the Famine: Social Vulnerability and Dislocation During the Finnish Famine of the 1860s'. In Declan Curran, Lubomyr Y. Luciuk and Andrew G. Newby, eds., 124–44, *Famines in European Economic History: The Last Great European Famines Reconsidered*. London: Routledge, 2015.
Walke, Anika, 'Split Memory', *Slavic Review* 77, no. 1 (2018): 174–97.
Zetterberg, Seppo, *Getting There Together: 150 Years of Vr*. Trans. Andrew Fisher. Helsinki: WSOY, 2012.

9

SPAIN'S 'HUNGER YEARS'

A lack of musealisation of a traumatic past

Miguel Ángel del Arco Blanco and Deborah Madden

For decades, Spain has struggled to come to terms with its dictatorial past. In the twentieth century, this Southern European country was ruled by two authoritarian regimes (Miguel Primo de Rivera, 1923–30 and the long-standing dictatorship of Francisco Franco, 1939–75) and suffered a brutal, internecine Civil War (1936–39). These authoritarian regimes suffocated the burgeoning democratic social movements and political parties that were borne out during the First World War and flourished during Spain's Second Republic (1931–39). Ignited by the Nationalists' coup d'état in July 1936, the Civil War left around half a million dead and cumulated in the brutal dictatorship of General Franco that would last almost four decades. After the dictator's death in November 1975, Spain began its precarious transition to democracy, which was ratified by the 1978 constitution and the first democratically elected government since 1936, most prominently the left's resounding electoral victory in 1982. Spanish society, however, would have to wait until almost three decades after Franco's death for activism and policies on public memory to gain momentum.

Memory capacity is limited not only by neural and cultural constraints, but also by the psychological pressures of the historical context in which one lives or regimes of power. This makes for an intense relationship between 'active' and 'passive' forgetting, as described by Aleida Assmann.[1] In Spain, the Franco dictatorship was instrumental in trying to foster active forgetting of the country's tumultuous past through censorship, myth-making, or even violence. A 'social forgetting' took place that reflected the tensions between the public silence imposed by the dictatorship on the one hand and the private memory that remained hidden and stored until it came to light in democracy on the other.[2] Until well into the twenty-first century, democratic

DOI: 10.4324/9781003391524-13

institutions did not promote active remembrance of what happened; thus, until the historical memory movement began to gain ground in 2000, the most bloody, brutal elements of the Civil War and Francoist dictatorship were not fostered by the public memory of the democratic Government: murders, court martials, property seizures, purges, and torture. It was also the case of Spain's post-Civil War famines (1939–42 and 1946) and 'hunger years' (1939–52), a period characterised by food shortages, mass starvation, rampant disease, and malnutrition. If efforts to commemorate and musealise the Civil War and Franco's dictatorship were meagre and sparse, collective memory of the famine and shortages of the bleak post-Civil War years were even more elusive, obfuscated, and obscure. Accordingly, this chapter aims to explain the dearth of commemorations, monuments, places of memory, and museums about Spain's hunger years from a historical perspective. It will also consider some examples that show progressive efforts to acknowledge, explain, and promulgate this period in Spanish history.

To this end, it is necessary to contextualise our discussion with consideration for the influences on Spain's collective consciousness, particularly following the inception of the dictatorship in 1939. The first section of the chapter centres on these ideas, detailing the myths propagated about the famine and hunger years by the Francoist state, which is critical to understanding the public silence regarding the official memory of the regime. We also outline public policy cultivated during the Transition to democracy (1975–82), detailing how the 'pact of forgetting' (or 'pact of silence') shaped public debate about the past and the lack of justice for crimes committed during the Civil War and dictatorship. In the second section, we discuss the genesis of Spain's historical memory movement, the so-called 'memory wars', the country's recent memory laws (2007 and 2022), and the burgeoning historiography about the Spanish famine. We will illustrate how, in all elements of this public debate, the famine and post-Civil War hunger were all but absent. Finally, we shift focus to developments and progress regarding Spain's memory of hunger: firstly, in reference to the identification and analysis of individual and intergenerational memories; and then through the limited efforts to musealise this period. We conclude with a consideration for recent commemorative practices about Spain's famine and hunger years, which, to our mind, represent the beginning of a public memory about the famine that has been lacking up until now.

Memory politics in Spain (1939–2000)

After General Francisco Franco's Nationalist forces declared victory on 1 April 1939, the Franco regime proclaimed 1939 as the 'year of victory'. Such a commemoration underscores the propagandistic, antagonistic approach the state cultivated during its reign, particularly during its first decade in power. In accordance with this 'culture of victory', the Civil War was characterised as a 'Crusade' for a 'true Spain' (identified with tradition, Catholicism, and Castile) that defeated the 'anti-Spain' (represented by the Republic, liberalism, and Marxism).[3] However, as triumphant processions lined the streets of Spanish cities, the most brutal years of the Spanish famine (1939–42) took hold. During this period, more than 200,000 people died due to food shortages or illnesses related to malnutrition. While the impact of the Civil War should be taken into account, historians have revealed that this period is better understood as a 'man-made' famine, caused by the autarkic interventionist model adopted by the regime.[4]

The regime's victory propaganda entirely silenced the existence of the famines that occurred, both in the immediate aftermath of the Civil War and in 1946. The causes of the post-War years known as the hunger years (1939–52) were also distorted, when the living standards of Spaniards plummeted and the economy stagnated. Public memory about the Francoist regime focused on eulogising the Nationalists' victory and commemorating the 'heroes' and 'fallen martyrs' who died 'for God and Spain', leaving Republican experiences forgotten, many of whom were incarcerated in prisons and concentration camps, murdered and buried in the mass graves throughout the country.[5]

Francoism also utilised its propaganda to obfuscate, occlude, and misrepresent the famine and hunger years. The famine was completely erased: according to official state discourses, it had not occurred. Deaths from starvation and the exponential growth in deaths from diseases such as tuberculosis, typhus, and diphtheria did not appear in the press, nor in speeches by Francoist officials. The brutal post-Civil War years were deemed an innate consequence of three factors that, according to Francoist rhetoric, were beyond the state's control: a persistent drought ('*pertinaz sequía*') that impeded food supply throughout the 1940s; the fallout from the Civil War; and consequences of international isolation.

Rather than acknowledging the hardships faced by Spaniards, the state capitalised on romanticised conceptualisations of food to defend its autarkic, isolationist policies. Propagandistic newsreels (*Noticiario y Documentales Cinematográficos*, commonly referred to as NO-DO)—disseminated from 1943 to 1975 and screened in Spanish cinemas—promoted local foodstuffs. One example is 'La naranja y su riqueza' ('Oranges and their Richness', 1951), which promotes the health and financial benefits of trading oranges, with no reference to the famine or malnutrition faced by Spaniards.[6] In another NO-DO entitled 'Arroz y paella' ('Rice and Paella', 1955), 'the grain—loaded with symbolic meaning that can be harnessed by the regime—positions Spain as an important rice-producing nation thanks to state intervention and autarkic policies'[7] (Image 9.1).

Erasure and manipulation of this hunger past resulted in Francoist mythology about the famine infiltrating into the collective imagination. Many Spaniards held the view that mass hunger was an organic consequence

(a)

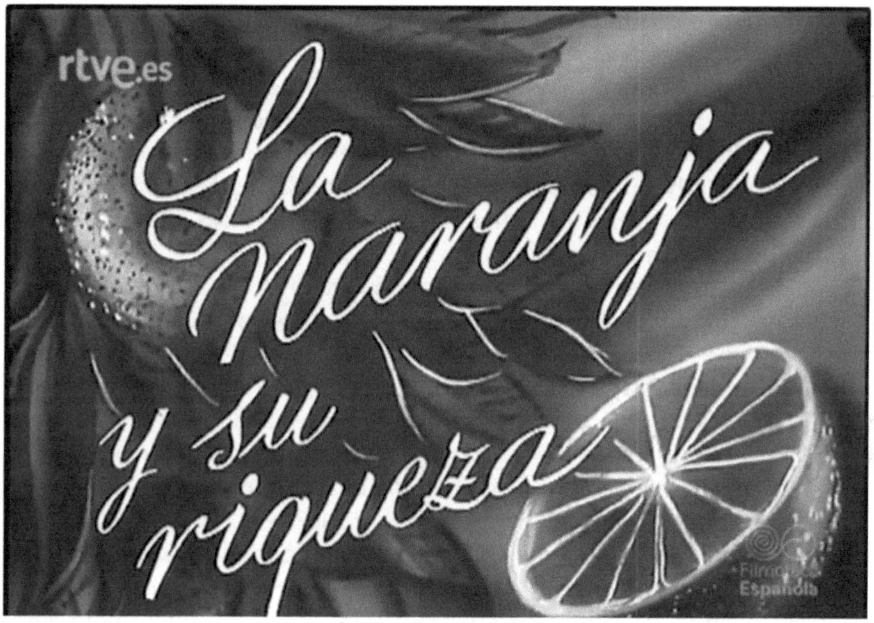

(b)

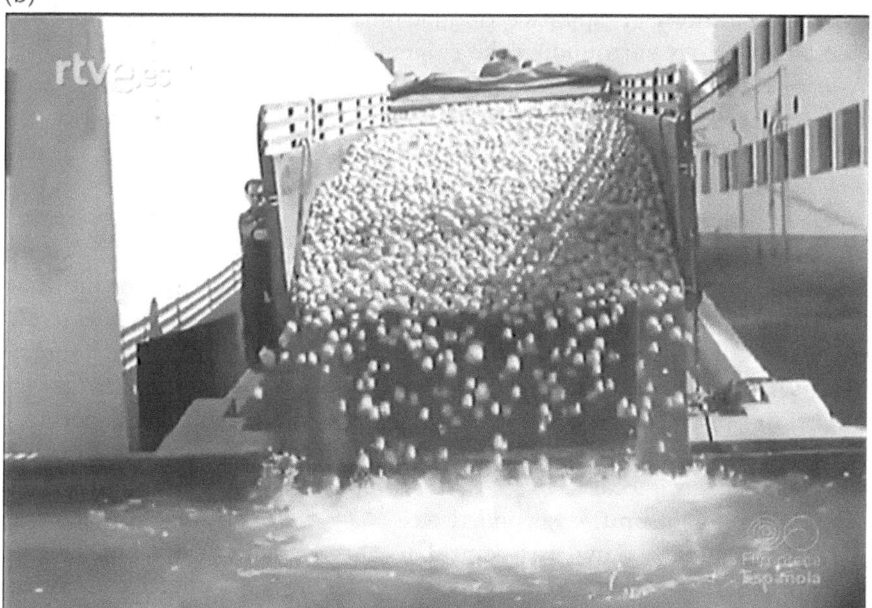

IMAGE 9.1 a and b. Francoist romantic conceptualisation of food: 'La naranja y su riqueza' documentary ('Oranges and their Richness'). Imágenes, Revista Cinematográfica. La Naranja y su Riqueza. No-Do, 1 January 1951, number 340.

of war and, when the situation improved in the 1950s, considered any improvement in their standard of living as evidence of the regime's success.[8] The fact that Spain was then a mainly agrarian country with poor communications and that the famine developed especially in the south of the country, far from Madrid and other parts of the country, contributed to the 'invisibility' of the famine. The absence of a coherent narrative on shortages, rationing, and poverty during early Francoism speaks to a 'silenced', fragmented history that remained unspoken within the individual and family spheres and, as we shall see, would take decades to come to light.[9]

Throughout the regime, the dictatorship reinforced such mythology, particularly from 1959 when collective consciousness about the Civil War began to evolve. The conflict was no longer understood as a 'crusade' and began to be understood as a 'struggle between brothers' for which the Second Republic was responsible. The regime's legitimacy was no longer centred on the war but now rested on having brought 'peace' and economic growth to Spain; in reality, however, the '25 Years of Peace' celebrated in 1964 were utterly disingenuous, while economic developments resulted from input and pressures from the United States.[10] The cult of economic success occluded memory of the famine: in the latter years of the regime—*tardofranquismo* ('late Francoism')—the state took credit for improving the standard of living, when it had in fact been responsible for more than a decade of economic stagnation. The myth of 'Spain's economic miracle', in this sense, replaced the previous mythology surrounding the enigmatic hunger years.[11]

After Franco's death in November 1975, reconciliation—rather than justice or vengeance—was critical to the country's precarious transition to democracy (1975–82).[12] Driven by pro-democracy social movements, the so-called Transition was, somewhat ironically, orchestrated by Francoist elites, particularly those more in favour of reform, known as the '*aperturistas*' ['progressives'] and democratic opposition. This period was characterised by a 'pact of forgetting' ('*pacto del olvido*'): a cross-party agreement that advocated amnesty to ensure that a democratic system would be effectively implemented. Fearing a repetition of the bloody Civil War, the country looked to the future, 'leaving the thorniest aspects of the past behind'.[13] Scholarship on post-Francoist Spain frequently echoes this loaded political discourse, referencing victims' 'forgotten' or 'silenced' histories, with some critiquing this terminology given that it obfuscates the covert ways that Spaniards shed light on this shrouded past.[14]

The 1977 Amnesty Law was central to this complex process of transitioning to a democratic state, which provided amnesty for crimes committed during the Civil War and dictatorship. Political prisoners were freed and tacit 'gag rules' impeded legal and political critique of Spain's dictatorial past, as the core principles of this law encapsulated the political mood of the period: moving forward, towards a fresh start that leaves the past behind.[15] For some, this meant that the most traumatic elements of the past were 'forgotten' for pragmatic purposes. For others, it signified a governmental silencing of the past, obfuscating any public memory about the war and dictatorship, which resulted in 'forgetting' the victims and silencing their stories.[16] A salient example of these tensions was the non-commemoration of the Civil War in 1986, as Felipe González's Socialist government upheld the state-sanctioned silence by declining to officially commemorate the 50th anniversary of the outbreak of the conflict.

At the same time, there was an institutional political, social, and legal pushback against the collective forgetting that shaped the post-Franco years. We know, for example, that some regions such as Extremadura, Navarra, and La Rioja exhumed the bodies of Republicans from mass graves on behalf of their families. Without equipment or support from the authorities, some decided to provide a dignified reburial to their loved ones who had been murdered by Francoist troops.[17] Academic interest in the Civil War and dictatorship was also whetted: to mark the 50th anniversary of the conflict in 1986—which was ignored by the Socialist government—dozens of conferences were organised, resulting in numerous publications, with an estimated 15,000 works produced.[18] The 'insatiable curiosity' of Spanish citizens was 'satisfied by a deluge of popular publications, television programs, and films', as cultural production proved a productive alternative to formal political debate.[19] While Spanish society utilised cultural output to recuperate collective memory about the past, neither the famine nor the post-Civil War hunger years were focalised.

Memory politics (2000–present)

The relationship between the state, Spanish society, and the country's violent past began to evolve in the twenty-first century, with the year 2000 marking a turning point. It was this year that forensic methods were first used to excavate a mass grave in Priaranza del Duero (León). Moreover, the Association for the Recuperation of Historical Memory (ARHM) was founded, with the aim of unearthing the remains of the regime's victims. A social movement began to gain ground that advocated for the exhumation of murdered Republicans, providing dignity to the victims, and commemorating the past. Propelled mainly by Spain's third generation—known as the 'grandchildren's generation'—who argued that victims' rights, truth, and justice were central to Spanish democracy—this movement demanded retribution for the 'silenced' crimes of the dictatorship, which ranged from execution, torture, and extrajudicial imprisonment to the loss of livelihood, exile, and the forced adoption of babies.[20] In 2007, the first of two memory laws—the Historical Memory Law—was passed by the governing Socialist Party.

Spain is an example of the difficulties of dealing with harrowing pasts. As a society marked by trauma and violence, it has faced the challenge of building a democratic collective memory through post-conflict memorialisation. The historical memory movement forced debates about the past into the open, initiating what has become known as the memory wars. The political left is in favour of implementing policies to confront the past, though tensions remain as to how and to what extent this should be realised. On the other hand, such measures have provoked backlash from the right. In 2002, the conservative People's Party government released a statement to mark 25 years of democracy in Spain, in which they reiterated that it was imperative to 'avoid in all cases the opening up of old wounds'.[21]

Conflict regarding historical memory reflects a society that remains divided by the Civil War and regime. The 'obituary wars' during this period exemplify this: relatives of Republicans published obituaries in honour of their deceased loved ones, outlining when they were killed, by whom ('the fascists') and why ('for defending democracy'); in the conservative press, the descendants of the victorious Nationalists did the same.[22] This competing memory phenomenon occurred regarding monuments dedicated to the fallen by the Francoist state: many town halls took measures to remove them from public spaces, facing resistance from citizens on the political right.[23] Spanish society needed to confront, engage with, and reflect on the past. When doing so, however, bloodshed, deaths, and disappearances took precedent.

Ongoing ideological conflicts have intensified with the introduction of the Democratic Memory Law, ratified in October 2022.[24] The far-right Vox and conservative People's Party voted against the bill, while the ARMH—still one of Spain's most-prominent grassroots organisations—criticised the measures as insufficient.[25] Tabled by the ruling Socialist-Podemos coalition and passed thanks to support from left-wing and nationalist parties, this new legislation furthers the ground broken by the 2007 Historical Memory Law, pledging to expedite the unearthing of mass graves, investigate historical human rights violations, provide reparations to those persecuted, wrongfully imprisoned and tortured, criminalise the exaltation of Francoist dictatorship, and remove all remaining pro-Francoist monuments from the country (discussed further in the next section). Spain's memory wars therefore not only exemplify competing memory cultures, whereby conflicting narratives co-exist and play out in contemporary political dialogue—in consonance with Michael Rothberg's conception of collective memory as 'the past made present'—but also speak to the ways in which nations 'legitimise their political claims and policies by referring to their pasts'.[26]

As evidenced by the foregoing, Spain's memory laws aim to foster understanding about the country's democratic history, 'preserve and maintain victims' memory of the war and Francoist dictatorship, through the pursuit and knowledge of truth'.[27] To this end, Spain's history was framed in relation to war, specifically in relation to the global conflicts that devastated Europe, as Spain's Civil War acted as an ideological precursor to the international confrontation between fascism and democracy. In accordance with literature on contested memories and victimhood, the ideological factions of the Spanish conflict are understood within 'a global frame of reference'—considering themselves to be oppressed by Marxism or fascism in accordance with their political affiliation. Thus, Spain is part of the multi-directional memory of the traumatic European twentieth century.[28] There is, however, no reference to the devastating, politically motivated famines that occurred during these years, ravaging women and men throughout Spain. The law clearly outlined that 'forgetting is not compatible with democracy'.[29] At the same time, it has not led to a state-funded museum about the Civil War and regime, nor due recognition for the harsh effects of the famine and hunger years, which were direct consequences of the state's propaganda and autarkic economic system. Thus, though Article 3 of the new law outlines the state's conceptualisation of victims to include all whose rights were impeded, including 13 distinct categories, there is no explicit reference to the victims of the hunger years, nor to the regime's failed economic, trade, or agricultural strategies that exacerbated the famine.

Political discourses and government initiatives have tended to focalise violent oppression and mass murder, occluding the critical impact of food shortages, rationing, starvation, malnutrition, disease, and poverty that brutalised Spain's population during the Civil War—particularly in Republican-controlled regions (predominantly the East and Southeast of the country, including Madrid, Barcelona, and Alicante)—and during the hunger years. In response to decades of silence regarding Francoist violence, contemporary governmental policies tend to prioritise the location and excavation of mass graves, extraction of Francoist monuments and memory sites, and the criminalisation of pro-regime rhetoric, with the broad aim of providing long-overdue dignity, recognition, and respect to victims. Similarly, historical memory activism focalises the violent persecution of the vanquished Republicans and the ongoing excavation of mass graves.[30] Legacies of the famine, on the other hand, rarely come to the fore in the recuperation of Republican historical memory.[31]

A lack of formal recognition of hunger can also be explained in relation to limited critical interest in the famine, which has been rectified in recent years. As we have outlined above, Spain's famine was occluded and silenced by the regime's propaganda. Archives were inaccessible to researchers. After the dictator's death, research about the war and dictatorship flourished, with particular attention paid to state violence and repression. Research that centres on the post-Civil War years has been a burgeoning field since the 1990s, specifically in relation to socioeconomic development, the consolidation of the regime, and the evolution of state structures and policy. Seminal research was published that disproved Francoist myths and revealed the bleak reality of Spain's post-Civil War landscape. Historians have uncovered the dire economic circumstances caused by the state's autarkic model, a fascist-inspired interventionist policy that reinforced the victors/vanquished binary.

With regards to the commemoration of hunger, then, the Spanish case represents a relatively logical anomaly. On the one hand, collective memory of Spain's traumatic past has been muted, stunted, and repressed, at least until the reification of the 2022 memory law. Political and legal efforts to confront the past, moreover, have focused on violence and oppression, while historians have only recently begun to explore the causes and impact of the famine, having previously considered mass hunger an organic consequence of war and the devastating violence of the Francoist state. The fact that Spain's famine has only relatively recently come to light has shaped and informed collective memory and policies about the hunger years, in relation to both commemoration and musealisation.

Popular culture, memorialisation, and musealisation of hunger in Spain

As we write this chapter, there are still no monuments dedicated to the Francoist famine in Spain. This dearth of monuments could be explained due to three main factors: the prevalence of Francoist myths, particularly given the belated, limited legal interventions by Socialist-led democratic governments; the emphasis on bloodshed and (mass) murder in Republican historical memory; and the fact that historiography on Francoism has only recently recognised the political implications of the famine. Despite sharing some social, political, and environmental conditions that engendered famine in other European countries throughout the twentieth century, the Spanish case is distinct in as much as there is no coherent national narrative that can be exteriorised onto a monument.[32] Whereas the Ukranian *Holodomor* (1932–33) exemplifies the brutality of Soviet occupation in such a way as to reinforce national solidarity, Spain's famine years evoke a myriad of tensions. Rather than a centralised national narrative, as is this case in relation to other European famines, Spain's history of hunger is fragmented by ideological and geographical factors that problematise a consolidated, democratic account. As we shall see, historiography on memories of hunger elucidates a collective history that is inflected by multifaceted personal and political tensions; an affective, fragmented history that is, perhaps, too allusive to be reified in a material site.

In order to explain the lack of commemoration and the absence of a coherent, unified discourse about collective memory of hunger in Spain, we must consider the insidious influence of the Francoist dictatorship. As we have outlined, the famine was not formally recognised by the regime. That said, a legacy and collective memory of hunger did indeed take root during the dictatorship, enduring until the democratic era due to its poignant impact on Spain's collective consciousness. The post-War novel is a salient example, a genre published under Francoism. In *Nada* ('Nothing', 1944), Carmen Laforet delineates the bleak and hopeless life of a female student in post-Civil War Barcelona. Camilo José Cela's masterpiece *La colmena* ('The Beehive', 1951) weaves a complex narrative of the inhabitants of 1950s Madrid, where hunger, the black market, and hardship are commonplace. In the seminal *Tiempo de Silencio* ('Time of Silence', 1962), psychiatrist Luis Martín-Santos paints a gritty picture of Spain's capital, with Madrid plagued by poverty, disease, and misery.[33] This cultural, collective memory of hunger would survive the death throes of Francoism, with the quotidian realities of hunger and the brutality of the post-Civil War years recurring as a common trope in Spanish literature. The work of Juan Marsé (*Si te dicen que caí*; 'If They Tell You I Fell', 1973), Agustín Gómez Arcos (*El niño pan*; 'The Bread Boy', 2006), and María Beneyto's poetry (*Biografía breve del silencio*; 'Brief Biography of Silence', 1975) are popular examples.[34]

Nevertheless, the dictatorship's strict censorship, restrictions on individual liberties, and the corrupting influence of state propaganda shaped cultural output under Francoism.[35] Memories of hunger were restricted to the individual and family domains. Rather than remaining covered in silence, stories of suffering, survival, and resistance were exteriorised in 'embodied memories', which shaped eating habits, food practices, and attitudes.[36] Women, many of whom were widowed or whose Republican husbands were imprisoned or exiled, were key, not only to ensuring their families' survival, but also to the transmission of lived experience, which contributed to the post-memory of the Spanish famine. As Carlos Gil Andrés observes, '[t]he memory of hunger, poverty and hardship of the post-Civil War era is a territory populated by female voices, hands, and perspectives'.[37] In rural areas, women resorted to collecting herbs, finding substitute ingredients, and relying on the black market to provide for their families. Traumatic memories of hunger and shortages were passed down to those who did not experience them firsthand, via modified recipes and intergenerational communication about a dormant history.

That said, it is also critical to recognise the difficulties many survivors face in their efforts to share or exteriorise these memories, as evidenced by oral histories from this period.[38] Some studies have elucidated how many Republican women struggled to articulate traumatic memories of sex-based violence, which included head-shaving, sexual abuse, and the forced ingestion of castor oil. At the same time, testimonies and oral histories speak to a subconscious unwillingness to recognise the hunger, starvation, or deprivation suffered by one's own family; to acknowledge and confess one's own wanting, seemingly, would constitute weakness, victimhood, or vulnerability. One woman recalling the post-Civil War era in Logroño (La Rioja, Northern Spain), for instance, is somewhat self-contradictory, explaining that though there was 'no money', 'we didn't go without food'.[39] Some confess to the scarcity of resources and criminal practices relied upon to source food, and yet, do not admit to having experienced hunger.[40] Other cases demonstrate how women and men that lived through this period find it difficult to talk about the famine and the methods they resorted to source food, with hunger stigmatised and considered a source of personal and familial shame. Accordingly, experiences of hunger are often delineated in relation to others, never to oneself.[41] It is, therefore, challenging and problematic to piece together a coherent narrative about this period, much less musealise these years, as those with intimate knowledge of the famine suppress or occlude their stories. The 'silencing' of the hunger years, in this sense, corrupts personal memories as individuals—unwittingly or not—reinforce this occlusion through self-censorship.

Recent years have borne witness to a growing interest in the famine years. Films such as *Pan's Labyrinth* (Guillermo del Toro, 2007) and *Pa Negre* ('Black Bread'; Agustí Villaronga, 2010) reflect on the bleak post-Civil War years, explicitly linking food and the struggle for survival with the power of the state and post-war violence. Similar themes are explored in contemporary literature, most notably in the best selling novels of Almudena Grandes and graphic novels such as Paco Roca's *Regreso al Edén* ('Return to Eden', 2020), which, using personal and familiar stories, explores intergenerational memories of hunger, deprivation, and the cultural and social capital of bread as a source of survival.

In the heritage sector, however, commemorations of hunger and famine are lacking. While the Francoist regime constructed a 'memory network to their fallen', democratic governments have yet to commission a monument to commemorate the famine.[42] Republican sites that do exist reflect the 'atomized Republican memory: a myriad of individual, unrelated memorials, not linked by any master narrative, any route or any central mnemonic anchor (a national museum or monument)'.[43] Memory places dedicated to the commemoration of Republican history are intimately related to Spain's landscape, with this traumatic past memorialised in such a way as to engage with an ongoing dialogue; to use Pierre Nora's *lieux de mémoire* paradigm, such sites constitute a 'material' (or physical) entity of memory, a 'symbolic' reification of anti-Francoist history, and a 'functional' site that facilitates the act of remembering and (re)constructing collective memory.[44]

The majority of these memory sites commemorate incidents of violence and conflict. Salient examples are the recovered bomb shelter Refugi 307 and Republican anti-aircraft battery Turó de la Rovira, both in Barcelona, and the plaques placed by successive Socialist Prime Ministers in 1988 and 2009 in Almudena Cemetery, Madrid, to commemorate the execution site of the 'Thirteen Roses', a group of women sentenced to death in August 1939 for terrorism.[45] Monuments have also been erected to commemorate acts of resistance and experiences of exile. A cement sculpture in Santa Cruz de Moya (Cuenca) was placed in 1991, in honour of the anti-Francoist guerrilla fighters whose resistance continued into the post-Civil War years, dedicated to the 'Spanish guerrillas who died in the struggle for peace, liberty and democracy'. In La Vajol (Girona), near the border with France, a small monument was constructed in 1999 to remember those forced into exile, mirroring the numerous dedications placed in French territory.

Spain's famine and 'hunger years', on the other hand, have not been commemorated with a monument or memory site; a curiosity that can be explained by the dynamics and politics of Spanish history. The construction and popularity of the Famine Memorial in Dublin (Ireland) and the Holodomor Victims Memorial in Kiev (Ukraine), which commemorate the devastating famines in Ireland (1845–49) and Ukraine (1932–33), should be understood in relation to both countries' history of colonialism and occupation, making the memory of a traumatic national past a cohesive national narrative for the now-independent nations. The Spanish famine, on the other hand, can be traced back to a bloody Civil War and a vengeful dictatorship that impeded reconciliation. As Spain still struggles to confront and harmonise its traumatic past, constructing a coherent narrative about a famine that reinforced and exacerbated the victors-vanquished dichotomy remains elusive, problematic, and, indeed, inherently political.

The obstacles and difficulties in relation to confronting the past in Spain have impacted and shaped how monuments are devised and narrativised in Spain. One of the country's most famous sites is 'Mirador de la Memoria' ('Viewpoint of Memory') in the Valle de Jerte, Extremadura (South-Western Spain), a region that was particularly brutalised by the famine and post-Civil War depravation. Inaugurated in 2009 by a memorial association, the site is a visual manifestation of the 2007 Historical Memory Law, erected to commemorate and remember the regime's victims.[46] The ambiguity of how post-Civil War Spain and memories of the famine integrate into the collective imagination is encapsulated by the symbolism of this monument: consisting of four nude figures (three males and one female) that overlook the vast panorama, the statues allude to hunger through the imbrication of the body, vulnerability, and Spanish landscape. Yet, the figures do not suggest malnutrition (one male figure has a protruding stomach; the female statue has full breasts and thighs). The sculptor of the work, Francisco Cedenilla (the grandson of a Republican who was executed and whose remains lie in an unmarked mass grave), remarked in an interview that he wanted to represent 'those forgotten by the Civil War', depicting 'figures thinking about all of the people who suffered as a consequence of conflict, like those in 1936'; they do not belong to either side, nor do they represent a particular class, age, or sex.[47] After its installation, the monument was shot at by protesters and restored by its creator, reflecting how the site delineates the violence of the

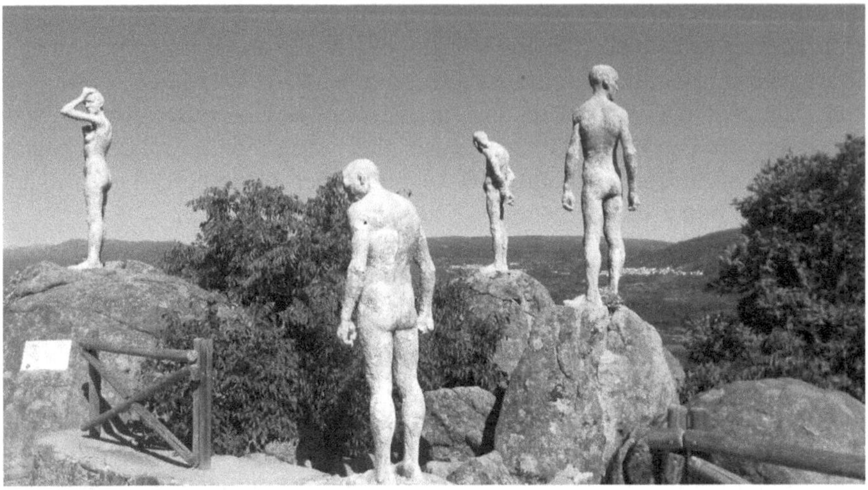

IMAGE 9.2 'Viewpoint of Memory'. Sculptor: Francisco Cerdenilla Carrasco, 2009. Wikicommons.

War, disassociating it from the Francoist famine. Famine and hunger, in this sense, are conspicuously omitted, as this core facet of Republican collective memory—and, indeed, histories of the Civil War more broadly—remains an unspoken trauma of Spain's past (Image 9.2).

Monuments are invested with history and marked by the period in which they were erected. The same can be said of the Spanish famine. The best example of this is the Valle de los Caídos (Valley of the Fallen), the so-called 'national monument to those who gave their lives for God and for Spain'. Construction began in 1940, and the site was inaugurated on 1 April 1959—the 20th anniversary of the Nationalists' victory in the Civil War—to extol the Francoist rebels. The Valley is a grandiose, imposing place carved out of the rock. A monumental cross that dominates the landscape presides over a basilica and tombs of the 'fallen', surrounded by symbols that exalt victory in a war conceived as a 'Crusade' against 'anti-Spain'. Many 'heroes and martyrs' of the Francoist side were buried here, and so were the remains of Republican prisoners. The site exemplifies how Spain's landscape is scarred by its violent past, as the remains of at least 30,000 anonymous Spaniards lie in mass graves on this site.[48] The remains of Franco himself were buried next to the basilica's main altar, alongside José Antonio Primo de Rivera, the leader of Spain's fascist party who was assassinated during the Civil War. The silence and pain of the rock occlude a history of pain and hunger, as the Valley was built by the forced labour of Republican political prisoners, who faced brutal working conditions and meagre food rations, resulting in numerous deaths from exhaustion, disease, and malnutrition.

In recent years, the monument has been the subject of political intervention. On 24 October 2019, Franco's body was exhumed and reinterred next to his wife in a cemetery in El Pardo, on the outskirts of Madrid. Orchestrated by the Socialist Prime Minister Pedro Sánchez, the removal of Franco's body was an effort to rework the politics of a (taxpayer-funded) mausoleum that had long been a site of fascist commemoration.[49] The site has been (re)renamed to its former title—the Valle de Cuelgamuros—and the government has opened a contest for ideas to 're-signify' the monument and turn it into a 'centre of interpretation'. As it stands, no official communications have considered the critical role of hunger, starvation, and shortages in the site's history.

With the government focused on converting the Valley into an 'interpretation centre', an opportunity has been missed to build a museum dedicated to the war and dictatorship, which, like the famine, is not mentioned in the 2022 Democratic Memory Law.[50] A virtual, international museum, however, has been developed, unrelated to governmental initiatives: the Virtual Museum of the Civil War, orchestrated by (mostly international) academics and inaugurated in 2022.[51] Financed by Canadian institutions, with some contribution from the Spanish government, the museum is free to access and organised into nine thematic galleries. The site centres on the Civil War period (1936–39) and, though there is a section dedicated to 'memory', there are no explicit references to the famine or hunger years. While the museum does include objects related to food practices and shortages during the conflict—such as the 'bread bombs' dropped by Nationalist soldiers during the 1939 siege of Madrid, and the Nazi-inspired 'One Dish Meal' introduced to fund welfare programmes—its temporal focus means that much of the famine is yet to be musealised.

With this in mind, we now turn to the exhibition initiatives that speak to a growing interest in the famine and the hunger years in Spanish museums, which builds on former projects that centred on war, exile, and concentration camps in post-Civil War Spain.[52] In 2016, 'Campo Cerrado: Art and Power in Post-War Spain' was inaugurated at the Reina Sofía National Museum of Contemporary Art (MNCARS) in Madrid, with the aim of publicising lesser known cultural output so as to re-think this period. As outlined by the organisers, this exhibition 'questions topics such as the scarcity or irrelevance of cultural or artistic activity during the 1940s and outlines and image of the time that resists schematisation'. Though the exposition interrogated a critical period of the hunger years by elucidating cultural and artistic activity from this period, references to food, famine, and shortages were absent.[53]

Food practices have been focalised in two exhibitions organised by the History Museum of Catalonia: 'Menús de guerra. Cocina de vanguardia y superviviencia' (Food of War. Avant-guard Cooking and Survival, 2014); and 'El Farcell de la postguerra' (The Post-War 'Bundle', 2018).[54] While the former centres on the War—outside the temporal parameters of the famine and hunger years—'El Farcell de Posguerra' confronts this oft-overlooked period of Spanish history. The title of the exhibition encapsulates the social perspective of the project, as the 'bundle' was the scarf used by the working classes to transport black-market supplies. With items including ration cards, magazines, the press, culinary objects, and propaganda, the exhibition explores food practices and supply policies during the hunger years. Indirect allusions to hunger are delineated through references to the black market (both large and small scale), failure of ration cards, increased prices, and the ineffective food aid policies implemented by the regime's welfare programme (Auxilio Social). One core strength of the exhibition is the inclusion of concrete examples of foodstuffs and daily life post-war difficulties, highlighting events and facts that occurred throughout Catalonia and Barcelona so as to disseminate collective memory about survival during this brutal period. That said, 'El Farcell' limited its corpus to food practices, with no reference to starvation or rampant disease. Nor was the cause of the stark drop in living conditions explored, as both the famine and its origins remained on the periphery.

A more concerted effort to explore the origin and impact of Spain's hunger years is central to the 2022 exhibition, 'La hambruna silenciada: El hambre durante la posguerra franquista, 1939–1952' ('The Silenced Famine: Hunger in Post-War Spain').[55] The exhibition is divided into five sections: the conceptualisation of the famine, origins, consequences, popular responses to hunger, and collective memory. With references to all of Spain interspersed throughout the collection, the broader scope of this project speaks to the vast research that underpins it; financed by numerous bodies, 'The Silenced Famine' was curated by academics specialising in the Spanish hunger years (Miguel Ángel del Arco Blanco and Gloria Román Ruiz). Supported by public and private funding initiatives from regional (Granada Provincial Council and University of Granada), national (Ministerio de la Presidencia), and private institutions (BBVA Foundation), the event was conceived as a travelling exhibition with plans to tour other Spanish cities throughout 2023 and 2024. Findings from numerous academic projects are disseminated, as well as testimonies sourced from archives or via interviews with survivors. The core aim of 'The Silenced Famine' is to verify, substantiate, and explore the Spanish famine, drawing links with other European famines of the interwar period. The fundamentally political causes of the famine are depicted in the promotional poster, which constitutes a military boot stamping on a loaf of bread, depicting violence, masculinity, brutality, and—fundamentally—the regime's control of bread, which functions as a metonym for food and Spain, given its omnipresence in the Spanish diet. While the exhibition includes artefacts from the post-War years (such as ration cards, recipes, propaganda, and publications), 'The Silenced Famine' can be epitomised by its aim to end the silence imposed by the brutal legacy of famine, hunger, and deprivation in Francoist Spain (Image 9.3).

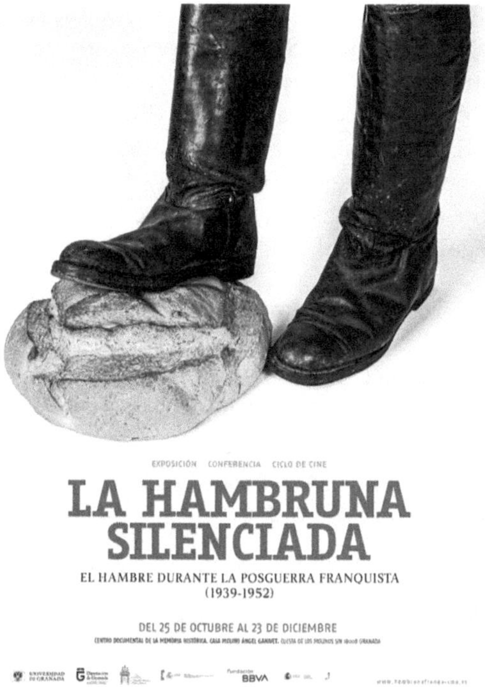

IMAGE 9.3 Promotional poster of 'La hambruna silenciada'. Author: Alfonso Aguilar (Perroraro). Source: Miguel Ángel del Arco Blanco.

Concluding remarks

The dearth of monuments and musealisations of the Spanish famine can be explained by the regime's propaganda and denialist policies, which cultivated a series of myths that silenced and distorted reality. The (re-)arrival of democracy in Spain and the years that followed were characterised first by 'forgetting' and, more recently, by the difficult recovery of historical memory, which saw the mobilisation of associations, public debate, and state policies—introduced exclusively by Socialist-led governments—that focalised identifying, recognising, and dignifying the victims of Francoist violence. Collective memories of hunger, however, remained dormant, delineated indirectly in cultural production, and restricted to transgenerational memories within personal and familial domains. After the dictator's death, Spanish historians focused on interrogating the most violent elements of the war and regime, with interest in the post-Civil War years—Spain's hunger years—and the famine growing in recent years. Accordingly, recent historiography has uncovered the political and economic origins of the Spanish famine. The combination of the foregoing factors explains the scarcity of public memory about hunger and famine in (post-)Civil War Spain. More recent years have borne witness to promising initiatives that musealise this core component of Spanish history, recuperating memories of hunger and bringing them to public attention. Looking ahead, more exhibitions and public commemoration of Spain's famine are to be encouraged, particularly by drawing out comparisons with other European famines, as are explicit references to legacies of hunger in political, governmental, and legal reforms.

Notes

1 Aleida Assmann, 'Canon and Archive', in *Cultural Memory Studies: An International and Interdisciplinary Handbook*, eds. Astrid Erll and Ansgar Nünning (Berlin: Walter de Gruyter, 2008), 97–8.
2 For the term, see Guy Beiner, 'Disremembering 1798? An Archaeology of Social Forgetting and Remembrance in Ulster', *History and Memory* 25, no. 2 (2013): 35–6.
3 See Javier Rodrigo, *Cruzada, paz, memoria; La guerra civil en sus relatos* (Granada: Comares, 2013).
4 See Miguel Ángel del Arco Blanco and Peter Anderson, eds., *Franco's Famine: Malnutrition, Disease and Starvation in Post-Civil War Spain* (New York: Bloomsbury Academic, 2021). Miguel Ángel del Arco Blanco, ed., *Los "años del hambre": historia y memoria de la posguerra franquista* (Madrid: Marcial Pons, 2020).
5 See Miguel Ángel del Arco Blanco, *Crosses of Memory and Oblivion: Monuments to the Fallen of the Spanish Civil War (1936–2022)* (London; New York: Routledge, 2023).
6 See the following clip: https://www.rtve.es/play/videos/revista-imagenes/naranja-su-riqueza/2864782/, accessed 24 January 2023.
7 See the following video: https://www.rtve.es/play/videos/revista-imagenes/arroz-paella/2867138/, accessed 24 January 2023; Lara Anderson, *Control and Resistance: Food Discourse in Franco Spain* (Toronto; Buffalo; London: University of Toronto Press, 2020), 38.
8 Xavier Moreno Juliá, 'Maria y Miquel: memorias de guerra y posguerra en España, 1936–1955', *Historia, Antropología y Fuentes Orales* 1, no. 21 (1999): 67–81.
9 See Del Arco Blanco's 2021 interview in the press: Héctor G. Barnés, 'La hambruna española que fue borrada de la historia: ¿y si mató más que la guerra?' ['The Spanish famine that was erased from history: and did it kill more than the war?'], *El Confidencial*, 16 February 2021. https://www.elconfidencial.com/cultura/2021-02-16/gran-hambruna-espanola-muertos-guerra_2945088/, accessed 24 January 2023.
10 See Rodrigo, *Cruzada, paz, memoria*; Asunción Castro and Julián Díaz, *XXV Años de paz franquista: Sociedad y cultura en España hacia 1964* (Madrid: Sílex, 2017), 11–6.
11 See Michael Richards, *After the Civil War: Making Memory and Re-Making Spain Since 1936* (Cambridge: Cambridge University Press, 2013). Also see Antonio Cazorla Sánchez, *Fear and Progress: Ordinary Lives in Franco's Spain, 1939–1975* (Chichester: Wiley-Blackwell, 2010).
12 Many mark the Socialists landslide electoral victory in 1982 as the end of Spain's transition to democracy.
13 Paloma Aguilar, 'Transitional or Post-Transitional Justice? Recent Developments in the Spanish Case', *South European Society and Politics* 13, no. 4 (2008): 417–33.
14 Seminal scholarship that draws on this paradigm includes: Paloma Aguilar, *Políticas de la memoria y memorias de la política* (Madrid: Alianza, 2008); Ofelia Ferrán, *Working through Memory: Writing and Remembrance in Contemporary Spanish Narrative* (Lewisburg: Bucknell University Press, 2007); Carlos Jerez-Farrán and

Samuel Amago, eds., *Unearthing Franco's Legacy: Mass Graves and the Recovery of Historical Memory in Spain* (Notre Dame, IN: University of Notre Dame, 2010). For criticism of the 'forgetting narrative', see, for example, Ángel Loureiro, 'Pathetic Arguments', *Journal of Spanish Cultural Studies* 9, no. 2 (2008): 225.

15 Stephen Holmes, 'Gag Rules or the Politics of Omission', in *Constitutionalism and Democracy*, eds. Jon Elster and Rune Slagstad (New York: Maison des Sciences Press, 1988), 19–58.

16 Santos Juliá, 'Echar al olvido. Memoria y amnistía de la transición', *Claves de la Razón Práctica*, 129 (2003): 14–25. Seminal scholarship that draws on this paradigm includes: Paloma Aguilar and Leigh A. Payne, *El resurgir del pasado en España* (Madrid: Taurus, 2018), 27–8; Fernández, *Políticas de la memoria y memorias de la política*; Ferrán, *Working through Memory*; Jerez-Farrán and Amago, *Unearthing Franco's Legacy*.

17 Paloma Aguilar, 'Memoria y transición en España: Exhumaciones de fusilados republicanos y homenajes en su honor', *Historia y política* 39 (2018): 291–325.

18 Julio Aróstegui Sánchez, *Historia y memoria de la guerra civil: Encuentro en Castilla y León, Salamanca, 24-27 de septiembre de 1986*, 3 vols. (Valladolid: Junta de Castilla y León, 1988); Juan Andrés Blanco Rodríguez, 'El registro historiográfico de la guerra civil, 1936-2004', in *Guerra civil: mito y memoria,* eds. Julio Aróstegui Sánchez and François Godicheau (Madrid: Marical Pons, 2006), 373-406.

19 Carolyn P. Boyd, 'The Politics of History and Memory in Democratic Spain', *The Annals of the American Academy of Political and Social Science* 617, no. 1 (2008): 136.

20 Paloma Aguilar and Clara Ramírez-Barat, 'Generational Dynamics in Spain: Memory Transmission of a Turbulent Past', *Memory Studies* 12, no. 2 (2016): 213–29; Ofelia Ferrán and Lisa Hilbink, 'Introduction: Legacies of Violence in Contemporary Spain', in *Legacies of Violence in Contemporary Spain: Exhuming the Past, Understanding the Present*, eds. Ofelia Ferrán and Lisa Hilbink (New York; London: Routledge, 2017), 1.

21 Olivette Otele, Luisa Gandolfo and Yoav Galai, 'Introduction: Absence and Trauma in Post-Conflict Memorialisation', in *Post-Conflict Memorialization. Missing Memorials, Absent Bodies*, eds. Olivette Otele, Luisa Gandolfo and Yoav Galai (Cham: Palgrave Macmillan, 2021), 3–7. Quoted and translated in Paloma Aguilar and Leigh A. Payne, *Revealing New Truths about Spain's Violent Past: Perpetrators' Confessions and Victim Exhumations* (London: Palgrave Macmillan, 2016), 13.

22 Ignacio Fernández de Mata, *Lloros vueltos puños: el conflicto de los desaparecidos y vencidos en la Guerra Civil Española* (Granada: Comares, 2016).

23 Del Arco Blanco, *Crosses of Memory and Oblivion*, Chapter 9.

24 BOE, 'Ley 20/2022, de 19 de octubre, de Memoria Democrática', https://www.boe.es/buscar/act.php?id=BOE-A-2022-17099, accessed 24 January 2023.

25 The ARMH statement is available on their website: https://memoriahistorica.org.es/contundente-critica-de-la-armh-a-las-deficiencias-del-anteproyecto-de-ley-de-memoria-democratica-del-gobierno, accessed 24 January 2023.

26 Michael Rothberg, *Multidirectional Memory: Remembering the Holocaust in the Age of Decolonization* (Stanford: Stanford University Press, 2009), 3; Otele, Gandolfo and Galai, 'Introduction', 2.

27 'Ley 20/2022, de 19 de octubre, de Memoria Democrática'.

28 Jie-Hyun Lim, 'Victimhood Nationalism in Contested Memories: National Mourning and Global Accountability, Memory and Political Change', in *Memory in a Global Age: Discourses, Practices and Trajectories*, eds. Aleida Assmann and Sebastian Conrad (London; New York: Palgrave Macmillan, 2010), 138. Rothberg, *Multidirectional Memory*, 3.

29 'Ley 20/2022, de 19 de octubre, de Memoria Democrática'.

30 See Paul Preston, *The Spanish Holocaust: Inquisition and Extermination in Twentieth-Century Spain* (London; New York: W. W. Norton & Company, 2012).
31 See, for example, Emilio Silva and Santiago Macías, *Las fosas de Franco: Los republicanos que el dictador dejó en las cunetas* (Madrid, Temas de Hoy, 2005).
32 Miguel Ángel del Arco Blanco, 'Las hambrunas europeas del siglo XX y el lugar de los *«años del hambre»*', in *Los «años del hambre»: historia y memoria de la posguerra franquista*, ed. Miguel Ángel del Arco Blanco (Madrid: Marcial Pons, 2020), 37–8.
33 Carmen Laforet, *Nada* (Barcelona: Ediciones Destino, 1944); Camilo José Cela, *La colmena* (Buenos Aires: Emecé, 1951); Luis Martín-Santos *Tiempo de silencio* (Barcelona: Seix Barral, 1962).
34 Juan Marsé, *Si te dicen que caí* (Mexico City: Novaro, 1973); Agustín Gómez Arcos, *El niño pan* (Barcelona: Cabaret Voltaire, 2006); María Beneyto, *Biografía breve del silencio* (Alcoy: Imp. La Victoria, 1975).
35 In her analysis of popular culture in the hunger years, Helen Graham explains that, throughout the 1940s, 'the regime attempted to exercise cultural hegemony through the dissemination of what could be called an archaising vision', via educational materials, folklore, monuments to Nationalist soldiers, comics celebrating 'heroic crusaders' and religious dramas. See 'Popular Culture in the "Years of Hunger"', in *Spanish Cultural Studies: An Introduction, the Struggle for Modernity* , eds. Helen Graham and Jo Labayni (Oxford: Oxford University Press, 1995), 237. For this reason, critical literature about the regime and post-Civil War years was often published abroad; *La Colmena*, for instance, was initially published in Buenos Aires.
36 Gloria Román Ruiz, 'Echoes of famine. Effects of the embodied memories of the Spanish Hunger Years (1939–1952) on survivors' subsequent food practices and attitudes', *Memory Studies Journal* 17, no. 4 (2023): https://doi.org/10.1177/17506980231155569, accessed 24 January 2023. See also David Conde-Caballero, Borja Rivero-Jiménez and Lorenzo Mariano-Juárez, 'Memories of hunger, continuities, and food choices: An ethnography of the elderly in extremadura (Spain)', *Appetite*, 164 (2021): 105–267.
37 Carlos Gil Andrés, '"Tengo grabado todo aquello": La memoria de los años cuarenta tiene nombre de mujer', in *Los «años del hambre»: historia y memoria de la posguerra franquista*, ed. Miguel Ángel del Arco Blanco (Madrid: Marcial Pons, 2020), 39.
38 David Conde Caballer, Borja Rivero Jiménez, and Lorenzo Mariano Juárez. *Vidas sin pan: el hambre en la memoria de la posguerra española* (Granada: Comares, 2022).
39 Quoted in Gil Andrés, 'Tengo grabado todo aquello', 37.
40 Ibid.
41 David Conde Caballero, *Hambre: una etnografía de la escasez de posguerra en Extremadura* (Badajoz: Diputación de Badajoz, 2021), Chapter 10.
42 Conxita Mir Curcó and Josep Gelonch Solé, 'Presentación', in *Duelo y memoria: Espacios para el recuerdo de las víctimas de la represión franquista en perspectiva comparada*, eds., Conxita Mir Curcó and Josep Gelonch Solé (Lleida: Edicions de la Universitat de Lleida, 2013), 11.
43 González-Ruibal, 'Beyond the Mass Grave', 99.
44 Pierre Nora, 'Between Memory and History: Les Lieux de Mémoire', trans. Marc Roudebush, *Representations*, 26 (1989): 19 u.
45 See https://www.barcelona.cat/museuhistoria/en/heritages/els-espais-del-muhba/muhba-refugi-307, accessed 24 January 2023; and https://www.barcelona.cat/museuhistoria/es/patrimonios/los-espacios-del-muhba/muhba-turo-de-la-rovira, accessed 24 January 2023.

46 'Viewpoint of Memory' came to international attention in 2018 when it was featured in the acclaimed documentary *The Silence of Others* (*El silencio de otros*, dir. Almudena Carracedo and Robert Bahar), which centres on the ARMH and the excavation of Spain's mass graves.
47 'Francisco Cedenilla: El monumento tiroteado no se identifica con ningún bando', *El Periódico de Extremadura,* 28 January 2009, https://www.elperiodicoextremadura.com/caceres/2009/01/28/francisco-cedenilla-monumento-tiroteado-identifica-45201805.html, accessed 24 January 2023.
48 Some suggest the number of bodies could be anywhere between 40,000 and 70,000. See Andrea Hepworth, 'Site of Memory and Dismemory: The Valley of the Fallen in Spain', in *The Memorialization of Genocide*, ed. Simone Gigliotti (London; New York: Routledge, 2016), 52.
49 Sebastiaan Faber, *Exhuming Franco: Spain's Second Transition* (Nashville: Vanderbilt University Press, 2021), 6.
50 'La transformación del Valle de los Caídos y otros retos pendientes en memoria histórica', *El País*, 31 March 2021, https://elpais.com/espana/2021-03-31/la-transformacion-del-valle-de-los-caidos-y-otros-retos-pendientes-en-memoria-historica.html, accessed 24 January 2023.
51 *Spanish Civil War: A Virtual Museum.* See https://www.vscw.ca/, accessed 12 April 2024.
52 For example, exhibitions curated by the Centro Documental de la Memoria Histórica (Historical Memory Documentation Centre) in Salamanca, which is amongst the country's most important Civil War archives, focused on artists, writers, and photographers in post-Civil War Spain, rather than on the daily life of famine, poverty, and hunger.
53 See the following website: https://www.museoreinasofia.es/exposiciones/campo-cerrado, accessed 24 January 2023.
54 For the exhibition website of *El Farcell de Posguerra*, see the following link: https://www.mhcat.cat/exposicions/exposicions_realitzades/el_farcell_de_la_posguerr, accessed 24 January 2023.
55 See the exhibition website: https://www.hambrunafranquismo.es/actividades/15-exposicion-la-hambruna-silenciada-el-hambre-durante-la-posguerra-franquista-1939-1952, accessed 24 January 2023.

References

Aguilar, Paloma, *Políticas de la memoria y memorias de la política.* Madrid: Alianza, 2008.

Aguilar, Paloma, 'Transitional or Post-Transitional Justice? Recent Developments in the Spanish Case'. *South European Society and Politics* 13, no. 4 (2008): 417–33.

Aguilar, Paloma, 'Memoria y transición en España: Exhumaciones de fusilados republicanos y homenajes en su honor'. *Historia y política* 39 (2018): 291–325.

Aguilar, Paloma, and Clara Ramírez-Barat, 'Generational Dynamics in Spain: Memory Transmission of a Turbulent Past'. *Memory Studies* 12, no. 2 (2016): 213–29.

Aguilar, Paloma, and Leigh A. Payne, *Revealing New Truths about Spain's Violent Past: Perpetrators' Confessions and Victim Exhumations.* London: Palgrave Macmillan, 2016.

Aguilar, Paloma, and Leigh A. Payne, *El resurgir del pasado en España.* Madrid: Taurus, 2018.

Anderson, Lara, *Control and Resistance: Food Discourse in Franco Spain.* Toronto; Buffalo; London: University of Toronto Press, 2020.

Arco Blanco, Miguel Ángel del, ed., *Los "años del hambre": historia y memoria de la posguerra franquista*. Madrid: Marcial Pons, 2020.

Arco Blanco, Miguel Ángel del, 'Las hambrunas europeas del siglo XX y el lugar de los «*años del hambre*»'. In Miguel Ángel del Arco Blanco, ed., 23–54, *Los «años del hambre»: historia y memoria de la posguerra franquista*. Madrid: Marcial Pons, 2020.

Arco Blanco, Miguel Ángel del, 'Famine in Spain during Franco's Dictatorship (1939-1952)'. *Journal of Contemporary History* 56, no. 1 (2021): 3–27.

Arco Blanco, Miguel Ángel del, *Crosses of Memory and Oblivion: Monuments to the Fallen of the Spanish Civil War (1936–2022)*. London; New York: Routledge, 2023.

Arco Blanco, Miguel Ángel del, and Peter Anderson, 'Famine, not hunger?'. In Miguel Ángel del Arco Blanco and Peter Anderson, eds., 1–16, *Franco's Famine: Malnutrition, Disease and Starvation in Post-Civil War Spain*. New York: Bloomsbury, 2021.

Aróstegui Sánchez, Julio, *Historia y memoria de la guerra civil: Encuentro en Castilla y León, Salamanca, 24-27 de septiembre de 1986*, 3 vols. Valladolid: Junta de Castilla y León, 1988.

Assmann, Aleida. 'Canon and Archive'. In Astrid Erll and Ansgar Nünning, eds., 97–107, *Cultural Memory Studies: An International and Interdisciplinary Handbook*. Berlin: Walter de Gruyter, 2008.

Barnés, Héctor G., 'La hambruna española que fue borrada de la historia: ¿y si mató más que la guerra?. *El Confidencial*, 16 February 2021. https://www.elconfidencial.com/cultura/2021-02-16/gran-hambruna-espanola-muertos-guerra_2945088/, accessed 24 January 2023.

Beiner, Guy, 'Disremembering 1798? An Archaeology of Social Forgetting and Remembrance in Ulster', *History and Memory* 25, no. 2 (2013): 9–50.

Beneyto, María, *Biografía breve del silencio*. Alcoy: Imprenta La Victoria, 1975.

Blanco Rodríguez, Juan Andrés, 'El registro historiográfico de la guerra civil, 1936-2004'. In Julio Aróstegui Sánchez and François Godicheau, eds., 373–406, *Guerra civil: mito y memoria*. Madrid: Marcial Pons, 2006.

BOE, 'Ley 20/2022, de 19 de octubre, de Memoria Democrática', https://www.boe.es/buscar/act.php?id=BOE-A-2022-17099, accessed 24 January 2023.

Boyd, Carolyn P., 'The Politics of History and Memory in Democratic Spain'. *The Annals of the American Academy of Political and Social Science* 617, no. 1 (2008): 133–48.

Castro, Asunción and Julián Díaz, *XXV Años de paz franquista: Sociedad y cultura en España hacia 1964*. Madrid: Sílex, 2017.

Cazorla Sánchez, Antonio, *Fear and Progress: Ordinary Lives in Franco's Spain, 1939–1975*. Chichester: Wiley-Blackwell, 2010.

Cela, Camilo José, *La colmena*. Buenos Aires: Emecé, 1951.

Conde Caballero, David, *Hambre: una etnografía de la escasez de posguerra en Extremadura*. Badajoz: Diputación de Badajoz, 2021.

Conde-Caballero, David, Borja Rivero-Jiménez and Lorenzo Mariano-Juárez, 'Memories of Hunger, Continuities, and Food Choices: An Ethnography of the Elderly in Extremadura (Spain)'. *Appetite* 164 (2021): 105–267.

Faber, Sebastiaan, *Exhuming Franco: Spain's Second Transition*. Nashville: Vanderbilt University Press, 2021.

Fernández de Mata, Ignacio, *Lloros vueltos puños: el conflicto de los desaparecidos y vencidos en la Guerra Civil Española*. Granada: Comares, 2016.

Ferrán, Ofelia, *Working through Memory: Writing and Remembrance in Contemporary Spanish Narrative*. Lewisburg, PA: Bucknell University Press, 2007.

Ferrán, Ofelia, and Lisa Hilbink, 'Introduction: Legacies of Violence in Contemporary Spain'. In Ofelia Ferrán and Lisa Hilbink, eds., 1–20, *Legacies of Violence in Contemporary Spain: Exhuming the Past, Understanding the Present*. New York; London: Routledge, 2017.

'Francisco Cedenilla: El monumento tiroteado no se identifica con ningún bando', *El Periódico de Extremadura*. 28 January 2009. https://www.elperiodicoextremadura.com/caceres/2009/01/28/francisco-cedenilla-monumento-tiroteado-identifica-45201805.html, accessed 24 January 2023.

Gil Andrés, Carlos, '"Tengo grabado todo aquello": La memoria de los años cuarenta tiene nombre de mujer'. In Miguel Ángel del Arco Blanco, ed., 23–45, *Los «años del hambre»: historia y memoria de la posguerra franquista*. Madrid: Marcial Pons, 2020.

Gómez Arcos, Agustín, *El niño pan*. Barcelona: Cabaret Voltaire, 2006.

Graham, Helen, 'Popular Culture in the "Years of Hunger"'. In Helen Graham and Jo Labayni, eds., 237–45, *Spanish Cultural Studies: An Introduction, the Struggle for Modernity*. Oxford: Oxford University Press, 1995.

Hepworth, Andrea, 'Site of Memory and Dismemory: The Valley of the Fallen in Spain'. In Simone Gigliotti, ed., 43–64, *The Memorialization of Genocide*. London; New York: Routledge, 2016.

Holmes, Stephen, 'Gag rules or the politics of omission'. In Jon Elster and Rune Slagstad, eds., 19–58, *Constitutionalism and Democracy*. New York: Maison des Sciences Press, 1988.

Jerez-Farrán, Carlos, and Samuel Amago, eds., *Unearthing Franco's Legacy: Mass Graves and the Recovery of Historical Memory in Spain*. Notre Dame, IN: University of Notre Dame, 2010.

Juliá, Santos, 'Echar al olvido. Memoria y amnistía de la transición'. *Claves de la Razón Práctica* 129 (2003): 14–25.

'La transformación del Valle de los Caídos y otros retos pendientes en memoria histórica', *El País*. 31 March 2021. https://elpais.com/espana/2021-03-31/la-transformacion-del-valle-de-los-caidos-y-otros-retos-pendientes-en-memoria-historica.html, accessed 24 January 2023.

Laforet, Carmen, *Nada*. Barcelona: Ediciones Destino, 1944.

Lim, Jie-Hyun, 'Victimhood Nationalism in Contested Memories: National Mourning and Global Accountability, Memory and Political Change'. In Aleida Assmann and Sebastian Conrad, eds., 138–62, *Memory in a Global Age: Discourses, Practices and Trajectories*. London; New York: Palgrave Macmillan, 2010.

Loureiro, Ángel, 'Pathetic Arguments'. *Journal of Spanish Cultural Studies* 9, no. 2 (2008): 225–37.

Marsé, Juan, *Si te dicen que caí*. Mexico City: Novaro, 1973.

Martín-Santos, Luis, *Tiempo de silencio*. Barcelona: Seix Barral, 1962.

Mir Curcó, Conxita, and Josep Gelonch Solé, 'Presentación'. In Conxita Mir Curcó and Josep Gelonch Solé, eds., 11–8, *Duelo y memoria: Espacios para el recuerdo de las víctimas de la represión franquista en perspectiva comparada*. Lleida: Edicions de la Universitat de Lleida, 2013.

Moreno Juliá, Xavier, 'Maria y Miquel: memorias de guerra y posguerra en España, 1936-1955'. *Historia, Antropología y Fuentes Orales* 1, no. 21 (1999): 67–81.

Nora, Pierre, 'Between Memory and History: Les Lieux de Mémoire', trans. Marc Roudebush. *Representations* 26 (1989): 7–24.

Otele, Olivette, Luisa Gandolfo and Yoav Galai, 'Introduction: Absence and Trauma in Post-Conflict Memorialisation'. In Olivette Otele, Luisa Gandolfo and Yoav Galai, eds., 1–13, *Post-Conflict Memorialization: Missing Memorials, Absent Bodies*. Cham: Palgrave Macmillan, 2021.

Preston, Paul, *The Spanish Holocaust: Inquisition and Extermination in Twentieth-Century Spain*. London; New York: W. W. Norton & Company, 2012.

Richards, Michael, *After the Civil War: Making Memory and Re-Making Spain Since 1936*. Cambridge: Cambridge University Press, 2013.

Rodrigo, Javier, *Cruzada, paz, memoria; La guerra civil en sus relatos*. Granada: Comares, 2013.

Silva, Emilio, and Santiago Macías, *Las fosas de Franco: Los republicanos que el dictador dejó en las cunetas*. Madrid: Temas de Hoy, 2005.

Román Ruiz, Gloria, 'Echoes of famine: Effects of the embodied memories of the Spanish Hunger Years (1939–1952) on survivors' subsequent food practices and attitudes'. *Memory Studies Journal* 17, no. 4 (2023): 10.1177/17506980231155569, accessed 24 January 2023.

Rothberg, Michael, *Multidirectional Memory: Remembering the Holocaust in the Age of Decolonization*. Stanford: Stanford University Press, 2009.

AFTERWORD[1]

Cormac Ó Gráda

The preceding contributions have raised many difficult questions and have answered them well. Why, they ask, are monuments commemorating past famines in Scotland in the 1840s, in Spain in the 1930s–40s, and in the Netherlands in 1944–45 so few, while commemorations of the Great Ukrainian Famine of 1932–33 are ubiquitous (Gouriévidis, Chapter 7; Del Arco Blanco and Madden, Chapter 9; De Zwarte and Jensen, Chapter 4)? Why did such *lieux de mémoire* remain contentious in Finland for a century or more after the event they commemorated (Boerman, Chapter 8)? Why does the main monument commemorating the Greek famine of 1941–44 depict 'a woman and a child, when adult men and the elderly were the main famine casualties, and […] is situated in Athens, when other localities suffered more than the capital' (Hionidou, Chapter 5)? Why are the treatments of past famines so different in Soviet, Irish, and Finnish textbooks (Bobeldijk, Chapter 2)?[2] Why is memorialisation in Ireland and in Scotland, to some degree at least, being channelled into present-day environmental and climate justice concerns (Gouriévidis, Chapter 7), while elsewhere famines are weaponised to sustain old enmities (Kudela-Świątek, Chapter 6)?[3]

One reason why memories and commemorations of famines are often so divisive is that the human agents and institutions who get blamed for them are also blamed for other things. Publicly commemorating events that divided people in the past, and particularly the recent past, is difficult; publicly commemorating events that divide them in the present is even more difficult. One solution is to stay silent or to forget. The Irish politician and co-operative activist Horace Plunkett famously advised the Irish at the turn of the last century that 'history was for Englishmen to remember and Irishmen to forget'.[4] Echoing Plunkett's advice almost a century later, the (unionist)

DOI: 10.4324/9781003391524-14

literary critic Edna Longley admonished the (nationalist) Irish for 'rhetorical memory' or for 'remembering *at*', and quipped that it would be wise for Ireland to erect a statue of Amnesia 'and forget where we put it'.[5] Another option is a memory that heals, but that works only after conflicting memories 'have been woven together into a narrative'.[6] Some might say that something akin to this was achieved in Ireland during its recent Decade of Commemorations (spanning the period between the introduction of the first Irish Home Rule Bill in 1912 and the admission of the Irish Free Sate into the League of Nations in 1923),[7] but it is far too soon for such healing in Ukraine or Moldova or, in a different context, post-Troubles Northern Ireland. For several decades in post-war Germany, revanchist memories of the *Vertreibung* (expulsion) of millions of mainly Eastern European *Reichsdeutsche* and *Volksdeutsche* made commemorating the events surrounding it contentious.[8] Only by 2008 had there been enough 'healing' for the Federal Government to allow the creation of a permanent exhibition of the exodus within the *Haus der Geschichte* (House of History) in Berlin.

Yet another option, as in Derry in Northern Ireland, is to allow different sides to narrate their own versions of the past separately (through the Museum of Free Derry and the Siege Museum, respectively), but even that presumes a reconciliation of sorts: an agreement to differ. The Irish Famine Museum in Strokestown, which pioneered the 'musealisation' of famines, set out from the start to allow a voice to differing perspectives on the events that they describe.[9] While the museums in Derry are about *not* forgetting, Strokestown was an exercise in retrieving a long-ago event that had been almost, if not entirely, forgotten.

Time plays a role. Oral histories of the Great Irish Famine of the 1840s are rich and important in their own way. They are history from below and focus on aspects often neglected in other evidence. Because they date mainly from the 1930s and 1940s, however, they lack the raw hurt evident in the oral histories of survivors of the Chinese Great Leap Forward of 1959–61 or the Greek Famine of 1941–44 (Hionidou, Chapter 5).[10] Irish memories of the 1840s also tended not to name names, either of those who died or those who treated them harshly, 'open[ing] the way for a version of famine history in which the descendants of those who survived all become vicarious victims'.[11] Context matters too. The sesquicentennial of the Great Irish Famine in the mid- and late-1990s, which began as the Northern Ireland Troubles were drawing to a close and the Celtic Tiger starting to purr in the South, spawned a wave of commemoration and memorialisation unmatched during the previous century and a half. For the most part, the commemoration steered clear of recrimination and provocation. While it certainly did not downplay the famine as cataclysm or the roles of ideology, indifference, and prejudice in exacerbating it, its focus was more prescriptive than resentful.

Both in Ireland and abroad, the sesquicentennial inspired dozens of new memorials, great and small, national and local.[12] Among them, Rowan Gillespie's much-admired group sculpture on Custom House Quay and John Behan's representation of a famine 'coffin ship' in Murrisk, Co., Mayo, have gained iconic status.[13] A gift to the state from philanthropist Norma Smurfit and unveiled by President Mary Robinson in May 1997, the former is described on its creator's website as 'dedicated to those Irish people forced to emigrate during the nineteenth–century Irish Famine', while the latter is Ireland's National Famine Memorial. Curiously, perhaps, both sculptures focused on emigration, forgetting that those who suffered most were those for whom emigration was never an option.

Gillespie and Behan also produced famine sculptures on the other side of the ocean, in Toronto and New York, respectively. Gillespie's monument in Toronto replicated the doleful themes of his Dublin work. It depicted 'a pregnant woman in a shawl; an emaciated figure lying prostrate on the ground; a man screaming; a man hunched over with starvation and sickness; and a man with his arms raised toward the CN Tower and the yacht club marina, as if invoking, "Yes, I'm here, and I'm your responsibility"'.[14] Whereas seven of Gillespie's sculpted figures left Dublin, there were only five in Canada: a poetic (if not strictly accurate) measure of the hardship of the crossing. Behan's *Arrival*, commissioned by the Irish government in 1997 and presented as a gift to the United Nations four years later, painted a more upbeat picture. Since 2001, it has stood outside the United Nations headquarters in New York and depicts orderly passengers disembarking or waiting to disembark in New York. Behan's work was described by then Taoiseach (prime minister), the characteristically upbeat Bertie Ahern, as a celebration of 'the Irish people who travelled the world in search of a new life and all the nations and countries which welcomed them and offered them a chance for that better life'.[15] Like in other recent Irish Famine memorials in Boston and Philadelphia, it is almost as if the Famine emigrants who had embarked on 'coffin ships' in Ireland disembarked at a mid-nineteenth century equivalent of highly efficient airport terminal—and lived happily ever after. And that too is a distortion. True, most of those who landed in America made better lives for themselves, but a significant minority did not. The contrast between Ahern's upbeat message and the bleak scenario depicted by Gillespie in Toronto could not be starker. Behan's publicly funded memorial recalled the self-confident Ireland of the Celtic Tiger, very distant from the past; Gillespie's is a more traditional view of the migrants' fate in the New World.[16] Who to remember, what to forget? These memorials also recall many of the issues raised in this book.

Where did these Irish sculptors find their inspiration? Gillespie's research did not engage much with scholarship on the Irish Famine. The insight for his Dublin work came from photographs of Holocaust victims and memories of an anorexic sister who died young, and from whom Gillespie 'knew very well the vacant look of the starving'. For the Toronto memorial, he drew inspiration from his mother's family, which had emigrated to Canada 'in famine times', only to return to Ireland 'when my grandfather became a judge in the newly formed Irish Free State'.[17] According to Gillespie, the interval between the Dublin and Toronto sculptures allowed his ideas to mature. Behan, too, looked into his heart; later, he revealed how pleased he was to have been 'allowed to have a personal interpretation of probably the most significant element of Irish history, the Famine'.[18] Perhaps the sculptors should have consulted the historians more. Or perhaps not, because, as the essays in this book amply corroborate, memorials are less about history than about how we—or somebody else—choose to represent the past.

Commemoration is by definition a collective and communal act, and there is a tendency to represent famines as communal, collective tragedies too. Hence, the frequent use of highly collective language in commemorative literature, as in the following statement from the Ukrainian Institute of National Remembrance:

> As a result of the Holodomor, Ukrainian society became, and has largely remained, traumatized, like other post-genocide societies. Tens of millions of survivors went through unbearable suffering and could not completely recover from their experiences … Famine trauma passed from parents to their children on a conscious and unconscious level.[19]

The same may be said of Ireland's President Michael D. Higgins' uncharacteristically insular remark (in the course of a trilingual speech in Cuba in 2017) that Ireland's Great Famine was 'so deeply tragic as to be too traumatic to recall.'[20] In history, statements like those are contestable. They gloss over the inequalities that characterise all famines and airbrush out of the reckoning those who collaborated with the authorities and those who survived by mistreating or neglecting the most vulnerable (cf. Kudela-Świątek, Chapter 6; De Zwarte and Jensen, Chapter 4). They imply that 'our' suffering was somehow unique. They also ignore the resilience of survivors and rely on the controversial assertion that trauma can be transmitted by a collective from one generation to the next.[21]

Irish communal memory, though not Irish historical research, also tends to flatten the suffering in the 1840s: everybody suffered, more or less equally. The suggestion by the late Frank McCourt, famous as the author of *Angela's Ashes* (1996), that 'in the racial unconscious of the Irish there must be some demon tormenting us over food' is a classic Irish example of shared remembering (or might perhaps be called preferred remembering), as is literary critic Luke Gibbons's famous aphorism about Ireland being 'a first world country with a third world memory', which Irish President Mary

McAleese later recycled with the more prescriptive 'We are a vibrant first-world country, but we have a humbling third-world memory'.[22] Or take the epigraph on the dust jacket of novelist Marita Conlan-McKenna's *The Hungry Road* (2020): 'as a nation starves, heroes must emerge'. Words and phrases like 'the Irish', 'us', 'we', and 'a nation' are everywhere. But, alas, there isn't much 'we' or 'us' in famines, and heroes are scarce too.[23] The hallmark of famine is inequality, and what later generations like to remember is not necessarily what happened. History suggests that there is a temporal dimension to all this. In the early stages of a crisis, there is more room for philanthropy and collaboration. Then, as the crisis worsens, concern gives way to neglect and solidarity to antagonism. It is surely no accident that nearly all the small number of incidents of cannibalism during the Irish Famine so far identified occurred in 1848 or 1849.

The dimensions and durations of the famine being remembered and commemorated also matter. The Dutch Hunger Winter Famine of 1944–45 yields a great deal of evidence for communal solidarity and a highly functional civil society, and in particular, great concern for children.[24] Almost certainly, the social capital of Dutch society kept mortality down for the duration of the famine. But it must be remembered too that this was a brief famine happening at a time when the prospect of liberation was in sight. As Leningrad *blokadnik*, Iura Riabinkin confided in her diary, 'I feel that, to turn myself back into what I used to be, there would have to be hope, the conviction that tomorrow or the day after my family and I will be evacuated'.[25] And it was likewise true in Bengal during the summer of 1943. For a time, popular expectations were buoyed by official propaganda that there was enough food for everybody—the mantra from the authorities was 'sufficiency'—if only it were spread around. But as soon as H. S. Suhrawardy, the minister responsible for civilian food supplies admitted that 'we have erred, and the main thing now is for us to get together and do what we can', people realised that they had been lied to, and 'a paralysing sense of calamity' set in.[26]

Famines and the Making of Heritage is a scholarly endeavour, but it is also explicitly prescriptive. Part of its message is that the history of famine, however horrific, can be a force for good. That is not a new message. In the wake of the murder of a rapacious moneylender in the Irish midlands in 1849, a newspaper reporter opined that 'poverty leads to the majority of the crimes in Ireland', and added that 'well would it be for the ruled, were the rulers to bear it in mind'.[27] Much more recently, addressing the crowd at the grave site of would-be Irish famine refugees in Grosse-Ile in Quebec in August 1994, Mary Robinson, an inspirational figure at the time, drew parallels between the mass deaths there and what she had witnessed firsthand in Somalia in 1992. A few years later, Robinson remarked at a gathering in Chicago that 'for every lesson children of Irish heritage learn about the Famine Relief of 1847, they should learn an equal one about the debt burden of the 1990s. For every piece of economic knowledge they gain about the crops exported from Ireland during the famine years, let them come to understand the cruelty of today's markets, which reinforce the poverty and helplessness of those who already experience hunger'.[28] More directly, one would hope that learning more about the causes and symptoms of famine in the past might reduce the likelihood of famines in the future.

Famines and the Making of Heritage is also a reminder that dispassionate discussion of some famines is difficult, particularly when transnational conflict is involved. Yet even in those cases, it should not be forgotten that class and culture divided people, and not all conflict was transnational; in the Irish case, for example, the Great Famine was not simply an event in Anglo-Irish relations. Can historians produce scholarly narratives of those famines, commonly evoked to stress transnational conflict, that can heal? It would be great if they could. Literature can do this, but can history? Alas, the causation works more readily in chronological reverse: reconciliation facilitates more dispassionate historical research. Take, for example, the state-run Holodomor Research and Education Centre in Kviv, which in 2018 set out as one of its tasks 'to conduct research on the history of the Holodomor of 1932–1933, the genocide of the Ukrainian nation'.[29] That shuts out eminent historians such as Sheila Fitzpatrick and Stephen Wheatcroft,[30] who fully accept the catastrophic dimensions of the 1932–33 famine and Josef Stalin's central role in it, yet are reluctant to call it a genocide.[31]

Our responsibility as historians of all hues is, above all, to establish what happened in the past as best we can, no matter how inconvenient that may be for people in the present. This means rejecting censorship in all its forms, engaging in dispassionate discussions, and continuing comparative and interdisciplinary analysis. Where histories are difficult, we can only hope that the truth as we see it can also heal, but we cannot guarantee that. It is usually easier for academics who engage with the past to 'decommission mindsets'—in the wise words of US peace envoy Senator George Mitchell[32]—than for the millions caught up in conflicts where the past is not yet history.

Notes

1 Thanks to Breandán Mac Suibhne, Fionn Ó Gráda, and Máire Ní Chiosáin for reading a draft of this afterword at very short notice. Remaining errors are my own.
2 See also Henrik Forsberg, 'If They Do not Want to Work and Suffer, They Must Starve and Die: Irish and Finnish Famine Historiography Compared', *Scandinavian Journal of History* 43, no. 4 (2018): 484–514.
3 See also Mary Robinson, 'Cherishing the Irish diaspora', 2 February 1995, https://president.ie/en/media-library/speeches/cherishing-the-irish-diaspora, last consulted 21 September 2023.
4 Horace Plunkett, *Ireland in the New Century* (London: John Murray, 1904), 26.
5 Edna Longley, 'Northern Ireland: Commemoration, Elegy, Forgetting', in *History and Memory in Modern Ireland*, ed. Ian McBride (Cambridge: Cambridge University

Press, 2001), 230–1. Such sentiments have been aired and analysed more recently in David Rieff, *In Praise of Forgetting: Historical Memory and Its Ironies* (New Haven: Yale University Press, 2016); and in Guy Beiner, *Forgetful Remembrance: Social Forgetting and Vernacular Historiography of a Rebellion in Ulster* (Oxford: Oxford University Press, 2018).

6 See T. G. Ashplant, Graham Dawson and Michael Roper, 'The Politics of War Memory and Commemoration: Contexts, Structures and Dynamics', in *Commemorating War: The Politics of Memory*, eds. Ashplant, Dawson and Roper (New York: Routledge, 2004), 20. See also Graham Dawson, 'The Meaning of "Moving On": From Trauma to the History and Memory of Emotions in "Post-Conflict" Northern Ireland', *Irish University Review*, 47, no. 1 (2017): 82–102.

7 See Department of Foreign Affairs (Ireland), 'Commemorations and Reconciliation', https://www.dfa.ie/our-role-policies/northern-ireland/commemorations/, last consulted 21 September 2023.

8 See Christian Noack, Lindsay Janssen, and Vincent Comerford, eds., *Holodomor and Gorta Mór: Histories, Memories and Representations of Famine in Ukraine and Ireland* (London: Anthem Press, 2012).

9 'Musealisation' has not yet made it to the *Oxford English Dictionary*, but four contributions in this collection (Corporaal and de Zwarte, Boerman, Gouriévidis and del Arco Blanco and Madden) use the term, and *muséalisation* can be dated back to 1991 on JSTOR. The Museum of the Defence and Siege of Leningrad predated Strokestown by a few years (1989), but it is less a dedicated famine museum than a resistance museum. See also Nuala C. Johnson, 'Where Geography and History Meet: Heritage Tourism and the Big House in Ireland', *Annals of the Association of American Geographers* 86, no. 3 (1996): 551–66.

10 See also Xun Zhou, *Forgotten Voices of Mao's Great Famine, 1958–1962* (New Haven: Yale University Press, 2013).

11 Cormac Ó Gráda, *Black '47 and Beyond: The Great Irish Famine in History, Economy, and Memory* (Princeton: Princeton University Press, 1999), 212.

12 The list on *Wikipedia* (https://en.wikipedia.org/wiki/List_of_memorials_to_the_Great_Famine) is long but by no means complete. For images of the Custom House Key and Murrisk monuments, see https://www.sculpturedublin.ie/famine/) and (https://curiousireland.ie/the-national-famine-memorial-murrisk-co-mayo-1997/.

13 For an excellent study of the history and etymology of 'coffin' ships, see Cian McMahon, *The Coffin Ship: Life and Death at Sea during the Great Irish Famine* (New York: New York University Press, 2021).

14 As described by James Patterson, 'Why is there a monument to 1,186 Irish emigrants in Toronto?', *The Irish Times*, 17 July 2017, https://www.irishtimes.com/life-and-style/abroad/why-is-there-a-monument-to-1-186-irish-emigrants-in-toronto-1.3157615, last consulted 21 September 2023.

15 'Arrival', https://www.un.org/ungifts/arrival

16 The preceding two paragraphs draw on Cormac Ó Gráda, 'Famine Monuments and Famine Memories', in *Ireland—the Matter of Monuments*, eds. Colleen M. Thomas and Paula Murphy (Liverpool: Liverpool University Press, 2024), forthcoming.

17 Roger Kohn, *Rowan Gillespie: Looking for Orio* (Dublin, O'Brien Press, 2007); Emily Mark-FitzGerald, 'Rowan Gillespie', *Sculpture Dublin*, https://www.sculpturedublin.ie/artist-biography-rowan-gillespie, last accessed 21 September 2023.

18 Brian McAvera, 'Deconstructing John Behan (an interview)', *Irish Arts Review* 30, no. 4 (2013): 84.

19 Ukrainian Institute of National Remembrance, *HOLODOMOR: Communist Genocide in Ukraine* (https://uinp.gov.ua/elektronni-vydannya/holodomor-communist-genocide-in-ukraine).

20 https://president.ie/en/diary/details/president-attends-the-launch-of-a-translation-of-star-of-the-sea-by-joseph/speeches, last accessed 21 September 2023.
21 Dawson, 'The Meaning of "Moving On"'.
22 Frank McCourt, 'Scraps and Leftovers: A Meditation', in *The Irish Americans*, ed. J. V. Mullen (Evanston, Ill.: McDougal Littell Publishing, 1996), 218; Luke Gibbons, *Transformations in Irish Culture* (Cork: Cork University Press, 1996), 3; Elaine Lafferty, 'President tells Americans of Ireland's "special ethos"', *Irish Times* (website), 18 September 1999, https://www.irishtimes.com/news/president-tells-americans-of-ireland-s-special-ethos-1.228679, last accessed 21 September 2023.
23 This is, of course, not to deny the heroism of some. See Brendan Mac Suibhne, *Subjects Lacking Words? The Gray Zone of the Irish Famine* (Cork: Cork University Press, 2017), 8–11; and Christine Kinealy, Jason King, and Gerard Moran, eds., *Heroes of Ireland's Great Hunger* (Cork: Cork University Press, 2021).
24 Ingrid de Zwarte, *The Hunger Winter: Fighting Famine in the Occupied Netherlands, 1944–1945* (Cambridge: Cambridge University Press, 2020), Chs. 7–8.
25 As cited in Alexis J. Peri, *Minds Under Siege: Rethinking the Soviet Experience Inside the Leningrad Blockade, 1941–45*. PhD dissertation, Berkeley: University of California, 2011), 85.
26 Cormac Ó Gráda, *Eating People is Wrong and Other Essays on the History and Future of Famine* (Princeton: Princeton University Press, 2015), 74, 78.
27 As cited in Cormac Ó Gráda, 'Behold a Pale Horse: Horrors and Heritages of Famine', *Studies* 111, no. 442 (2022): 139.
28 Mary Robinson, 'Why commemorate the Irish Famine? Address to the Irish Fellowship Club, Chicago', 1995. https://www.president.ie/en/media-library/speeches/why-commemorate-the-great-irish-famine-address-by-mary-robinson-to-the-iris.
29 For this quotation, see Holomodor Museum (Kviv), 'Holomodor Research Institute launched its official site', 5 September 2020, https://holodomormuseum.org.ua/en/news-museji/holodomor-research-institute-launched-its-official-site/, last accessed 21 September 2023.
30 On Fitzpatrick and Wheatcroft, see *Explaining History Podcast*, 'Sheila Fitzpatrick's view on Collectivisation', 28 March 2023, available at: https://explaininghistory.org/2023/03/28/sheila-fitzpatricks-view-on-collectivisation/; Claire Weiss, 'An interview with economic historian Stephen Wheatcroft on the Soviet famine and historical falsification', *World Socialist Website*, https://www.wsws.org/en/articles/2023/07/10/qutp-j10.html, last accessed 21 September 2023.
31 The previous four paragraphs build on Ó Gráda, 'Behold a pale horse'.
32 As cited in Archbishop Eamon Martin, 'Our inability to decommission mindsets has prevented us from achieving the kind of conflict transformation envisioned in the Good Friday Agreement', *Irish News*, 9 April 2023.

References

Ashplant, T. G., Graham Dawson and Michael Roper, 'The Politics of War Memory and Commemoration: Contexts, Structures and Dynamics'. In T. G. Ashplant, Graham Dawson and Michael Roper, eds., 3–86. *Commemorating War: The Politics of Memory*. New York: Routledge, 2004.

Beiner, Guy, *Forgetful Remembrance: Social Forgetting and Vernacular Historiography of a Rebellion in Ulster*. Oxford: Oxford University Press, 2018.

Dawson, Graham, 'The Meaning of "Moving On": From Trauma to the History and Memory of Emotions in "Post-Conflict" Northern Ireland'. *Irish University Review* 47, no. 1 (2017): 82–102.

Department of Foreign Affairs (Ireland), 'Commemorations and Reconciliation', https://www.dfa.ie/our-role-policies/northern-ireland/commemorations/.

Forsberg, Henrik, 'If They Do not Want to Work and Suffer, They Must Starve and Die: Irish and Finnish Famine Historiography Compared'. *Scandinavian Journal of History* 43, no. 4: 484–514.

Gibbons, Luke, *Transformations in Irish Culture*. Cork: Cork University Press, 1996.

Johnson, Nuala C., 'Where Geography and History Meet: Heritage Tourism and the Big House in Ireland'. *Annals of the Association of American Geographers* 86, no. 3 (1996): 551–66.

Kinealy, Christine, Jason King, and Gerard Moran, eds., *Heroes of Ireland's Great Hunger*. Cork: Cork University Press, 2021.

Kohn, Roger. *Rowan Gillespie: Looking for Orio*. Dublin: O'Brien Press, 2007.

Lafferty, Elaine, 'President tells Americans of Ireland's "Special Ethos"'. *Irish Times*. 18 September 1999, https://www.irishtimes.com/news/president-tells-americans-of-ireland-s-special-ethos-1.228679.

Longley, Edna, 'Northern Ireland: Commemoration, Elegy, Forgetting'. In Ian McBride, ed., 230–53. *History and Memory in Modern Ireland*. Cambridge: Cambridge University Press, 2001.

McAvera, Brian, 'Deconstructing John Behan (an interview)'. *Irish Arts Review* 30, no. 4 (2013): 84.

McMahon, Cian T. *The Coffin Ship: Life and Death at Sea during the Great Irish Famine*. New York: New York University Press, 2021.

MacSuibhne, Breandán, *Subjects Lacking Words? The Gray Zone of the Irish Famine*. Cork: Cork University Press, 2017.

Mark-FitzGerald, Emily, 'Rowan Gillespie'. *Sculpture Dublin*, https://www.sculpturedublin.ie/artist-biography-rowan-gillespie.

McCourt, Frank, 'Scraps and Leftovers: A Meditation'. In J. V. Mullen, ed., 216–21. *The Irish Americans*. Evanston, IL: McDougal Littell Publishing, 1996.

Noack, Christian, Lindsay Janssen, and Vincent Comerford, eds., *Holodomor and Gorta Mór: Histories, Memories and Representations of Famine in Ukraine and Ireland*. London: Anthem Press, 2012.

Ó Gráda, Cormac, *Black '47 and Beyond: The Great Irish Famine in History, Economy, and Memory*. Princeton: Princeton University Press, 1999.

Ó Gráda, Cormac, *Eating People is Wrong and Other Essays on the History and Future of Famine*. Princeton: Princeton University Press, 2015.

Ó Gráda, Cormac, 'Behold a Pale Horse: Horrors and Heritages of Famine', *Studies* 111, no. 442 (2022): 134–9.

Ó Gráda, Cormac, 'Famine Monuments and Famine Memories'. In Colleen M. Thomas and Paula Murphy, eds., *Ireland—the Matter of Monuments*. Liverpool: Liverpool University Press, forthcoming.

Patterson, James, 'Why is there a monument to 1,186 Irish emigrants in Toronto?'. *The Irish Times*, 17 July 2017, https://www.irishtimes.com/life-and-style/abroad/why-is-there-a-monument-to-1-186-irish-emigrants-in-toronto-1.3157615.

Peri, Alexis J., Minds Under Siege: Rethinking the Soviet Experience inside the Leningrad Blockade, 1941–45. PhD dissertation, University of California, Berkeley, 2011.

Plunkett, Horace. *Ireland in the New Century*. London: John Murray, 1904.

Rieff, David, *In Praise of Forgetting: Historical Memory and Its Ironies*. New Haven, CT: Yale University Press, 2016.

Robinson, Mary, 'Cherishing the Irish diaspora'. 2 February 1995. https://president.ie/en/media-library/speeches/cherishing-the-irish-diaspora.

Robinson, Mary, 'Why commemorate the Irish Famine? Address to the Irish Fellowship Club, Chicago', 1995. https://www.president.ie/en/media-library/speeches/why-commemorate-the-great-irish-famine-address-by-mary-robinson-to-the-iris.

'Sheila Fitzpatrick's view on Collectivisation'. 28 March 2023, https://explaininghistory.org/2023/03/28/sheila-fitzpatricks-view-on-collectivisation/.
Weiss, Claire, 'An interview with economic historian Stephen Wheatcroft on the Soviet famine and historical falsification'. *World Socialist Website*, https://www.wsws.org/en/articles/2023/07/10/qutp-j10.html.
Zhou, Xun, *Forgotten Voices of Mao's Great Famine, 1958–1962*. New Haven, CT: Yale University Press, 2013.
Zwarte, Ingrid de. *The Hunger Winter: Fighting Famine in the Occupied Netherlands, 1944–1945*. Cambridge: Cambridge University Press, 2020.

INDEX

Note: Locators in *italics* represent figures and page numbers followed by 'n' denote endnotes.

FSC
www.fsc.org
MIX
Papier | Fördert
gute Waldnutzung
FSC® C083411

Kolibri 360 GmbH
Ferdinand-Jühlke-Straße 7
99095 Erfurt, Deutschland
produktsicherheit@kolibri360.de